D1222635

Lady Tennyson's *Journal*

Lady TENNYSON'S *Journal*

Edited with an Introduction by
JAMES O. HOGE

University Press of Virginia
Charlottesville

The publicaton of this volume is sponsored
by the VPI Educational Foundation, Inc.

THE UNIVERSITY PRESS OF VIRGINIA

First Published 1981

Library of Congress Cataloging in Publication Data
Tennyson, Emily Sellwood Tennyson, Baroness, 1813–1896.
Lady Tennyson's journal.
Includes index.
1. Tennyson, Alfred Tennyson, Baron, 1809–1892—Biography. 2. Poets, English—19th century—Biography. 3. Tennyson, Emily Sellwood Tennyson, Baroness, 1813–1896. 4. Wives—Great Britain—Biography. 5. Tennyson family. I. Hoge, James O. II. Title.
PR5581.T39 1981 821'.8 [B] 80-21387 ISBN 0-8139-0876-0

Printed in the United States of America

Frontispiece: Lady Tennyson, from the portrait (1862) by G. F. Watts, R.A. The original is in the Tennyson Collection at the Usher Gallery, Lincoln, England. (Courtesy of Lord Tennyson and the Lincolnshire Library Service)

To Carol and our son, Tyler

Contents

Illustrations

MAP

Acknowledgments

In the course of working on this edition I have benefited by the influence and assistance of others whom I wish to thank for their contributions. First of all, I would particularly like to express my appreciation to Cecil Y. Lang, who has so generously given me counsel through the years. Once again he has taken time away from his own work to help improve mine. He must know as well as I how futile it would be for me to attempt to explain or to express thanks for all he has contributed to the completion of this book. Suffice it to say that he remains both my most perceptive critic and my staunchest supporter.

I am also profoundly grateful to the late Sir Charles Tennyson. It was he who first encouraged my interest in his grandmother more than a decade ago, and without his support this edition would not have been undertaken. And I wish to thank the present Lord Tennyson for allowing me to publish Lady Tennyson's Journal and to quote from her unpublished letters and from Hallam Lord Tennyson's unpublished *Materials for a Life of A. T.* For a variety of reasons my appreciation is due Christopher Ricks, Edgar F. Shannon, Jr., Jerome H. Buckley, Dwight Culler, Robert H. Super, Catherine B. Stevenson, June S. Hagen, and Nancy Clausen. Nor can I fail to mention the debt I owe my colleagues Richard L. Hoffman, James L. W. West III, Arthur M. Eastman, C. L. Hardy, and A. J. Colaianne for their advice and friendship.

The staffs of both the Carol M. Newman Library of Virginia Polytechnic Institute and State University and the Ilah Dunlap Little Memorial Library of the University of Georgia have been consistently generous with time, resources, and invaluable suggestions about tracing and identifying a host of obscurities. Among the many who assisted me in these two libraries I want to thank by name Anita Malebranche, Charles W. Haney, Hazel Hubbard, and Vivian Phillips. I am also deeply indebted to the Lincolnshire County Library Service for permission to publish this Journal and to quote from various unpublished letters, and I want to express my gratitude to the staff of the Tennyson Research Centre for the great help they have provided during my several visits there. In addition I am under obligation to the staff of the Library of Congress for gracious assistance and to The Huntington Library, San Marino, California, for permission to quote from Lady Tennyson letters located there.

I wish to thank Leota Williams for her generous and tireless labors in helping me get the final manuscript ready for publication. And, finally, I must thank my wife Carol for pressing upon me the importance of finishing this book before our son Tyler could divert my attention to other responsibilities. (He has now done so.)

Blacksburg, Virginia James O. Hoge

Editorial Method

Lady Tennyson's Journal, two large hand-written volumes bound in green, cloth-covered boards, now in the Tennyson Research Centre, is a redaction, or epitome, made from a number of earlier diaries and journals that spanned a quarter of a century. None of these "original" journals of Lady Tennyson's have survived. Most likely her son Hallam destroyed them in 1896 or 1897 once he had completed work on *Alfred Lord Tennyson: A Memoir.* Hallam Tennyson used the Journal extensively in writing his *Memoir*, the two-volume biography of Tennyson that was preceded by the unpublished ten-volume "Draft for Materials for a Life of A.T." and the privately printed four-volume *Materials for a Life of A.T.*, both of which are also in the Tennyson Research Centre. While working on his various versions of the *Memoir*, Hallam occasionally wrote his own inserts or marginalia on certain pages of the manuscript Journal. And some of these additions or editings of Hallam's actually appear in the published *Memoir* as if they were legitimate parts of Lady Tennyson's Journal. I, of course, am not concerned with pointing out inaccurate quotations in the *Memoir*, but I have deleted from the Journal all of Hallam's additions. Hallam also sometimes crossed or blotted out passages in the Journal that he evidently thought indiscreet or indelicate. Whenever possible, such passages have been reinstated, again in order to restore the Journal to its unedited state. Finally, a few entries from Lady Tennyson's earlier journals which do not appear in the epitome Journal are recorded in Hallam's *Materials for a Life of A.T.* Such authentic entries from the *Materials* are printed here in brackets with their source noted.

In transcribing and editing the Journal, I have attempted to reproduce Emily Tennyson's language and style, including various errors and peculiarities, with as little alteration of any kind as possible. Accordingly, I have observed the following editorial principles:

1. In order to do justice to the individuality of Emily Tennyson and to preserve the spontaneity of her entries, I have retained nearly all of her verbal idiosyncrasies. Her ampersands, dashes, and abbreviations have been permitted to stand, along with incomplete sentences and misplaced upper-case letters. Incorrect punctuation has been corrected and missing marks of punctuation added only in those rare cases when the reader would obviously be confused or misled. All misspellings have been retained, but superscripts have been normalized and unconscious repetitions corrected. When I have found it necessary to emend, I have done so silently, provided no substantive change is involved.

2. Since a new paragraph among the Journal entries usually indicates a change of date, even when no new date is set down, I have for

the most part preserved Emily Tennyson's paragraphing. However, in some instances when she arbitrarily begins new paragraphs for no logical reasons of style, emphasis, or chronology, I have joined two or more of her paragraphs to reduce the number of unnecessarily brief entries.

3. Ellipses indicate the omission of the few words or sentences that I have judged so awkward, trivial, or repetitious as to hinder or trouble the reader. All ellipses are my own.

Abbreviations

AT	Charles Tennyson, *Alfred Tennyson* (London: Macmillan, 1949).
Letters of E. T.	*The Letters of Emily Lady Tennyson*, ed. James O. Hoge (University Park: Pennsylvania State University Press, 1974).
Materials	Hallam Tennyson, *Materials for a Life of A. T.*, 4 vols. (Privately printed, Tennyson Research Centre).
Memoir	Hallam Tennyson, *Alfred Lord Tennyson: A Memoir by His Son*, 2 vols. (London: Macmillan, 1897).
T.R.C.	Tennyson Research Centre, Lincoln, England.

Introduction

After the death of the poet laureate in 1892, Lady Tennyson spent most of her time assisting her son Hallam (second Baron Tennyson) with his prodigious task of preparing the Tennyson *Memoir*. Together she and Hallam collected, sorted, and assembled an extraordinary mass of materials related in various ways to Tennyson's life and works. Lady Tennyson gathered and inspected all extant letters to the poet, and she worked at recovering every available letter written *by* Tennyson, as well as the many letters she herself had written during forty-two years of married life.[1] And, in addition to selecting and arranging hundreds of letters and other items for her son's convenience, Lady Tennyson prepared her own final Journal.

From immediately after her marriage in June 1850 until shortly before her nearly fatal collapse in the autumn of 1874, Emily Tennyson kept a running account of life in the Tennyson home. Though she by no means made an entry for every day during that period of twenty-four years, certainly there are no sizable gaps, and she was particularly scrupulous in noting every occurrence of the slightest moment involving her husband. The epitome Journal put together after the poet's death is the product of a laborious combining of the several initial journals to form a more convenient and usable whole. Since Emily compiled her final Journal solely as a source of information for Hallam, one would suppose that she deleted certain items of highly personal material preserved in her antecedent diaries. Nonetheless, her Journal, as we have it, is a treasure trove of information about the Tennysons' daily life, and it enables us to see both the laureate and the entire Tennyson family circle more clearly than ever before.

[1]See *Letters of E. T.* More than three-quarters of Emily Tennyson's letters are to family and close friends, including many of the leading literary and political figures of the day, but there are others, mostly of a business or official nature, to persons she knew casually or not at all. Emily also wrote a number of letters for Tennyson, but most of these bear the poet's signature and, therefore, must be considered his letters. The vast majority of Emily's holograph letters are located in the Tennyson Research Centre, Lincoln, England. Other large groups are at Yale, Harvard, Indiana, the Huntington Library, and the Boston Public Library.

It is important to emphasize that Emily intended her Journal for her son's eyes only, and she was thus little concerned about either the style or the structure of her writing. The Journal, then, is in no sense a literary composition, and it possesses only the most simple and rudimentary form. Emily simply set down her recollections of each day's happenings as they came to her, and she made little attempt to separate the trivial from the noteworthy in her entries. Indeed, she had very few principles of selectivity, and though she did select, as must any writer, her Journal is a curious and sometimes bizarre mixture of the trifling and the profound. It is altogether in keeping with her habit, for example, to juxtapose an account of her sons' morning romp with their tutor on the High Down to a careful record of Tennyson's reading during the previous fortnight. Unquestionably the survival of much of the material here is accidental, and one wonders whether the days for which no entry appears were not often omitted more by chance than by design.

All the same, Emily's primary purpose in keeping her Journal over the years was to preserve a record of Tennyson's daily life, and where he is concerned little is left to chance. Day by day she records what the poet reads and writes, what he says, where he goes, and whom he sees. She periodically indicates his state of health, his mood, his plans for composition, revision, and publication, his reactions to praise or blame, his opinions on a host of topics, and (most important of all from her point of view) she describes Tennyson's relationship with herself and with their sons, Hallam and Lionel. Emily's marriage to Tennyson consummated a love match that endured altogether more than fifty years, and her great love for her husband, growing ever stronger through the years, is manifest throughout her Journal.[2] When they were alone, or with Hallam and Lionel, at Farringford or Aldworth, Tennyson and his wife spent most of their time together. Emily gives countless

[2]Tennyson first met Emily Sarah Sellwood, the eldest daughter of Henry Sellwood, a Horncastle solicitor, in Holywell Wood, immediately adjacent to the Somersby Rectory, in 1830. After the marriage of Tennyson's brother Charles (who later took the surname Turner) and Emily's sister Louisa in 1836, Emily and the poet saw each other frequently, and in 1838 they became engaged. Although financial distress forced Tennyson to break the engagement two years later, he never ceased loving Emily, and he again proposed marriage in late 1847 or early 1848. This time, however, Emily refused, apparently fearing Tennyson's religious skepticism, and it was not until the spring of 1850 when she read his *Elegies*, later titled *In Memoriam* at her suggestion, that Emily agreed to marry Tennyson. All the same, she apparently had been fervently in

descriptions of evenings spent with the poet discussing Kant, Dante, Milton, Shakespeare, Chaucer, Dryden, or the Greek tragedians, or, at other times, talking of politics or of shared religious interests, their conversation often turning to the Resurrection and the Atonement or to the immortality of the soul. Tennyson delighted in reading aloud, and he frequently entertained friends and special guests by reading or reciting particular favorites from his own verse. When he read or recited to Emily alone, he sometimes reverted to poems they both held most dear—*Maud*, *In Memoriam*, the "Wellington Ode," "The Holy Grail," or "Guinevere"—but he was more inclined to read his wife his new compositions, asking her thoughts and her advice. Tennyson welcomed Emily's criticism of his poems, and, though as a rule she enthusiastically approved what he had written, he invariably reworked his compositions in accordance with her suggestions when she demurred. Tennyson, who valued the opinions of few, resented the censure of virtually everyone, but he always sought and to a degree even relied upon Emily's ideas concerning all literary matters, and he usually took her judgment as final.

Emily frequently shows the poet engaged in domestic chores, sometimes with her, sometimes alone, and it is the picture of Tennyson the country squire tirelessly and meticulously tending his Isle of Wight estate, and later his Sussex summer home, that more than anything else gives the Journal its unique ambiance. Here we see Tennyson working diligently to improve his beloved Farringford, clearing away brush and replacing it with new shrubs and trees, preparing the farm land for proper husbandry, making hay, building his hideaway cottage in Maiden's Croft, and rolling the lawn by moonlight.[3] And in later years we find him similarly employed at Aldworth, digging or planting his garden, landscaping with shrubberies and

love with the poet ever since 1836, even though for many years she thought their union impossible. H. Drummond Rawnsley, a Lincolnshire cousin of Emily's, wrote that during the years apart Tennyson and Emily "ate out their hearts in secret" (*Memories of the Tennysons* [Glasgow: J. MacLehose and Sons, 1900], p. 71), and his brother, Willingham Rawnsley, asserted that Emily "always thought of him, and they each kept the sacred fire alight in their hearts" (*Tennyson, 1809–1909: A Lecture* [Ambleside: George Middleton, 1909], p. 19).

[3]A few years after buying Farringford, Tennyson built a crude little cottage where he subsequently did much of his writing near Maiden's Croft, a meadow immediately adjacent to the Farringford lawn. Maiden's Croft was named by the monks of the Abbey of Lyra, Normandy, who owned the land before Walter de Ferringford acquired it in the fourteenth century.

trees, both exotic and domestic, laboring to surround his new home, as he had the old, with laurustinus, lilacs, and barberries, with elms, pines, holly, and Euonymus Europoeus. Quite often Emily assisted her husband with these homely occupations, as far as her health allowed, and when he was away from home, she supervised everything, at times even tending the poultry and other small livestock herself.[4] When Tennyson returned from his often protracted trips away from home, there were sometimes several nights of backgammon with the boys or at other times delightful evenings gathered around Emily's piano, while she played Haydn, Beethoven, or Mozart, or perhaps her own settings of Tennyson's poems.[5] And we see all four as often outdoors playing battledore and shuttlecock, or inspecting and directing the seemingly endless construction of Aldworth, or crossing the grounds of "dear old Farringford" and mounting the High Down to gaze at the sea.[6] Surely one of the Journal's most humorous passages, and, oddly enough, one

[4]Emily Tennyson was bothered from girlhood by a spinal disorder which fostered the physical debility that plagued her throughout much of her life. Although Carlyle was probably not wholly incorrect in his observation that Tennyson's wife seemed constantly "sick without a disorder" (*Thomas Carlyle: Letters to His Wife*, ed. Trudy Bliss [London: Victor Gollancz, 1953], p. 272), Emily was undeniably a slight, frail woman, and virtually every Victorian who found occasion to record his impressions of her testifies to her constitutional weakness. Neither in her letters nor in her Journal, however, does Emily often complain of ill health, apart from fatigue, and despite her general physical infirmity she maintained a remarkably complete and efficient control over all domestic doings at Farringford and Aldworth right up until the week of her death. Ellen Terry, who came to Farringford in 1864 as the bride of G. F. Watts, remembered Emily as "a slender-stalked tea rose" who amazed her by managing absolutely everything in the Tennyson household while lying on her crimson sofa in the drawing room (Joanna Richardson, *The Pre-Eminent Victorian* [London: Jonathan Cape, 1962], p. 289).

[5]Emily was an accomplished pianist who composed as well, often setting her husband's poems to music. Usually she wrote her Tennyson songs after hearing the poet read the verse she was to set, and her settings were intended to give an impression of his readings. Emily printed several of her Tennyson settings, including "The Song of the Alma River," "The City Child," and "Minnie and Winnie," and in 1891 she allowed the Polish pianist Mlle. Janotha to present a number of her songs in concert at St. James's Hall.

[6]In June 1867, when he first asked James Thomas Knowles to design his summer home in Black Horse Copse, Blackdown, high in the Sussex North Downs, Tennyson wanted nothing more than a modest four-room house. Emily envisioned a grander dwelling from the start, however, and she soon assumed full responsibility for Knowles's efforts, with Tennyson offering little more than mild protests to each proposed addition. Construction dragged on interminably, and by the time Aldworth was completed in late 1869 even

of the most moving, is Emily's description of Tennyson, Hallam, and Lionel all yoked together to pull her little invalid carriage about the Farringford estate, a service largely reserved for herself but on rare occasions also offered to ailing female guests.

The Journal is valuable first of all, just as Emily intended, for what it tells about Tennyson. However, we should not underestimate its importance as a repository of information about Emily Tennyson herself. Emily always wrote hurriedly, and the spontaneity of her entries, formless and disheveled as they are, adds immeasurably to their value as an authentic record of her thoughts and feelings. She wrote down her widely varied recollections without imposing on them any structure other than that necessarily provided by chronological order. But her artless presentation, like her arbitrary inclusion of trivia, testifies to the fact that Emily never wrote with an eye to publication and suggests that she probably recounted events very much as she remembered them. Emily in fact was incapable of insincerity, and her honesty and candor are as obvious in her Journal as they are in her letters. Equally apparent here are her intellectual curiosity and her broad reading and knowledge, as well as her saintly tolerance and unselfishness and her remarkable kindness to everyone, especially to all those who frequented the Tennyson home—family, friends, servants, even uninvited guests.

Emily was hostess, friend, and confidante to many eminent Victorians, and a number of them remark particularly on her erudition and on her powers as a conversationalist.[7] At dinner and afterwards in the drawing room she held her own with Lear, Longfellow, Jowett, Gladstone, Dean Stanley, the duke of Argyll, Clough, the Brownings, and countless other luminaries, and she charmed everyone with her intellectual prowess and with her sprightly, often unexpected, rejoinders. Though we do not have her conversation, Emily's Journal allows her to speak, and it underlines our impression of her as a woman whose fragile appearance belied her great inner strength and

---

Emily had begun to lament the constant presence of workmen. To be sure, they would have been gone months before had not Emily requested and directed a score of last-minute expansions and improvements for both house and grounds.

[7]Among those most impressed by Emily's conversation was Theodore Watts-Dunton, who stated at the time of her death that she had always seemed to him destined from birth "to hold a high place as a conversationalist, brilliant and stimulating" (*The Athenaeum*, August 15, 1896, p. 227).

who continually surprised people with her vigorous spirit and her determination.[8]

There is little doubt that Tennyson's marriage in June 1850 was the single most crucial event in his life. From youth he had struggled to escape "the madhouse of self" that entrapped him just as surely as it did the speakers of *Maud* and "Tithonus" and "Locksley Hall," and Emily enabled him to lose himself in another person as he had not done since the death of Arthur Henry Hallam. Lonely, self-tormented, troubled by religious uncertainties and doubts about his own abilities, Tennyson probably exaggerated little when in 1845 he confessed to Aubrey DeVere "that he must marry and find love and peace or die."[9] Once she decided that neither his chronic melancholia nor his religious skepticism was beyond her curative powers, Emily devoted herself completely to Tennyson, quieting his sense of unrest, curbing his tendency to brood and fret, encouraging his halting social instincts, and protecting him from those irritants most likely to disturb his comfort and his happiness. During their forty-two years of marriage she never tired of working to shield the poet from vexations, while encouraging him in every conceivable way, reassuring him when he questioned either his powers or his prospects, supporting him with her own unwavering emotional stability. Tennyson himself was certainly strong in spirit as well as physique, but his strength was vulnerable and inconstant, whereas his wife's, threatened by fewer incertitudes, was rarely shaken.

In addition to protecting her husband's emotional well-being in so many ways, Emily managed all financial affairs at Farringford and Aldworth, handled the bulk of Tennyson's voluminous correspondence, copied his poems and helped prepare

[8]Even Harold Nicolson, who blamed Emily for spoiling Tennyson as an artist by soothing his romantic discontent, admits that there was undeniably "something more positive in Mrs. Tennyson than the evanescent, wistful charm which is generally attributed to her" (*Tennyson: Aspects of His Life, Character and Poetry* [Boston: Constable, 1923], p. 157). Just the same, Nicolson succeeded in nurturing the idea that Emily exercised a smothering influence on Tennyson's noblest, wildest poetic impulse and that she must bear responsibility for encouraging the creation of more of the tender, sentimental little poems that earned her husband the "School-Miss Alfred" sobriquet before his marriage. Several recent Tennyson scholars have been more inclined to agree with the Tennysons' friend James Spedding, the impeccable critic and man of taste, who observed to the poet in 1870 that "domestic happiness" had apparently had no "demoralizing effect" upon his verse. And Spedding concluded, "Your touch is as delicate and vigorous and your invention as rich as ever" (Spedding to Tennyson, January 15, 1870, T.R.C.).

[9]Wilfrid Ward, *Aubrey DeVere: A Memoir* (London: Longmans, 1904), p. 72.

them for publication, saw to his table and his wardrobe, tended to their sons, directed the endless comings and goings of visitors, and kept the poet largely undisturbed. In short, Emily must be given paramount credit both for rescuing Tennyson from the tragic self-absorption that warped his youth and for managing his home and continuing to minister to his personal needs in a manner designed to promote his contentment and to leave him free to write. Shortly after Tennyson's death James Knowles, who knew both husband and wife as well as any outsider during their last two decades together, expressed the conviction that the world owed to Emily's perpetual love and care "many years of Tennyson's prolonged life and many of his immortal Poems."[10] Although she never stood in awe or hesitated to criticize or correct, Emily adored Tennyson, and, though without question he was periodically restless and troubled even after he married her, she tempered the periods of discontent and enabled him to survive them. Emily's Journal reveals, as nothing else can, the many facets of her care and her love, growing all the more tender through time. "For me I cannot separate her from him," wrote Henry Graham Dakyns, as he struggled to find words to describe Emily and to express his feelings about her.[11] Emily also felt the two to be inseparably one, and in December 1892, two months after her husband died, she wrote to Annie Fields that it was the most blessed thing for her "to live with him still and to feel that he lives for good in so many."[12]

If Emily erred in any way in her management of home and family, it was in overexerting herself in her perpetual labor of

[10] Knowles, "Aspects of Tennyson," *Nineteenth Century*, 33 (January 1893), 188.

[11] Dakyns to Hallam Tennyson, August 13, 1896, T.R.C. Henry Graham Dakyns (1839–1911), the poet and classical scholar, lived at Farringford as tutor to Hallam and Lionel Tennyson from February 1861 until September 1863, when he became a classics master at Clifton College.

[12] Lady Tennyson to Annie Fields, December 9, 1892, Huntington Library. The wife of James T. Fields (1817–81), the American author, editor, and publisher, Annie Fields was a friend and correspondent of Emily's from the time of the Fieldses' first visit to Farringford in 1859. Mr. and Mrs. Fields visited the Tennysons again in 1869, this time accompanied by Mabel Lowell, the twenty-one-year-old daughter of James Russell Lowell. In 1869 when Emily received a copy of Mrs. Fields's *Asphodel* (1866), which was dedicated to herself, she wrote to express her appreciation, but she also voiced dissatisfaction with one detail in the dedication: "Am I wrong," she said, "in asking that [it] might be To Mrs 'Alfred Tennyson' when it is reprinted in England—Mrs. Emily Tennyson would mean an unmarried sister—and you see I am bound not quietly to give up the honour" (October 5, 1869, Huntington Library).

love. As early as 1861 Benjamin Jowett, master of Balliol and the Tennyson's dear friend, pleaded with her to exercise more discretion lest she ruin her health:

> *I fear that I cannot be mistaken in observing that you get weaker especially during the last year. It grieves me to see you who care for the most trifling wants of other people so helpless about yourself. Please do not be unpractical in a matter of such extreme importance: but get change of air and give up work (Mt. Atkinson [the Freshwater vicar] could answer all the letters that ought to be answered equally well) and get the best advice. Do not throw away your life in the performance of imaginary duties which are really unimportant. . . . It is not the letterwriting etc. but your life and preserve* [*sic*] *that are the real good and blessing in the house. Your unselfishness really passes into a sort of apathy or indolence about self which is quite wrong.*[13]

But Emily did not heed Jowett's advice. Instead of curtailing her activities, she grew all the busier as Tennyson's fame expanded, and she spent more and more time entertaining the poet's acquaintances and either censoring or answering his mail. In addition, she found it increasingly difficult, but also increasingly necessary, to protect him from the machinations of publishers and the incursions of "Cockneys."[14]

Although physically strenuous, the many trips with Tennyson to London or Lincolnshire or abroad must have been refreshing for Emily.[15] Nonetheless, it was shortly after their return to Farringford from the 1874 tour of France and the Pyrenees that Emily suffered the collapse that very nearly ended her life. Her own slender account of the breakdown, which appears as her final Journal entry, dated simply "September 1874," provides few details, but unquestionably she had finally pushed herself too far. At the time Tennyson wrote of her condition to James Knowles, laying particular blame on Emily's ceaseless letter writing: "She has overwrought herself with the multifarious correspondence of many years, and is now suffering for it. I trust that with perfect quiet she will recover; but it will never again do for her to insist upon answering every idle fellow who writes to me. I always prayed her not to do so but

[13]Jowett to Lady Tennyson, May 12, 1861, T.R.C.

[14]Tennyson's label for the Isle of Wight tourists who infringed on his privacy.

[15]Tennyson, of course, was born at Somersby, Lincolnshire, at his father's rectory, and Emily was from Horncastle, a mere seven miles away. During their married years the Tennysons often visited the Charles Tennyson Turners at Grasby as well as other Lincolnshire relatives.

she did not like the unanswered (she used to say) to feel wroth and unsatisfied with me."[16]

Emily's doctors ordered that she exert herself at nothing if she valued her life, and indeed she never again was able to act as Tennyson's secretary or his amanuensis. All the same, she did recover to a great extent. Within six months she had resumed control of virtually all household affairs, and by early 1877 she was even writing letters again, though she now addressed few outside the family. Of course, she lived on for nearly twenty years, and her attitudes and her outlook on life remained as youthful and sanguine as ever. Always rather pallid and thin, "monastic" in appearance said John Addington Symonds,[17] Emily nevertheless retained her lovely auburn hair and her perfect complexion, and she never really looked or acted old. Her relish for life continued undaunted, and though near the end she confessed that people and things had "grown very shadowy," she also declared that her interest in the affairs of England, and for that matter the entire world, had not in the least diminished. "Perhaps the desire that I could in any way influence [the world] according to what I believe to be right is more passionate than ever," she wrote in 1891. "If it were not so it would be hard indeed to go on living."[18]

During her last months Emily remained at work on her Journal, further condensing the whole and recopying illegible sections, as her failing eyesight permitted, sometimes dictating her revisions to Hallam's wife, Audrey.[19] She also spent a good deal of time entertaining and caring for her beloved grandchildren,[20] but even in old age her full and busy life at home never

[16] Quoted in Knowles, "Aspects of Tennyson," pp. 187–88.

[17] *The Letters of John Addington Symonds*, ed. Herbert M. Schueller and Robert L. Peters (Detroit: Wayne State University Press, 1967), I, 512.

[18] Lady Tennyson to Annie Fields, May 26, 1891, Huntington Library.

[19] In June 1884 Audrey Boyle married Hallam Tennyson and moved to Farringford, which remained home for the rest of her life. Audrey grew to be quite close to her father-in-law, and during his final years she was largely occupied in assisting Hallam with his work as Tennyson's amanuensis. Audrey was also Tennyson's favorite companion on his long daily walks, and she was so fascinated by what he said on a wide range of topics during their many treks around the Isle of Wight that she periodically set down his most memorable remarks. Her recently published notebook is a valuable source of information about Tennyson's preoccupations during the last decade of his life ("Talks and Walks: Tennyson's Remarks and Observations, 1870–92," ed. James O. Hoge, *JEGP*, 77 [January 1978], 53–71).

[20] Hallam and Audrey Tennyson had three sons: Lionel Hallam (b. 1889),

caused her to forget the outside world. One of her very last letters celebrates the proposal at Oxford to allow women to compete for the B.A. degree,[21] and another touches on her fear that England, and indeed all of Europe, may have grown complacent about the possibility of military attack, a lifelong concern she shared with Tennyson: "Who in these days of steam is to defend Europe in case of an incursion from China or from South America or Africa if not Europe itself. . . . War Baba [Tennyson] hated, war we hate, but I fear the time for peace has not come."[22]

On August 5, 1896, Emily suffered an attack of influenza that was soon complicated by severe congestion of the lungs. As always, she minimized her pain, but by the ninth her condition had worsened markedly, and that night Dr. G. R. Dabbs, the Tennyson family physician, told Hallam that his mother would not recover. She died at dawn the next morning with her devoted Hallam at her side, and she was buried in the Freshwater parish churchyard, barely a mile from Farringford.[23] Letters of sympathy came to Hallam and Audrey from all over the world, from both intimate and casual acquaintances, some of the latter having met Lady Tennyson no more than once, from statesmen and educators, from the poet's friends and their wives. Herbert Warren, president of Magdalen College, Oxford, spoke of how Emily had encouraged and protected her husband and of "the saintliness of her spirit—the purer for suffering, the stronger out of weakness."[24] And Marian Bradley, wife of George Granville Bradley, the longtime headmaster of Marlborough, wrote of how she had always looked up to Emily and of "what a raising influence she was in my life." "I used to call her my 'Madonna,'" Mrs. Bradley continued, "and say that I came to her to be sprinkled with

---

Alfred Aubrey (b. 1891), and Harold Courtenay (b. 1896), the last born only three months before his grandmother's death. Lionel and his wife, Eleanor, the daughter of Frederick Locker-Lampson, had two sons, Alfred Browning Stanley (b. 1878) and Charles Bruce (b. 1879), the late Sir Charles Tennyson, who died in 1978.

[21] See her March 7, 1896, letter to her niece Agnes Weld, *Letters of E.T.*, p. 369. It was not until 1920 that Oxford did grant degrees to women.

[22] Lady Tennyson to Agnes Weld, May 10, 1895, *Letters of E.T.*, pp. 367–68. "Baba" was the grandchildren's pet name for Tennyson.

[23] Lionel Tennyson died of jungle fever in 1886 on the way home from India, where he and Eleanor had been visiting Lord Dufferin in connection with Lionel's work in the India Office.

[24] Warren to Hallam Tennyson, August 14, 1896, T.R.C.

her pure water from the dust that contact with the struggles of life in the world and of worldly people was apt to smother one in."[25]

A few moments before her death Emily said to her son that most of all she had tried to be a good wife, and when Hallam assured her that none could have been a better wife to his father, she spoke what were to be her final words, "I might have done more."[26] For once Lady Tennyson was wrong. If one may borrow from Lady Monteagle's 1892 tribute to the laureate as one "who did so much more than any other living man to lighten the Darkness and silence of Death," surely it can be said that Emily Tennyson truly lightened Tennyson's darkness as no other could have done.[27] She brought him peace at Shiplake Church on June 13, 1850,[28] and she preserved a large measure of that peace in his life for the next forty-two years, saving Tennyson the man and, thus, Tennyson the poet.

[25] Mrs. Bradley to Hallam Tennyson, August 12, 1896, T.R.C.

[26] Emily's last words are inscribed in Hallam Tennyson's hand on the inside of the front cover of volume one of his four-volume *Materials*.

[27] Elizabeth Spring-Rice, Lady Monteagle, to Lady Tennyson, October 12, 1892, T.R.C.

[28] Many years after his marriage Tennyson remarked, speaking of Emily, "The peace of God came into my life before the altar when I wedded her" (*Memoir*, I, 329).

The Journal

1850

[Summer]

In your Father's study there was not an attic but a cheerful room with a Bay window with red curtains & a bust of Clive.[1]

Days of affliction however were at hand. Great family sorrow and then on your Father's part an entire loss of property. Tormented by an unbusinesslike agent on whom he could not depend for the regular payment of rent from Grasby, he sold the estate and was induced by a speculating neighbour to put the proceeds of the sale and other money into a wood-carving project.[2] The brothers & sisters except Frederick & Charles gave up also some of their possessions & to your Father's horror he found that in his absence his Mother had signed away her all. He however threatened instant exposure if this agreement were not cancelled & so it was cancelled. That most loving & generous of brothers-in-law your Uncle Edmund Lushington subsequently insured the life of this speculator & so speedily rescued part of your Father's money for the speculator dropt down dead a short time after—a tragic end, is it not, to speculation?[3]

[1]The Journal opens abruptly with this reference to Tennyson's study at High Beech, Epping, where the Tennysons moved after they relinquished Somersby in the summer of 1837 and where Lady Tennyson visited the poet several times before they broke their engagement in 1840. Apparently Lady Tennyson took all of this first section of the Journal from her "Narrative for Her Sons," an account of the early acquaintance, courtship, honeymoon, and first three years of marriage, which she wrote for Hallam and Lionel Tennyson in December 1869. (See "Emily Tennyson's Narrative for Her Sons," ed. James O. Hoge, *Texas Studies in Literature and Language*, 14 [Spring 1972], 93–106.) I am unable to account for the fact that the Journal opens here in the middle of the "Narrative for Her Sons" rather than at the beginning. In addition to the published "Narrative," two other unpublished versions are preserved in the Tennyson Research Centre, but this Journal account is in some respects unlike any of the other three.

The bust in Tennyson's study was that of Robert Clive (1725–74), the famous soldier and founder of the empire of British India.

[2]See *AT*, pp. 186–88, and *Memoir*, I, 220–21, for complete accounts of Dr. Matthew Allen's abortive "Pyroglyphs" project, which absorbed all of Tennyson's meager savings, along with a £500 legacy left him by an aunt of Arthur Hallam's and the proceeds from the sale of a small property at Grasby that he had inherited from his grandfather.

[3]Tennyson regained much of his lost capital in 1845 as a result of the foresight

About this time were great family sorrows & these eventually in 1840 made my Father deem it advisable that the correspondence which he had allowed between us should cease.[4] In ourselves there was no change. Whether I did rightly in yielding I cannot tell. My Father's love I never doubted, but [I] was divided between two duties and years of great misery were consequent on my decision. With my Father I was perfectly happy as well I might be. In whatever respect I have been worthy to be your Father's wife I owe to him for he read to myself & sisters the best historians & poets and encouraged me to read them, books of science & theology & all that could help life besides.[5] Your Father and I did not meet again until we met at that then happy & delightful house, Park House. Your Father was believed to be in Italy so I went to see your Aunt Cecilia who was very dear to me & faithful thro' all as was Aunt Tilly.[6] Your Father appeared unexpectedly before breakfast. I returned home to Hale as soon after as I could.[7] Then [May] we met at my cousin's house a month before we married.[8] In all these years I had lost courage and I don't know if I should ever have ventured to become his wife knowing the greatness of the responsibility had not Kingsley not merely encouraged but urged me—Thank God.[9] Before this your Uncle Edmund had again

---

and kind action of Edmund Lushington (1811–93), the husband of Tennyson's sister Cecilia, whose marriage (1842) the poet celebrates in the epilogue to *In Memoriam.*

[4]The correspondence prohibition in effect terminated the engagement of some three years.

[5]See Emily Tennyson's account of her youth, particularly as it involves her father, Henry Sellwood, in "Recollections of My Early Life," in *Tennyson and His Friends*, ed. Hallam Tennyson (London: Macmillan, 1911), pp. 1–7.

[6]These aunts were Cecilia Tennyson Lushington (1817–1909) and Matilda Tennyson (1816–1913). Cecilia and her husband, Edmund, lived at Park House, near Maidstone, the county town of Kent. Matilda was virtually a permanent "guest" of the Tennysons from the time of her mother's death in 1865 until the poet's death.

[7]In 1848 Emily Tennyson and her father moved from Horncastle to Hale, West Surrey, where they lived together until her marriage in June 1850.

[8]In May 1850 Tennyson and Emily met at the Shiplake home of Drummond and Catherine Rawnsley. The son of the rector of Halton, near Somersby, Drummond Rawnsley was a close friend of Tennyson's from boyhood; his wife, "Kate," was the daughter of Sir Willingham Franklin and thus Emily's first cousin. Rawnsley married the Tennysons the following month, and Tennyson subsequently wrote "To the Vicar of Shiplake," expressing his gratitude for the "gift" of "such a wife" as Emily Tennyson.

[9]Charles Kingsley (1819–75), author of *Alton Locke* (1850), *The Water Babies*

come forward with loving generosity & offered to give up his carriage horses to help us. Of course we could not allow this.

Then [June 15] we went to the Hotel at Linton.[10] In those days solitary enough. We had both been at Linton before but not together. We enjoyed our rambles to Waters-meet & the Valley of Rocks. We went there on horseback, I on a donkey which proved rather an unmanageable beast. He dismounted and gave me the horse & to my delight when we met country people they evidently quite understood the state of things and bowed to him most respectfully. We returned by Exmoor Forest expecting a forest but we only saw a very few trees on a hill. There were however Red deer near them. We also went to Glastonbury. To me it was very pleasant to see the wild Tors of the country whence my Father's family came and at Glastonbury we lunched in the Refectory built by one of them (I am told) as the Pilgrim's Hospital.[11] The oriel window and the room with black outsteps leading to the dais now being part of the George Inn.[12] In after years it seemed a very pleasant coincidence that he, the last Abbot but one, should have been the only Abbot buried in the Chancel near the real or reputed grave of King Arthur.

Then we went to Clifton and to my horror some injury to a nail having made a painful little laceration necessary the doctors gave him Chloroform, then a new thing. I was turned out of the room and heard him shout as if hallooing the hounds. The chloroform was not of the best and had blistered his poor chin. Then we went to Bath and afterwards to Cheltenham to see his dear Mother & the rest of the family living there.

(1863), and other works, was curate at Eversley nearby and a friend of the Rawnsleys. The major role Kingsley played in Emily Tennyson's decision is also documented by Hallam Tennyson on the front leaf of volume four of his "Draft for Materials for a Life of A.T." where he has written: "Charles Turner urged that [there] should be no delay of the marriage and his advice was strenuously backed up by Charles Kingsley and consequently it took place forthwith."

[10]The account of the wedding, included in "Narrative for Her Sons," is omitted in the Journal, which picks up here two days after that ceremony.

[11]The Sellwoods were an old and landed Somersetshire family whose estates had comprehended a vast portion of the county for generations before the family moved to Aldworth, Berkshire, in the late eighteenth century. Little is known of any member of the Sellwood family before the eighteenth century, with the exception of Abbot John de Selwode, a native of the East Woodlands, near Frome, who was elected fifty-seventh abbot of Glastonbury on November 15, 1457.

[12]The George and Pilgrims' Inn, built in High Street in 1470, now a hotel.

Mirehouse. James Spedding discovered that [we] were at an Hotel in Keswick, called on [us] and pressed [us] to go to Myer House.[13] [My] first acquaintance with this good & wise & delightful friend. Most kind was [our] reception and [our] visit very pleasant. Excursions on lake and mountain which [we] enjoyed and the family circle which could not fail to be interesting. The father a fine old English Gentleman and the brother Tom looking as if he had walked down from some stately picture of Velasquez.

Afterwards having from his cousins the Boynes the offer of Brancepeth, from the Marshalls of Coniston that of Tent Lodge, Coniston, & from Miss Heathcote that of her cottage, we chose Tent Lodge as most suitable to our fortunes & set off there [late July].[14]

Most kind were his old friend Mary Marshall (Spring Rice) and our drives with her on the mountains & our rowings on the lake, he rowing, I steering, were delightful in among the water lilies or by some clump of Firs where the Herons were watching us or to some island or the further shore where we one day found a scrap of newspaper left by some picnic party with the names of one of his uncles & one of mine. At [*illegible*] Coniston I saw Carlyle for the first time. He was staying there. When your Father presented me to him, he looked at me for a

[13]James Spedding (1808–81), author and essayist, editor of *The Works of Francis Bacon* (1857), was a Cambridge Apostle and Tennyson's lifelong friend. After this initial meeting with Tennyson's bride at the Speddings' home, Mirehouse, in Keswick, Spedding gave Aubrey DeVere "an excellent account of Mrs. Tennyson, saying that she is very good, sensible, and anxious to make her husband write poetry. She is thirty-seven years old, and has much beauty, and they are happy together" (Ward, *Aubrey De Vere*, p. 158). Again, Spedding was "deeply impressed with Alfred's happiness and serenity" when he dined with the Tennysons at Chapel House on March 11, 1851 (*AT*, p. 261).

Occasionally Emily Tennyson lapsed into the third person, evidently thinking that she would thus expedite Hallam Tennyson's writing of the *Memoir*; but she subsequently changed most of her pronouns back to the first person, both here and in the "Narrative for Her Sons." I have changed the person [in brackets] where she neglected to do so.

[14]In 1828 Gustavus Frederick Hamilton, 7th Viscount Boyne (1797–1872), had married Emma Maria, daughter of Maj. Matthew Russell and Mrs. Elizabeth Russell, the elder sister of Tennyson's father, Dr. George Clayton Tennyson. Earlier in 1850 the Boynes had succeeded to Brancepeth Castle, the ancient home of the Neville family, in Durham. Several others also offered honeymoon houses, but the Tennysons decided to visit Tent Lodge, the home of James Marshall and his wife, Mary, the sister of Tennyson's old Cambridge friend Stephen Spring-Rice. They stayed with the Marshalls at Coniston from the end of July until mid-October, when Tennyson began looking for a permanent home.

second from head to foot & then gave me a hearty shake of the hand. Your Father made me rather nervous, I dare say, listening to what I said to him at dinner, & no doubt was rather nervous himself when he heard me say, "Mr. Carlyle, you know that that is not sane." Next day, I think, he came to call and hearing me cough & seeing a window open behind me he quietly shut it. He was ever invariably most kind to me.

While there [mid-August] Edmund Lushington, Mr. Patmore, Mr. Woolner, Mr. Kirkpatrick visited [us] and he made [me] known to his old friends, Aubrey de Vere & his delightful mother, who were staying with the Marshalls.[15] Aubrey de Vere, he said, looked like a young Seraph. Then as now he was a delightful companion. [We] saw also Franklin & Ellen Lushington, & Mr. Lear, the Monteagles.[16] Among acquaintances

[15]Coventry Patmore (1823–96), the poet, is best remembered for *The Angel in the House*, which he published in four separate volumes, *The Betrothal* (1854), *The Espousals* (1856), *Faithful Forever* (1860), and *The Victories of Love* (1862). Patmore's other books of verse include *The Children's Garland* (1862), which he wrote with his first wife, Emily (d. 1862), and *The Unknown Eros and Other Odes* (1877).

Thomas Woolner (1825–92), the sculptor, was long an intimate friend of the Tennysons. In 1851 and 1855 Woolner did plaster medallions of Tennyson; he completed his marble bust of the poet (now in the Library, Trinity College, Cambridge) in 1857. In 1867 Woolner showed a three-quarter medallion of Tennyson at the Royal Academy; he finished a draped bust in plaster in 1874; and his final Tennyson study, the bearded bust (now in the National Gallery, Adelaide), was completed in 1876. Woolner also did a bronze medallion of Emily Tennyson in 1858 which he exhibited at the Royal Academy.

Kirkpatrick = unidentified.

Aubrey DeVere (1814–1902) was an Irish poet and dramatist. After becoming well acquainted with Emily Tennyson, DeVere expressed his high opinion of her in a letter of September 24, 1854, to Isabella Fenwick: "I regard her as one of the 'few noble' whom it has been my lot to meet in life; and with a nature so generous, and so religious a use of the high qualities God has given her, I cannot but hope that the happiness accorded to her after so many years of trial, may be more and more blessed to her as the days go by" (Ward, *Aubrey DeVere*, pp. 227–28).

[16]Franklin Lushington (1823–1901), Edward Lear's friend and brother-in-law of Tennyson's sister, Cecilia; judge to the Supreme Court of the Ionian Islands from 1855 until 1858. In September 1855 the Tennysons selected Lushington to be official guardian for their sons, Hallam and Lionel, in the event of their own deaths. Ellen Lushington was his wife.

Edward Lear was a dear friend of both Emily and Tennyson, and through the years Emily became his particular confidante. It was Lear who in 1859 decided, "computing moderately, that 15 angels, several hundreds of ordinary women, many philosophers, a heap of truly wise and kind mothers, 3 or 4 minor prophets, and a lot of doctors and schoolmistresses fall far short of what Emily Tennyson really is" (*AT*, p. 319).

The Monteagles were Thomas Spring-Rice, 1st Baron Monteagle of Bran-

made at Tent Lodge Mrs. Fletcher was one of the most remarkable.[17] She had known Walter Scott & his friends intimately and seemed worthy to have known them. She told among other things of travelling tailors who used to recite fragments of Ossianic poems before the days of Macpherson. They recited in Gaelic.

The ever-changing aspect of lake and mountain was, of course, a continual source of delight. Day by day lordly wreaths of storm clouds across the mountains & sunlit clouds like bright spirits or a rainbow in the lake are recorded or the pleasure of gathering grass of Parnassus or Stags Horn moss or . . . of seeing the Touch-me-not, a balsam with a yellow tube flower whose seed vessels coiled in their spirals burst when touched with rather a loud crack. The interest of hearing that thirteen wild swans had been seen just before Christmas by Mr. Beaver, a resident near the lake, which had alighted within sight of his window, also of the wild black bird in his garden which had learned to call his dog "Bonny Bonny" in the tone and manner of a maid servant then in his service & so distinctly that the dog had been seen running at the call. . . . [We] went to Rydal Mount and back home but did not go in.

Of one wild stormy night during Edmund Lushington's visit there is a record for [our] bed-room window was broken & [we] had to take up [our] quarters in another room. . . . But the pleasant days at Tent Lodge came to an end. The Marshalls most kindly offered [us] to take up our abode at Tent Lodge and Lady Ashburton wished [us] to live in one of theirs at Pepper-corn rent.[18] [We] were very grateful but thought it best to go house-hunting for [ourselves] & that ever hospitable Park House received [us] meanwhile.

---

don (1790–1866), and his second wife, Marianne (d. 1889), eldest daughter of John Marshall of Hellsteads, Cumberland. Spring-Rice was secretary to the Treasury in Earl Grey's administration from 1830 until 1834, and he served as chancellor of the Exchequer in Melbourne's second administration, 1835–39.

[17]Eliza Fletcher (1770–1858) was the widow of Archibald Fletcher (1746–1828), the Scottish reformer and author. Her well-known *Autobiography of Mrs. Fletcher of Edinburgh* was published in 1875 under the editorship of her daughter, the widow of Sir John Richardson.

[18]Harriet Mary Baring (1805–57) was the daughter of George John Montagu, 6th earl of Sandwich, and wife of William Bingham Baring, 2d Baron Ashburton (1799–1864). Lady Ashburton later entertained Tennyson at her celebrated Christmas literary party of 1855.

October

14th. [We] left for Cheltenham and travelled with Mr. Matthew Arnold then in the hey-day of youth. Next day lunched at the Birminghams' & arrived at his Mother's house. . . . On the 21st [we] went to Somerset House. Thence [we] went to the Henry Taylors at Mortlake and met Mr. Edward Villiers & Mrs. Cameron, Mr. Taylor, then to see the likely houses in the neighbourhood.[19] [Our] first sight of Mrs. Cameron with whom [we] were afterwards so intimate. That day she was a delightful picture in her dark green silk with wide open sleeves, the dress fastened by a silk cord round the waist and having the courtly charm of manner which was one of her many phases & one which became her right well.

23rd. Went to Park House by Rochester.

November

6th. On the morning of the 9th a letter came from Col. Phipps offering him the Laureateship.[20] That night he had had a dream that the Queen and the Prince had called on him at his Mother's and been very gracious, the Prince kissing him which made him think "very kind but very German." He had told this to [me] before the letter from the private secretary was brought to [us]. It promised that no birthday ode should be required. After some consideration the office was on the 13th accepted. On the 14th Monckton Milnes arrives and having been told the story of the dream & the laureateship wrote it off to Germany

[19] Edward Villiers = unidentified.

Mrs. Cameron was Julia Margaret Cameron (1815–79), wife of Charles Hay Cameron, the former president of the Indian Law Commission; famous for her portrait photography, as well as for her volcanic energy and her extravagant generosity. Tennyson was particularly fond of Mrs. Cameron, though she was forever inveigling him to sit for her photographs or to submit to a variety of her eccentric demands. The poet often complained that Mrs. Cameron's portraits gave him much unwanted publicity, but he would endure for her sake what he would tolerate from no one else.

The friend of Wordsworth and Southey as well as Tennyson, Henry Taylor (1800–1886) was both a longtime officer in the colonial service and a successful poet and man of letters, best remembered for his verse drama *Philip van Artevelde* (1834).

[20] Col. Charles Beaumont Phipps (1801–66) was an equerry to the queen at Osborne House, near East Cowes on the Isle of Wight.

as he told us at luncheon.[21] He stayed the 15, 16, 17th and was very amusing. He kindly said that if ever we would come & stay with him at Fryston, we should have a wing of the house to ourselves. Miss Horton, Mr. Venables, Mr. Crawford were other guests.[22]

House-hunting again. During this week there he read nearly all *Twelfth Night* & *King Lear* to [us].

[21] Richard Monckton Milnes was 1st Baron Houghton (1809–85).

[22] Miss Horton = unidentified.

George Stovin Venables (1810–88), the Cambridge Apostle, barrister and essayist, was a lifelong friend of the poet's.

Crawford = unidentified.

1851

January

20th. [Upon arriving] at Warninglid we found the dining-room and his room & [our] room more comfortable than might have been expected.[1] I had had the good fortune to bring with [me] from [my] Father's house an excellent Cook and Housemaid. Milnes & her sister Matilda made matters much easier than they might otherwise have been.[2] Next morning he had a long walk and heard the birds sing as he had never heard them sing since he left Somersby, and he ate a good breakfast for him on his return. However that day we were blown out of the dining-room & he was smoked out of his room & the rain went more than halfway thro' our bedroom and the storm was so loud we could not sleep so he got up & read some of the books we had unpacked the evening before.

21st. He had a walk again before breakfast and then wrote out the Seizure-Cataleptic alterations in *The Princess* while I packed his things to go house-hunting once more.

Milnes and [my] yard-wand went with him to measure the rooms of houses in the neighbourhood but they found no house likely to suit, so he went off to Twickenham and slept at the Castle. Workmen hammering away every day during his absence to make the house a little more tenantable & comfortable before his return. He returned to stormy nights again in which we could not sleep and finally after consulting a doctor at Horsham whether I might travel, we paid our year's rent and rates & taxes.

February

2nd. And bade farewell to Warninglid and he with his accustomed tenderness drew [me] in a garden chair some two miles over

[1]The Tennysons' first home was at Warninglid, near Horsham, in Sussex, where they settled on January 20, 1851. The house soon proved unsatisfactory, however; its remoteness was especially intolerable because Emily was expecting her first child in April.

[2]Milnes and Tilly were maids who assisted the Tennysons in their move to Warninglid.

the rough road guarding [me] from every jolt on [our] way to the Talbot Inn.

3rd. Arrived at Shiplake. He much enjoyed his time there with Drummond and sometimes Mr. Kingsley and Mr. Barsun. Drummond's father, Mr. Rawnsley, Rector of Halton, was also there and Alice Wright, a lively cousin of his. The birds sang delightfully and the buds of the lime trees were crimson in the sunlight and the weather often enjoyable and the walks in the terrace pleasant. The water was much out from rain in the nights and occasionally in the days and one day he saw a double shadow of himself, one from the sun, one from the water. We read *Alton Locke.*[3]

Many days he went house-hunting in the neighbourhood but without success.

18th. We set off for Park House and slept at the Clarendon [Hotel] where I fell down a little step tho' warned by him a minute or two before and made myself very ill. He doctored the sprained foot water-care fashion with loving care.

20th. We arrived at Park House & there I was for some time under a doctor's care.

23rd. He went up to Franklin Lushington's rooms for the Levee & for House-hunting and saw Chapel House in Town.[4]

24th. We read *Alton Locke*, drove about in search of the Court-dress. Man recommended by Mr. Rawnsley but could not find him & so had to give up the Levee on the 26th.

Rogers hearing of this kindly sent for him & offered him his own dress which had been worn also by Wordsworth and had been promised to the Wordsworth family as an heir-loom.[5] The coat did well enough but about other parts of the dress there was some anxiety as they had not been tried on.

[3]The importance of Charles Kingsley's *Alton Locke* as a source for *Maud* has been suggested by Sir Charles Tennyson: "Alfred and Emily both read *Alton Locke*, and the story of the tailor poet particularly moved Alfred" (*AT*, p. 260). J. B. Steane describes the resemblances of *Maud* to *Alton Locke* in detail in his *Tennyson* (London: Evans Bros., 1966), pp. 93–94, 111–12.

[4]On March 11, 1851, the Tennysons moved into Chapel House, Twickenham, where they resided until they secured Farringford in November 1853.

[5]Hearing of Tennyson's difficulties about a Court dress, Samuel Rogers offered his own suit, which Wordsworth had once worn on a similar occasion.

March

3rd. A. went again to London and stayed at Sir Alexander Duff-Gordon's.[6] He went in the evening to Lord John Russell's party put off from last week by the change of ministry & was introduced to Bunsen & the Duke of Argyll.[7] The Duke in after days & to the end of his life one of his most valued friends.

4th. A. went to a soireé at Bunsen's.

5th. Dined at the Marshalls.

6th. Got well thro' the Levee. Mr. J. G. Marshall & Sir. A. Gordon were both with him and he talked with Lord Monteagle who introduced him to Sir George Grey.[8]

7th. A. gave the news of the agreement with Mr. Clifton for Chapel House having been signed. Joyful news for [us] both.

8th. Our servants went to Chapel House but found all comfortless, Mr. Clifton having misunderstood about the day.

10th. We left Park House & A. gathered there the first Daffodils from the Park and Ellen went out in the rain to get me a nosegay. We slept at Rochester.

11th. Grigsby, the Park House coachman, arrived to look after us and our luggage and at London Bridge Station we found the Marshalls delightfully luxurious carriage with Butler and coachman & groom waiting for us. Grigsby being there, we sent back the groom and got wonderfully well over the journey to Chapel House, thanks to all this care & kindness. Mr. Marshall & Mr. Taylor & the Welds[9] looked after us. Mr. Spedding also & the Patmores dined with us.

[6] Sir Alexander Duff-Gordon (1811–72), husband of Lady Lucie Duff-Gordon (1821–69), the brilliant literary hostess and friend of Heine.

[7] Baron Christian von Bunsen (1791–1860) was a Prussian diplomat and scholar. He was Prussian minister to London from 1842 until 1854.

George Douglas Campbell, 8th duke of Argyll (1823–1900), was a scientist, poet, chancellor of the University of St. Andrews, secretary of state for India, 1868–74, and Lord Privy Seal, 1852–55, 1859–66, 1880–81. Argyll was of great importance to Tennyson in his relations with the Court, and it was he who wrote to Tennyson on March 25, 1862, conveying the queen's command for the laureate's initial visit to Osborne. Argyll introduced Tennyson to the House of Lords in March 1884.

[8] Sir George Gray (1799–1882) was a statesman who served as home secretary under Russell, 1846–52, and under Palmerston, 1855–58 and 1861–66.

[9] Emily's sister Anne and her husband, Charles Richard Weld (d. 1869), assistant secretary and historian of the Royal Society from 1845 until 1861.

25th. Father pays us his first visit. Looking at the Bishop, he fell backward down-stairs & bruised his eye & his legs. Alfred walks before breakfast; short walks, not like the long Warninglid walks. Duty walks and alas! without pleasure.

April

3rd. He saw the first swallows in the Thames. Mrs. Marshall & Mr. Taylor come from time to time. They are most good to me.

12th. Our Father goes.

20th. [Our] first child born.[10]

July–October

Italian journey. In Paris [we] saw the Brownings on [our] way from Italy to England.[11] They came to [us] at the Hotel Donores[?] where [we] were staying. Mr. Browning friendly then as he was to the end. She very fragile-looking with great spirit-eyes met [me] more as a sister than a stranger. Saville Morton came also & his wild laugh sounded thro' the corridors.[12] The Brownings came to say goodbye but [we] were out. [We] found on [our] return two beautiful Paris nosegays exactly alike. The flowers of both arranged in a sort of Grecian pattern (in colours beautifully mixed).

Having the greatest gifts, he never got his due meed of praise from the world.

[10]On April 20, 1851, the Tennysons' first child was born dead, likely as a result of Emily's fall at the Clarendon Hotel on the journey from Shiplake to Park House.

[11]The Tennysons left for their first trip abroad together in early July and returned to Chapel House before the end of October.

The Brownings were, of course, the poets Robert (1812–99) and Elizabeth Barrett (1806–61).

[12]Saville Morton (d. 1852) was for many years correspondent of the *Daily News* in Paris.

1852

[April 3]

Saturday before Passion Week. We go . . . to A.'s old friend's, Mr. Rashdall, Vicar of Malvern. A man so beloved that he had emptied the dissenting chapels. The congregations coming to his church services held sometimes in a field. We drive to Eastnor castle to see the wild daffodils tho' the Somers[1] were absent. A flowery record of spring wood anemones, primroses, dog-violets, cowslips, hyacinths at Lord Beauchamp's,[2] Cowley Park & different places in the neighbourhood. The pear trees covered with blossoms, like springing and falling fountains, charmed us much and the British Camp interested us greatly.[3]

We see Mr. Dobell[4] from time to time & Mr. Foxbury, Mr. Harris. We look at different houses in the neighbourhood but to all some objection is found. We go to hear Mr. Dibdin preach and rejoice in the earnestness of his faith. A. is much interested in a long talk he has with him. During our visit he reads Wordsworth's *Apocalypse* to me.[5] We left the land of Apple blossoms & Plum blossoms and flowering shrubs and trees of many sorts which had so much delighted us and bade farewell to our kind host and went to Cheltenham for about a fortnight, & then returned home on June 16th bringing our sister Matilda with us. He and his sister went to the Exhibition & saw Millais' *Ophelia* & *The Huguenots*.[6] A. was much delighted with both but much the most with *The Huguenots*. Our neigh-

[1] Charles Somers, 3d Earl Somers (1819–83), and his wife, Virginia (1827–1910), daughter of James Pattle of the Bengal Civil Service. Eastnor Castle, located two miles southeast of Hereford, was built in 1812 by the 1st Earl Somers.

[2] Henry Beauchamp, 5th Earl Beauchamp (1829–66), M.P. for West Worcestershire until 1863, when he succeeded his father as earl.

[3] The camp was located atop Herefordshire Beacon (1,370 ft.), legendary scene of the capture of Caractacus by the Romans in A.D. 75.

[4] Sydney Thompson Dobell (1824–74), a "Spasmodic" poet and critic. Tennyson's *Maud* is reminiscent of Dobell's poetry, particularly *Balder* (1853), which the laureate often praised.

[5] *The Prelude* (1850) VI.617–40.

[6] Both paintings were first exhibited in 1852. John Everett Millais (1829–96) used Elizabeth Sidall (later Mrs. D. G. Rossetti) as his model for *Ophelia*.

bours, Dr. Parish, the incumbent of our Chapel, Mr. Scooner, a clergyman at Twickenham, call. Mr. Archibald Peel, of whom from this time we see a great deal and whom [we] like much, takes A. to Marble Hill & points out the Avenue in which Sir Walter Scott places the interview between Jeanie Deans & Queen Caroline, and A. occasionally takes advantage of the permission kindly given to walk in the grounds.[7]

Franklin Lushington, the Patmores, Mr. Woolner dine with us & we spend happy days chiefly in our little garden.

A. reads some of Herschel's *Astronomy*[8] to me & we have long talks together until July 7th when he goes up to sleep at Mr. Spedding's rooms on his way to the sea. My Father and the Welds come to us and my Father remains with me during A.'s absence. Mr. Venables, Mr. Peel also visit me. A. goes to Whitby, Scarborough, and Grasby. He likes the new vicarage there & thinks the country looking pretty. My Father leaves and A. returns & we have drives in the Park and our little Hallam is born on the 11th of August.[9]

From the first A. watched him with profound interest. Some would have smiled to see him bringing our baby in his Bassinet to the drawing-room when no guest was there. He wrote "Out of the Deep, My Child" to him ("De Profundis"). He was christened at Twickenham, 5 October. There was some question as to the name. A. with a loud voice said "Hallam," & Mr. Hallam[10] looked pleased tho' jokingly he said afterwards in Sutton they were afraid he might be a fool so they would not call him Alfred but they called him Hallam. The guests were: Mr. Hallam, Mr. Maurice, Mr. & Mrs. Brookfield, Mr. & Mrs. James Marshall, Mr. Henry Taylor & Aubrey, Mr. & Mrs. Cameron, Mr. Venables, Sir Alexander & Lady Duff Gordon, Mr. Palgrave, Mr. [*illegible*], Edmund Lushington, Charles &

[7] Archibald Peel, whom Tennyson first met in 1851, was the son of Gen. Jonathan Peel of Marble Hill. The Jeanie Deans–Queen Caroline interview occurs in *The Heart of Midlothian*.

[8] John Frederick William Herschel, *Outlines of Astronomy* (London, 1849).

[9] On the same day Tennyson wrote of the birth to his friend John Forster, Dickens's biographer: "I have seen beautiful things in my life, but I never saw anything more beautiful than the mother's face as she lay by the young child an hour or two after, or heard anything sweeter than the little lamb-bleat of the young one. I had fancied that children after birth had been all shriek and roar, but he gave out a little note of satisfaction every now and then, as he lay by his mother, which was the most pathetic sound in its helplessness I ever listened to. You see I talk almost like a bachelor, yet unused to these things" (*AT*, p. 269).

[10] Henry Hallam (1777–1859), the historian and father of Arthur Henry Hallam.

Louisa Turner, Charles, Anne, & Agnes Weld, Matilda Tennyson, Drummond Rawnsley, Stephen Spring-Rice, Mr. Browning, Mrs. & Miss Bolton, Mr. Archibald & Miss Peel.[11] Mr. James Marshall, Mr. Hallam & Mr. Maurice were sponsors. Mrs. Browning too ill to come tho' they had stayed in England on purpose. Mr. Carlyle's letter got thrown aside in the hurry of moving. Mr. Tom Taylor[12] came next day by mistake. Mr. Charles Spring-Rice did not come thro' another mistake. Mrs. Henry Taylor & Catherine Rawnsley kept at home by their babies. Mr. Scooner performed the service. Drummond Rawnsley gave the haunch of Venison, the best I had ever tasted. There were flowers and beautiful peaches & other fruit & the best champagne we could get. Milnes made so perfect a breakfast that it was thought to have come from Gunters & we were proud.

After this the funeral of the Duke of Wellington came [November 18]. A most impressive sight. A.'s ode[13] was written before he had seen it. Later at Farringford I had a dream that the Duke came to our home to see us. He rose to shake hands with me & I feared the cold hand of death but it proved a warm living hand. The river is so much out that we are afraid of damp for our little Hallam & take him to Lord Howard de Walden's[14] house at Seaford. In the garden was a pretty fence made apparently of two rows of saddleback tiles. He likes the walks near the sea & to Alfriston. Sometimes from the house waves playing at hide & seek over the bank may be seen. There we made acquaintance with Mr. Fitzgerald's brother. Mr. Lear came to us there and A. said perverted our Hallam from the pure protestant worship of morning light on the bedpost to that Romanism of a gay dancing [*illegible*].

[11] Among those attending Hallam Tennyson's christening were F. D. Maurice (1805–72), the Christian Socialist and Cambridge Apostle; William Henry Brookfield (1809–74), rector, school inspector, and later chaplain in ordinary to Queen Victoria, and his wife, Jane (1821–96), the intimate friend of Thackeray and first cousin of Arthur Hallam; Henry Taylor and his son Aubrey; Francis Turner Palgrave (1824–97), editor of *The Golden Treasury*; Tennyson's brother Charles and his wife, Louisa, Emily's youngest sister; Charles Weld, his wife Anne, Emily's other sister, and their daughter, Agnes; and Tennyson's old Trinity friend Stephen Spring-Rice (1814–65).

[12] Tom Taylor (1817–80) was the famed dramatist, journalist, and editor of *Punch*.

[13] "Ode on the Death of the Duke of Wellington," published November 16, 1852, Tennyson's first separate publication since becoming poet laureate.

[14] Charles John Howard, earl of Suffolk and earl of Berkshire (1804–76). Howard was styled Viscount Andover and also Lord Howard (of Walden).

1853

The Marshalls being at Brighton we afterwards took a small house in Kemp Town for a time where we had our little Hallam vaccinated. Thinking that it would in future be an interesting link in the generations, we took him to Mr. Rogers, one of his breakfast mornings reminding me, no doubt, of the other but more slender link when some years before I had been asked to dance by Mary Chaworth's "Jack Musters" as he was called by his familiars.[1] Mr. Rogers was most kind. He kissed the baby boy & said in his courtly way to Mother, "Mrs. Tennyson, I made one great mistake in my life. I never married."

Then went to Farnham house-hunting again. Here we saw Mr. Kingsley who came to visit us and whose talk was as ever interesting. Hallam spent his first birthday at Grasby where we took him after having been at Whitby, Redcar, & Richmond. He [Tennyson] had left to go to Scotland alone, the cold of Whitby having been too much for Hallam.

My husband ill three weeks in Edinburgh. Ludovic Colquhoun[2] very kind to him. "The Daisy" written then. The Englands were so good as to lend him their house. He joined me at Grasby afterwards and Frederic[3] was also there. Later [October] he went to Bonchurch to his friends the James Whites, Edmund Reek, & Feildens.[4] From them he heard of Farringford as a place that might possibly do for us. He went and found it looking rather wretched with wet leaves trampled

[1]Musters was the dashing, fox-hunting squire who married Byron's first love, Mary Chaworth.

[2]Ludovic Colquhoun (1807–54), Tennyson's Scottish friend with whom he had become acquainted while the two men were taking the water cure together at Dr. C. M. Gulley's establishment at Umberslade Hall in the spring of 1847. A great admirer of Tennyson's poetry, Colquhoun occasionally wrote poems himself, and in 1852 he sent the Tennysons a sonnet celebrating the birth of Hallam.

[3]Tennyson's brother Frederick Tennyson.

[4]James White (1803–62), author and curate, lived much of his life in Bonchurch, Isle of Wight, where he wrote a number of Scottish historical tragedies and other historical and miscellaneous writings.

Edmund Reek = unidentified.

The Feildens = unidentified.

Farringford House, circa 1853, before Tennyson added his library tower. (National Portrait Gallery)

into the downs. However we thought it worth while to go and look at it together. The railway did not go further than Brockenhurst then and the steamer, when there was one from Lymington, felt itself in no way bound to wait for the omnibus which brought as many of the passengers as it could from the train. We crossed in a rowing boat. It was a still November evening. One dark heron flew over the Solent backed by a Daffodil sky.

We went to Lambert's, then Plumbley's Hotel[5] . . . smaller than now. Next day we went to Farringford & looking from the drawing-room window thought "I must have that view" and I said so to him when alone. So accordingly we agreed with Mr. Seymour to take the place furnished for a time on trial with the option of purchasing.[6]

November

24th. We left Chapel House, to be occupied for the remainder of the lease by our Mother, and arrived at Lymington sleeping at the Hotel as we feared to take our Hallam over the Solent in a row-boat.

25th. A great day for us. We reached Farringford. It was a misty morning & two of the servants on seeing it burst into tears saying they could never live in such a lonely place. We amused ourselves during the autumn. I would by sweeping up leaves for exercise and by making a muddy path thro' the plantation into a Sandy one. We were delighted with the snowdrops & primroses in the plantation & by the cooing of the Stock-dove & the song of the Redwings.

[5]The best hotel in Freshwater, Isle of Wight, in its day.

[6]Mr. Seymour owned Farringford, together with the surrounding grounds, until the Tennysons bought it from him in 1856.

A picturesque, fifteen-room country house, Farringford stands about a mile from the southern shore of the Isle of Wight on a little eminence just north of the high chalk cliffs that rise five hundred feet above the sea. Although the land attached to the house became the property of one Walter de Ferringford in the fourteenth century, Farringford itself was not built until around 1800. Despite its extensive views, Farringford was as isolated as Tennyson could have wished. Dense pine, elm, holly, and laurel sequestered it on the north; a thick belt of elms secluded the house from behind; and to the east lay the great cliffs and the sea. Arthur Paterson has observed that "no wild bird's nest was ever better hidden than was Tennyson's home in 1853" (Helen Allingham and Arthur Paterson, *The Homes and Haunts of Tennyson* [London: Adam and Charles Black, 1905], p. 18).

1854

February

28th. A. makes "a bower of rushes" in the kitchen garden facing the down. Sitting there we heard the sound of the cannon practising for the Crimea. Their booming sounded somewhat knell-like. He found the little carriage in the village in which for so many years he drew me about when I could not walk[1]—a constant source of pleasure to us.

March

16th. Our Lionel born. A. when he heard of it was watching in the little study under the bedroom and saw Mars in the Lion culminating. This afterwards determined us to give our baby the name of Lionel—a family name before proposed among others.[2]

April

The little carriage was soon in requisition & I was taken by A. to see the "wealth of Daffodils" in the wilderness and we admired the rose-coloured & green sheaths of the Lime leaves as they lay like flowers under the trees and a great many things besides. Edmund Lushington and Mr. Patmore had been staying with us about a week and they insisted on taking me up the down[3] two days. The view delighted me and we were interested by a mirage which we saw on the top of the down as we ascended. There seemed a great river with black islands in it. All the air along the line of the down became visible in moving waves.

[1] For comments on Emily's physical fragility, see the Introduction, pp. 4, 8–9 and *Letters of E. T.*, pp. 7–8.

[2] The sight of Mars culminating in the Lion seemed particularly significant to Tennyson, for at the time a declaration of war against Russia appeared to be imminent. Within the fortnight war was declared and soon thereafter the Tennysons' second son was christened Lionel.

[3] The High Down (now Tennyson Down) overlooks the sea, where Tennyson walked each day and where he often took Emily for private outings, the poet drawing his wife along in her special carriage.

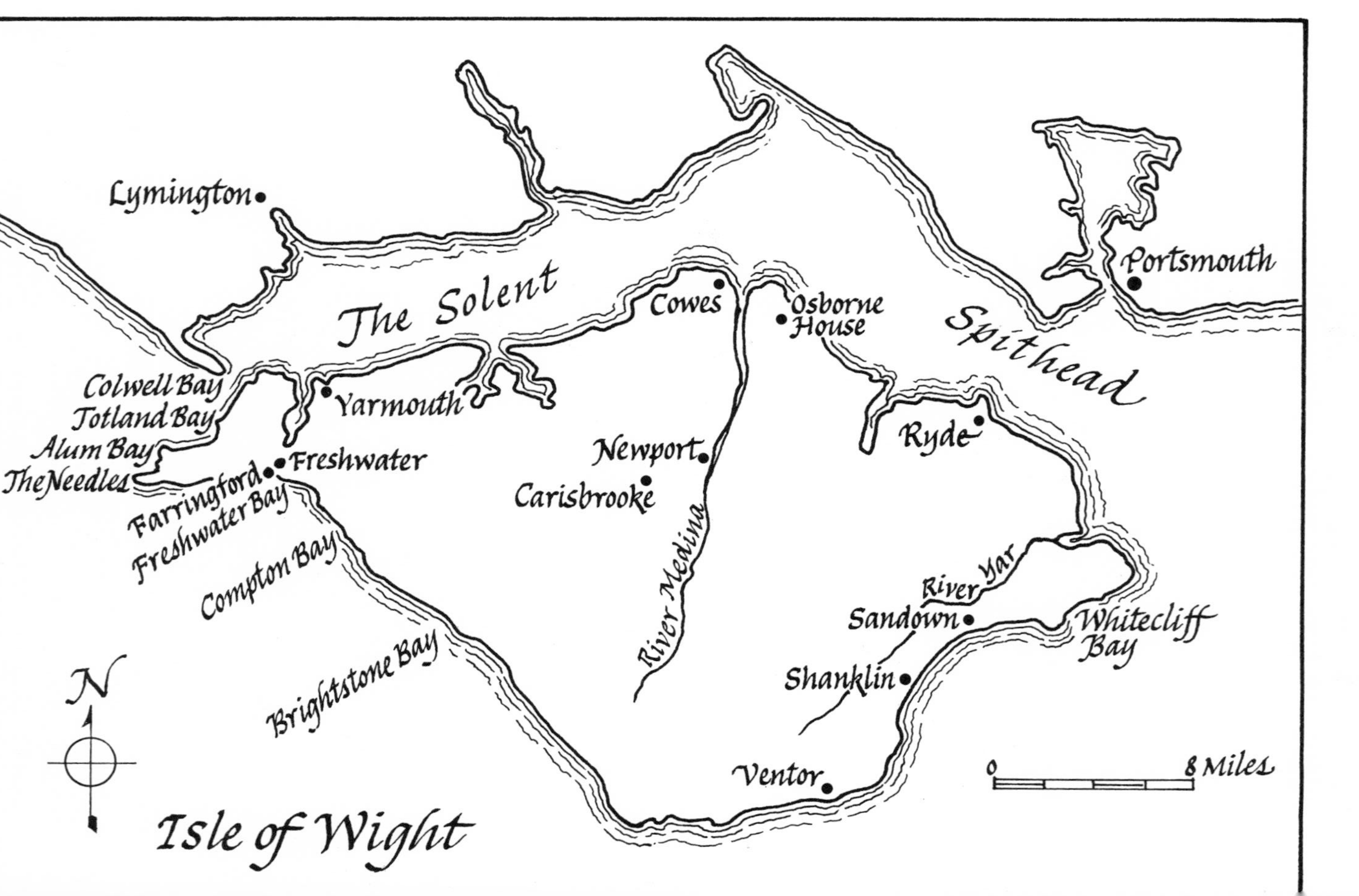
Lymington
The Solent
Cowes
Osborne House
Portsmouth
Spithead
Colwell Bay
Totland Bay
Yarmouth
Alum Bay
The Needles
Freshwater
Farringford
Freshwater Bay
Newport
Carisbrooke
Ryde
River Medina
Compton Bay
River Yar
Sandown
Whitecliff Bay
Shanklin
Brightstone Bay
N
Ventor
0
8 Miles
Isle of Wight

May

15th. The three gentlemen went up to London together.

23rd. A. returned.

25th. Mr. FitzGerald came & stayed about a fortnight. Delightfully amusing he was. He often went out with his sketch book and brought us home sketches and horned poppies and orchids and yellow daisies. In the evening he translated Persian odes for A. who had hurt his eye while I was shut up in my room by poring over a small printed Persian Grammar which, with other Persian books whose type seemed to be trying, I confess [*illegible*] to have hidden away. Some evenings Mr. FitzGerald played to us beautiful airs from Mozart, Handel, or some old English composer. His memory for music was wonderful.

June

3rd. Franklin Lushington came.

6th. Our Lionel was christened, he being one Godfather, Mr. FitzGerald standing proxy for Drummond Rawnsley & I for Emma Hamilton Russell who had been thrown out of a carriage & was confined to the sofa.[4] On returning from Church we found Sir John Simeon.[5] This was my first introduction to a friend who was to be so much to us both as long as he lived. A. had met him before.

Mr. Isaacson (the Rector), Mr. Bateman, Mr. Sheriff & a friend of his dined with us. Franklin Lushington made sketches & left us on the 9th. He liked the place. When strong enough I helped A. to work in the garden. He took some very long walks in the great heat, to Bonchurch once and back, sometimes over the shingly shore, other walks almost as long to Newport & back & to Newtown. He knocked himself up but did not tell me.

[4] As a result of this accident Emma Maria Russell Hamilton (Lady Boyne) was confined to Brancepeth during early June.

[5] Sir John Simeon (1815–70) was the Roman Catholic squire of Swainston Hall, near Newport, eight miles east of Farringford. He became one of the laureate's dearest friends, and he is immortalized in Tennyson's "In the Garden at Swainston."

July

25th. A letter from Edmund Lushington telling of his sister Louisa's death at Avignon on the 17th, a grievous loss. With the intellect of the family she had great sweetness and humility and was beloved by all I think.

The abundance of wild flowers was delightful to us. St. John's wort (a mystical plant as he called it), common centaury, common agrimony, the small campanula on the down, Law-wort, Flea-wort, & the lovely little Lady's tresses.

August

11th. We kept our little Hallam's birthday by taking him & our servants to Alum Bay. Hallam to his exceeding delight driving the donkey. Afterwards he was taken to Scratchell's Bay in a boat, A. & the servants with him. I had to go home with nurse & baby.

12th. I saw A. off on the Solent with Mr. Grant for Christchurch, Corfe Castle, Swanage.[6] Near there they found an old Waterloo man who delighted them. They slept at Bournemouth one night, then Mr. Grant was obliged to return. A. went on to Glastonbury, Wells, Cheddar Cliffs, and came home on the 21st and was ill afterwards.

29th. Mr. Mundy came and we had a pleasant talk about Lincolnshire people. He left the next day.

September

1st. Sir John & Lady Simeon came to luncheon bringing his brother & sister, Baron de Schroeter, and Aubrey de Vere & all

[6]Grant was Sir Alexander Grant (1826–84), best remembered as principal of Edinburgh University, where he devised the remarkably successful tercentenary celebration in 1884. Grant was appointed a public examiner in classics at Oxford in 1856, the same year he became 8th baronet of his line, and in 1863 he became vice-chancellor of the University of Bombay. In 1865 he was nominated director of public instruction for the presidency of Bombay, a position he held until he returned from India to accept the post at Edinburgh in 1868.

Located a few miles from the New Forest, Corfe Castle was built on the Purbeck Downs soon after the Norman Conquest. A favorite residence of King John, the castle occupies the site of the hunting lodge where Edward the Martyr was assassinated in 979. Also found on the peninsula known as Purbeck Island, Swanage is a charming little resort and watering place.

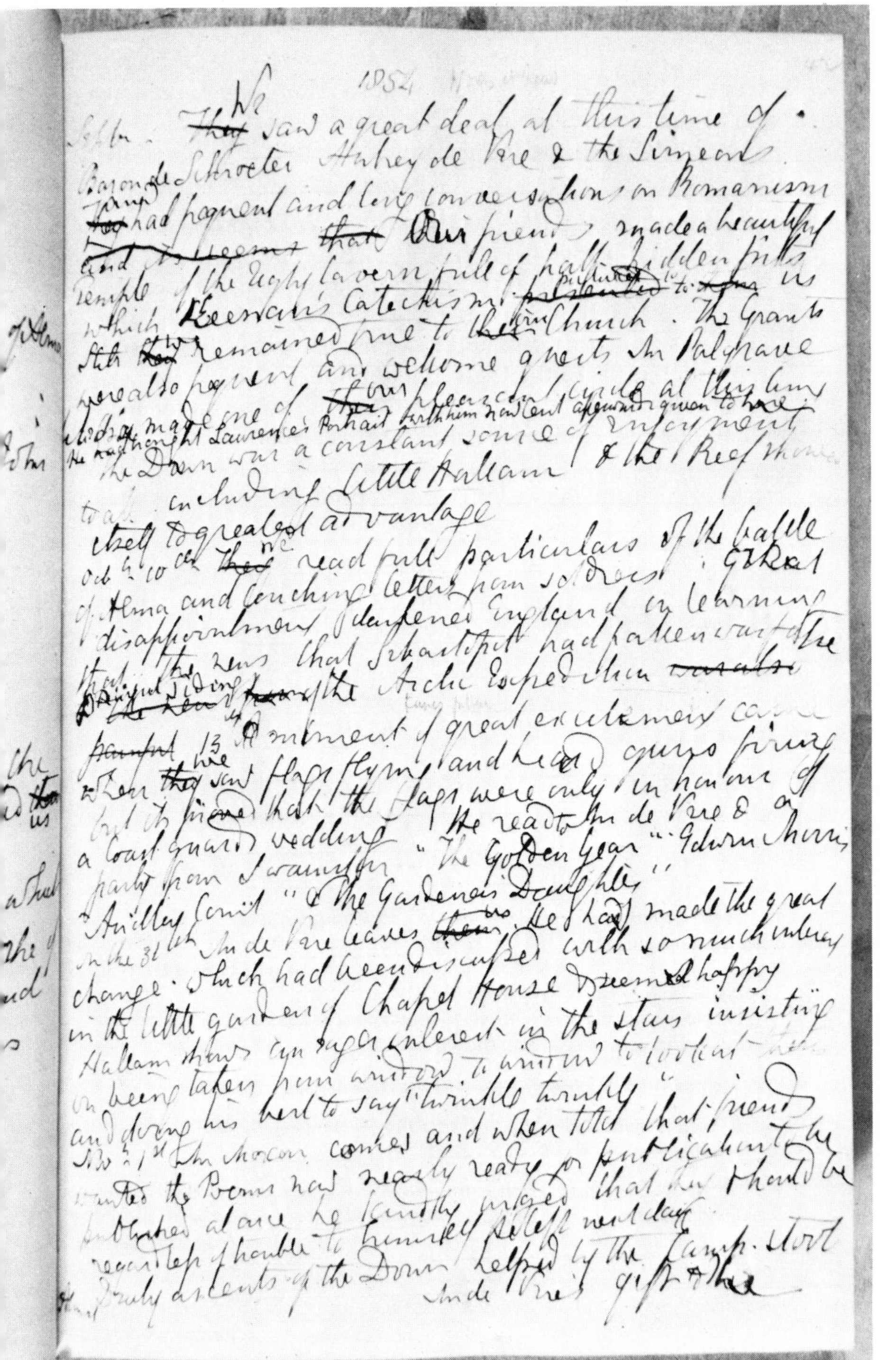

A facsimile of Lady Tennyson's handwriting from Journal entry for the autumn of 1854. (Courtesy of Lord Tennyson and the Lincolnshire Library Service)

except Lady Simeon & myself went to Alum Bay & then in a boat to the Needles taking Hallam with them.[7]

The Baron interested us greatly. His ardent love for souls being so rare.

6th. Aubrey de Vere comes to stay with us & Franklin Lushington, Edmund being also here.

We saw a great deal at this time of Baron de Schroeter, Aubrey de Vere, & the Simeons and had frequent and long conversations on Romanism and it seems that our friends made a beautiful Temple of the Ugly Cavern full of half-hidden pits which Keenan's Catechism[8] pictures to us. Still we remained true to our church. The Grants were also frequent and welcome guests.[9] Mr. Palgrave also who made one of our pleasant circle at this time; he had brought Laurence's Portrait with him, now lent, afterwards given to me.

20th. The battle of Alma.[10] A. read his "Maud" to Sir John.[11]

The down was a constant source of enjoyment to all, including little Hallam & the Reef showed itself to greatest advantage.

October

10th. We read full particulars of the battle of Alma and touching letters from soldiers. Great disappointment darkened England

[7]The first Lady Simeon was the former Jane Baker, daughter of Sir Frederick Baker.

Baron Th[eodore?] H. de Schroeter was a frequent quest of the Tennysons during his late summer (1854) stay with the Simeons. When he visited Farringford, the baron was tireless, and also somewhat tiring, especially to Emily Tennyson, in his efforts to convert the laureate's family to Roman Catholicism.

The Needles are a series of large angular rocks that protrude from the sea and form a line eastward from the shore immediately below the High Down.

[8]Stephen Keenan, *Controversial Catechism* (Edinburgh, 1846).

[9]Sir Alexander Grant's wife was the former Susan Ferrier, daughter of Professor James Frederick Ferrier of St. Andrews.

[10]All through the summer and autumn of 1854 Tennyson and Emily followed the developments of the Crimean War as they were reported in each day's *Times*. On September 17 the Allies landed in the Crimea, and a few days later followed the successful battle of the Alma.

[11]According to legend, it was at the suggestion of Sir John Simeon that the early lyric "Oh! that 'twere possible" was expanded into a longer work which eventually became *Maud*. However, Tennyson must have long thought of doing something more with "Oh! that 'twere possible," though Simeon's suggestion may indeed have spurred him on (*The Poems of Tennyson*, ed. Christopher Ricks [London and Harlow: Longmans, 1969], p. 1037).

on learning that the news that Sebastopol had fallen was false. Painful tidings of the Arctic Expedition.[12]

13th. A moment of great excitement came when we saw flags flying and heard guns firing but it proved that the flags were only in honour of a Coast guard wedding. He read to Mr. de Vere & a party from Swainston "The Golden Year," "Edwin Morris," "Audley Court," & "The Gardener's Daughter." On the 31st Mr. de Vere leaves us. He had made the great change which had been discussed with so much interest in the little garden of Chapel House & seemed happy. Hallam shows an eager interest in the stars, insisting on being taken from window to window to look at them and doing his best to say "twinkle, twinkle."

He reads many of Campbell's poems, some of which he had read to me on the little yellow sofa near one of the drawing-room windows at Somersby & I said that if I lived to teach the boys, the patriotic songs should be among the first they should learn.

November

1st. Mr. Moxon[13] comes and when told that friends wanted the Poems now nearly ready for publication to be published at once, he kindly urged that they should be regardless of trouble to himself. He left next day. Almost daily ascents of the Down helped by the Campstool, Mr. de Vere's gift to me.

8th. Looking from the Beacon and seeing the White Cliffs reflected in the beautifully clear sea, their violet gray shading looked to us tender & sad.[14] Perhaps the landscape seemed so

[12]Sir John Franklin (1786–1847), the Arctic explorer and Emily Tennyson's maternal uncle, was lost in the Arctic regions in 1847. Relics and further intelligence from Franklin's final expedition were obtained from the Eskimos in 1854.

[13]Edward Moxon (1801–58), Tennyson's publisher since 1832. It was largely because of Moxon's determined persuasion that Tennyson published his 1842 *Poems*, ending his decade of silence and establishing himself as a major poet. For complete discussions of the Moxon–Tennyson relationship, see Harold G. Merriman, *Edward Moxon: Publisher of Poets* (New York: Columbia University Press, 1939), pp. 169–87, and June Steffensen Hagen, *Tennyson and His Publishers* (University Park: Pennsylvania State University Press, 1979), pp. 58–118.

[14]On the south coast east of Farringford rises St. Catherine's Hill (781 ft.), which is crowned by the remains of a fourteenth-century beacon known as the "Pepper Pot."

sad for the sorrowful news of the death [*illegible*] of the pious neighbour Colonel Hood.[15]

14th. We read that touching account of the Scotts Grays & [*illegible*] how they devoted themselves at Balaclava.[16] The writer says that their "ears are frenzied by the monotonous, incessant cannonade going on for days together." Some Captain compares the appearance of the troops to the turning of a shoal of mackerel. We are almost afraid to open the newspapers now. Every day we go up the down or sweep up leaves & burn them. Sir John, Mr. Edmund Peel & Mr. & Mrs. Augustus Peel come. Mr. Millais comes on the 22nd and is beguiled into sweeping up leaves & burning them in the intervals of making sketches of Hallam & myself.

25th. He leaves. We have had talks as to the limits of realism in painting. A. hates overrealism.

December

2nd. A. writes "The Charge of the Light Brigade" & sent it to *The Examiner.*[17] We hear of the dreadful storm at Balaclava on November 14th & are shocked to know of the loss of the winter clothing of the troops in the *Prince* & of so many transports besides & alas also of so many lives.[18]

Souvestre's account of the Bretons[19] interests us very much. Their glory in the name of Christians, the fact that their most popular songs are religious, that when the cholera was among

[15]Col. Francis Grosvenor Hood (1809–55) led the third battalion of grenadiers at the Alma in 1854 and was subsequently shot in the trenches before Sevastopol.

[16]The Scottish Highland companies distinguished themselves in the charge of the Heavy Brigade at Balaclava on October 25, 1854. Years later Tennyson commemorated the event in "The Charge of the Heavy Brigade at Balaclava," first published in March 1882.

[17]"The Charge of the Light Brigade" was first published in the *Examiner* on December 9, 1854.

[18]During a dreadful storm on the night of November 14, 1854, thirty-two English transports were wrecked on the Euxine, along with ships such as the *Prince* and the *Sea Nymph*, which foundered with all on board. The *Prince* was a particularly grievous loss as it was laden with an immense quantity of ammunition, as well as beds, blankets, and warm clothing for the troops and medical supplies for the hospitals.

[19]Emile Souvestre, *Les derniers Bretons* (Paris, 1854).

them they would not listen to the doctors until they put their advice in a song set to a National Air strikes us much.

He reads some of Dante's *Inferno* to me & then Virgil's Hades. The thought of Russia & of our soldiers is so absorbing that Hallam's games are of Russia or he falls down & says, "this is the way the Russians fall when they are killed." He loves to talk of the poor soldiers who have no butter & no toast. He sings "Rule Britannia" with great ardour & is always asking for pictures of her. His love for her has almost superseded that of the stars tho' he does look at them still.

A. reads Homer's Hades to me. We read Ferrier's *Institutes of Metaphysics.*[20]

We keep Christmas by his blowing bubbles for the children who have pretty wreaths of laurel & holly on their heads. He is invited to meet his friends at the Grange[21] but cannot go. Mr. Palgrave & his brother[22] at the Hotel & often with us. Charles Weld also comes.

[20] James Frederick Ferrier, *Institutes of Metaphysics: The Theory of Knowing and Being* (London, 1854).

[21] The home of Lady Ashburton, located near Alresford, Hampshire.

[22] William Gifford Palgrave (1826–88), the son of Sir Francis Palgrave and brother of Francis Turner Palgrave. Palgrave was for some time a Jesuit missionary in Syria and Arabia. In 1865 he severed his connection with the Jesuits, became an English diplomat, and served, successively, in Abyssinia (1865), Turkish Georgia (1870), the West Indies (1873), Manilla (1876), Bangkok (1879), and Uruguay (1884).

1855

January

10th. A. reads "Maud."

12th. Poems from Hazlitt's *Selection.*[1] Mr. Tuckerman[2] & his brother, pleasant Americans, bring a note of introduction from Mr. Robertson once a clergyman at Burley. On coming up to the house they see a yellow light strong enough to cast their shadows & those of the trees. No Aurora & no meteor visible but the clouds slightly luminous, the night otherwise pitchy dark. The Tuckermans dine two or three days & walk & talk. It's interesting to see how they cling to the thought of the old English home.

Day by day we are saddened by the seemingly hopeless news from the Crimea. Such terrible incapacity & neglect judging from the *Times* & also partly from private accounts.

A robin in the house so tame that it let me take it in my hand & when A. was reading to me it sat near us by the fire.

February

1st: Very cold, the snow folding in & out of the hedge like drapery. A. reads some of the *Idylls* of Theocritus to me. "Hylas," "The Ile of Cos," & "The Syracusan Women," also the first poem of "Maud" in the rough.

Whirling snow in the driving east wind. One of the finest American Pines half blown down. He read some of Edgar Poe's Poems to me two or three evenings, then the beginning of "Maud" & the Mad Song and one night all "Maud."[3]

Our poor little Lionel has been suffering from Eczema after vaccination. The golden mist of Hallam's hair . . . and notice

[1] William Hazlitt, *Select Poets of Great Britain* (London, 1825).

[2] Frederick Goddard Tuckerman (1821–73), the Massachusetts sonneteer.

[3] See *Maud* II, 239 ff. In February 1855, when *Maud* was all but completed, Tennyson wrote the "mad scene," which he inserted between "Oh! that 'twere possible" and Part III, thereby making the transition between the two parts less abrupt.

of six volumes of *Punch* bound, the gift of Messrs. Bradbury & Evans, cheer the wintry weather.[4]

A. reads *Othello* to me in three nights, then two Acts of *Macbeth*, then finished *Macbeth* & read *Richard III* in three evenings. Afterwards *Henry IV* [*illegible*]. We like to hear the Shrove Tuesday ditty of the Village children about white bread, fat bacon, apple pie, Mother's Day & other things that could not be made out by us. Lionel delights in warlike songs. In one of our rash walks up the down A. got a chill & was very unwell.

Mr. Woolner came & on the 5th began A.'s Medallion.

16th. The crocus wreath began to burn.

19th. Mr. Woolner left. I thought the medallion very beautiful, very fine & shiny, the best likeness that has been made.

Mr. Woolner leaves on the 19th. He gives Hallam a bit of Virgin gold from Australia. "Loola" was very kind to him & was a great darling with him.

21st. Fast day, so stormy we could not go to church nor get out at all except that A. breathed the air for a few minutes.

March

Spring Birds & flowers duly chronicled, each one hailed with gladness. Each varied aspect of Down & sea giving first delight. A letter from Mr. Ruskin kindly asking A. to see his Turners, Mr. Woolner having spoken of his desire to see them.[5] A. says to me "Cold & clearcut face."[6] View exquisitely beautiful. Snow sparkling in Blackgang.[7]

30th. Heard the first Stock-Dove.

[4]Frederick M. Evans (1803?–70) and William H. Bradbury (1832–92) were employees of Moxon's publishing company and managers of that company from 1858 until 1864. Evans and Bradbury published *Punch* from the mid-1850s until Evans's death in 1870. Shortly thereafter the firm became Bradley, Agnew, and Company.

[5]Woolner served as intercessor between Tennyson and Ruskin, expressing the poet's desire to see the Turner collection in the National Gallery. Ruskin wrote to Tennyson, stating his pleasure in the laureate's interest and his desire to show him the Turners (see *Memoir*, I, 383).

[6]See *Maud* I.88–101.

[7]Blackgang Chine is a steep ravine located eleven miles due east of Farringford.

31st. He read a good deal of "Maud" again.

April

2nd. A. finished Goethe's "Helena" to me.[8] We only admired the classical part & the lines, "Dort hinten still im Gebirgtal hat" and "Nicht nur Verdienst, auch Treue" and a little also the Vine chorus & Rock chorus.

3rd. Were to have gone to see the Baltic Fleet off but the storm of wind & rain prevented us. A letter comes from Mr. Tom Taylor announcing his intended marriage.[9]

5th. We drive to Newport, he on his way to Bonchurch whence he returns on the 8th and tells me wonderful scientific facts of which he has heard from Dr. Mann.[10] The one cowslip [*illegible*] in the Park had been spared for his return.

Shakespeare several evenings. Anne Weld & Agnes stay a few days having come over from Pardwell with Mrs. Leacock & Mrs. Cuthbert, her sister-in-law, who returned the same day.

We accompany the Welds to Newport & go to Swainston. All there very kind & pleasant but we are bad guests for however gladly we welcomed our friends at home, we felt that our work and therefore our chief pleasure was there & that there we must for the most part be. At Swainston [we] met Mr. Silvera, a priest who interested [us], & [we] were taken to see Sir Henry & Lady Mary Gordon[11] who were not at home but the Housekeeper who had been Miss Gordon's nurse took us over the chief rooms and about the grounds pointing out the oaks her young lady had planted & taking all the hearty delight in everything belonging to the family so seldom found now. We were charmed with the old rooms & the oriel windows looking out on the grassy terrace with the pretty village church where

[8] See "Helena Fantasmagoria, Interlude to Faust," the third act of *Faust*, Part II.

[9] On June 19, 1855, Tom Taylor married Laura Barker, third daughter of the Rev. Thomas Barker, vicar of Thirkleby, Yorkshire.

[10] Dr. R. J. Mann, an enthusiastic amateur scientist with an especially keen interest in astronomy. In 1856 Mann published *Maud Vindicated*, a spirited defense of Tennyson's embattled monodrama.

[11] Sir Henry William Gordon (1818–87), the brother of Charles George ("Chinese") Gordon, and his daughter. After twenty years in the army, Gordon entered the Ordnance Department in 1855. He was made controller in 1870, and in 1875 he became commissary-general.

tower & spire were seen from among the fir trees or in the near sloping park or the more distant down. Mr. Godley[12] dined with us at Swainston. Hallam & Johnnie[13] wild with delight, Hallam much the wildest. Lady Simeon ill in bed but Sir John kindly insisted on taking us to see Mr. Nun's beautiful flowers.

25th. A. reads "Maud" in the morning & we go home afterwards. He reads to me some of Wiseman next evening, some of "The Lady of the Lake."[14] Primrose, rose-coloured sheath of the Sycamore leaves, Cuckoos, Nightingales, all sights and sounds of April delighted us. I write out "Maud."[15]

May

1st. We hear of Franklin Lushington's appointment to a judgeship in Corfu. We admire the deep-red catkins hanging from the topmost branches of the Black Poplar against the blue sky. Also the white glistening buds of the Elms.

The end of the Chapel House lease had come & we put away books & papers & go to Twickenham, parting[?] to Cowes. We call on old friends there.

We go to Somerset House & see Edmund & Franklin Lushington, Mr. Lear, & Mr. Spedding. Two or three days afterwards he goes to Mr. Spedding's rooms. We take the children to the Crystal Palace and we had hoped that Edmund & Franklin Lushington would have come with us, but their poor Eddy[16] was too ill.

Anne Weld & Charles Tennyson & Major Sanky[17] did ac-

[12] An Isle of Wight neighbor of the Tennysons.

[13] John Stephen Barrington Simeon (1850–1909), the son of Sir John Simeon and 4th baronet, M.P. from 1895 till 1906.

[14] Wiseman was undoubtedly Cardinal Nicholas Patrick Stephen Wiseman (1807–65), archbishop of Westminster. Tennyson was likely reading in Wiseman's three-volume *Essays on Various Subjects* (London, 1853).

The Lady of the Lake was Sir Walter Scott's narrative poem, written in 1810.

[15] From the time of their marriage until her nearly fatal collapse in 1874, Emily Tennyson served as her husband's principal amanuensis. She wrote out the various versions of poems as Tennyson completed them, and she always prepared his final copy for the press.

[16] The Edmund Lushingtons' only son, Edmund, died in 1856 at the age of thirteen.

[17] Possibly William Sankey (1822–92), who was raised to the rank of general in 1881.

company us & Major Sanky & Mr. Ruskin dined. Lady Franklin & Sophy Cracroft in the evening.[18] We go to the Exhibition & return to Twickenham again & take the children to Kneller Hall.[19] We go to the Welds' party & met among many others Matilda & Horatio Tennyson,[20] Mr. Lear, Mr. Spedding, & Mr. Venables.

31st. To Park House. Poor Eddy very patient & sweet. The devotion of his Aunt beautiful to see. The Park House party go to Eastbourne but we leave our children with their nurse & set off for Oxford. Very shaky & with beating hearts we saw it. Dr. & Mrs. Scott kind.[21]

[*June*]

A. brings my breakfast to me in my room, both of us were terribly nervous & I too stupid to understand that Mr. Gardiner, the clergyman at Hale whom I would much like to have seen, was himself. I thought him some one else. A. said that when he sat in the Balliol garden the shouts from the Theatre seemed to him like the shouts of the multitude in early Christian times. When they cried "Christians to the Lions." In the theatre there some shouts so overwhelmed me that I thought I must·have left it particularly those that followed A.'s name. However the great doors opened & he came in looking calm & dignified tho' pale. I grew calm too & so put the minds of the Miss Scotts more at ease about me. More than kind they were. A. sat down on the steps nearly under Lord Derby. Then there was one shout for *In Memoriam*, one for "Alma" & one for "Inkermann." The sea of upturned faces was very striking from where he was & I was. While others went to the laying of the

[18] Lady Franklin was the widow of Emily's uncle Sir John Franklin.

Sophy Cracroft was a special friend of the Tennysons whom they frequently saw in London. She was the daughter of Thomas Cracroft and his wife, the sister of Sir John Franklin.

[19] This was originally the home of Sir Godfrey Kneller (1646–1723), the painter, located in Great Queen Street.

[20] Horation Tennyson was a younger brother of the poet's.

[21] The Tennysons went to Oxford for the poet to receive the doctorate of letters. The degree ceremony, thrilling for both Tennyson and his wife, was held in the Sheldonian Theatre.

Dr. Robert Scott (1811–87) was select preacher at Oxford, 1853–54 and 1874–75; master of Balliol College, Oxford, 1854–70; and dean of Rochester, 1870 until his death. Mrs. Scott was the former Mary Jane Ann Scott, daughter of Maj. Hugh Scott.

foundation stone of the museum we walked to Magdalen College, A. in his scarlet robe. While we were admiring the cloisters a student accosted us & kindly offered to take us to his room that we might have a good view but we had not time to avail ourselves of his offer. We called on the Grants & the Cowells.[22] Only Miss Grant at Home who was so good as to offer her brother's smoking-room while we were in Oxford. We met all at Magdalen in the evening. He had long talks with Mr. Gladstone & Montalembert & was introduced to Dr. Wellesley.[23] Nothing could exceed Mrs. Cowell's kindness who got me a chair, tea, cloak & all I wanted making me fear for herself lest she should suffer by so exposing herself to the draughts of the cloister. We did little more than walk thro' the crowded room & return.

Next day Mr. Arthur Butler and Prof. Max Müller were so good as to take us about.[24] First we went to the Museum & in approaching we met Dr. Wellesley who had kindly come to show us the Raphael Sketches[25] & it made me ashamed to see him running about with a chair that I might never have to stand, but everybody was as kind as could be. We saw the beautiful illuminations in the Bodleian Library then we went to Christchurch meadows & hall & to New College Gardens. In the evening Professor Johnson[26] showed us the Nebulae in Cas-

[22] Edward Byles Cowell (1826–1903) and his wife, the former Elizabeth Charlesworth. Cowell matriculated at Magdalen Hall, Oxford, in 1850, and during the six years of his university life he became acquainted with Edward FitzGerald, Tennyson, Thackeray, and Benjamin Jowett among other notables. In 1867 Cowell assumed the newly founded professorship of Sanskrit at Cambridge University, where he remained until his death.

[23] Montalembert was Charles Forbes René, count de Montalembert (1810–70). He succeeded his father as a peer of France in 1831; he was born in London, spent much of his youth there, and visited England in 1855, 1858, and 1862.

Dr. Henry Wellesley (1791–1866) was a scholar, antiquary, and patron of Italian studies. Wellesley was appointed vice-principal of New Inn Hall, Oxford, in 1842, and he served as principal from 1847 until his death.

[24] Arthur Butler is probably Arthur Gray Butler (1831–1909), fellow of Oriel College, Oxford, in 1856 and later a dean and tutor of Oriel from 1875 until 1897.

Friedrich Max Müller (1823–1900) was the orientalist and philologist and Taylorian professor at Christ Church, Oxford, from 1854 until 1868. Max Müller served as curator of the Bodleian Library from 1856 until 1863 and again from 1881 until 1884.

[25] The Raphael sketches are housed in the Fortnum Gallery at the Ashmolean Museum.

[26] Manuel John Johnson (1805–59). Professor Johnson took charge of the Radcliffe observatory in 1839, and he remained at Oxford as professor of astron-

siopeia, generally invisible to the eye, resolved. Wonderful points of light with wide spaces of dark sky between. A strange & delightful feeling of strange worlds. We saw also the ring Nebulae in Lyra & the double star in the middle of the Great Bear's tail & he another in Hercules. It is impossible to express what it was to us both to see what we had for years so longed to see. The Professor most kind, we were both charmed with him and forgot the large party into which we were unexpectedly ushered. Professor Adams[27] was there and so also was Max Müller. I had first seen Oxford when six years old . . . when a summer's sunset gilded the domes & churches. Then it seemed a fairy city to me and now it looked like a dream of the Middle Ages. We left Oxford with a grateful feeling of the kindness we had received from all. We slept at Somerset House & went next day to Twickenham & A. brought our children from Park House.

7th. We reach home again. "Maud" was finished which added to the delight of returning.

8th. A. reads [me] one of Jowett's Essays, a gift which we found on our return. We had brought Stanley's[28] gift with us too that pleased us much. We went to Swainston & found the Goldschmidts on the road coming to us.[29]

---

omy until his death. Johnson was popular in the university, and the observatory became in his time a resort of the leaders of the Oxford Movement, including John Henry Newman.

[27] Arthur Robarts Adams (1812–77), the barrister and fellow of St. John's College from 1835 until his death.

[28] Arthur Penrhyn Stanley (1815–81), the liberal theologian and Oxford Professor of Ecclesiastical History; dean of Westminster from 1864 until his death.

[29] The Goldschmidts were Johanna Maria ("Jenny") Lind (1820–87), the popular vocalist, and her husband, Otto Goldschmidt, the conductor. The Goldschmidts met on the Continent in 1849 and were married in 1852. Jenny Lind's personal charm rivaled her glorious voice, and during the course of her many appearances in England, spread over nearly forty years, she achieved a level of popularity reached perhaps by no other singer in England. Emily was much taken with Jenny Lind during her several visits to Farringford in early May 1871. Several days after their initial meeting Emily described the visit on May 3 in a letter to Hallam: "Madame Goldschmidt sang some of Handel's Milton very finely & one piece from Elijah. . . . She is full of fun & of feeling & of power. She told me her shyness was so great that she used to feel life was not worth having her suffering was so great the day of singing & the day before

Mr. Lear and Mr. Peel came to us & Mr. Bradley[30] called, the beginning of our acquaintance with this good and able and affectionate friend.

The wealth of wild flowers is a continual source of delight to us. We filled a bowl with orchis—like sunrise, as he said, and with campanula & other wonderful flowers which could rival any bowl filled from a greenhouse as we thought. . . .

My Father came & next day, August 6th, we take the children to the Warren to call on the Bradleys, & see Mrs. Bradley for the first time. She was preparing tea among the furze bushes to celebrate her little girl Edith's birthday.

August

6th. He sends the "Balaclava Charge" to be printed for the soldiers as they want it & the Chaplain of the S.P.G. tells that we could not do a greater service than to send them copies on slips.[31] We sent 2,000 slips, I think, & they are to have another 1,000 if wanted.

A. reads Margaret Fuller[32] to me. We keep Hallam's birthday by an expedition to Brook ourselves & our servants. A beautiful day. Stock-doves cooing continually in the morning. A letter from Mr. Lear giving little hope of Henry Lushington's life.[33]

---

but at the time the love of her art overpowered all other feeling—When some one asked her here if she was shy about singing she said; have you ever talked with a man on the eve of being hanged or guillotined? If so you may know what I have felt" (May 10, 1871, T.R.C.).

[30] George Granville Bradley (1821–1903), headmaster of Marlborough, 1858–70, master of University College, Oxford, 1871–81, and dean of Westminster from 1881 till his death. The Tennysons first became acquainted with Bradley and his wife, Marian, in the summer of 1855, when the Bradleys were vacationing at Alum Bay. Soon they were fast friends, and in 1860 the Bradleys took a house near Freshwater expressly to spend their holidays near Farringford.

[31] A chaplain from the Society for the Propagation of the Gospel serving in the military hospital at Scutari wrote to Tennyson informing him that he could perform a great service for the British troops by sending out copies of "The Charge of the Light Brigade." The poet accordingly sent the chaplain two thousand copies of the "Charge" in the original version, as he now realized that the changes made in the poem for its publication in the *Maud* volume were not improvements.

[32] *Memoirs of Margaret Fuller Ossoli, Consisting of Her Autobiography and Notices of Her Life*, ed. J. F. Clarke, R. W. Emerson, and W. H. Channing (London, 1852).

[33] Henry Lushington (1812–55) was the brother of Edmund and Franklin Lu-

13th. My Father left us & we went on the down, saw more butterflies I thought than I had seen in my whole life together before. . . . We began *Margherita Pustula.*[34] On the 14th we heard from Edmund Lushington of his brother Henry's death at Paris. A great loss to all. His brother Franklin had arrived too late to see him alive. A. reads "Ecclesiastes" to me which he had once read to Henry Lushington, also "Solomon's Song."

16th. Henry Lushington laid to rest beside his Father & Mother at Boxley. News of Sveaborg came.[35] Hallam delighted, shouting "down Sebastapol."

18th. News of the French & Sardinian Victory on the Tchernaya.[36] I at least enjoyed a scramble over the rocks from Colwell Bay to Totland with the Mundys who were staying with us now. At their request A. reads "The Charge of the Light Brigade" to them & afterwards the "Ode to the Duke of Wellington" & some of Campbell's Songs.

19th. A. reads the last hours of Oliver Cromwell to them.[37] Next day the Mundys leave. We examine a quicksilver fly thro' the microscope, also a cocoon which looks like a honeycomb of burnished silver, the eggs like the crumbs of Whiters bread.

A great thunderstorm, Blackgang Chine ghostly white in the moonlight, a grand black thunderous cloud between the moon & the glorious paths of moonlight. On the sea lightning all over the heavens. There was a hollow voice in the thunder & the storm lasted many hours. Next night the moon came up over the down & he said it was like Michael Angelo's sunrise in the Medici Chapel at Florence.[38] The head over the giant shoulder.

---

shington; chief secretary of the Maltese government from 1847 until his death. Lushington's loss weighed heavily upon Tennyson, to whom no friend had been closer since the death of Arthur Hallam. He is one of the three memorialized in "In the Garden at Swainston."

[34] *Margherita Pusterla* was Cesare Cantù's enormously popular historical novel (1838) concerning religious persecution in thirteenth-century Spain.

[35] In the late summer of 1855 the British navy bombarded and heavily damaged the Russian fortress of Sveaborg in the harbor of Helsinki.

[36] The August 18, 1855, French and Sardinian victory on the banks of the Thernaya.

[37] Tennyson owned *Oliver Cromwell, Lord Protector: Letters and Speeches, With Elucidations by Thomas Carlyle* (London, 1850).

[38] The sculpture of *Aurora* atop the sarcophagus of Lorenzo de'Medici, duke of Urbino, in the New Sacristry, Medici Chapel.

29th. A. left for the Peak & I taught Hallam for the first time to say his prayers.

September

3rd. A. returned in an open boat, the bow slapping the wave each time it falls, the sea being very rough.

We went to meet him but he had not arrived by the steamer, the hour of which had been changed, but, tho' I asked both postman & Captain, neither told me this but left me sick at heart not finding him. After his long ramble in the Forest & his rough passage he had to walk home for there was no Fly. However he arrived at last. He had not been to the Peak but had enjoyed his week at Salisbury . . . & in the New Forest. This last most of all. His descriptions of the fire of the sun in the Fern, a background to the boles of the great Beeches; of the purple glow of the heath & of the delicious heath air all of which I love so dearly revived my old wish to see the Forest. In a clear & rather rapid stream he had seen a cow standing with cataracts of light from the four legs. In one old part of the New Forest he had found the ground under the trees quite covered with leaves of wood sorrel. In other parts the ground was bare, in others covered with beautiful grass.

4th. I was walking in the garden with Hallam after A. had gone in when Mr. & Mrs. Frederick Pollock[39] drove up & introduced themselves to me. They had dined & so went to Alum Bay while we dined and came to us in the evening & got him to read some of "Maud." Having unpacked their things at the Hotel they slept there and came next morning after breakfast. We sat in our reed hut in the kitchen garden and after a time he finished "Maud." The Pollocks dined with us at luncheon & they returned to their children.

Next day the Grants came to High Down Villa, a red house built during our absence from home, a most unwelcome sight opposite our Farm Gate.[40] However the Grants were welcome

[39]William Frederick Pollock (later Sir, 1815–88) of the illustrious family descended from David Pollock, saddler to George III. Pollock was appointed a master of the Court of Exchequer in 1846, Queen's Remembrancer in 1874, and, in 1876, senior master of the Supreme Court of Judicature. His wife, Juliet, was the daughter of the Rev. Henry Creed of Corse, Gloucestershire.

[40]High Down Villa, also called simply the "Red House," was subject to lease and was most often occupied by visitors from the mainland. The Tennysons stayed in the "Red House" the last two weeks of May 1856 while extensive renovations were in progress at Farringford.

inhabitants. So able & cultivated & friendly a man as Mr. Grant could not be otherwise than a delightful neighbour.

Mr. Palgrave, also ever a welcome guest, arrives next day & we walked with him & the Grants, one or more, dined with us from time to time. We had interesting conversation. We superintended trimming a thorn to open a view of Brook point and took Hallam up to the down & built chalk towers & demolished them, "the smoke" giving exceeding delight to the little boy.

On the 9th with joy & thankfulness checked in part by past false reports, we heard of the fall of Sebastapol. This time the report was official. After dinner at which Mr., Mrs., & Miss Grant and also Mr. Stokes & Miss Cotton, as well of course as our guest Mr. Palgrave, were present, he read "The Tapestried Chamber" & being in high spirits he made every one very merry with his talk.[41]

17th. Mr. Palgrave went & A. read "Maud" in walks on the down, the sound of the stock-doves' wings among the trees in the Park as he lay on the seat under the Cedar, a beautiful sound. A. read some of the *Symposium* to me in the evening. A very happy evening. Next day after a glorious walk on the down he read the new poem in "Maud."

The day after Mr. Grant & his friend Mr. Porte called & asked us all to go out with them in a boat. We all went & found the sea so very rough as we neared the point that we did not round it but hoisted sail & returned. The sky was bright & the waves fine & the old sailor's humorous remarks amused us.

Pleasant walks & pleasant evenings with Mr. Grant & Mr. Porte.

24th. Miss Grant takes leave.

25th. A. went to the dentist in London, Mr. Grant & Mr. Porte with him as far as Basingstoke. Lady Grant tells me that she has planted a bit of myrtle which A. gave her meeting her in the hall one day when she dined here & that she had given a bit to Miss Grant & also to a Shropshire lady. He will be quite ashamed of having so much made of his little bit of myrtle. In

[41] Henry Sewell Stokes (1808–95), the Cornish poet and close friend of Charles Dickens. Among his chief works are *The Lay of the Desert* (1830), *Rhymes from Cornwall* (1871), and *Poems of Later Years* (1873).

Tiny Cotton, who later married Capt. T. C. S. Speedy, was the daughter of Benjamin T. Cotton, a conservative candidate for Parliament from the Isle of Wight in 1879. Miss Cotton was one of Emily Tennyson's most intimate young friends.

"The Tapestried Chamber," a short story by Sir Walter Scott, was first published in *The Keepsake* in 1828.

obedience to his wish that I should not miss my daily walk I go up the down day by day & I am very sorry that he should not see the splendid harvest morn.

27th. He dined at the Brownings & had a very pleasant time. Read "Maud." The two Rossettis came in the evening.[42]

Lady Grant tells me that Sir Graham Hamond[43] had charmed his eighteen guests into sitting intent while he read them "The Charge of the Six Hundred" which she had taken him & had not seen before. Also she told how one cold winter's morning Sir John Simeon had repeated it to the Hunters waiting on some hill for the scent or something else, & how they all listened & seemed to forget what they had come there [for].

30th. Thanksgiving Day. So rainy no one could go to church so I read the Prayer appointed for the day at evening prayers at home. He dined with the Camerons & met Mrs. Brookfield, Mr. Spedding, Mrs. Bayley & Miss Crawford and read "Maud."[44]

October

1st. He dined at the Welds and enjoyed looking at his sketches in Brittany. Mr. Spedding & Frederic[45] were also there.

2nd. He arrived about half nine from Cowes, our usual route in those days. A Mr.— comes from Nottingham to see him, an Artisan. We ask him to dinner. He wants to hear some of "Maud." A. reads all. We fear that the poor man must have been hurt that we knew nothing of his poems which he had sent. They had been acknowledged and one reads something of every book to see if it ought to be read & then if it seems that it ought not, one throws it aside & it is forgotten but not without a pang thinking how much it has cost the writer and what high hopes have perhaps been built upon it. One really could do

[42]Following their meeting, Dante Gabriel Rossetti said of Tennyson in a letter to William Allingham: "He is quite as glorious in his way as Browning in his, and perhaps of the two even more impressive on the whole personally" (*Memoir*, I, 390n).

[43]Sir Graham Eden Hamond (1779–1862), of Afton Manor, Norton. Hamond was made a captain in the Royal Navy in 1798 and became an admiral of the fleet in 1862.

[44]Louisa Bayley (née Pattle) was Mrs. Cameron's sister and the wife of Henry Vincent Bayley, later judge of the Supreme Court in Calcutta.
Miss Crawford = unidentified.

[45]Frederick Tennyson.

nothing else but read small books of poems & pass judgment on them if one read all sent. The very letter writing takes not unfrequently till 2 or 3 or even four o'clock in the day and all to no purpose save that of courtesy as far as the stranger part goes. But we were sorry for this pilgrim from a distant county. He was very good about the matter.

The saddest incident (rather most tragic) of this kind was one at Chapel House when an old Waterloo Soldier brought his twelve books on the battle of Waterloo. He had taught himself to read & write (I believe that he might write these). He wanted to know if they should be published. "Great images loomed" sometimes thro' words of the old man's creation but A. was obliged to say that "they could not be published as a whole" but that Publishers might accept parts for magazines. The dear old soldier came & carried away his twelve books in their oak case (I think it was). We asked him to come & see us but he never came again.

At this time we have the pleasure of seeing again a good deal of the Swainston party. One day we had an exciting slide down to Alum Bay, the clay path wet from recent storms. We came up with our feet in eel baskets. The Kents are with the Simeons. Milton, part of Hallam, Carlyle's *Cromwell*, our evening readings now.

14th. A letter from the Senior Chaplain (Crimea) asking for a thousand more copies of "The Charge." A. reads part of *King John* to me.

17th. Franklin Lushington & Mr. Lear come. A long talk with F.L. in the morning then he walked with A. nearly all over the farm. Sir John Simeon comes with Mr. Deane. I forget Friday & fish which spoils my dinner, theirs being spoilt. However Mr. Lear's singing made us forget this whatever else it brought to mind. He sang for two or three hours. The whole of "Mariana," the whole of "The Lotos Eaters," "Ellen Adair," "Tears idle tears," "Let the solid ground." Then go by "Oh that 'twere possible." All his own settings.[46] Next morning we breakfasted at half past six to see him & F.L. off. When they were gone we counted seven capes all glorious in the golden morning mist.

[46] Edward Lear set a number of the laureate's poems to music, and he often played and sang his settings on his visits to Farringford. According to Sir Charles Tennyson, Lear's settings "were always sincere and permeated with the spirit of the words," and they were among the few settings approved by Tennyson himself, who found that they cast "a diaphanous veil over the words—nothing more" (*AT*, p. 441).

Then we went up to the Attic & looked through the telescope to try & watch their boat & we thought we saw a boat & Mr. Lear said it must have been theirs for no other boat was crossing. I put F.L.'s "Points of War" & his brother Henry's two poems to music. When we have given [up] Mrs. Cameron & Julia[47] both, they arrive with their little German maid Katchen, all thro' the storm & the rain. A. reads to us some Milton. He is most good in reading to me in the evenings.

Next day while they had walked to the Light House, Sir John Simeon & Sir George Baker[48] came. Sir John charmed with Mayall's photograph of A. which Mrs. Cameron had had framed & brought down. . . .[49] We talked all the evening speculative talk dear to A. & to me.

Next evening he reads some of Shakespeare's sonnets, two of Milton's, & others to us and next day after church part of *Samson Agonistes*. We go in the afternoon to church whenever able, the morning service being too long for my strength except on Communion Sundays when I go for that service only.

Visits to Afton & Norton made in a not very luxurious Donkey chaise. On one occasion Julia's foot having gone thro' the moment she stept into it. However we went merrily on.

Sir John & Lady Simeon & Sir George Baker came to dinner. The children were made to walk over the table, nothing loath. All very merry. Mrs. Cameron played on the piano & Julia sang & Sir John & A. made high shouldered ghosts. We wished for Aubrey de Vere. Strange to say a letter came from him next day. We were not frequent correspondents. Mrs. Cameron summoned hastily home by her little Charlie's illness.[50]

One day we go up the down and are charmed by magical effects of cloud. Other days we sweep up leaves. He reads two or three of Edgar Poe's poems to me one evening, another an Essay in *The Westminster Review* on Intuitive Proof of God from design. The wild flight of birds delightful, walks up the down, sweeping leaves, evening reading, one night an interesting

[47] The Charles Camerons' daughter.

[48] George Augustus Baker (1728–1866), the third son of Sir Robert Baker of Dunstable House, Surrey. Baker did not succeed to the baronetcy; he was for many years rector of Ibstone-cum-Fingest, Oxfordshire.

[49] This Tennyson photograph was taken by John Edwin Mayall (d. 1867), the popular artist and photographer who kept a shop in Regent Street from 1852 until his death. Probably this is the Mayall photograph of the poet that appeared on the title page of the *Royal Edition* (1881).

[50] Charles Cameron was a son of Charles and Julia Margaret Cameron.

letter in *The Times*, another part of *The London Review* on "Maud."[51]

Kind letters from Mr. Ruskin & Mr. Tuckerman.

A. reads me some of Thackeray's *Humourists of England*.[52] By A.'s desire I read *The Newcomes*. Some parts I grant tender & beautiful but others seemed to me heart-withering & I do not wonder that there is no youth among the young now if this is the food on which they feed.

After sweeping of leaves & burning them in which Hallam, happy boy, joins, we play at Backgammon . . . to spare his eyes from reading, but he generally reads to me a little first. Another kind letter from Mr. Ruskin, but he does not accept A.'s invitation to visit us, only says he should like it.

December

8th. Very cold but we go to church notwithstanding. He reads some of St. John & Jowett's Essay on the Atonement.[53]

Burn leaves & dig & put sand & ashes in the shrubbery.

12th. We make a bonfire of leaves & burn the box with all the pipes in it, he having first put the last bit of tobacco into his study fire thinking that he would give up smoking.

An Italian comes with his Hurdy-gurdy & when we had given him some money, he asked if he might come & warm himself by the fire. We talked a little in Italian to him & he told us he came from Genoa. A letter from Mr. Brimley.[54] An interesting one from Mr. W[oolner] telling of a relation who had

[51] The essay "Theism" ran in the October 1855 *Westminster Review*, pp. 167–85. The same month an unsigned review of *Maud, and Other Poems* appeared in the *London Quarterly Review*, pp. 213–29.

[52] William Makepeace Thackeray, *The English Humourists of the Eighteenth Century* (London, 1853).

[53] Included in his *Epistles of St. Paul to the Thessalonians, Galatians, Romans* (1855), the "Essay on the Atonement" expresses Jowett's vehement moral objections to popular Evangelical doctrine. The essay was attacked as unorthodox, and among some conservative churchmen it aroused widespread prejudice against Jowett, which was rekindled in 1860 by the publication of his *Essays and Reviews*. Throughout his troubles at Oxford the Tennysons remained loyal to Jowett, and they gave this bold investigator of theological questions their unqualified support.

[54] George Brimley (1819–57), the essayist, a regular contributor to the *Spectator* and to *Fraser's Magazine*. Brimley wrote an article on Tennyson's verse that was contributed to the Cambridge Essays of 1855.

been roused from a state of despondency by "The Two Voices." He came to Ryde for change and on the evening of his arrival saw for the first time A.'s poems. He read "The Two Voices," burst into tears & soon returned quite restored to his family.

I read some of Plutarch's "Theseus" to A. in Langhorne's *Lives*[55] for we said we must read these Lives.

Mr. Brodie comes by Mr. Monteith's desire to make a bust of A.[56] Very cold weather.

15th. A. goes to Newport to consult Sir John Simeon about our own affairs. He as ever most kind.

19th. Mr. Grant & Mr. Jowett come. Still very cold.

20th. Too cold for me to join their walk.

21st. Mr. Brodie goes. A. reads "Maud."

23rd. Mr. Palgrave arrives. A., Mr. Jowett, & Mr. Grant go to church. A. reads some Milton.

24th. We put up Holly & evergreens in the rooms. Mr. Stokes dines with us; Mr. Grant's cousins, the two Miss Cottons & their brothers, & Miss Way, their cousin, come in the evening. The circle becomes formal & A. insists on a game of Blindman's buff so we had a good child's game of English Blindman's buff which I for my part enjoyed. A great thunderstorm to-day & there had been one before in the night.

27th. Mr. Jowett & Mr. Grant & Mr. Palgrave leave us. A very pleasant time we have had with them. Many interesting talks. Mr. Palgrave lent us Macaulay to read & *Esmond* & Mr. Grant gave A. Goethe, and Keightley's *Milton* & *Hiawatha*.[57] They were also most kind in bringing the children books & toys & in playing at ball with both & in having all manner of gambols with Hallam in which baby was too young to join.

28th. Charles Weld came to us while we were in the plantation

[55] *Plutarch's Lives*, translated by John and William Langhorne, 6 vols. (London, 1770).

[56] The Scottish sculptor William Brodie (1815–81) began a bust of Tennyson in late 1855.

Robert Monteith (1812–84), whom Tennyson visited at his country house on the Clyde in 1853, was an old friend from Cambridge days.

[57] Thomas Babington Macaulay, *The History of England*, 5 vols. (London, 1849–61).

Thomas Keightley, *An Account of the Life, Opinions, and Writings of John Milton* (London, 1855).

having walked from Newport. He read us "A Pardon" from his tour in Brittany which interested us.

29th. He read "Carnac," also interesting.

30th. A. & I went to church.

31st. To-day he had to go [to] the Grange.

1856

January

1st. A letter from him written at Southampton & enclosing Mr. Jowett's kind letter received just as I had been saying to myself, "It is dreary without him." Charles makes a kite for the children to their exceeding delight. Lionel asks if Hallam will go to the sky with a string. I try in vain to secure some pleasant companion for Charles. He leaves me on the 2nd & I am very sorry that he should have had so dull a visit.

My daily letter from A., even on the 8th when he returns.

4th. A very kind letter also from Mr. Brookfield telling about him. During his absence there was a wonderful meteor over the Solent, but I did not see it.

9th. He read me some of Eckermann's conversations with Göethe.[1] We are very cozy in the Study with the large screen across the window. We are still brave enough to go up the down sometimes.

12th. Molière's *Tartuffe* & *Don Juan*.

14th. Mr. Estcourt[2] comes to look over the place for us with a view of our purchasing. Merwood[3] walks with us. . . . Molière these evenings and a little Eckermann. A. goes out at night.

18th. We learn that Russia has accepted the proposals of peace. . . . The children much excited by the stranding of a ship near Brook. A. carves some ivy leaves from nature in Apple-tree wood. In spite of its hardness they are very well carved.

20th. After church in the afternoon he reads to me about the London Poor.[4]

[1]Johann Peter Eckermann, *Conversations with Goethe in the Last Years of His Life*, translated by S. M. Fuller (London, 1839).

[2]A Harbottle Estcourt, deputy governor of the Isle of Wight.

[3]Merwood worked for the Tennysons as gardener and handyman until April 1860.

[4]Tennyson read to his wife from Henry Mayhew's *London Labour and the London Poor* (London, 1851).

22nd. Sir John Simeon fetches A. to Swainston.

24th. He looks in at the Drawing-room window having returned to me while Sir John is at Ryde. He tells me of the Saxon king found in his tunic, a net work of gold, & of Romans & Saxons lying side by side in the same tombs.

25th. I walk with him on his way to Swainston. As it is the first time I have appeared on the road my appearance causes some excitement.

Walked in the fields & met Merwood who asks me about plowing the orchard. I say that I will write to A. Merwood is an idyllic sort of man, he can neither read nor write. He is very shrewd. I talk to him sometimes about farming matters. A peace comes to one from the quiet here and one feels it good to have one's home & I hope feels thankful for the beautiful home tho' I for my part should prefer one on some heathy hill on the mainland when I think of the difficulty of getting to my Father if he were ill.

Finished Macaulay & read some of Eckermann. Letters from A. who is now at Ventnor with the Manns. He has seen Saturn pretty well. All the rings seemed to him one except the dark ring where it crossed the bright.

February

1st. He tells me of the beautiful octuple system in Orion which to the naked eye looks like rather a faint star under the lower star in Orion's belt.

4th. He comes home while I am on the Down. We read part of *The Misanthrope* together. A. had been going to copy Sinnett's[?] lovely passage on young children but Sir John lends him the book for me.[5] A. reads me the picture of Nimuë (Vivien) & Merlin.[6]

5th. Up the down. He reads me that book of *The Odyssey* about the dead.

6th. We dig or rather hoe in the garden. He begins *The Odyssey* to me. I feel that in his beautiful *viva voce* translations, quite lit-

[5]This perhaps was a work by Mrs. Jane Sinnett, who published *A Child's History of the World* (1853) and other children's works.

[6]Tennyson began work on "Merlin and Vivien," first published in 1859 as "Vivien," in February 1856.

eral, I get as much as it is possible to have of the true spirit of the original.

7th. Rainy & stormy, we do not get out. While we are playing with the children in the drawing room, Mr. Woolner arrives about the second book of *The Odyssey* in the evening. We have in these days two or three pleasant walks & every evening *The Odyssey.* Lady Simeon & Miss Simeon call.

16th. A. & Mr. Woolner dine at Swainston.

19th. Sir John returns with them to dinner & likes Mr. Woolner's medallion of me.[7]

22nd. We send a servant to Chapel House to look to the packing of our furniture.

24th. A. reads Lowth's Isaiah.[8]
A. takes me out when the days are sunny & I sit in the arbor. Mr. Woolner most kind to the children.

28th. The bust looks nearly finished. Difficult work for Mr. Woolner as A. is not at all fond of having his face copied & will only spare a little while at night when Mr. Woolner has to take a candle in one hand & model as he can.[9]

The snow-drops are beautiful & the Russian violets which A. brought from Steephill castle thriving & deliciously sweet.

29th. We have been waiting more than six weeks for a decisive answer about the price of this place. We long for a settled home & in spite of the difficulty of getting to & from this, we like it too well to wish to leave it.

March

1st. A. finishes *The Odyssey.* I very sorry it is done.

2nd. He reads the book of Esther and a good deal more from the Bible.

4th. He began *Hamlet.* He digs in the garden every day.

[7]The bronze medallion of Emily Tennyson which Woolner exhibited at the Royal Academy in 1859.

[8]*Isaiah,* translated and annotated by Bishop Robert Lowth (London, 1778).

[9]Apparently Tennyson was a very difficult subject. Previously Woolner had had trouble with the second Tennyson medallion (1855), which Anne Weld criticized but which Emily Tennyson finally approved (see *Letters of E. T.*, p. 76).

5th & 6th. Hamlet.

7th & 8th. As You Like It.

9th. He reads "The Sermon on the Mount" and a good deal besides in the Bible.

10th. Mr. Butler calls.[10] We ask him to dinner & he comes. He admires the bust which is finished.

11th, 12th, 13th. Twelfth Night.

13th. Much Ado About Nothing.

14th. Mr. Butler dines & A. reads "Maud." A. digs almost every day & sometimes walks with Mr. Woolner. I not well enough.

15th. Mr. Woolner leaves us. A. finishes *Much Ado.*

16th. Our Lionel's birthday. Mrs. Cameron sends "The Poems in Memoriam & Maud" beautifully bound to Hallam thinking it his. Poor little Lionel had only our small gifts, but bubbles blown which pleased both children much. Hallam ran after "the beautiful birds" with great glee and opal worlds which burst leaving nothing but smoke behind half awed them both.

17th. A. began *Measure for Measure* in the evening. He walked alone on the down the harshest wind being too much for me.

The 18th brought a petition for a National Song for Wales. I obliged to order our furniture to be warehoused because we cannot get an answer about this place.

19th. Heard the Stock dove for the first time this year. A. said the exquisite song to me from "Merlin" ("Vivien").[11] He has set to work in earnest on the poem now. Wind changed to N.W. after having been so long in the East. *Measure for Measure* this evening.

20th & 21st. "Merlin."

24th. Mr. Venables, Mr. & Mrs. Tom Taylor arrive. Delightful Beethoven from her & some settings of A.'s songs.

[10]Henry Montague Butler (1833–1918) was Charles Vaughan's successor at Harrow, where he served from 1859 till 1885, when he was appointed dean of Gloucester. In 1886 he became master of Trinity College, Cambridge, and in 1889 he was appointed vice-chancellor of that university. Butler wrote of visiting the Tennysons at Farringford and Aldworth in his "Recollections of Tennyson" (*Tennyson and His Friends*, ed. Hallam Tennyson, pp. 206–21): "To go to either of Tennyson's beautiful homes, to see him as the husband of his wife and the father of his sons, was to me and mine for many years a true pilgrimage, both of the mind and of the heart" (p. 221).

[11]"Merlin and Vivien," ll. 385–96, 444–47.

25th. Mr. Richard Doyle[12] arrives & Sir John Simeon dines with us. Mr. Doyle had a stormy passage in an open boat & lost his hat. He wrapt himself in his plaid & the woman screams at the gray ghost when he goes to buy a hat. The steamer had gone to look at the gun boats. A. & the Taylors see them first near the Needles like wild fowl on the water. Mr. Venables took cold yesterday & did not join in the walk but stayed with me & we talked for hours. A delightful companion he is. Mrs. Taylor sings her own settings of some of A.'s poems. "The Sisters,"[13] "The Miller's Daughter," "The Brook" are what we like best. A great gift for music she has.

26th. The Taylors and Mr. Doyle go to see the hounds throw off at Swainston. A. & Mr. Venables walk over later. All return in the evening.

27th. A. got cold yesterday & so does not join in the walk to Brook, has a warm bath instead. Miss Cottons & Miss Way in the evening. Music again.

28th. Sir John Simeon & Mr. Pollen[14] dine with us & Dr. & Mrs. Mann come in the evening. Our guests walked to Alum Bay & home by Totland Bay before dinner.

29th. *Twelfth Night.*

30th. A. reads "Merlin" ("Viven") to Mr. Venables & me in the Study.[15] I am glad that he agrees with me in thinking it so grand.

31st. Sir John Simeon & Mr. Pollen come with Mr. Estcourt. Mr. Pollen & Dr. Mann walk to the Needles & delight to watch the sea birds. Meanwhile we have a grand consultation with Mr. Venables & Sir John about Farringford. They had kindly given up the Hunt to help. Most kind both of them. Both wish us to buy it. Mr. & Mrs. Taylor leave us. Sir John takes the rest of the party to Swainston except Dr. & Mrs. Mann who come to stay with us. We are sorry to lose our pleasant guests.

[12]Richard ("Dickie") Doyle (1824–83), the artist and caricaturist. Doyle was a regular contributor to *Punch* from 1843 until 1850, when he resigned his connection with the paper in protest against its vehement attacks upon papal aggression.

[13]"The Sisters" is "We were two daughters of one race."

[14]Probably Richard Hungerford Pollen (later Sir, 1815–81), 3d baronet, who in 1863 succeeded his uncle, Sir John Walter Pollen.

[15]Hallam Tennyson wrote the word *finished* beside this entry to indicate that "Vivien" was complete in its revised form when Tennyson read it to Venables and Emily on the 30th.

April

1st. Dr. & Mrs. Mann work in their own room. I too tired to do anything. We have some of the Essay in the evening.

3rd. They go. We dine early with them & talk in the evening.

4th. He takes me out in the garden a little & reads "Merlin." I read "Enid & Geraint" to myself before.[16] We hear the Stock Dove in the Elm.

5th. A. begins *The Tempest.*

6th. The children meet him with a cowslip in his hand. A. reads the 12th, 14th, 15th, 16th Chapters of St. John to me.

7th. He begins *The Iliad* to me.

8th. Iliad.

9th. A. brings me white violets & primroses. Mr. Grant comes unexpectedly. Comes again in the evening & hears "Merlin" after I have gone to bed. He gives me Robertson's "Sermons"[17] & brings Blake's "Job," a gift to A. from Mr. Jowett.

10th. A. finishes writing out "Merlin" and gives it to me to read. I read one of Robertson's sermons and like it much. Mr. Grant comes while we are in the garden and wheels ashes in the wheelbarrow for A. A. & I talk in the evening.

11th. He reads me the beginning of the first book of King Arthur. Three days following I have read "Merlin" to myself, also some of Matthew Arnold's poems and Browning's.

12th. He reads some of the *Purgatorio.* A. plants potatos. I watch. Mr. Sheriff calls to take leave. We read Robertson's sermons and like them very much. Mr. Grant dines with us & walks with A. at night.

14th. A letter from Mr. Estcourt saying that Mr. Seymour accepts our terms.[18]

[16]Although Hallam Tennyson states that "Geraint and Enid" was begun on April 16, 1856 (*Memoir* I, 414), his mother's entry indicates that the poet had begun the idyll somewhat earlier that spring. The poem was printed privately in 1857 at Canford Manor as "Enid, an Idyll" and was included in the 1859 *Idylls* as "Enid." The title "Enid" was expanded to "Geraint and Enid" in 1870, and the poem was divided into two parts in 1873.

[17]Frederick William Robertson, *Sermons Preached at Trinity Chapel, Brighton,* ed. Struan E. Robertson, 4th ser. (London, 1855–63).

[18]In early April 1856 the Tennysons decided to purchase Farringford. Terms

16th. A. brings me a little bit of the first of the *Idylls of the King.* I walked in the garden while he was planting Potatos. In the evening he reads me some of *La Mare au Diable.*[19] A most kind invitation to Coniston from the Marshalls.

17th. Read Robertson's *Sermons* & Johnson's *Chemistry of Common Life,*[20] write letters as usual, & between while I make manuscript books for him. I walk in the garden while he digs. Read some of *Hiawatha.* We send for Merwood to know the rent of the orchard & beg him not to let doves & other birds be shot. He told me that I had my wish of Rooks building in the trees for some had built there. He reads some *La Mare au Diable.* Mr. Grant comes about seven & tells us that he has to go next week about the Chair of Moral Philosophy. The Plum tree which fell in the winter, tho' only attached by a little bit of bark to the soil, is blossoming as if it were in the ground. A. & I planted the Barberry which we had brought with us.

19th. We re-potted the oleanders & planted the large Alexandrian laurel, which had years ago been given me from Wrangle, near our bower.

21st. Aunt Franklin & Sophy Cracroft drive over from Cowes & return after dinner. Sir John & Lady Simeon hail us in the down lane but cannot stay because they brought Johnnie & baby. Mr. Grant stayed to dinner. Drummond Rawnsley arrives.

22nd. Our servants went thro' the Fleet arrayed for the Review[21] to-morrow & were charmed with the day.

23rd. We set off about half past seven with Drummond & Mr. Grant for Yarmouth with a wretched white pony and we feared we should be too late but in reaching the Solent bar we saw other carriages & the little *Solent* just coming out of the Lymington river. The Simeons with Mr. Godley and Mr. Wynn and Sir James Carmichael, the Croziers, Hamonds, A. Court Holmes, Captain were also on board.[22] All very kind. The sea

---

were soon agreed upon with Mr. Seymour, and by May their furniture stored in London was fetched for the home they now owned.

[19] George Sand's *La mare au diable* (1846).

[20] James Finlay Weir Johnston, *The Chemistry of Common Life,* 2 vols. (Edinburgh, 1855).

[21] The Grand Review of the Fleet.

[22] Among the dignataries aboard the little *Solent* were John Robert Godley (1814–61), the close friend of Edward Gibbon Wakefield, with whom he had planned and helped found the community of Canterbury, New Zealand;

was calm & the passage to Yarmouth seemed short. We steamed past the stately ships & the gun boats & the block ships & the floating batteries all dressed with their wreath of flags. The yellow sands swarmed with people clustering like bees. Here & there red coats enlivened the mass. The *Victory* stood up proudly in the midst of the harbour. We heard a salute, then the *Victory* manned arms and soon the Royal Yacht with its three tall masts each bearing a flag came out of harbour. Every ship saluted. The smoke curled along the whole line six miles long, I was told, & then cleared partly away & we saw the ships & the distant hills beginning to appear. A beautiful sight. Soon the Queen's Yacht passed us & the ships manned arms & we heard the cheer of the *British Tar* and the *Solent* cheered too. It was pleasant to hear A.'s voice cheering. I waved my handkerchief. As we passed at the head of the lines I thought of the avenue of Sphinxes, the great ships stood so still and grand. But at times one could not help wishing for the old sails. We steamed along behind the Queen's Yacht. The two hours of the royal luncheon seemed long but then came a magnificent sight. The whole fleet passed the Queen, wheeled round the Pivot Ship & returned. The Pivot ships looked grand with their yards manned. All through the Review we caught now & then distant sounds of "God Save the Queen." As we returned the gun boats were attacking South sea castle.[23] A cloud of smoke with occasional flashes. The sound was to our ears surprisingly little both of this and of the salutes but in reality so great that it shook the windows at Farringford. Now came the parting salute to the Queen & then we steamed back to Yarmouth & arrived about nine at home & found a pretty tea set out on the round table in the drawing room with hot meats on a side table. Sir John with his friends, Mr. Wynn, Mr. Godley & Sir James Carmichael, in addition to our own party. I am glad we have seen this great sight, glad too that it was on St. George's Day & Shakespeare's birthday. It was pleasant to watch the enjoyment of the little Simeons & A. Court Holmes. I see Louisa & Mary Simeon to-day for the first time (Two dear friends to-

---

Charles Wynne Griffith Wynne (1780–1865), M.P. for Carnarvonshire, 1830–32; Sir James Robert Carmichael (1817–83), 2d baronet, an intimate friend of the Simeons; A. Court Holmes, a neighbor of the Tennysons and a descendant of Henry Holmes (d. 1738), of Yarmouth, lieutenant-governor of the Isle of Wight; and the family of Col. Richard Pearson Crozier of West Hill, Freshwater.

[23]Located a few miles southeast of Portsmouth, Southsea Castle, now a modern fort, was built by Henry VIII. On the nearby esplanade are a number of naval memorials, including the anchor of the *Victory*.

be).[24] I longed for my Father who was himself to have been a sailor. How he would have delighted in the day.

24th. Drummond walks on Afton down with A. & hears a few lines of King Arthur & is shown the new poem in "Maud."[25] We dined early with him & he walks afterwards to the Ferry. Mr. Grant in the evening.

25th. A hue & cry after his new great coat. I fear it was lost in the boat. He has to go to Oxford without it. We hope soon to see him again. A. read me the Peleus of Catullus all except the Fates. Merwood came to tell us of white sand which he thought would do for glass-making. Afterwards he brought some lime & told us of building stone and the best chalk pit of the place all on our land. I went in to attend to A.'s warm bath & afterwards Mr. Watson arrived with his two daughters bringing a letter from Norton Lodge. They asked to look over the place where they had spent a happy year. I showed the girls all the rooms.

29th. A. reads me some of *Troilus & Cressida* and makes letters with bricks for our Hallam.

30th. This morning a letter comes from Mr. Venables saying that Mr. Chapman pronounces the title of Farringford good. We have agreed to buy, so I suppose it is ours. Went to our withy bed, such beautiful blue hyacinths, orchises, marsh marigolds and cowslips. Wild cherry trees too with single white blossom. The park has for many days been rich with cowslips and furze

[24] Sir John Simeon's daughters. Louisa Simeon ("Louy") became the Tennysons' particular friend; she frequently stayed at Farringford when her father was away in London or elsewhere and was accepted almost as a daughter. Shortly before her death Louy (then Mrs. Richard Ward) recalled her feelings as a young girl for Farringford and for Emily Tennyson: "I was sometimes allowed to drive over to Farringford with my father, and, need I say, I looked forward to these as the red-letter days of my life. Not only were the talk and intellectual atmosphere intoxicating to me, but I became passionately attached to Lady Tennyson. Praise of her would be unseemly; but I may quote what my father was fond of saying of her, that she was 'a piece of the finest china, the mould of which had been broken as soon as she was made.'" She was, Mrs. Ward continued, "so helpful, so tender, full of the wisdom of one who had learnt to look upon life and all it embraces from one standpoint only, and that the very highest!" (*Tennyson and His Friends*, ed. Hallam Tennyson, pp. 309–10).

[25] For the second edition (1856) of *Maud*, Tennyson added three stanzas to the opening section; mitigated the attack on the peace-party in I.x; and added I.xix (on the mother's deathbed), and II.iii (on Maud's death), as well as a stanza at the very close of the poem.

in flower. The elms are a golden wreath at the foot of the down, we admired the mespilus in flower and the apple trees with their rosy buds. He dug the bed ready for the rhododendrons. A thrush was singing among the other birds, as he said "mad with joy." At sunset the burning splendour of Blackgang Chine, and St. Catherine's, and the red bank of the primeval river contrasted with the turquoise blue of the sea (that is our view from the drawing-room) make altogether, a miracle of beauty. We are glad that Farringford is ours.

Look over the inventory of the Seymour furniture & mark what we should like to have. Went on with *Troilus & Cressida* but A. says that he cannot read all to me. Our two little games of Backgammon.

May

2nd. We had a delightful time in the plantation and admired the Beech leaves coming out of their long brown tender spiral buds & the rich red brown sycamore leaves rising gracefully from their gorgeous crimson sheaths. In two or three other trees we have noticed the flowers coming out together with the leaves from the same sheath.

3rd. A. walks to Alum Bay. The water was low so that he could see the Bay from a greater distance than he had ever seen it before. He said that he had never seen it so fine. We see a field thick with white Narcissus.

4th. Thanksgiving for Peace—Go to Communion. Walk in the fields with the children who are much excited calling the birds to come & eat food that we have put for them under the Elm before the Drawing-room window. Poor little Hallam coloured with disappointment as they flew by unheedful of his call "Come birdies it is very good."

5th. Mr. Isaacson[26] called & we subscribed to the church at Constantinople. I take the children to Captain Hamond's. We pass the rest of our neighbours on the road & so could not call. No neighbours could suit us better. All so kind & friendly & not expecting us to give great dinner parties or to join them. A. & I went to look at shells & chalk which Merwood had put for us in the Greenhouse & then to see if the potatos he had planted were sprouting. I brought home a huge netting needle given

[26] The Freshwater curate.

me by Mrs. Hamond hoping that A. would learn to make nets for the garden as my Father does.

6th. A. begins Chaucer's "Knight's Tale" to me. The night before he had read Dryden's[27] that we might compare the two. Chaucer's beyond compare I think.

7th. These days east wind & rain. A. finishes the "Knight's Tale."

8th. He walks before breakfast & brings me flowers. Mr. Seymour asks thro' Mr. Sewell to have the house for packing. I begin separating books. A. reads me "The Man of Law's Tale," Dame Custan[ce], which I admire extremely.

9th. A. walks before breakfast. He reads me "The Monk's Tale" of the three men hunting Death to kill it.[28] We have a little Backgammon afterwards, have been packing a little to-day.

10th. A. walks again before breakfast. Merwood comes to ask about making a private road for us to the Down. A. goes with him to look about it & then returns to take me out because it is so beautiful.

He goes to Swainston to meet the Monckton Milneses, I do not go because of the packing. A beautiful evening sad without him.

11th. Go to church, beautiful day. Sunset gorgeous colours of the rainbow on the shoulder of Afton down, distance lovely as can be.

12th. Mr. & Mrs. Monckton Milnes come with Sir John & Lady Simeon & A. to luncheon. A. took Mr. & Mrs. Milnes into the plantation. Sir John stayed behind to help me by taking down the books & then followed them & missed them. I had a pleasant talk with Lady Simeon. When our friends had gone we went all over the Farm buildings with Merwood even up the ladder into the granary.

13th. In the midst of all our confusion while all imaginable things strewed the drawing-room & the bookshelves were bare & the chairs & tables dancing, Prince Albert came.[29] We wish things

[27] Dryden's translation "Palamon and Arcite," in *Fables, Ancient and Modern* (1699).

[28] Obviously Lady Tennyson has in mind "The Pardoner's Tale."

[29] The prince consort declared his intention of bringing the queen to Farringford during the next several days. However, the queen never came, and the Tennysons were able to finish their redecoration and refurnishing without further interruption.

had instead been looking their best to have done him honour. One of the gentlemen with him gathered a great bunch of cowslips which the Prince admired very much & took them himself. One dropt & I kept it for the children as a memorial. A nightingale was singing while he was here I think. It had been singing delightfully all the morning close to the house. Afterwards A. & I had a very pleasant walk in the fields. He took me to that field where the great bunches of white Narcissus grow. The steep sand bank in it is very pretty. After dinner he came to fetch me that I might see the beautiful view from the North attic where he was sitting because his own was piled up with books & other things.

14th. After dinner we go to the Red House which has since been Villa Doria, High Down Villa, Locksley. Mr. & Miss Seymour & a man servant arrive.

15th. Sir John Simeon, the Milneses, & Mr. Stephen de Vere called on their way to Alum Bay.[30] We did not go. It rained so they had their luncheon at the Inn there & return for us. We go to Swainston.

16th. The Milneses leave. Sir John & Lady Simeon, Mr. de Vere, & ourselves go to Osborne. All except Mr. de Vere leave our names. The drive very pleasant. Mr Wagy[?] Prosser[31] comes to dinner. Mr. de Vere plays some old Church music. Very beautiful.

17th. We return from our pleasant visit. We like our host & hostess more & more. We drive in an open carriage against a brisk west wind & enjoy it much. Soon after our arrival at our temporary home we have a message from Lambert[32] telling us to expect the Queen, for orders for her reception had been given at Yarmouth and one of the carriages was to be in readiness to take HM to Freshwater Gate & the Prince had said to Captain F. on leaving Farringford, "It is a pretty place, it is a pretty place. I shall certainly bring the Queen to see it." We dressed our children in their rose-coloured dresses and all went into the Farringford garden to receive HM, not liking to go into the house tho' we did have rugs spread on the narrow path left

[30] Sir Stephen Edward DeVere, 4th baronet (1812–1904), was M.P. for Limerick, 1854–59; he succeeded his brother, Vere DeVere, as 4th baronet in 1880. In 1886 he published his finely turned *Translations from Horace*.

[31] Possibly James Prosser (1789?–1877), vicar of Thame, Oxfordshire, and chaplain of Thame union from 1841 until 1871.

[32] The landlord of Plumbley's Hotel, Freshwater.

between packages in the entrance hall. However the Queen did not come probably because of the stormy morning. Edmund[33] comes to dinner.

18th. A. & Edmund walk & admire a glorious bank of blue hyacinths waving in the wind.

19th. The Queen lays the foundation stone of the new Military Hospital so we do not expect her to-day. Mr. Palgrave & Mr. Sellar come to dinner.[34] A little before A. & I had had a delightful walk which had led us in returning by the brook that runs thro' Steep wash green. I praised its beauty to a man working in one of the cottage gardens. He said we do not think of it being near. I dare say it seems pretty to strangers. He told us that it was never dry.

20th. I spent my Louy's[35] birthday partly in writing letters partly in expecting the Queen, for orders had again been received at Yarmouth.

21st. Captain Crozier told us that the Prince had put the cowslips in water meaning to make cowslip tea of them for the Queen & himself.

22nd. Miss Seymour goes.

23rd. Mr. Sellar leaves us. We like him exceedingly. Mr. Seymour calls to take leave & we hear that they are sorry to go.

24th. Mr. Palgrave goes. A. reads me part of the Review on Ruskin in the *Quarterly*.[36]

26th. We go up to Farringford with Lambert to look at the furniture for which he is good enough to bid for us.

27th & 28th. Sale days. The week uncomfortable what with the sale & the children not being happy here.

29th. Go up to look at things and find a plain gold ring, a wedding ring we think, in a bed-room.

30th. The sweeps come. We look over our purchases with the auctioneer's clerk. Get to the Red House late for dinner. The evening splendid. Sunlight among the trees in the field seen

[33] Edmund Lushington, Tennyson's brother-in-law.

[34] William Young Sellar (1825–90) was the noted Virgilian scholar and professor of Latin at Edinburgh University from 1863 until his death.

[35] Emily's sister Louisa Turner.

[36] "Modern Painters," *London Quarterly Review*, 98 (April 1856), 208–35.

thro' our kitchen garden beautiful. The ducks made a pleasant noise in that pleasant lane leading to our back gate. They sailed about snapping their bills catching some of the innumerable insects.

31st. Went to Communion, then to Farringford & rang at the front door as he told me & he opened it to me & we went about the house & garden.

June

1st. We began to unpack things & to take them into the house. Went back late to dinner. Weather most beautiful. We admire the view from the farm yard where the wall fringed with flowers over the garden gate is the foreground.

3rd. Unpacking again. Capt. & Mrs. Crozier bring Col. Ferber to see the rooms. Putting out beds on the grass. Splendid days.

4th. Unpacking still. We get the children's day nursery ready for them & I help E. to make Hallam's & Gandy's[37] beds. We stay to welcome our children to their home. They run about delighted and Hallam asks, "May I stay?" Then we go to dine at the Red House and come home by the garden. A beautiful evening. We stop at the barn & look at Merwood's bits of carpet which he thought might do for us. I had sent to beg that he would not wait but there he sat in the barn his carpet spread out of doors. My A. gathered a rose and gave it to me as we walked thro' the kitchen garden. We went in at our back door. An evening to be remembered. A. gave me a welcome to our home which will be ever dear to memory. We had our tea in the drawing room. A. read me some of "Enid." It seemed as if we were the people of those old days. A Stag's horn beetle (I think it was) came into the room with a harp-like sound. We put it out & it sat on the window frame looking in at us & we admired its bright black eyes & its horns like the leaves of a Fan Palm, only they were brown yellow.

5th to 15th. Joiners mending many breakages. Great scrubbings going on, placing of furniture, hanging pictures, planning carpets, with occasional delight of glorious view of the Light-House glittering in the distance with laurels twinkling in the foreground under gloom of trees or of cliffs & sea gem-like.

[37] Gandy was the children's nurse.

15th. A. reads "Griselda"[38] to me, a favourite with me, and "Enid" as far as it is done & we weed in the garden. He reads also some of Sidney Smith's life.[39] Glad to see the great peonies we planted in the plantation growing.

18th. We go up the down, very beautiful & very delightful. Sain foin makes the hill crimson in a long slip. Pretty dwarf roses & great tracts golden with lady's fingers in other parts. We water & weed a little after rain.

21st. A pleasant walk in the fields. A. reads me a bit of Cambises.[40] I am glad that we both like Chaucer so much.

22nd. Go to Church. A. reads me some of the epistle to the Romans. Baby runs in with two Bee orchises gathered near the Gate. I never saw any before & I am glad to see them. We admired the reflection of the clouds soft in the still sea. We saw a great ship pass majestically with troops from the Crimea & could not but think of the happy hearts that ship would make. How cold & blank the drawing room felt when I returned.

24th. All this week I bind manuscript books for A. & weed his potatos & his "clearing."

27th. The Simeons come & like the house better with our furniture. They say it looks more homey. They go with me to the potatos & the children bring Lady Simeon some tea.

July

2nd. A. arrives unexpectedly, brought news of a sad possibility respecting our affairs.[41] He showed the noblest disregard of it much as the reality would affect us. I can never forget it. He admires the rooms.

3rd. We go into the withy bed to look for flowers. It is so much of a jungle we can scarcely get in & we are glad to find the willow herb we planted last year thriving. . . . In the evening

[38] "The Clerk's Tale." Tennyson's Enid was his version of the patient Griselda.

[39] Lady Saba Holland, *A Memoir of the Reverend Sydney Smith, with a Selection from His Letters*, edited by Mrs. Austin, 2 vols. (London, 1855).

[40] Evidently "The Summoner's Tale."

[41] Tennyson had been informed that the bank in which was lodged all the money he had collected for the purchase of Farringford might suspend payment. He did lose some £200 but had feared the loss would be far greater.

we went to look at the beautiful wild garden rose bush in the wilderness which made him think of Sunday mornings at Somersby when his Mother used always to gather a white rose.

4th. Charlie's[42] birthday. A. & I went to watch Merwood's progress with the water-pipes. What beautiful white sand! Found the children playing in the chalk pit as we went up the down. Gandy at her crochet work. Built a castle for them & shot it down, gave them wild roses & returned home with them. Many wild flowers about & on the down the thyme is beautiful.

6th. Went to Communion & afterwards in the garden heard A.'s low whistle & found him lying by the strawberry bed under the trees nearest the wall. We walk in the fields. A beautiful day.

8th & 9th. Backgammon these nights. My birthday. Delightful letters from my Father & Louy, & from A. "Why did you not tell me?" Better than a hundred letters had he written them.

10th. Mr. Peel comes. Mr. Bradley calls. Mr. & Mrs. Seymour call on their way to Chale. I promise to let them know if we let Farringford next year. The Bradleys come to Villa Doria (our Red House). Mr. Cotton calls. I busy planning a new Dairy. We receive a firefly which Mr. Smith has been so kind as to let Mr. Patmore send us. There are two raised lamps of yellow light behind its eyes, also a long slit in the body likewise bright with yellow light which we did not see at first until we had put it in water. We send it back by post. The children very pleased with it. The Bradleys send us a neck of Venison & dine with us.

11th. Mr. Bradley brings us his little basket carriage to look at. A meeting of the children. Little Arthur drives our Hallam & Lionel. The Bradleys & Mr. Peel dine with us.

12th. The beautiful contributions for the bazaar arrive from Grasby. The Bradleys in the evening. Edmund arrives at nearly twelve. All the servants gone to bed except Gandy who finds some cold lamb for Edmund. A. & I come down to him & Mr. Peel not knowing we are with him also comes down & kindly offers his room.

13th. A long talk with Edmund. Mr. Bradley calls. Sarah Hayward's most kind contributions to the bazaar.

14th. Mr. Peel & Edmund go at 7 in the morning. I busy in mak-

[42] Charlotte Elwes who later married Tennyson's brother Horatio.

ing an Inventory of all the things in the house. We discover a great well of water in the cellar which must be drained away as we never mean to use the hot water apparatus running thro' two floors of the house. Drains bad as they have never been before. Bradleys in the evenings.

15th. Inventory again. A. persuades me to go up the down with him. Air warm, down very sweet, flowers beautiful, centaury just coming out. Mr. Bradley calls. I sent off my Bazaar things to Lady Worsley Holmes.[43]

September

26th. On our way from Gloucester we pass encampments and barrows on the downs and reach Salisbury.[44] How pure & beautiful the Cathedral & how striking the tombs between each pair of pillars. It was the Friday afternoon service and we heard "He was despised" sung. Very affecting to both of us. We meant to have taken Gandy & the children next morning but it was a pouring rain. It cleared however a little before we started and we have a delightful passage, quick & sunny, and a bright drive home. Both the children very merry. Hallam exclaims, there is Farringford, as he comes to the bell & is very excited at getting home. How cheerful & airy & beautiful home looks!

28th. Hallam will not believe it is Sunday because it rains. For our Welsh we only read the Hundredth psalm to-day.

29th. How gem-like the beauty of our view towards Blackgang looks. We make out a little of "Enid" in Welsh[45] & in the evening I play some Welsh airs & A. reads as much of his "Enid" as is sufficiently finished.

30th. We go up the Down. A. reads me the beginning of *Troilus & Cressida.*

[43]Probably Elizabeth, Lady Worsley-Holmes, wife of Sir Henry Worsley-Holmes of Appuldurcombe, Isle of Wight.

[44]During the mid 1850s Tennyson made several autumnal trips to Salisbury, Glastonbury, Amesbury, and the New Forest in search of materials and impressions for his poems on the Arthurian legends.

[45]Tennyson's "Enid" was founded on "Geraint, Son of Erbin" in Lady Charlotte Guest's translation of the *Mabinogion*. Tennyson also read the *Mabinogion* in the original Welsh.

October

1st. Mr. Moxon comes for a few hours. Very kind about advancing us money. A. goes with him as far as he goes on the way to Swainston. The road not yet done.

2nd. A. cannot return to-day as he had intended because of the rain.

3rd. He walks home to-day. We look at the little American edition which is very pretty.

5th. After Communion sit in the Arbour with A. & he walks on the down at night. The stars are splendid. He talks with the coast guard who says how much happier the French sailors are than ours. I hope it is not so. Our new post-bag looks like home.

6th. Every day A. walks with me about the garden & the fields.

7th. (I think it is) We get Mr. Lee's kind note & *The Lives of the British Saints*[46] and what he has copied about King Arthur—26 or 27 pages of copy book.

8th. So much letter-writing that some days I have no time even for a little Welsh Bible.

10th. Very fine. I take a holiday from letter-writing & have a ride in the Rocking-Chair in the garden while A. clears out Quitch.

11th. Quitch again tho' it is rainy & misty. I get A. to read me a good part of "Maud" before it goes for a second edition.

13th. 14th. A bit of "Enid" these two evenings.

15th. Mr. & Mrs. Patmore cross in an open boat. Rash the landlord says in the storm.

16th. A luncheon party of fifteen to meet Mr. & Mrs. Albert Hamburgh.[47] The A. Court Holmeses, Simeons, Capt. & Mrs. Hamond, . . . Mr. Cornwall Simeon,[48] Mr. & Mrs. Clough. Everybody very kind.

17th. A. with his Quitch again. The Cloughs come to dinner. Very taking they are.

[46] *The Lives of the English Saints*, ed. John Henry Newman (London, 1844–45).

[47] The Albert Hambroughs lived at Steephill Castle, Ventnor, Isle of Wight.

[48] Cornwall Simeon (1820–80), Sir John Simeon's brother.

18th. "Enid" in the evening. The Patmores delighted.

21st. "Merlin." The Patmores think it still grander. They are so kind. They take long walks in the morning that I may not be tired.

22nd. We hear from Park House that dear little Eddy was taken from them on the 20th. A boy of great promise & Edmund's only Son. Very sad.

23rd. The Patmores go to Swainston. I like them more and more.

24th, 25th, 26th, 27th. Isaiah one evening & Chaucer the other evenings. Walking & sweeping leaves. Very pleasant days.

29th. Mr. Dempster arrives in the evening having been grounded two hours the [*illegible*] having to obey. He sings "The May Queen" to us.[49]

30th. Walks with A. in the morning to the Needles and sings to the children & in the evening to us.

31st. Miss Cotton & Miss Southwell come to hear Mr. Dempster sing in the evening. The Simeons call. A. walks on Afton Down in the morning.

November

1st. A. walks with Mr. Dempster to the Ferry. Chaucer.

3rd. The Simeons in the evening. Very pleasant evening.

4th. Beautiful day again, walking, sweeping leaves, & Chaucer.

5th. We hear that we have lost only 200 in the Ding Bank troubles. We feared that it might have been much worse & we are glad & thankful. A. has put down all "Enid" to read to me & reads it this evening. These delightful walks & readings do me a great deal of good.

6th. Very indifferent news of my dear Father. A. very good to me. He reads me the alterations in "Enid." The big screens he has put up for me in the drawing room amuse the children very much. Baby says he is going up a mountain.

8th. Send the photographs of A.'s medallion & mine to my Father for his birthday.

[49] William Richardson Dempster (1809–71) was a composer and public singer. He set "The May Queen" to music and composed music for most of the songs found in Tennyson's longer poems.

11th. "Enid."

12th. "Merlin."

13th. Dr. Mann shows his microscope to Merwood & to us. The butterfly's tongue a coiled bracelet of filagree gold, the silk worm's spiracle, a splinter of Fir wood & one of Mahogany. All wonderful & beautiful.

14th. A. & I set off for Park House. The short angry white waves rather alarm one. The spray makes us wet at first but the boat goes smoothly. The sun is bright but the wind cold. My A. protects me from it with numberless cloaks & wrappers. We dine at Somerset House & Poor Edmund meets us at the train & dines there too.

15th. To the Dentist & then to Park House.

16th. We talk about different things and about Eddy. The place looks splendid with the autumn leaves in the sunshine.

17th. "Enid" to-night after a day of talking.

18th. We go to see the Tom Lushingtons[50] at the Stacey House. They come to dinner.

19th. They come again to dinner and we go afterwards to London.

20th. Dentist, Aunt Franklin, Sophy Cracroft, LeFroys, Mr. Woolner, Mr. Palgrave, L. Simpkinson, Mr. Buchanan.[51] Read in the evening. A. buys Physical Atlas & other books & hears people asking for Tennyson's Poems for prizes, gives the name of Weld for his purchases.

21st. We return home, leave London in a fog but find only a light mist with gray clouds in the country. The children's joyful greeting "I am very glad to see you" as they run & skip with

[50] Tom Lushington (1815–58), the brother of Edmund, Henry, and Franklin Lushington, and his wife, Mary (née Lushington), a member of another branch of the family.

[51] The LeFroys were John Henry LeFroy (1817–90; knighted 1877) and his first wife (d. 1859), the daughter of Sir John B. Robinson. In 1857 LeFroy was appointed inspector-general of army schools, and in 1868 he became general of ordnance. Subsequently he served as governor and commander-in-chief of the Bermudas from 1871 until 1877 and as governor of Tasmania from 1880 until 1882.

L. Simpkinson = unidentified.

Buchanan was possibly William Buchanan (1777–1864), the London picture dealer and author of *Memoirs of Painting* (1824).

beaming eyes very delightful. Dr. Mann reports the progress of drains & stoves which he has been so good as to superintend for us. The children very pleased with the numbers of Schnorr's Bible[52] which we brought them, Grandpapa's gift.

27th. "Aurora Leigh" from Mr. Browning.

December

3rd. A letter to say that all is settled about Farringford. A letter misses the owner, changes the place of payment, so all these days we have been anxious & now we are glad & thankful that the place is our own. Today Mr. Isaacson calls & talks a long while about troubles in the Parish which troubles us. A. remarks to me on the news coming as it does on the day we have heard that Farringford is our own. I finish "Aurora Leigh" today. I go out & find A. at the Leaf heap which he has kept up very diligently these days that I might not smell the drain work which has been going on. He reads to me the first part of *Julius Caesar*. The boys very happy getting jogged both together on his knees.

4th. A letter from poor Mother. Very cheerful but telling us that one eye fails.

6th. These days reading Johnston's *Agricultural Chemistry* & Villemarque's *Bardes Bretons.*[53]

7th. Communion. Two wrecks of Fruit Vessels & two poor men drowned.

9th. See to the planting of crocuses, mezereon, Lilacs which came yesterday & to the building of a stove in the Greenhouse. A. rolls the grass by moonlight & goes to the sea. Stormy.

10th. Stormy again but Mrs. Cameron's good Ellen comes with Arnoll's fittings for the drawing room fireplace notwithstanding.

11th. A. dines with Captain Crozier and meets Capt. & Mrs.

[52] *Schnorr's Bible Pictures*, compiled by Julius Schnorr von Carolsfeld (Leipzig, 1855–60).

[53] James Finlay Weir Johnston, *Elements of Agricultural Chemistry and Geology* (Edinburgh, 1842); Hersart De La Villemarqué, *Poèmes des Bardes Bretons du VIe siècle* (Paris and Rennes, 1850).

Fenwick,[54] Miss Jean Murdock, Capt. & Mrs. Hamond & has a very pleasant evening. A great thunder storm. While he is away his books in the new shelves—the Welsh shelves & others. He is surprised to find them done.

12th & 13th. Stormy still. A. rolls the grass.

15th. Sir John Simeon comes to lunch & to hear "Enid." The Arnoll brick stove in the Greenhouse lighted for the first time. It answers very well.

16th. Plumbers, Glaziers, Carpenters, Bricklayers, a fearful array of workmen. We get the Greenhouse made tidier. The Barometer has taken a most wonderful leap of about a quarter of a circle in one day & of half the circle in two or three days.

17th. We hear of Horatio's engagement to Charlotte Elwes.[55]

18th. Mr. Palgrave arrives unexpectedly and comes laden with books, a welcome sight to us. I perceive the beginnings of baby's illness.

20th. A. reads half "Enid."

21st. Mr. Henry Smith calls while I am with poor baby. I send word that A. is on the down. He finds him & Mr. Palgrave & comes in the evening with Miss Price. They are very kind & agreeable.

22nd. A. goes to the Coal-meeting at the Rectory, finishes "Enid" in the evening. Mr. Palgrave delighted.

23rd. We persuade Mr. Palgrave to stay. A. reads a little Milton.

24th. Mr. Palgrave goes, a beautiful day he has, we are sorry he is going. Afton party call. Captain & Mrs. Hamond come. The Capt. brings a Turkish pipe for A. and they kindly press me to go with him to the Jubilee on the 30th.[56] Were things otherwise I should like to go but of course I cannot leave baby.

25th. A. & I alone. We have a grand Yule log & our baby is rather better. Dr. Mann's powder sent in a letter has done him good.

A. digs diligently & rolls & reads "La Petite Fadette"[57] & the

[54]Probably the Percival Fenwicks. The third son of Col. William Fenwick, Percival Fenwick (1820–63) was promoted to lieutenant colonel in 1859 and held that rank until his death in Madras.

[55]Horatio Tennyson married Charlotte Elwes at St. Laurence in April 1857.

[56]The Jubilee was a celebration in honor of the John Simeons.

[57]George Sand, *La Petite Fadette* (Paris, 1849).

first book of *Paradise Regained*. To the children he says "Ye Mariners of England" & they repeat it with great glee.

30th. He goes to the Hamond Jubilee & takes Mr. Stokes. In spite of the beautiful white gloves with which I provide him & which he wears, he does not dance. He talks to Sir Graham of Nelson. Sir Graham shows A. his portrait & promises to show him a Panorama of the battle of Copenhagen. He takes Mrs. Grosvenor Hood to supper. Every one very kind & friendly. Mr. Stokes gives him one of his Garland bits for the children.

31st. We were to have gone to Swainston for the Christmas tree to-morrow but can not because of baby tho' he is much better. He reads me The Spanish Armada[58] & we look at Wilmot's book together.

[58]Probably *The History of the Spanish Armada* (London, 1759).

1857

January

1st. A beautiful day. A. reads me some of Shakespeare's Sonnets & other things. Baby out a little to-day & has meat again.

2nd. Sir John Simeon & Mr. Pollen lunch with us, admire our boys, & the Illustrations to his poems. He reads some Burns to me.

A. rolls diligently.

6th. A. reads to me some of the seven poems hung up in the Temple of Mecca & tells me that these were the true inspiration of "Locksley Hall."[1] He wonders that he has never read them to me before & told me this. 2nd and 3rd Books of *Paradise Regained.* The Haunch of Venison. Gray's "Eton."[2] He rolls in the daytime.

10th. Mr. Archibald Peel comes. He & A. go up the down at night. I see a white owl in the Ilex.

11th. We go to Church & they go down to the sea at night after A. has read the 4th book of *Paradise Regained.*

12th. Sir John Simeon & his brother Cornwall come to dinner. We have a pleasant evening.

13th. Some of the Afton party in the evening. Ghost stories, "The Tapestried Chamber" & others.

14th & 15th. Shakespeare's "Let me not."[3] A little "Maud" & a great deal of talk.

16th. "Maud." I leave before the sad part.

17th. Mr. Peel rushes suddenly to Chester. I write letters to know what chance he would have for Newport. Capt. Hamond kindly calls to talk to me & say he is too late. A. walks to

[1] Among the several sources which may well have influenced Tennyson's ideas for "Locksley Hall," Sir William Jones's prose translation of the *Moâllakát,* the seven Arabic poems hanging in the temple of Mecca, was likely most important.

[2] Thomas Gray, "Ode on a Distant Prospect of Eton College."

[3] Sonnet 116.

Swainston to meet one of the candidates & his friend Mr. Beau mont.[4] I send forward his portmanteau that he may go on to Bonchurch for he has not been well these last days & I think he wants change. I look after the garden walks & the little gate into "The Wife's Walk" for A.

21st. A letter from Sir John saying that A. will return to-day. Lady Simeon, Miss Simeon, & Mr. Bonham Carter[5] bring him. He sees the gate & approves.

22nd. We look after the workmen & he reads me some of *Hamlet* in the evening.

23rd. Workmen, rolling, & some *Richard III.*

24th. Workmen again, some *Henry VI.*

25th. The 55th Chapter of Isaiah. Too stormy for Church.

26th. We walk a little in the Wife's walk. He reads me some of *Timon.*

Hamonds, Croziers, Afton party all very kind in coming to see us. No formality of calls returned. They know I have too much to do to pay visits often. Walks about the fields these days. The land seems much impoverished. A. reads some of Garth Wilkinson on Egypt to me.[6] Review of Swedenborg in the February *Fraser*[7] which A. reads to me.

February

1st. Go to Communion & hear a bird sing while waiting at the Church door more sweetly than almost any I ever heard. A wood Lark, I think. A. reads Swedenborg's *Heaven & Hell.*

3rd. A. begins to translate the *Prometheus Bound* of Aeschylus to me.

4th. He burns leaves in Maiden's Croft as he did yesterday and h gets me the long bench to lie down upon & gives me his cloak Smoke & flames very beautiful when Merwood put in the Brambles. Little feathery tongues of flame. Most beautiful da

[4] An Isle of Wight neighbor and friend.

[5] John Bonham-Carter (d. 1884), M.P.

[6] Tennyson was reading James John Garth Wilkinson's *Improvisations from Spirit* (1857).

[7] "Emmanuel Swedenborg," *Fraser's Magazine*, 55 (February 1857), 174–82

A. reads me part of an Essay from the *Quarterly* of October on Physionomy [*sic*].[8]

5th. We go out to the field with cinders & lime. We have a long talk with Merwood on farming matters. A. draws me in Mr. Bradley's little carriage with a view of buying it. I am reading the last volume of Lord Mahon[9] which interests me extremely. A. reads to me of Fergusson's *Architecture.*[10] Mr. & Mrs. Lewis call.

6th. A. drives me in Mr. Bradley's carriage to see whether it will do for us. It shakes too much unfortunately. Mr. & Mrs. Lewis come in the evening.

7th. We spread ashes just outside the iron fence & then go into the Avenue field & consent to the cutting down of three small Elms in the way of the Plough. A. sees Merwood feed his sheep & talks to him about the Moon. I finish Lord Mahon, sorry that it is come to an end.

9th & 10th. We look after workmen & A. reads *Macbeth* to me.

11th. We pour quicklime & put cinders under the Chestnut trees in the Park. The green moss turns a beautiful red.

13th. The children delighted with the help they think they give in hauling down trees. We see Jupiter & Venus near each other. A splendid sight. The days have been beautiful, frost at night but sunny days not cold.

Lady Simeon calls to look after us. Very kind she is. A. reads all Milton's Sonnets to me & some of Cicero on Immortality.

Backgammon, A. not being well enough to read.

17th. Mrs. Charles West[11] & her sister Charlie come all the way from St. Laurence's cottage to breakfast. Walk to the beacon with A. & return after tea. A. goes with me to find the lost seat of my stool.

Walks in the fields & gardens & on the down. Birds sing delightfully, the sea mews cry. A. puts his cloak over me that I

[8] "Physiognomy of the Human Form," *London Quarterly Review*, 98 (October 1856), 247–68.

[9] Philip Henry Stanhope, Viscount Mahon, *History of England from the Peace of Utrecht to the Peace of Versailles*, 7 vols. (London, 1836–54).

[10] James Fergusson, *The Illustrated Handbook of Architecture*, 2 vols. (London, 1855).

[11] The first wife of Dr. Charles West (1816–98), the well-known physician and author of *Diseases of Women* (1856).

may see Jupiter from his study window. He sees him from the room silvering a cloud. A. reads to me the reign of John in Sharon Turner,[12] some of Burton's *Anatomy of Melancholy* in the evenings.

21st. Mrs. Cameron comes with Charlie & Henry. . . . A. makes the path up to Maiden's Croft.[13]

22nd. &shows Mr. & Mrs. Cameron the wilderness & Maiden's Croft & garden & farm yard.

23rd. Mr. Estcourt & Woodford come to look over the Farm & to settle things & Sir John in the kindness of his heart rides over to see if he can help. Mr. & Mrs. Cameron, Julia, & Mr. Charles Henry Cameron[14] dine with us. The Afton ladies in the evening.

25th. A. brings me violets & primroses at breakfast time. The pretty little basket carriage which Mr. Archibald Peel has kindly chosen for us arrives. Mr. C. H. Cameron leaves. We begin our half-past six o'clock dinner. Hitherto we have dined at five or half-past & our friends say have kept our clocks half an hour too fast. Very likely. There is no very exact record of time here. A. works till one generally when we lunch & as soon as they are old enough our boys dine with us. A. walks & works out of doors with me & when they are old enough we have them with us in the afternoon.[15] He reads me some of Spedding's *Bacon.*[16] Delightful to me.

26th. Carts of seaweed on the Park. The Simeons & Camerons to dinner.

27th. The children a pretty happy sight in the wilderness. Hard-

[12] Sharon Turner, *The History of England during the Middle Ages*, 5 vols. (London, 1825).

[13] Arthur Paterson offers an enchanting picture of Maiden's Croft as "a very quiet and sheltered spot far from habitable places, facing the lonely Down, and sheltered by trees to north and east, . . . a favorite haunt of Tennyson's" (Allingham and Paterson, *The Homes and Haunts of Tennyson*, pp. 9–10).

[14] The brother of Charles Hay Cameron.

[15] Emily Tennyson obviously wrote the latter portion of this entry in later life after her sons were grown, most likely when she was reducing her various earlier journals to this epitome Journal.

[16] *The Works of Francis Bacon*, ed. James Spedding, R. L. Ellis, and D. D. Heath, 14 vols. (London, 1857–74).

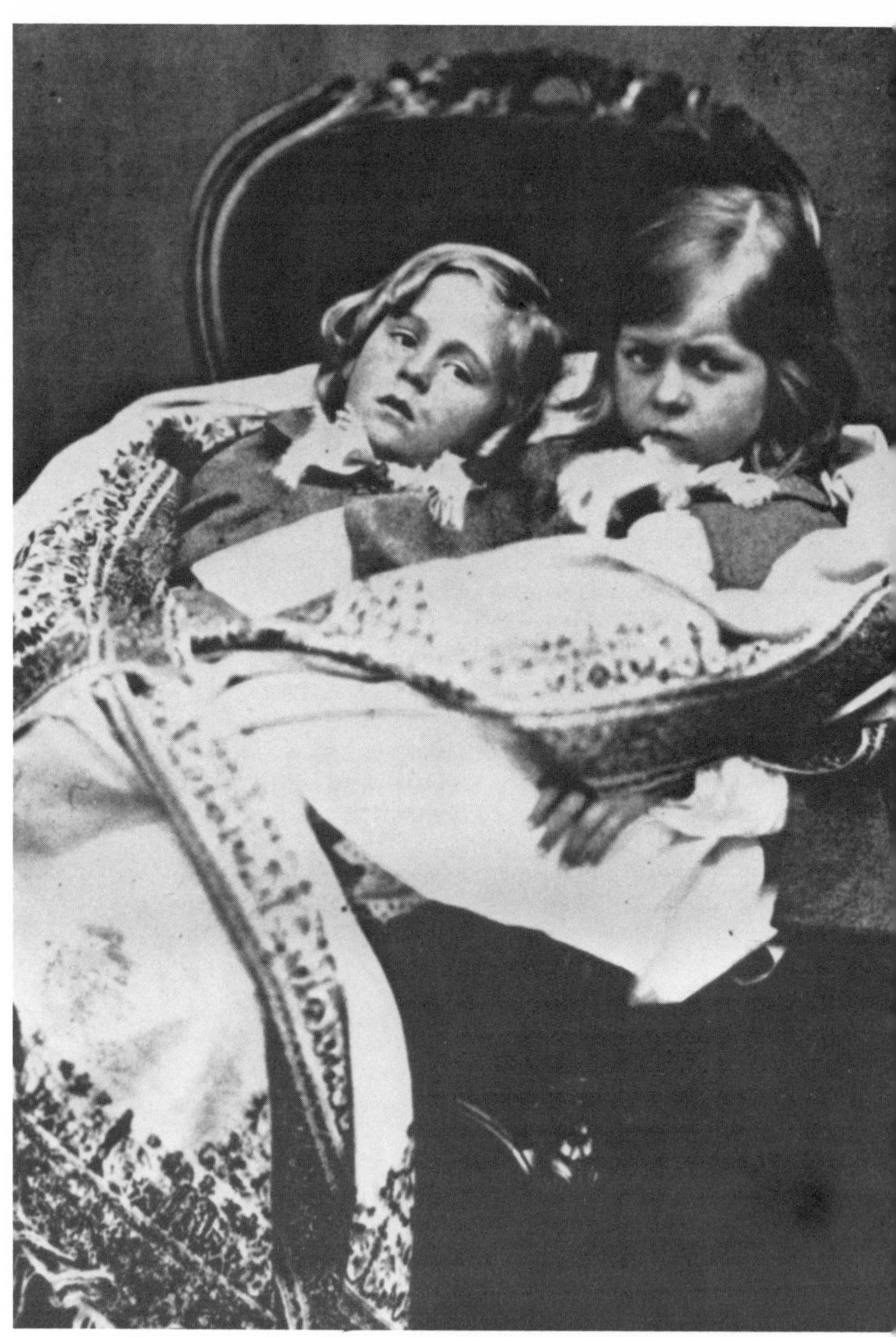

Hallam and Lionel Tennyson. Photograph by Lewis Carroll at Coniston in 1857. (Tennyson Research Centre Collection, Lincoln, courtesy of Lord Tennyson and the Lincolnshire Library Service)

inge[17] leading Lionel by the hand, Hallam leading all. Then they come each with a bunch of snowdrops or primroses. Hallam runs with his rosy cheeks to kiss me then I have a kiss from all.

28th. Mr. & Mrs. Cameron & Julia come to tea that they may hear. "Enid."

March

1st. After Communion A. & I walk in the fields & then call on the Merwoods & taste her Currant & greengage wines.

A blackbird sings with something of the sweet sad note of that which charmed me at Hale. I think I never heard another like it. The thrushes mad with joy. There is a continual ripple of song either from starlings or redwings. Daily meetings with the Camerons.

2nd. "Merlin" read.

3rd. I promised to go with A. & them to Swainston if it were fine. It was misty & I did not go.

4th. Mr. Cameron & Julia find us marking Maiden's Croft as we do these days, A. & Me.

6th. Mr. Cameron dines & they plan a visit to Bonchurch & A. wants me to go but it seems more prudent that I should stay at home. I write many letters after having turned the clay a little in Maiden's Croft & Pathacre as A. bid me.

9th. A. returns late. I amuse myself with my Piano waiting for him.

10th. A. takes Julia & Hardinge to the Meet at Afton. Her Mother is in bed & a mistake about the carriage for me & we do not like to disappoint Julia. I hear the first dove. Mrs. Cameron comes to dinner.

11th. A. reads some of *The Wisdom of Solomon*[18] to me & tells me the passages he marked when reading it to Arthur Hallam.

12th. In the fields again. Mr. Warburton[19] comes while we are at

[17] Hardinge Cameron, son of Charles and Julia Margaret Cameron and namesake of 1st Viscount Henry Hardinge (1785–1856).

[18] Probably James Creighton's *An Enquiry into the Nature of That Wisdom Which Solomon Possessed in an Eminent Degree* (London, 1805).

[19] Possibly Rowland Eyles Egerton-Warburton (1804–91), the poet.

dinner & stays with us. Mrs. Cameron in the evening. Mr. Warburton leaves next morning. Mrs. Cameron in the evening.

14th. We in Pathacre spreading earth & lime when Mr. Cameron comes to walk. It is so windy. A. soon tired of walking, comes again with him to Pathacre. He thinks it too windy for me to stay & finished the work alone. Mr. Cameron has gone to fetch Mr. Prinsep[20] who has brought a hundred violet roots for us. A. goes to the sea which has been rolling with a grand continuous roll. Hallam asks if Mr. Prinsep will have an ugly nose again. I puzzle for a moment & remember the naughty Princess of the Fairy story. The flower of the wood laurel beautiful now. A. reads to me a little Milton.

15th. Mrs. Cameron, Mrs. Prinsep, Julia & Alice to nursery tea. A. reads me more chapters of *The Wisdom of Solomon.*

16th. Sir John & Lady Simeon come to luncheon & bring Johnnie to meet the little Camerons at Lionel's birthday dinner. Mrs. Cameron, Hardinge, & Alice come afterwards with a fire balloon & little lamps of Noah's Ark flags & such things. They find us in Hill Close breaking chalk & they come trooping back with all the children. The fire balloon catches fire while the gentlemen are racing with the children. Mrs. Cameron & Ellen deck the furze bush with toys & lamps & we draw lots. I so tired that A. will not have anyone in the evening. Our guests depart after five o'clock tea. . . . These days work again in the fields. The gulls make a wild noise every day now. Mrs. Cameron & Mrs. Prinsep[21] to dinner or in the evenings. I receive Froude's *England*[22] from Mr. Warburton—a most welcome gift.

23rd. We dine with the Camerons after our usual field work. Mrs. Cameron gives me Henry Taylor's poems beautifully bound in crimson. Hardinge brings me home. A. stays & reads the scene from *Pericles.* I finish copying "Enid."

24th. The Camerons go to Swainston & come for "Merlin" in the even.

25th. A. reads to me some of Froude. Very pleasant to me. The first lark to-day, I think. Merwood finds a bat sleeping in an

[20] Henry Thoby Prinsep (1793–1878), the Orientalist and Indian civil servant and master of the celebrated Little Holland House, Kensington.

[21] Sarah Monckton Prinsep, one of the famous Pattle sisters, as was Julia Margaret Cameron; mistress of Little Holland House.

[22] J. A. Froude, *History of England, from the Fall of Wolsey to the Death of Elizabeth,* 12 vols. (London, 1856).

old Ash tree which he cuts down in the Rue. He brings it into the drawing room & it awoke & flies about but at last it is caught & put out of the window. We cut down a dead Acacia for A.'s desk.

26th. He works always in the fields & I look on. We talk this evening & he goes late to the Camerons & finds four military men there. They had all been dragging the Bay & he brings a basket of Fish home with him. Holland had gone to bed & hears him pumping for he had found a tub & had put the fish in & was pumping over them.

27th. Sir John & Mr. & Mrs. Cameron dine. Mrs. Prinsep in the evening. Sorry that she is going. Next morning Sir John leaves & A. walks with him to the hotel taking R. Doyle's picture of the view from Farringford & Miss Sewell's[23] Lake Tennyson in New Zealand, so named by Mr. Frederic Weld, to be framed. . . .

April

1st. A. reads some of the paper on Rats in the *Quarterly*.[24] It makes one feel an affection for them, telling how they lead about & take care of the blind & how they have attached themselves to man. It also tells how the old British rat, being weaker than the Hanoverian, it fights in companies whenever it can.

3rd. Polling day here. The grass looks very rich where we have put the clay & Merwood the seaweed. . . .

6th. I send off the last proof sheets of the Illustrated Edition.[25] We put the cuttings of our hair & the children's in the ground round the cabbage roses. Look at the livestock on the farm with Merwood & tell him that the importation of Cattle from certain parts is forbidden because of murrain.

9th. We hear the first nightingale. A. reads me a little Froude in the evening.

10th. He goes on the Down & talks to the coast guard about Jesus

[23]Probably Anna Sewell (1820–78) of Yarmouth, only daughter of the author Mary Sewell. Miss Sewell is best remembered for *Black Beauty* (1877), which sold more than a hundred thousand copies within the first fifteen years after its publication.

[24]"Rats," *London Quarterly Review*, 101 (January 1857), 68–78.

[25]Moxon's published the *Illustrated Edition* in the spring of 1857.

Christ as we had been talking before he went out. "A great day to-day" (Good Friday), the coast guard began, & they talked on.

11th. Mrs. Cameron comes with Mr. Steven & lunches.[26]

14th. Captain & Mrs. Hamond dine with us. Julia & Mrs. Prinsep & the Afton young ladies in the evening.

15th. We go to St. Laurence for Horatio's wedding. The day beautiful, a delightful drive. Banks flowery with primroses circle the fine wall of the Undercliff which as A. says looks as if some old order of architecture, knolls gorgeous with furze backed by the sea. We went into the garden of the Black Gang Hotel. I looked down the path which Papa & I descended some twelve years ago. We think the garden of the St. Laurence Cottages a Paradise. Knolls of greenest, smoothest turf & primrose banks & walks, trees, a rocky stream, splendid flowers in beds & the sea for background. They kindly make me lie down in the drawing room & have my dinner there. A. & I go to the Pelham Cottage. The stars are bright & the rooks cawing at eleven o'clock. We stumble about for it is too dark to see the paths but make our way to the light in the house at last.

16th. Stormy clouds but only two little showers during the day & a good deal of sunshine. The little church gay with hothouse & greenhouse flowers. Charlie[27] looks very pretty in her wreath & veil & Horatio his very best. A pleasure to see their happy faces. The rooms & the breakfast table decked with primroses. All very cheerful. After breakfast we all dance under the Verandah. A. & I arm in arm. We throw a large horseshoe once belonging to a Lincolnshire cart-horse & our oldest old slipper after them for good luck. About three when the bride & bridegroom have left for Winchester. A. & I & Mrs. West drive to Bonchurch to call on Manns, Peels & Whites, the rest ride on horseback. Mr. Hamburgh, the Miss Sewells & their friend Miss Frederick, & Mr. Field's friend Mr. Latham,[28] & Dr. Mann dine. A. does the honours, Dudley[29] not being well enough. I sit near A. at dinner to my delight.

[26] Stephen was Leslie Stephen (later Sir; 1832–1904), the Cambridge don and skeptic, who in 1867 married Mrs. Cameron's niece Julia Jackson.

[27] Mrs. Horatio Tennyson.

[28] Possibly Henry Latham (1794–1866), the vicar, an occasional writer and lifelong student of the classics.

[29] Dudley George Cary Elwes (b. 1837), brother of Charlotte Elwes Tennyson.

17th. He walks with Eleanor[30] to see the Pillar named after A. by Dr. Kane of which Miss Sewell is so very [*sic*] as to make a water-colour drawing for us. After luncheon we return home. Another charming drive and a delightful welcome from the boys who come skipping downstairs singing in chorus, "I am so glad you're come home, I'm so glad you're come home," & to see how Hallam plays the host to us. We unpack the frigate which Mr. Peel has sent us to the joy of the children.

18th. Mrs. Cameron & Julia to tea with Mrs. Prinsep. We hear that Mr. Southey has been photographing the children.[31]

20th. Dr. & Mrs. Vaughan come.[32] A. reads a great part of Job to me.

22nd. A. mows. Mr. Arthur Stanley comes, goes up the down with A., dines & sleeps. Dessert in the drawing room. A very pleasant talk & a little bit of "Maud." Mr. Stanley never likes visiting the same place twice—Waste of time—or does not like disturbing 1st impressions.

23rd. Mr. Stanley goes after I have had a very pleasant talk with him. We cannot but be sorry that he must go.

24th. A beautiful Thomas à Kempis[33] sent me by Sir John as an Easter gift.

Woodford comes & we go about the Farm with him. A. reads me some of Colomba.[34] Mr. Reginald Southey's photograph of the boys arrives. One can trace some likeness to Hallam in that of Hallam little ruffian tho' he be. Lionel comes out still less distinctly but one is grateful. We look after the gates with Merwood. . . .

[30] Eleanor West, the sister of Harriet West of Wrawby, Lincolnshire, who in June 1860 married Arthur Tennyson.

[31] Reginald Southey (1835–99) was doctor, author, and amateur photographer. He wrote *The Nature and Affinities of Tubercle* (1867) and *The History of Bright's Disease* (1881).

[32] Charles John Vaughan (1816–97) was the famous Anglican divine and headmaster of Harrow, 1844–59, credited with introducing to that school the same standards of excellence Thomas Arnold established at Rugby.

[33] Thomas a Kempis, *The Following of Christ* (London, 1851). On the flyleaf is inscribed "Emily Tennyson from J. S." Obviously "J. S." is John Simeon and not James Spedding, the speculation on p. 162 of volume one of *Tennyson in Lincoln*, compiled by Nancie Campbell (Lincoln: The Tennyson Society, 1971).

[34] Undoubtedly a volume by or about the Celtic saint Colomba (Columba), also known as Columkille.

26th. A little bit of "Merlin."

27th. A. goes to London. Only a little open carriage comes for us. I say I fear that there is no room for you, my children. Poor Hallam's eyes fill with tears so we each take a child on our knees. Rather late for the steamer but A. rows after it & it stops & he gets on board. The dentist detains him longer than we expected. I look after calves, poultry, & vine, plant roses & clematis & woodbine near his chair in the corner of the kitchen garden (I call it his but he put it there for me), & one rose tree near our arbour, tie up lettuces for him, put pine branches in the hedge near where it is thin, get lilies of the valley for his room, write many letters, & read a little.

May

6th. His Acacia wood desk which I have had made for him out of one of our own Acacias comes & I write a letter to him on it.

Hallam writes his own letter to Papa to-day, 13th.

15th, 16th, 17th. A. writes every day but I am made sad. Some days by the negligence of the post office my letters coming two together instead of one every day. My days all much the same.

18th. He comes home to-day with Mr. Woolner & Mr. Vernon Lushington.[35] The photograph priceless (Cundall's),[36] so much the best I have seen.

19th. A delightful & very happy walk. The wilderness a paradise of flowers—blue hyacinths like the Heavens breaking thro' the earth, orchises, gorgeous crimson crown in the Pine trees. A. covered with sweet golden dust from them. The cedar brightening with the new leaves. A. read the "Ode to the Duke of Wellington" in the evening & told Mr. Lushington the song from "Merlin."[37]

20th. Horatio, Mr. Worsley, Mr. Wise & Dudley Elwes come in a boat & had to return at once because of the tide & so did not see

[35] Vernon Lushington (1832–1912), fourth son of Sir Stephen Lushington (d. 1877) of South Hill Park, Berkshire.

[36] Joseph Cudall (1818–95), the publisher. Cudall was a keen amateur photographer and was a member of the London Photographic Club, sometimes called the Calotype Club. Under the name of Stephen Percy, Cudall wrote *Robin Hood and His Merry Foresters* (1841) and *Tales of the Kings of England* (1850).

[37] "Trust me not at all or all in all" (see 11. 385–96, 444–47).

A. who had gone with the two gentlemen to Alum Bay.[38] He reads "Maud."

21st. They walk towards Compton Bay & he reads *Hamlet.*

22nd. Mr. Lushington brings me Rock-roses from the Cliff. Sun roses they are called because they open at sunrise & the petals fall at sunset. He & Mr. Woolner have a beautiful walk to Cliff End & admire the views from the lane leading to it.[39] A. reads "Audley Court" & other things. Mrs. Cameron sends me the Portfolio with Mr. Southey's photograph of the boys.

23rd. Mr. Lushington & Mr. Woolner go, with a hope on our part that they may come again before long. Mr. Wilberforce comes.[40]

24th. All go to Church. A. reads Milton.

25th. Milton.

27th. We admire the golden leaves of the Black Poplar bright with sunshine against the dark Fir trees.

28th. Mr. Wilberforce goes. Mother & Matilda come. A great deal of writing all these days.

June

1st. We send off "Enid" to Moxon!

3rd. Mr. & Mrs. Archibald Peel dine with us.

[38]Philip Stanhope Worsley (1835–66), the poet, was a member of the family of Worsleys of Gatcombe, Isle of Wight. Worsley's most successful works were his version of *The Odyssey* (1861) and his translation of the first twelve books of *The Iliad* (1865), both of them done in Spenserian stanzas.

Wise was probably John Richard de Capel Wise (1831–90), the author and ornithologist. Among other works Wise published *Shakespere: His Birthplace and Its Neighbourhood* (1860) and *The New Forest* (1862).

[39]Cliff End is the point where the High Down (Tennyson Down) ends in a sheer westward drop toward the Needles.

[40]Samuel Wilberforce (1805–73) was third son of William Wilberforce; dean of Westminster, 1845, and bishop of Oxford, 1845–69. At Oxford, Wilberforce faced great opposition from the low-church party, which suspected him of Papist learnings. His condemnation of *Essays and Reviews* in 1860, however, and his stern action on the case of John William Colenso occasioned a gradual rise in his popularity. In 1869 Wilberforce was appointed bishop of Winchester, and in that post he initiated and presided over the revision of the New Testament, a project not completed until after his death.

10th. I get up early to see dear Gandy off, obliged to send her away for fear of bad effects on our Hallam from favouritism to Lionel whom she had from the first. Dreary days of discomfort & sadness from parting.

11th. Mr. & Mrs. Peel walk to Alum Bay & The Needles with A. and dine with us.

12th. Sir John & Captain Simeon call. We walk & talk and are very glad to have them back again. A. resolves not to publish "Nimuë" ("Vivien") & "Enid" until he has a bigger book.

13th. We take the children for a walk in honour of our wedding day.

15th. Stormy East winds. Poor A.'s Hayfever very bad. He had scarcely anything of it last year.

17th. Horatio & Charlie come.

19th. Edmund & Cissy. Drives to Norton, Totland Bay, Needles, Alum Bay, Brook. Mr. Bayard Taylor comes. We are all sorry that he only stays one night.

29th. The Bradleys come & Miss Price. Edmund & Cissy go.

30th. Arthur Wright[41] comes.

July

1st. The Bradleys.

2nd. Horatio & Arthur go in a boat to the Needles. Bring home a gull & two guillemots (willies).

3rd. Arthur goes. Mr. Reginald Cholmeley[42] calls among others.

4th. Mr. Lear comes.

6th. Sir John & Lady Simeon dine here & Mr. George Coltman who is staying here. The Bradleys & Miss Price, the Afton party & Mr. Ellis & Mr. Rutsan. All charmed with Mr. Lear's singing.

[41] The longtime rector of Coningsby, Lincolnshire. Wright published "The Endowed Schools Act, 1869, Considered in Reference to the Counties of Lincoln and Nottingham" (1872), as well as a selection of Tennyson's verse in Latin and Greek (1882).

[42] Perhaps a member of the family of the Rev. Robert Cholmeley (1780–1852), rector of Wainflete from 1817 until his death.

7th. Mr. Coltman goes before we are up. We are touched by hearing him creep softly down stairs. Mr. Lear goes after having sung all the morning. Lionel throws himself on my knee & seems quite overpowered by music.

8th. An Italian sings to a kind of lyre.

9th. All our guests go. The first evening we have been alone for two months or more. A. busy examining the snakes' eggs which Merwood brought in yesterday having found them buried two or three feet down.

The snake hearts beat at least two hours after having been taken in the thin jelly sheath out of the leathery egg. A. puts my cloaks & cushions by the myrtle under the cedar tree & I lie down. The view splendid. He brings me the first lines which may be the nucleus of the parting of Arthur & Guinevere.

12th. We go with out children into the Hay field. The children very merry out with us. I have a very nice talk with A. in the evening.

13th. Hay field. The Bradleys, Miss Price, & Mr. O'Grady to tea.

14th. Splendid weather. A. drives with Mr. Bradley to Heathfield & then waters Nemophila & puts out Lilies of the Valley. Mr. Bradley in the evening. A pleasant talk after A. had read me some of Shakespeare's Sonnets.

15th. Mr. Bradley helps me to arrange the books before we leave home. He very kind. I working till one or two o'clock in the morning.

16th. Mr. Bradley comes to help & to say good-bye. We have a prosperous journey & go to Draper's Hotel. We go to Burlington House. A. sleeps there & dines.

17th. Burlington House & Cudall's to have the children photographed. We go to Little Holland House & are charmed with the House & gardens. Mr. Prinsep most kind. I am introduced to Mr. Prinsep & both A. & I to Mr. Watts.[43] Then we go to Argyll Lodge. No one at home.

[43] Watts was George Frederick Watts (1817–1904), the famous artist, a permanent guest at Little Holland House for nearly twenty-five years. Watts was a long-time friend of the Tennysons, and he painted both the poet (the well-known 1859 "moonlight portrait" and several others) and Emily Tennyson (1863). Arthur Paterson said of the portrait of Lady Tennyson, now located in the Usher Art Gallery at Lincoln, "It is a wonderful piece of characterization;

18th. We go to Grasby. Charley meets us at North Kelsey Station.

19th. We all—Louy, my Father, A. & I—receive the communion, Charley administering. We take our children to church for the first time in the afternoon. Both very good but Hallam asks whether the man will soon let him out.

20th & 21st. Drives. We go to Caistor. A. goes over the house which was his great Uncle's & for which, & the houses & farms belonging, Charley has had to take the name of Turner.[44]

24th. Children very pleased with flags & triumphal arch at Kelsey in honour of the opening of the school there yesterday.

25th. Charley drives A. and me to Bayons Manor.[45] Only Mrs. d'Eyncourt at home. She is very kind & shows us all over the house.

26th. We take our children to church in the afternoon & Hallam asks if Uncle Charley will leave his nightgown in church.

27th. The boys & I drive with A. to the Barnetby Station, see him off & bring back Harriet Wright.

29th. We drive to the Mausoleum at Brocklesby.[46] Children much pleased. Hallam wants to call to the Dead. He says there are giants there. We have drives with my Father.

30th. The boys charmed with the school feast for which we went yesterday to Caistor to buy cakes & toys, which they distribute, & Lionel astonishes the children by giving them flowers. They are very eager in the races for books. Hallam singling out a particular clergyman. Lionel, of course, following his example. The school children show great fancy in their dances to the Hurdy-gurdy of a wandering ministrel. Lionel charmed. The school children sing old English airs very well on the lawn. Then "God Save the Queen" & three lusty cheers & they depart.

. . . the great artist has caught the prevailing quality of the face—the tenderness and spirituality—a face not wanting either in its lines of strength" (Allingham and Paterson, *The Homes and Haunts of Tennyson*, p. 80).

[44] In March 1835 old Sam Turner died and left his estates at Grasby and Caistor to Charles Tennyson, thereafter Charles Tennyson Turner.

[45] The home of Tennyson's grandfather George Tennyson, which was inherited by his second son, Charles, who took the ancient name of d'Eyncourt.

[46] In the park near the village is the circular Mausoleum (1787–94) designed by James Wyatt.

August

1st. Our pleasant visit ends. I go with a sad heart. We walk down part of Charley's walk before going. He takes us to the Station. At Manchester A. & Mr. Woolner, our servants meet us & after luncheon we go to the Exhibition.[47] We are fortunate to find rooms at the Waterloo Hotel. Meanwhile A. & I see British shields & go to the Botanical gardens & admire the white & yellow water lilies & see the Victoria Regis. I meet a kind Quakeress while he is away a minute who speaks to me. I have tea, he soda water. We dress & go to hear Dickens read his "Christmas Carol" in the Free Trade Hall. Next morning Mr. Woolner breakfasts with us & we go again to the Exhibition, see Hunt's pictures, Turner's sketches & Mulready which please A. more than anything, I think, & me very much also. Gainsborough's beautiful portrait "The Blue Boy" & "Mrs. Graham."

We set off for Coniston before one. At the Station find Mr. & Mrs. Jewsbury,[48] Mr. Woolner & a Mr. Smith, I think, a gray gentleman who came years ago to see A. at Coniston & found him gone. We arrive at Tent Lodge between seven & eight & find that Mr. & Mrs. Marshall, Mr. Spring-Rice & Gandy have been several times to look for us. A. goes to dine with the Marshalls. Mr. Allingham comes in the evening.

2nd. Mr. & Mrs. Marshall call. They look so young & well & are so very, very kind.

6th. We dine with the Marshalls to keep A.'s birthday.

8th. Mr. Woolner arrives & Lionel claps his hands.

11th. A pouring rainy day for Hallam's birthday but Mr. Woolner is very kind in playing with the boy & when it clears in the afternoon Mr. Marshall & Julia[49] bring gifts (whips & a gun & Poems for little Children) & Julia had a good game with the boys & tea. Pleasant talks & walks [*illegible*] we have with all these pleasant friends—Mr. Stephen Spring-Rice and his daughter Ailene [and] his brother Aubrey included.

[47] The 1857 Manchester Exhibition.

[48] Mr. and Mrs. Frank Jewsbury, who had made the Tennysons' acquaintance at the Exhibition and with whom the poet subsequently spent an evening (see *AT*, p. 306). Frank Jewsbury was the brother of Geraldine Endsor Jewsbury (1812–80), the novelist and intimate friend of Jane Welsh Carlyle.

[49] The James Marshalls' daughter.

12th. Early in the morning we hear the sound of an axe. About nine the great Beech tree in front of the dining-room window falls. Mr. Marshall's kindness to A. who had said the house is too much shut up with trees. We have none [of] us been well.

14th. Alas! there has been a mistake as to the Beech cut down as Mrs. Marshall finds to her regret. A large Beech instead of a small one. Dr. Whewell,[50] Mr. Spring-Rice, his brother Aubrey, Julia, Ailene all come to us.

18th. A picnic on the Moor & A. reads "Maud" afterwards. We have had a happy day. Myriads of fish sporting in the lake. We see them among their emerald groves. We hear the owl hooting wildly & sadly at night & some other birds calling. Mr. Bywater[51] kindly insists on A.'s riding his cob & accompanies him himself. A. enjoys the ride & is the better for it. He loses his old watch. Mr. Bywater's man rides over the same ground in a vain search for it. He leaves slips of paper in the Farmhouses saying to whom the watch belongs & I take the children to look for it. The heath is delicious & there are many flowers of Grass of Parnassus but no watch. It comes back however found, I believe, by some labourer.

Finish Froude & *Tom Brown*[52] whom we think delightful.

24th. A. proposes Furness Abbey. [Mrs. Marshall] meets us in the Barouche. A delightful drive. The view where the plain & the rocks all come in together framed by the mountains particularly fine, I think. The Abbey imposing, so massive & such glowing stone. On our return in the train . . . we meet a kind, intelligent man who tells all about the quantity of Iron ore found in the mountains near the Duddon. The royalties seem to vex him.

Mr. Marshall takes us beautiful drives in Pony carriage or Barouche. A. reads me the new translation of "The Song of Solomon"[53]. . . .

30th. Mr. Marshall goes to Dublin for the British Association.

[50]William Whewell (1794–1866), Tennyson's tutor at Trinity College, Cambridge; Knightbridge professor of moral philosophy, 1838–55; master of Trinity College, 1841–66; and vice-chancellor of Cambridge in 1843 and 1856.

[51]Possibly John Ingram Bywater, father of Ingram Bywater (1840–1914), the humanist and Greek professor at Oxford.

[52]Thomas Hughes, *Tom Brown's School Days* (1856).

[53]Probably *The Song of Songs*, translated from the original Hebrew with a commentary, historical and critical, by Christian D. Ginsburg (London: Longman & Co., 1857).

We were in the boat & I caught sight of what seemed to me Mrs. Marshall's dress. We found her & Mr. Venables coming down the walk. Mr. Venables made a seat for us in the branches of Fir trees & we had a very nice talk. Day beautiful. They lunched with us & we rowed to the end of the lake. A. gathered there rushes at the mouth of the river for me. He landed on the island where we had landed years ago. The heathery hills made the waves purple. There was a long swell as we returned. Everyone takes such care of me I am ashamed. A. dines at the Marshalls'. He will not let me go because we are late.

September

1st. MM's kindness cannot be exceeded.[54] Among other walks Mr. Venables & A. go to the Three Lakes Point which A. pronounces one of the finest they have had. Before they go Mr. Venables reads us some of "The Prologue" to *The Canterbury Tales.* Very agreeable he is always in the evenings.

5th. A. & MM have had a walk & he has read old Ballads to us, "The Lord of Sin" & bits of others.

6th. Take the children to church but I resolve not to do so again as a general rule at present. I am sure it is not good for them. I could scarcely restrain Hallam from dancing during the sermon & he was continually asking me, "What does that mean?"—repeating the words. One day he wanted to know if the man were a soldier or a policeman for he talked about punishing him.

Mr. Marshall returns from Mount Frenchard, leave Victor in Ireland for a few days.

9th. I have a little talk with Mr. Venables. Sad to think that he goes to-morrow.

12th. A grand expedition to Langdale Pikes. We go in the Barouche to the little house at the foot of Dungeon Gill, then after the gentlemen have been up the Gill in a car, to Blea Tarn.[55] Mr. William Spring-Rice has left us on the road to Keswick after having shared our luncheon with us at the foot of Lingmoor.[56]

[54] MM is Emily Tennyson's abbreviation for Mary Marshall.

[55] Site of the Solitary's cottage in Wordsworth's *Excursion.* All the surrounding countryside has likewise been immortalized in *The Excursion.*

[56] Lingmoor Fell.

What grand walls of rock this and Silver How! and Lingmoor couches magnificently like a Lion at the foot of Langdale Pikes & what a fine sweep they make to the Valley, the moraine just beyond! Bowfell too is very imposing & the tarn wild as need be. I like this spot best of any I have seen among the Lakes. MM & I so tired we do not go down to dinner tho' I had much the best chance for I had A.'s arm to support me all the way after Mr. Marshall sat beside the clownish driver to keep him in order & prevent him from breaking us on the wheel by furious driving. A good-natured clown tho'. Mr. Williams[57] arrives. Mr. Cheetham & Mr. Clark come to luncheon next day.[58] Mr. Williams charms A. by Arab stories.

14th. The gentlemen set off for Wastwater. After a drive MM brings me to the gate of Tent Lodge & so ends the very pleasant visit to Mount Coniston.

16th. I drive & A. walks with MM afterwards & runs all the way when he has left the carriage which meets them not to keep me waiting longer than need be for dinner.

I do not go with the party to Buttermere & Keswick. Mr. William Warburton & Lord Ribblesdale[59] call.

Franklin Lushington comes for an hour or two before we start for Patterdale. Our poor little boys cry very much when we leave them. Small pleasure for me to go anywhere without them. However to-day I must. A most kind welcome from the William Marshalls. Music & the Conservatory in the evening. After A. has taken me to the seat where one sees the gorgeous flowers backed by lake & mountain, he & Mr. Marshall take me about the garden & to the Waterfall in a garden chair. Rainy in the afternoon but in spite of this we drive to Halstead where we can see but little of the mountains. JGM goes with us having arrived just in time before the drive to tell us of his geologi-

[57] Possibly Rowland Williams (1817–70), the Anglican divine. In 1862 Williams was prosecuted and suspended for one year by the court of arches for heterodoxy displayed in his contribution to *Essays and Reviews* (1860).

[58] Henry Cheetham (1827–99) was canon of Saffron Walden, Essex, 1856–58; bishop of Sierra Leone, 1870–81; and vicar of St. Mary's, West Cowes, Isle of Wight, 1882–88.

William George Clark (1821–78) was the celebrated Shakespearean scholar. Clark was a fellow of Trinity College, Cambridge, from 1844 until his death. He was joint editor of *The Cambridge Shakespeare* (1863–66), and he endowed the Clark lectureship in English literature at Trinity College.

[59] Thomas Lister Ribblesdale, 3rd baron (1828–76), who shot himself at Loeche les Bains, Switzerland.

cal rambles.[60] After in my room A. comes to bring me down to the conservatory which he says is quite a little bit of the East with the magnificent flowers & the crimson leaves & the long trailing plants drooping from the ceiling. All this is perhaps even more enchanting by lamplight than by sunlight except when the sun is in certain positions.

25th. I press the beautiful specimens of ferns which Mr. Marshall has given me & then we all go off in a boat this sunny morning. We go to the Devil's Chimney & until we can see Helvellyn, then we land in a pretty garden. After luncheon we bid farewell to Patterdale but have to wait for horses the Landlord at the Inn having had to send away forty people this morning.

26th. Mr. Dodgson comes to photograph.[61] Mr. William Spring-Rice, Miss Heathcote, Franklin Lushington arrive. Frank sings in the evening. MM is delighted. Miss Bulford kindly gives up her room to Miss Heathcote who goes next morning. Walks & drives.

29th. A letter from Carstairs to say that it is full till Monday so we do not go as we had intended. A. not having been well we have not given long enough notice.

October

1st. We got to the hotel at Inverary. We had not meant to go till next week. JGM & MM take us in the Barouche to Windermere. We very sorry to part from them, I need not say. On the road it begins to rain. We sleep at the railway Inn, Carlisle. Dreary rain when next day we reach Glasgow. . . .

3rd. We go up Loch Ling & Loch Goil by Glen Goil to Inverary. On the way we meet with a Mr. Mitchell whom A. had met ten years before in the Pass of Killiecrankie. He recognizes A. & kindly asks us to his house. We learn that the Duke has been summoned to Balmoral.[62] The Duchess is at Dunrobin.[63]

[60] JGM is Emily's abbreviation for James G. Marshall.

[61] This meeting at Tent Lodge was the Tennysons' first with Charles L. Dodgson (Lewis Carroll).

[62] Balmoral Castle was long the Highland home of Queen Victoria.

[63] The magnificent seat of the Duke of Sutherland, Dunrobin Castle incorporates the remains of an ancient fortress dating from 1097. The duchess of Argyll was Lady Elizabeth Georgiana (d. 1878), eldest daughter of the 2d duke of Sutherland.

4th. Lord Lorn[64] & his Tutor kindly call & try & persuade us to go to the castle but we do not like to go during the absence of the Duke & Duchess. We should not have come had not a letter from the Duchess missed. A rainy walk with A. in the Avenue. I see a splendid rainbow very broad over a mountain. Snow on the tops of some mountains, a great hailstorm & a thunderclap. Hallam exclaims with delight at the brilliant rainbow over the bridges & a wooded hill. I never saw one look so solid & so bright, I think. The mountains wild & beautiful in a pale evening light. The Moon on the lake. A. goes to the castle to say that we think of going away to-morrow. He is charmed with the grounds both by moonlight & sunlight. The evening bright & calm. He has tea & returns about twelve.

5th. The missing letter from the Duchess telling us of their plans & inquiring about A. Lord Lorn has also had a letter giving directions about our rooms & saying that he is to do his best to keep us at the castle. Very kind but I am homesick. The Tutor most considerate. He tries to reconcile us to going to the castle in the absence of the Duke & Duchess. We stay here to-day at all events. A. is taken out in the boat dredging & is much interested by the curious beasties found. After luncheon we have a wild drive to the waterfall & round by the fresh-water lake.

6th. Lord Lorn writes that the Duchess meant to leave Dunrobin early on Monday & hoped to be at the castle to-morrow & to find us there. Most kind, so we resolve to go there after luncheon. A very cordial welcome.

7th. Fast day. Afternoon church. A little before eight A. & I hear a knocking at the drawingroom window & find a white owl dancing on the ground & trying hard for admittance. . . . Soon after another knocking at the window of the Antiroom & the Duchess with Lady Edith & Mr. Charles Howard[65] come in having walked thro' the dark night from the Oban road. The dear Duchess had hired a steam vessel to come the quicker & had stayed for the Fast day service on the road.

[64]John Douglas Sutherland Campbell, later 9th duke of Argyll (1845–1914). The lordship of Lorn (or Lorne) was resigned in 1469 by Walter Stewart to Colin Campbell, 1st earl of Argyll, who from that date (as were his successors) was usually designated "Earl of Argyll, Lord Campbell and Lorn." By the nineteenth century the title "Lord Lorn" was commonly assigned to the eldest Argyll son and heir.

[65]Lady Edith Campbell (1849–1913), eldest daughter of the duke of Argyll, and Charles Wentworth George Howard (1814–79), fifth son of the 6th earl of Carlisle; M.P. for East Cumberland from 1840 until his death.

8th. A. in bed with a cold. The Duchess & Mr. Howard take me out for a drive. Next day we both drive with the Duchess & Mr. Howard. Dinner very pleasant, servants sent away.

10th. The Duchess goes with Lord Lorn & his brother Archibald to meet the Duke. Lady Emma Campbell drives with A. but we do not go far but have another drive with the Duke & Duchess.[66] A. reads "The Lotos-Eaters" & "Ulysses" in the evening.

13th. Our pleasant visit ends. The Duke & Duchess most kindly take us our first stage. The Day is beautiful. Loch Lomond as lovely as can be. Queen's Hotel at Glasgow very good.

We reach Carstairs before luncheon on the 14th. All very kind. Mr. Jenner comes to dinner. Mr. Alfred Trevelyan[67] sings.

15th. A. reads "Maud" in the morning. After luncheon we drive to the Falls of the Clyde.

16th. Mr. Monteith goes with us to the train.[68] We arrive late at Headingley. I too much knocked up to go down to dinner.

17th. We see what we have so much wished to see, the admirable mills & the beautiful little church. I go down to dinner but have to leave the table.

19th. Set off for Peterborough.

20th. We reach Park House & leave again on the 28th. Sad enough to leave them all. With Edmund & Cissy on the 27th. Frank goes with us to Aylesford. Reach Ashburton Cottage to luncheon.[69] Aubrey de Vere & Mr. Henry Taylor, Lady Charlotte Schreiber, her daughter, & her friends, Mr. & Mrs. Richards, are among those we see. . . .[70] Mr. Woolner, Holman

[66] Archibald Campbell (1846–1913), was the Argylls' second son, and Lady Emma Campbell (d. 1893) was the only sister of the duke of Argyll. In 1870 Lady Emma married Sir John McNeill (d. 1883).

[67] Alfred Wilson Trevelyan, 7th baronet (1831–91), who succeeded his uncle, Sir Walter Calverley Trevelyan, in 1879.

[68] Monteith is Tennyson's old Scottish friend Robert Monteith.

[69] Ashburton Cottage was the home of William Bingham Baring, Lord Ashburton, and his second wife, Louisa, Lady Ashburton (d. 1903).

[70] Lady Charlotte Schreiber (1812–95) was the Welsh scholar, formerly Lady Charlotte Guest. In 1833 Lady Charlotte married Sir Josiah John Guest (1785–1852), whose iron works at Dowlais she managed after his death until her marriage in 1855 to Dr. Charles Schreiber (d. 1884). Lady Charlotte is

Hunt, Mr. & Mrs. Patmore, Mr. Spring-Rice, Rossetti are all very kind.

November

3rd. We drive with Mrs. Cameron to see the Carlyles. Mr. Carlyle admits us tho' against rule to admit guests in the morning. We return thro' Wimbledon Park. Mr. Henry Taylor, Mr. Lear, Williams, Mr. Rossetti, Mr. Holman Hunt, Mr. Woolner dine. Lady Charlotte & her party come in the evening. All pleased with Mr. Lear's singing. A. reads the "Morte d'Arthur" & "Break, Break" after he has sent me to bed. Most hospitably, most kindly have we been received by our friends in their houses. We are grateful for all the enjoyment we have had.

4th. Still we joyfully return, for all the enjoyment we have had, to our own darling home. Day rainy at first. . . . Clear as we cross. Rosy streaks as we near home at sunset. The children lavish all manner of tender words on their home. A. reads me some Dante—the Francesca, Ugolino, Daniella, Farinata, Cavelcanti.[71]

5th. We write letters & go into Maiden's Croft & the garden. We find golden egg-like things on two sets of plants. These days about home & sweeping leaves after our old fashion. Our friends call.

10th. A little Lucretius.

11th. Odes of Gray, Coleridge & Shelley. Very delightful.

12th. Some Livingstone.[72]

---

remembered primarily for her translation of the *Mabinogion* from old Welsh manuscripts (1838–49).

The Richardses were Henry Brinley Richards (1819–85), the pianist and composer, and his wife. Richards served as a director of the Royal Academy of Music and was a professor there and elsewhere. His musical sympathies were mainly on the side of Welsh music, and he published, among many other songs, the "Harp of Wales" and "God Bless the Prince of Wales," which has become the Welsh national antham.

[71] See the *Inferno*, V, for Francesca; X, for Farinata and Cavalcanti; and XXXIII, for Ugolino. See the *Purgatorio*, XXVI, for Daniella.

[72] David Livingstone, *Missionary Travels and Researches in South Africa* (London, 1857).

16th. Sweep leaves too late & get cold. A. reads me some of Grove's Correlations.[73]

19th. Some of Béranger's Songs. Lucretius & Béranger. I go on with Livingstone to myself.

21st. A. works very hard in the garden all these days. My cold too bad to go out. A. reads me some of Harry Lushington's things. "La Nation Boutiquière," "Inhermann" & we agree that they are very noble.[74] How much we do miss him.

30th. A. reads me part of *Much Ado about Nothing*, rather in memory of Augustus Stafford whom he saw act Benedick in their college days, I think.[75]

December

1st. Sir John & his brother Cornwall Simeon call. More of *Much Ado* in the evening.

2nd. A. reads me "Sea Dreams." Very fine, I think.

3rd. A. walks to the Simeons, returns on the 4th. He makes an old woman for them with his hand & then I kissed them sitting with Papa on the floor to their great delight.

8th. Sir John fetches him to Swainston. Hallam whispering over and over again in Sir John's hearing, "Why does he go?" He returns next day, reads to me some of Jocelyn[76] two or three evenings but we cannot get on with it. Sir Alexander Grant's book[77] pleases me very much. A little *Hamlet* & "Comus."

[73] Sir William Robert Grove, *On the Correlation of Physical Forces*, the substance of a course of lectures delivered in the London Institution in 1843 (London, 1846).

[74] See Henry Lushington, *La Nation Boutiquière, and Other Poems, Chiefly Poetical* and *Points of War*, by Franklin Lushington (Cambridge, 1855).

[75] Augustus Stafford O'Brien Stafford (1811–57) attended Trinity College, Cambridge, with Tennyson and took an M.A. in 1832. Stafford was M.P. for North Northamptonshire from 1841 until his death. Arthur Henry Hallam, Richard Monckton Milnes, and Robert Monteith also took part in the March 19, 1830, performance of *Much Ado about Nothing* at Trinity College.

[76] Likely Jocelin de Brakelond, whose *Chronicle* Carlyle drew upon for *Past and Present*.

[77] Aristotle's *The Ethics*, with essays and notes by Sir Alexander Grant, 2 vols. (London, 1857–58).

19th. A lovely day. Mr. Palgrave comes. He comes always laden like Schiller's Lady from the Strange land.[78] The children delighted with the pictures of the Fairy Tales which he has kindly brought them. A. works the garden as usual and walks with me when I can walk.

23rd. Sir John dines with us.

24th. A. brings me a nosegay of white wild roses & tells me that there are plenty more in the hedge, also bramble flowers and a little bit of woodbine but this is rather withered. The holly wreaths just up. A. reads "Griselda" to us. A delightful evening.

25th. A beautiful sunny day. Went to Communion. A letter from Colonel Phipps asking by desire of the Queen that A. would write a stanza to "God Save the Queen" to be sung at a concert which is to be given at Buckingham Palace on the evening of the Princess Royal's wedding day.[79]

A. reads some of Rogers to us.

28th. Mr. Palgrave goes. We resolve after all to fight our way thro' Jocelyn.

30th. A letter from Colonel Phipps approving, I hope, of the two stanzas sent on the 27th. A. & I walk & sweep up leaves & burn them as usual.

[78] See Schiller's "Das Mädchen Aus Der Fremde."

[79] Tennyson wrote two additional stanzas to "God Save the Queen" to be sung at the State Concert which was to be given at Buckingham Palace on January 25, 1858, the wedding day of the Princess Royal to Crown Prince Frederick William of Russia.

1858

January

1st. Thankful indeed ought we to be that we begin the New Year as the old was ended in our happy daily round of work indoors & out or in pleasant walks when outdoors work could not be.

2nd. We decide on putting the little gate at the end of the Wilderness & we do finish Jocelyn.

3rd. A. reads me the histories of Jeptha & of Samson.

4th & 5th. *Morte d'Arthur.* Invitation to the Concert at Buckingham Palace. The Somersby pictures come. Every evening we act fairy tales & nursery stories for the boys, being Mother Hubbard or her dog or the Frog Prince or the Bird & Mouse or even Sausage as may be.

7th. Finish hanging the Somersby pictures. The boys find a little robin dead but still warm & Lionel kisses it over & over & makes me kiss it, & Hallam & A. make a grave for it in Hallam's garden between the Alexandrian laurel & the Russian violets & Lionel puts it in. They have made me carry it part of the way. A. tells them to say "God bless you" to it & we put some of the feathers which have fallen off into Lionel's garden. A. reads me the end of the *Morte d'Arthur.* It is awe-inspiring.

8th. He reads to me the beginning of his parting of King Arthur & Guinevere. Grand and gigantic almost awe-inspiring some of it seems to me.

9th. When the boys & I have done our "Plays," A. comes & reads their favourite nursery rhymes—Fox, My Lady Lea & the Three Huntsmen. He reads me the greater part of the History of Saul in "Samuel." Next evening Saul & David.

12th. We look about a site for the Summer House. Mr. Swinburne & his friend Mr. Hatch come & dine here.[1] A. reads

[1] Edwin Hatch (1835–89) was a theologian and intimate friend of Swinburne. Hatch's unpublished diary preserves his impressions of the Farringford visit on January 12, 1858: "Called on Tennyson . . . : first in morning when we talked not much, he being busy with his poem. Then at dinner with him and Mrs. Tennyson: stayed till long after midnight in his glorious little room, but what he said is to be remembered not here but in my soul for ever" (*The Swinburne Letters*, ed. Cecil Y. Lang [New Haven: Yale University Press, 1959–62], I, 14).

"Maud" & when I am gone upstairs, King Arthur's speech.[2]

15th. A. goes on with "Kings" & reads me more of his "Arthur & Guinevere," to my mind the grandest thing he has ever done & what he reads more beautifully if possible than anything else.[3] He sends the hundred copies of the Stanzas to Colonel Phipps for the Queen.

17th. He reads me Guinevere's speech. Four days he walks to the Needles & other days long walks.

21st. He comes into the Nursery & reads "The Sultan" to the children, also their favourite "Snow White & Rose Red," then "Briar Rose."

22nd. He finishes "Kings" to me which he has been reading almost every evening.

25th. Princess Royal's wedding day. I was telling Hallam what twins meant saying that they came into the world together, that he came alone, that Lionel did, that I did, upon which he indignantly replied, he, not you, you came down from Heaven with Papa.

A. makes the boys very happy by building a city for Hallam & defending while Hallam fires.

February

1st. Cities built again & again by the boys & A. He looks to the building of our Summer House & reads me in the evening Juvenal's 13th Satire in Latin & then translates it.

[2]"Guinevere," ll. 419–577.

[3]Emily Tennyson's high opinion of "Guinevere" was echoed the next spring, before publication of the first four *Idylls*, by the duke of Argyll, who wrote to Tennyson: "I can hardly tell you what an impression that lofty verse made upon us—and is calculated to make, I am certain, upon the world—I am not sure that I do not think it the finest thing you have ever written" (April 27, 1859, T.R.C.). Later that summer Argyll wrote to the poet again in praise of "Guinevere," this time conveying as well the impressions of Thomas Babington Macaulay: "Macaulay is certainly not a man incapable of *understanding* anything, but I knew His tastes in Poetry were so formed in another line, that I considered him a good test—and three days ago I gave Him 'Guinivere' [*sic*]. The result has been as I expected that he has been *delighted with it*, and he told me that he had been greatly moved by it—and admired it exceedingly. Altho' by practice & disposition he is eminently a Critic, he did not find one single fault" (July 14, 1859, TRC.).

5th. He takes me to look at the Summer House.

8th. He cuts down two little trees & reads "Chronicles" to me these evenings. Mr. Henry Marshall[4] calls.

10th. A. reads "Ezrah" & part of "Nehemiah." The children talk about the "Son of God." Lionel says, "You know, Hallam, what it means. This is our Sun & God's Sun is much larger & brighter & is called Jesus Christ." "No," Hallam says, "this is not it. We will ask Borton."[5]

A. reads me a little of Macnaghten[6] on Inspiration. We talk until it is too late to finish "Nehemiah."

13th. A. chops wood for logs & we do finish "Nehemiah." Macnaghten. Maccabees.[7]

15th. Sir John Simeon dines & sleeps & brings the children beautiful toys with which they are, of course, charmed. A. reads a bit of "Arthur & Guinevere." Sir John helps me to rig a boat for the children, walks with A. to the Needles & goes before our dinner. Maccabees in the evening.

17th. News of the taking of Canton Forts.[8] We begin *Faust* as we have neither of us read it or anything German for a long time.

18th. News of Canton taken. We look anxious at debates about the Government of India. In the evening *Faust.*

21st. "Defence of Guinevere."[9]

24th. Lord Dufferin sends his book[10] to A. A. reads me "Guinevere."

25th. "Deuteronomy," Hegel's *Philosophy of History*, Bede's *Ecclesiastical History* these evenings. . . .

[4]Perhaps Henry Marshall (1795–1874), the Surrey attorney.

[5]A Farringford cook.

[6]Probably a piece by Sir William Hay Macnaghten, 1st baronet (1793–1841).

[7]The four books in the Old Testament Apocrypha treating of the oppression of the Jews from 222 to 135 B.C.

[8]See the *Times* for February 15, 1858 (p. 8), for a complete account of British victories in December and January at Calcutta, Bombay, and Canton over various insurgent forces and Chinese insurrectionists.

[9]William Morris's poem (1858).

[10]Frederick Temple Hamilton-Temple Blackwood, marquis of Dufferin and Ava, *Letters from High Latitudes: Being Some Accounts of a Voyage in the Schooner Yacht "Foam" . . . to Iceland, Jan Mayen and Spitzbergen in 1856* (London, 1857).

March

1st. "Guinevere." A. pastes up part of the window to make me warm and makes a beautiful Snow Lady & puts a black hat on her. He reads to me about Arabia. He takes me to the Summer House and brings out the large bench & puts his cloak over me. Deliciously warm it is. I delight in the little rest. He reads me some of "Guinevere" again because I ask again & again for it.

5th. He reads to me the Life of Caedmon in Bede. We agree as to its beauty & that this is the sort of biography we like.

I have not been at all well lately. Never was there such a tender nurse as my A. & the little boys follow his example & put cushions and make me comfortable after their fashion and are very pitiful over me & very loving to me. He makes the boys very happy by building castles that they may knock them down. A. blows bubbles in the nursery to keep the children from me & then he finds them so beautiful that he comes down to me with bubbles & children that I may see the gorgeous skies & the pretty little landships & the little planets breaking off from their suns & the single star becoming a double star. The boys wild with delight.

I find him lighting a fire for me. He reads part of *The Tempest* to me. A great delight. He paints the seats of the Summer House & reads me "Guinevere." Surely a most noble & touching poem. Sir John dines. Very pleasant as he always is. Before he comes Lionel sits expecting him and says, "I want 'John Simeon' every day." To-day he brings the boys two beautiful little boats with oars. Next morning he plays with the children & goes with A. to Totland to see the great blocks of Granite for the Lighthouse & leaves us before dinner. A. reads me a bit of Bacon's *Advancement of Learning*. Some passages as noble and beautiful as ever were written, I should think. Next day the Invalid chair comes from Sir John.

15th. Eclipse of the Sun. The day so cloudy that we see nothing of it except a darkness of evening for a few minutes. A. & the servants went on the down. There they saw the Sun red & the moon very near. A. has worked very hard at copying "Guinevere" & brings it down to me finished at tea-time. The eve of our Lionel's birthday.

16th. The boys very happy with their ninepins. They are splendid, they say. A. plants yellow crocuses from pots to replace those eaten by mice that we may not miss our golden wreath this year. We have another in the South. He takes me out in the chair these days. Next day the Simeons kindly come to look after us. The first day she has left her baby so long.[11]

A. reads me some Brown's *Atomic Theory*, "Beneficence of Suffering" from the *Quarterly*, some of Lewes's *Goethe*.[12]

22nd. Mr. Warburton comes for a night. One day the guns begin firing briskly from the forts while Lionel is on the down gathering flints. He throws them down & looking at the Moon overhead asks what the Man is going to do to them.

29th. Mr. Jowett comes. Next day he helps A. to draw me in the chair thro' Maiden's Croft, St. George's Field, the Mead by the farmyard & the Park home.

31st. We have "Sea Dreams" in the evening.

April

1st. Mr. Newman[13] comes to tea and Mr. Jowett goes away with him afterwards to the Red House, so our delightful days with him as our guest end. Before he goes the children playing with him both fall in the grate. He snatches them up & they are not much hurt. A. reads the last chapters of "Zechariah" to me. Mr. Jowett has been so very good to the boys & they so (I fear) expressively affectionate to him. They will long remember their tossing in the blanket (Mr. Jowett's Shawl) which he and A. gave them in Mr. Jowett's room & their jumps in the carpet bags. The Druid Temples too. I have to make Druids for them.

A. takes me up to look at the summer house which he has painted & about our nine [*sic*] goes to Mr. Jowett.

5th. Storm of Rain & East wind. The weather-cock blown down. Next day Professor Tyndall & Harry Jones bring Mr. Pollock's book *New Friends* to Hallam.[14] They & Mr. Jowett dine with

[11] This baby was Stephen Louis Simeon (b. 1857), who in 1886 became private secretary to the secretary of state for Home Department.

[12] Samuel Brown, *Lectures on the Atomic Theory; and Essays Scientific and Literary* (Edinburgh, 1858); "Sense of Pain in Man and Animals," *London Quarterly Review*, 103 (January 1858), 99–120, George Henry Lewes, *The Life and Works of Goethe; with Sketches of His Age and Contemporaries*, 2 vols. (London, 1855).

[13] Francis William Newman (1805–97), the religious writer and brother of John Henry Newman. A fellow of Balliol College, Oxford, 1826–30, Newman was professor of Latin at University College, London, from 1846 until 1869. He acquired repute chiefly for the *History of Hebrew Monarchy* (1847), *The Soul* (1849), and *Phases of Faith* (1850).

[14] John Tyndall (1820–93), the scientist, superintendent and later honorary pro-

us. Mr. Newman & Mr. Dicey[15] come in the evening & are very agreeable. Rain & East wind continue.

8th. Professor Tyndall & Harry Jones call in the morning to take leave. Mr. Parker[16] comes. Next day Mr. Jowett dines with us & Mr. Newman & Mr. Dicey come in the evening. We like them much.

A. paints the Summer house & Mr. Parker walks. He kindly promises to lend us books. Mr. Jowett, Mr. Newman & Mr. Wadly in the evening. Sir John Simeon.

13th. Mr. Parker leaves us. His high aspirations as a Publisher interest us very much. Mr. Jowett dines in the nursery & then goes up with A. to talk about the two poems he has read[17] & to hear the third "Guinevere." A happy evening with A. He reads me about Dante in *Fraser*[18] & some of the *Leaves of Grass* by way of curiosity.

14th. Bad news of my Father. I send him photographs of the boys. Two days later most joyful news of his wonderful recovery. Beautiful weather but still cold enough for me to be glad of the shelter of the hedges in the delicious spot where A. takes me where the bank is brilliant with primroses & celandine & the sweet briar begins to smell & the beautiful purple violets & where the birds sing.

A charming note from Mr. Jowett to the boys. We look at

---

fessor of the Royal Institution, was frequently a guest of the Tennysons, particularly during the 1870s.

Harry Longueville Jones (1806–70) was a Welsh archaeologist. Jones was the founder (1846) and first editor of *Archaeologia Cambrensis*; in 1849 he was appointed inspector of schools for Wales, and he continued in that position until 1864. Among his most important works are his "Plan for a University for the Town of Manchester" (1836) and *Memorials of Cambridge*, with Thomas Wright (1841).

I am unable to identify Pollock's book.

[15] Francis William Dicey (d. 1888), the London portrait painter. Dicey exhibited seventeen pictures at the Royal Academy between 1865 and 1888, and he painted an especially fine portrait of the Prince of Wales which was engraved by William Bell Scott.

[16] John William Parker (1792–1870), the publisher and printer. Parker became printer to Cambridge University in 1836; he sold his London business to Longmans in 1863.

[17] Probably "Sea Dreams" and possibly an early draft of "The Grandmother," which Tennyson completed by July 1858.

[18] "The History of Italian Literature," *Fraser's Magazine*, 57 (April 1858), 426–39.

the newly planted trees in the belt & in these warmer days we go into Maiden's Croft, the garden & lawn. He reads a little Hegel to me. We hear of Mr. Moxon's illness. Some of Henry Taylor & some of the songs in *The Princess*. We hear nightingales these days & a cuckoo & I see a swallow. He reads to me some of the poems in Béranger's last volume & brings beautiful white nettle flowers which we agree would do well for capitals of pillars. It is a happy time for me with our little boys on each side of me on the sofa in the anti-room or Study reading to them nursery tales or nursery rhymes before our own evening reading. If it were not faithless I should be afraid of so much happiness as I have. A. reads me some of Kingsley's poems. I lie on the green bench near the Summer [house] while he plants the lilacs. He has drawn me in my little carriage all the way by himself except that I walked up our sandy road thro' the wilderness which this year he has covered all alone this year for the first time, I not having been well enough to help. Lady Simeon & Louy come just as we have returned home. We show them the beautiful flowers (Riviera Anemones, I think) growing wild in the plantation.

27th. After dinner next day A. & I talk of want of reverence for great men [*Page torn*]

28th. The box of books which Mr. Parker so kindly promised to lend us arrives & among them Kemble's last book,[19] a gift to A., also a garden net netted by my Father.

A. has the wood carved by William (Seaton) brought in for me to see. A. begins reading Motley[20] to me. A feeling of the freshness of youth comes over me. History read aloud recalls the feeling of the days when my Father used to read it aloud to me & my sisters.

After tea A. bids me go on with my music. He likes to hear me at it, he says. This too makes me think of all the pleasure my Father had in my music or rather in my singing as I did most evenings latterly to him but I cannot sing now. I sing to A. a little but am too weak and out of practice to sing decently. He takes me to look at the windows he has painted in the Summer [house]. I think they are beautiful.

[19] *State Papers and Correspondence Illustrative of the Social and Political State of Europe from the Revolution to the Accession of the House of Hanover*, ed. John M. Kemble (London, 1857).

[20] John Lothrop Motley, *Rise of the Dutch Republic*, 3 vols. (London, 1856).

May

1st. Books from Mr. Moxon. A beautiful present from Mr. Jowett. A Homer & a little Plato all bound in soft binding of Russian leather. We go on with Motley these evenings. It must be confessed that I think he is not just to Royal personages tho' on the whole his History is very interesting. We make a practice of looking [up] in Baxter[21] all the flowers we do not know. It was pleasant to see the glee with which Hallam rushed up to Lionel the other day saying, "Lionel, here is a crowfoot." The boys answer the nice letter to them from Mr. Newman & gather flowers to send him. Backgammon & I finish the English Hegel & read a passage in the German marked by Mr. Jowett.

7th. Hallam could scarcely be got to bed last night he is so delighted with Croker's stories from English History which I am reading to him.[22] He is very sweet & simple & tractable. Backgammon, A. not equal to reading these two nights.

9th. A. takes me into the garden & Merwood shows us a lovely little nest of a white throat hanging suspended under the canopy of ivy which hangs from the wall near the back gates. A. reads to me about Oldcastle in Sharon Turner. Next day Mr. & Mrs. James White & Lotty & Clara & Mr. & Mrs. Blackwood lunch with us & the boys dine & are very good & have a famous romp with Lotty afterwards while the rest of the party go with A. to Alum Bay.[23] A. talks to me when they are all gone as they do after evening tea. The day after he takes me to our Summer House in Maiden's Croft where I stay while he paints the floor.

13th. When we are out to-day he takes me from the summer house into the kitchen garden & the farmyard where Mrs. Merwood tells us some of the romance of the village. A. reads "The Grandmother" to me.

15th. I have the large table desk put into his dressing room & he likes it there because it is lighter than his little study & he writes out "The Grandmother" at luncheon. After dinner he fetches me to look at the view from the upper windows for the first

[21] William Baxter, *British Phænogamous Botany*, 6 vols. (Oxford, 1834–43).

[22] John Wilson Croker, *Stories for Children from the History of England* (London, 1817).

[23] Lotty and Clara were children of the James Whites.
The Blackwoods = unidentified.

time this year. Rich in its May beauty of golden gorse, flowering trees & yellow-green elms bathed in sunlight and green through the mist on the hills beyond the Solent.

Hallam begins his little History of England. He & Lionel dine with us at our luncheon & A. delights them by making them say bits of Greek. "Say about a tree falling," "Say Ye Mariners of England," "Say about the Soldier sleeping & coming back to his dear home."

19th. A. has to go to London to the dentist. The boys take me out, the Sardinian[24] comes & the boys rush down for money as usual & Hallam brings his soldiers & Lionel his farm to show him.

I do A.'s books & make manuscript books for him & get many of the summer flowers put into the beds. Every day A. writes to me.

25th. He says he would most likely come but may take another day. I get flowers from him & let the children stay up beyond their usual time, but he arrives long after they are in bed. Next day we hang up the Cromes[?] which he has brought in the Anti-room. Charles Weld comes & Mr. Fairbairn, & next day Mr. Henry Marshall dines with us & the next (June 1st) Mr. Wandby & the day after he comes in the evening & the day after Sir John Simeon & Col. Hall & then after this Mr. Wandby &, June 2nd, Charles Weld goes.[25] Very kind & pleasant he has been. A. takes me to hear a nightingale. One has been singing in the withy bed but I fear its nest is stolen, it does not sing to-day. The May was like snow on the hedge. . . . The withies too wore white with their silky down. A most happy outing I have had. A. tells me his plan for the "Maid of Astolat."

June

2nd. He takes me to the Attic to see the Judas Tree & the Pink Thorn. The view wonderfully lifted up & fine, green lights on

[24] A Freshwater organ grinder who periodically came to Farringford.

[25] William Fairbairn (later Sir; 1789–1874) was a renowned engineer. In 1860 Fairbairn received an honorary LL.D. from Edinburgh University, and in 1861 he assumed the presidency of the British Association. Fairbairn was created a baronet in 1869.

Wandby = unidentified.

Col. Hall was Col. T. [Thomas?] Hall of the Grenadier Guards of Killean, Argyll, and Baronald, Lanarkshire.

the slopes & many walls of rock seen not generally seen. We choose from Merwood's crooked oak sturdy wood for a chair which William Seaton is to make. We must put a seat under the Ilex near the front door for the Yarmouth view. Merwood tells us of a red-breasted nightingale which sings to them while working in the wood & comes hopping down among them. Also he tells us how he has been frightened by the flapping of the night hawk's wings when driving insects from the shelter of the trees. A. reads to me the recently published beginning of "Hyperion" & we agree that it is the first.[26] A snail on the drawing room window. We watch the blood flowing thro' it like smoke from head to tail. The children very much pleased. A. asks me at dinner whether I had ever put down Merwood's story of the Raven coming down on his white head when he was a Shepherd boy watching his flock. A. takes me out usual rounds & to our new seat under the Ilex. I never knew how glorious the woodbine could be until I saw it climbing high up the Ilex with the sunshine on it. But how beautiful everything looks & what delicious scents. I found a curious insect with saffron coloured worm-like body & a ruff of green wings round its neck. I opened the green closet in the study & Hallam exclaimed a worm! I found a melon-coloured oak caterpillar which had gnawed a hole more than an inch long & half an inch wide. The shavings were all round it.

9th. Poor A. has to go again to the dentist. Dreary work but his teeth must be attended to. I watch him off in the steamer. We have misty days. Lionel seeing a thick column of smoke go straight up says, "how smoky God will be!" Hallam replied, "Lionel, you should not talk so." "But it is true, Hallam, if all the smoke goes to Heaven, God will be as black as the funny man" (meaning the Ethiopian singer).

A. will have me drive every day & he writes every day. I send him some seringa & myrtle on our wedding day & Hallam insists on sending a bit of their cake.

One night I think I hear "the villainous centre-bits."[27] I get up & listen & feel still more sure that there is a grinding of glass. I light a candle & show it at the window & grown bolder

[26]The theory that "The Fall of Hyperion" is really a preliminary draft for "Hyperion" has met with little acceptance. However, there is some likelihood that the introductory colloquy with Moneta, in which the goddess upbraids the poet for having been "a dreaming thing, a fever of thyself," was in fact written before "Hyperion."

[27]*Maud* I.41.

go to the window myself & see a snail whose shell is grinding the glass. Presently an almost musical note succeeds. Hallam finds a Jackdaw on the down which has apparently been wounded for it cannot fly. He is exceedingly anxious that Borton should know how to make raw meat when I tell him the bird eats it raw not roasted. The Simeons & Mrs. Prettyman kindly come to see me. She brings her son & her grandson & niece, also Mr. & Mrs. A. Court Holmes & Mrs. Bonvene & her sister & Miss Fanny Crozier all take pity on me.[28] The boys make hay. Our violet-coloured Petunias & scarlet geraniums look very pretty with the Hay-cocks as a background.

23rd. I go early to the Ferry as A. says he may cross in an open boat. I wait about an hour & a half. Lady Hamond & Miss Caroline Hamond & Mrs. Grosvenor Hood[29] come & talk to me. A. arrives in a little boat from the steamer. The country looks very pretty as we drive home. We find the boys still up waiting for him. The box of pictures sent by Mr. Palgrave opened in honour of his return.

A. takes me our happy rounds. We go first to the roses. Mr. James, Mr. Wood, & his cousin come. "Jack" the Jackdaw flies away & is tempted back by a bit of meat when he is trying to get in at the nursery window. He stays a little while in his cage then flies away & we see him no more. We see the Bradleys again often now. Mr. Holman Hunt arrives. He seems so good and great that one can dream oneself with an Artist of the olden time. He races with the little Bradleys in the little cart & they & our boys have tea in the hay field. A pretty sight they are.

1st. Mr. Holman Hunt helps A. to trim the knee-feathers from the wreath of Elms over the sea view & to put a seat for me under the cedar. We go with the children to Captain Hamond's. They are wild with delight.

2nd. Mr. H. Hunt leaves us. Mr. Peel comes.

[28] Both Mrs. Prettyman and Mrs. Bonvene, the wife of Capt. Bonvene, were Isle of Wight friends and neighbors of the Tennysons.

Fanny Crozier was one of the West Hill Croziers, probably the daughter of William Pearson Crozier.

[29] The widow of Col. Francis Grosvenor Hood, Mrs. Hood lived at Heathfield, Norton, near Yarmouth.

6th. Mr. Peel goes & Sir John Simeon, the Bradleys & Philpotts[30] dine with [us].

Sir John leaves next day after luncheon & kindly wishes us to take Swainston on our way to Hampstead.

9th. We leave the well-loved place & arrive at Britannia Cottages. The Jesses[31] have done their best for us but the situation is damp.

11th. We take the children to the Zoological gardens. They are enchanted. A. gets a chair for me so I can go round with them. The Lions come & look at them & make a low growl as if they thought them dainty morsels just out of reach.

16th. Kind Mrs. Prinsep rescues us from our lodgings. The hostess does all she can for us but I think we should have had typhoid fever had we remained there, but no other lodgings could be found. While we [were] there Mr. Patmore walked over from Finchley to see us & they bring their children & one day come in a Fly to fetch us so we all go to see their home & return.

Our boys very happy at Little Holland House swinging and with help climbing trees in the garden. A. writes out some lines of the fair "Maid of Astolat" & reads them to me. Mrs. Cameron comes & Mr. Watts & Alice Prinsep return from Malvern & A. reads "Guinevere" & "The Grandmother" to them. Nothing can exceed the kindness of our hostess. We are introduced to Lady Somers.[32] Very beautiful & pleasant she is & she walks well which has a charm for me. We see Mrs. Dalrymple,[33] too, another of the very remarkable sisters. Mr. Woolner, Mr. Holman Hunt, Burne-Jones, the Brookfields & Mr. Henry Taylor, Mr. Val Prinsep,[34] & others. A. reads his "Guinevere" again & "Sea Dreams." I get warm clothing for A.'s Norway journey. As the carriage is nearly packed for leaving Little H. House, Mr. Charles Howard comes in saying he thought it looked rather like Inverary. Very pleasant to see him

[30]Probably Henry Philpott (1807–92) and his wife. Philpott served as master of St. Catherine's Hall, Cambridge, 1845–60, as vice-chancellor in 1846, 1856, and 1857, and as bishop of Worcester from 1860 until 1890.

[31]Tennyson's sister Emily and her husband, Captain Richard Jesse.

[32]Virginia, Countess Somers, the greatest beauty among the Pattle sisters.

[33]Sophia Dalrymple (1829–1911), another daughter of James Pattle and the wife of Sir John Warrender Dalrymple.

[34]Valentine Prinsep, the second son of Henry Thoby Prinsep of Little Holland House.

again. One of the kindest of men as he is. We go to Grasby. My Father more bowed but stronger and better notwithstanding these last years & the illness. Horatio & Charlie & Eleanor West staying in the house.

23rd. I go with A. to Hull. Horatio kindly accompanies me. Sad work. The day is dark & it thunders & it rains but there is a rainbow. Mr. Barrett & Mr. Tweedie,[35] his travelling companions, arrive. I had hoped to look at the berths but she stands out to sea. Next day a great storm arises & continues all night. I cannot but be anxious. Lewis & Albert Fytche come.[36] Charlie & Louy are so good. They will have me drive every possible day & he often drives me himself.

August

1st. A few lines from A. from Christiansund. Mrs. Barnard kindly thought of asking for my letter. We have no post. He says that he has given up the journey. Charley & Louy go for their little holiday. Nanny & Agnes come. My Father kindly gives the boys money to buy A. a birthday present & gives all the children gifts on Hallam's birthday. He has been looking forward to his birthday & much as he has longed for it, he is not disappointed. I never saw a creature happier than he is all days. He ends it by acting Fair Rosamund![37] My father drives with me every day.

16th. My A. returns, when we had almost given him up. I had just begged to have the clogged horses unclogged & we were watching the gambols of the horses when Borton ran up & said "Master," so away we went & found [him] just alighted looking fresh & well & brown after his three days at sea.

22nd. We all go to Communion. A. takes me & we go again to church in the afternoon. Mr. Cotten officiates to-day.

24th. We leave Grasby. My Father walks up the hill with A. We go to the Great Northern Hotel. Mr. Lear calls & Mr. Woolner & next day A. dines with the Camerons & the next we take the children to the Crystal Palace. Mr. Woolner goes with us. Mrs. Cameron, Charlie & Henry & Mr. de Vere meet us. Our Lionel

[35] Mr. Barrett is George Goodin Barrett (1816–95). Tweedie is perhaps William Menzies Tweedie (1826–78), the popular artist; primarily a portrait painter.

[36] These were Lincolnshire cousins of the poet.

[37] See "Rosamund's Bower," first printed in the *Memoir*, II, 197.

struck almost dumb with wonder & will go all the time with me in my chair. I persuade A. to go with Mrs. Cameron & dine at the Prinseps.

27th. We come home. A beautiful day. Admiral & Captain Crozier come on board the Steamer & I give the Admiral my red-lined cloak by way of flag & he waves it in honour of his little niece's birthday as we pass the house. . . . All looks delightfully & smiling in the house. A. & I walk down to the Merwoods. A. reads me some of Lewes's *Goethe* & next evening Julian's rebuilding of the Temple.[38]

September

1st. Mr. Rossetti, Captain Bridges, Mr. & Mrs. Dasent[39] in these days. Mr. Wandby very ill. A. goes to see him. He gives his canaries to the boys to their great delight & leaves his fossils in A.'s care. We find Ladies' Tresses & Flowers which we like very much. Every possible day he takes me out in the little carriage & the boys are delighted if they are allowed to help. Certainly the pleasure of being drawn about our pretty fields by him is far greater than could [be] to me from most drives, fond as I am of driving. One morning I saw the little fellows in their blouses on the landing walking hand in hand playing at taking a morning walk & wild walk it was. I think I never saw them look prettier. I stood at the bottom of the flight of stairs & at every turn they rushed into my arms. . . .

12th. A. goes up the Down to-night to see the Comet. I go with him to the Attic windows to look at it. It looked fine low down on the horizon over the beacon lights. Next day we call on the Bonvenes & the children go as far as the monument with A. on his way to Swainston. After dinner I play merry old dance tunes & the children dance. Lionel almost flying as usual. Hallam asked the other day whether the clouds were slippery; I ought to know for I was there before I came here. Next day he returns with Sir John & they come laden with Tomatoes which A. has begged for me because I had said that

[38]Tennyson probably read the account of the Temple's reconstruction in the Apocrypha, I Esdras 5.56 ff.

[39]George Webbe Dasent (later Sir; 1817–96), the Scandinavian scholar, and his wife, the former Fanny Louisa Delane of Old Bracknell, East Hampstead. Dasent was named assistant editor of the *Times* in 1845, and he held that position until 1870, when he was made commissioner of historical manuscripts. He was knighted in 1876.

they suited me & ours are not yet ripe. They bring also the precious "Sir Launcelot du Lac," so precious that I am afraid of having it in the house lest anything should befall it.[40] They take me to Maiden's Croft in my little carriage & then Sir John reads me some of "Sir Launcelot." He has to return to guests at home. Next day A. takes me all along the foot of the Down to the road to Farringford Farm. The air is delightful. The only drawback lest it should be bad for him to drag me so far. In the evening both before & after tea he reads "Sir Launcelot" to me.

"Sir Launcelot" again. The next day we have only been a little while in the Summer House, to which he has drawn me, when we hear Sir John's welcome rung & see him approaching with Mr. John Doyle.[41] They all three join in dragging me up the down. A delightful day & to me a very enjoyable outing except that I feared to overwork them. We all four lie down & talk. The gentlemen go back with us & have a little smoke & chat with A. before they return. He reads me in the evening about St. Sophia. We are unsettled, expecting Mr. Palgrave. These days again at the foot of the down. We see a lizard & weasel running out of the hedge.

22nd. We have the pleasure so often longed for of welcoming Mr. & Mrs. Maurice. A. had just taken me round by Maiden's Croft & the ploughed fields & the lane & we were standing near the wood house when they arrived. A. reads "Guinevere" after tea.

A rainy day so we send a note to Mr. Ludlow[42] at the Warren Farm instead of calling as we had intended. Sir John & Lady Simeon & Mr. John Doyle come to dinner. Very pleasant.

Next day Mr. Maurice comes down thinking to breakfast with the children & myself but we have already breakfasted. He is so good as to read Prayers for me. If one could but have them always read so! I never saw any except perhaps one who

[40]The Tennysons were well acquainted with Chrétien's twelfth-century Arthurian romance in which Lancelot del (du) Lac first appears. Apparently when the Welsh hero Llwch was introduced to the French in the eleventh century he became Lancelot du Lac and as such acquired a foster mother in the Dame du Lac.

[41]John Doyle (1787–1868), the painter and caricaturist. In 1829 Doyle produced in lithograph the first of his lightly satirical portraits of the leading political celebrities of his time, and under the pseudonym "H.B." he continued to produce his political caricatures until 1851. Among those luminaries he caricatured were Wellington, Brougham, Disraeli, Palmerston, and Melbourne.

[42]John Malcolm Ludlow (1821–1911), the Christian Socialist and friend of F. D. Maurice and Charles Kingsley.

seemed so to commune with The Most High. Mr. Ludlow calls. Mr. Maurice & I drive with the children to the Lighthouse. The gentlemen walk. A sunny day. The gentlemen are so kind as to take the children down to the Needles. Mr. Maurice is so very kind to them. He loses his hat while taking care of them. We make unsuccessful attempts to clothe his head with handkerchiefs. Mr. Ludlow offers his hat and at last we see all three gentlemen walking wildly on the down without hats & then Mr. Ludlow takes them to the Farm & Mr. Maurice returns in his hat. He & A. take Hallam home by the down. Mr. Ludlow dines with us. Mr. Charles Anderson[43] calls with Mr. Rossetti's card, walks with the gentlemen to Brook & comes in the evening. Mr. Maurice & I take the children to call on Mrs. Ludlow at the Warren Farm.

26th. Sunday Mr. Maurice reads the morning service to Mrs. Maurice, A. & myself. Hallam is with us. A. rejoices as much as I do in his reading. A. reads some Milton to Mrs. Maurice & me while Mr. Maurice is at church—"Lycidas."

Next day we prevail on them to stay a little longer. A. first takes me & then draws Mrs. Maurice in the little carriage to Maiden's Croft & when she has gone in they draw me up the down & home by the lane. Very pleasant talks in the evening. To-day Mrs. Maurice is too unwell to go in the little carriage. The gentlemen take me up the down again and the children with Borton go all the way to the Beacon with us. Mr. Maurice takes them by turns on his back! & they go with me by turns in the little carriage. Mr. Ludlow calls. Sir Alexander Grant, the Miss Ferriers & the Afton ladies come to tea. Harriet Wright arrives before dinner. A. reads "The Grandmother" and "Sea Dreams" in the dining-room after luncheon.

29th. Extremely sorry to part from Mr. & Mrs. Maurice. Who would not? Mr. Henry Marshall & Mr. Oliphant[44] lunch with us and afterwards go in a boat to Alum with Sir Alexander & Miss Ferrier, who brings the children beautiful toys. Harriet goes, we do not, but A. takes me up by the down by the steps he has made for me, the children with us. He & I talk a long time after dinner.

30th. The comet splendid.

[43]Charles Abercromby Anderson (d. 1872) was Inspector-general of Her Majesty's hospitals and fleets from 1869 until his death.

[44]Probably Francis Wilson Oliphant (1818–59), husband of Margaret Oliphant, the novelist. Oliphant was a skilled painter and designer of stained glass.

October

1st. These days Mr. Ludlow comes & Sir Alexander & Miss Ferrier & sometimes one or more of the Afton party. He reads "The Grandmother."

2nd. Sir Alexander & Miss Cotton want A. to walk with them but he in his goodness takes me up the down instead & afterwards he reads what he has done of "The Maid of Astolat" and next day Sir Alexander & Miss Ferrier dine with us & he reads "Guinevere," & Sir Alexander pronounces it the finest thing in the language. I know that it is said in the heat of a first hearing, still it is pleasant. We have the children taken out of bed to see the Comet. Lionel said to me next morning that he thought he was dead when he saw the comet & I was told that he said "Am I dead?" These delightful outings on the down do me so much good & I think I feel better to-day than I have done these two years. To-day A. takes a volume of the *Morte d'Arthur* & reads me a noble passage about the battle with the Romans. Some *Mabinogion* in the evening. Next day we all call on Mrs. Austin at Plumbley's Hotel & see Mdlle Von Zeschau.[45] A. goes to meet Mr. & Mrs. Roebuck at dinner at Swainston. I decline. We see the Comet with Arcturus shining brightly over the nucleus, & when A. returns he comes to my room & tells me that it has been a glorious sight. He saw the Comet as he was driving to Swainston & then at dinner & he said he must leave the table to look at it & they all followed. They saw Arcturus give a great leap when he got out of the Comet's tail.

Col. Hall, Mr. Ludlow, Mr. Herbert, Captain & Mrs. Hamond call, Sir Alexander & the Miss Ferriers & Miss Cotton also. He helps A. to race me up & down the garden. Next day Mrs. Austin, Mdlle. Von Zeschau, Sir Alexander, Mr. Herbert & Mr. Ludlow dine with us. The Afton ladies in the evening. When the gentlemen have betaken themselves to the smoking room & Mrs. Austin has gone, we dance a set of Quadrilles! & sing & play. A. takes me a long way towards the Lighthouse next day, Mdlle. helping. Mr. Ludlow goes part of the way. A. reads us a little Milton, that part where Eve tempts Adam. Comet fainter but fine. We see it from the staircase window.

Next night A. draws Astronomical Diagrams for Harriet.

[45]Mrs. Austin was Sarah Austin (1793–1867), the wife of John Austin, the jurist. Mrs. Austin (née Taylor) was a highly competent translator, and she also edited a number of works, including *Germany from 1760–1814* (1834) and the *History of Reformation in Germany* (1845).

Mdlle. Von Zeschau = unidentified.

The day after Sunday he reads the epistle & gospel & lessons & I [read] the *Psalms*. It is too rainy & stormy for church. Again one of our delightful outings & we still see the Comet from the upper staircase window & from his Dressing-room window. A. is just going to read Shakespeare to us when Sir Alexander and his party arrive unexpectedly to tea.

12th. A. not very well but he takes me notwithstanding into the fields. Well that we had not gone further for the handle of the little carriage breaks. Edmund & Frank arrive. How delightful to have Frank back in England! We talk merrily. Next morning misty moisty. Edmund has brought us "Frederic" to look at. Mrs. Austin & Mdlle Von Zeschau lunch with us & Mrs. Austin talks to Frank about Malta among other things & is very agreeable. Sir Alexander & his party in the evening. A little music. Next day A., Edmund, & Frank take me to the milestone between the Beacon & the Lighthouse.

Up late talking in A.'s room & get up early this next day to see Edmund off. A. & Frank take me up the down. We wait for the children & see the white Afton pony in the lane & wait for the party there also. The children go with us to the Beacon. A. & Frank, Sir Alexander, the Miss Ferriers, & Mdlle Von Zeschau go on, I very nearly to the Needles. A. stays with me, the rest of the party go on. A. sits beside me. Such a glorious afternoon. The sea calm & blue. Hurst Castle[46] & the Red Lighthouses glittering each with a star on its forehead, the sands so yellow, the hills of every hue, nothing could be more exquisite. Frank soon comes up to us & he & A. race home with me. The splendour & glory of the sunset one cannot soon forget. The Crescent moon stood over our down as we turned into the Wilderness from Maiden's Croft. We asked all to dinner & Coggie[47] rode off to Afton to invite the rest of the party there for the evening. A pleasant evening & late when the smoking party has left us. Frank sings to us. A. comes to send me to bed & then he reads "The Grandmother" to the rest & to Frank what he has done of "The Maid of Astolat."

Next morning I get up early to breakfast with Frank who sets off for Brighton. Lionel standing by the window, Hallam hears him say "dear Uncle Frank" for he has taken a great fancy to his Godfather. A. takes me out & we have a happy evening.

[46] Located approximately six miles to the south of Brockenhurst, at the mouth of The Solent, Hurst Castle was a coast defense during the reign of Henry VIII and was for a time the prison of Charles I.

[47] Apparently the daughter of Sir Andrew Snape Hamond.

16th. He reads "The Rape of the Lock" to me.

17th. Next evening when Sir Alexander & Miss Ferrier come we show them that grand Sonnet of Michaelangelo's which we have been reading in Vasari, also the beautiful account of Raphael's power over the Artists.[48] A. sends me to bed soon after ten & takes them up into the smoking room & reads "The Maid of Astolat."

18th. Mrs. Austin, Sir Alexander Grant & the Miss Ferriers come to say goodbye. Next day being rainy A. has a romp with the boys & reads bits of "Sir Launcelot" to me. Some of *Julius Caesar* after dinner & scraps of *Noctes Ambrosianae*[49] after tea. I take Harriet to the Ferry next day & afterwards A. reads some Milton to Matilde (Mdlle. Von Zeschau) and me. He reads the *Psalms* with Hallam & me on Sunday morning & we go to church in the afternoon. *The Merchant of Venice.*

28th. A letter about Mr. W. Moxon's extraordinary statements.[50] Two decisive letters answering soon found by me but the affair occupies nearly all our time & thoughts for some days. So much writing has to be done. Hallam with Bowerbird notions of adornment not being able to get flowers because of the rain scatters scraps of all kinds about the hall & the stairs in honour of Nanny's birthday & Lewis Fytche's wedding day. Next day Sir John Simeon dines & sleeps here & is as usual most sympathetic. A. reads the *Psalms* with us & lessons & epistle & gospel to us. He takes me out as usual every fine day. To-day the sun shines brightly & the birds sing sweetly.

Two very welcome gifts of late, Gladstone's *Homer* from Sir

[48] "To Giorgio Vasari," which Michaelangelo wrote soon after Vasari published his *Lives of the Painters, Sculptors, and Architects.*

[49] *The Noctes Ambrosianae of "Blackwood"* [by John Wilson, J. G. Lockhart, etc.], 4 vols. (Philadelphia, 1843).

[50] In early October 1858 William Moxon informed the Tennysons through Charles Weld that any new financial arrangement between Tennyson and the Moxon firm would have to wait upon settlement of a debt of £8,886.8.4, which Tennyson owed the estate of the late Edward Moxon. In a letter to the poet (Oct. 27, T.R.C.) Weld detailed Moxon's claim that "in consequence of *your* earnest solicitation his late brother had embarked in an unfortunate speculation of publishing an *Illustrated Edition* of your poems, of which he printed 10,000 copies and that 7,790 remained unsold. These are valued at £8,374.5; 2,080 copies of *The Princess* at £338; 400 of the *In Memoriam* at £76.13.4; and 600 of 'Maud' at £97.10—making altogether £8,886.8.4." The eldest Moxon brother, Charles, did not support William Moxon's spurious claim, however, and it was soon dropped.

Alexander Grant and Müller & Donaldson's *Greeks* from Mr. Parker.[51]

November

1st. From eleven to eleven we are looking for Moxon letters instead of being at Westfield where we are asked for the opening of the Ryde Museum. Charles Weld & Mr. Forster most kind in taking all sorts of trouble for us in this Moxon business. Nevertheless we have another weary day of letter hunting & letter writing. The great Ilex opposite the dining room planted in the year of the battle of Waterloo has split. This split is filled with clay & it is girded by strong iron chains & soon moves itself by its branches.

We are very happy every evening almost in the Study, the boys & myself on our three chairs side by side an arm round each & I reading "Reynard The Fox" to them. A. reads *A Midsummer Night's Dream* & some of Sir Francis Palgrave's.

6th. Matilde & Miss Gordon come to Maiden's Croft & tell us of the birth of Lady Gordon's daughter.

9th. We go to look at Merwood's new purchase of Sheepwash Farm. A pretty spot. I glad to find that Oleb spring runs thro' the green of which A. is Lord. So he who is so fond of a running stream is not quite without one. In the evening he reads me all that is done of "The Maid of Astolat." I get cloth & lining & have a cloak made to replace that which he has lost by way of surprise, but he has seen the bill for the cloth & noticed my sending out a bundle of dark wash!

10th. My Father's birthday. The children & I write to him & send white roses.

Next day I am busy preparing for his departure. A bitter east wind so he thinks that I must not go even to the Ferry & of a journey to London for me he will not hear & so he goes alone. I finish Palgrave, go on with Thorndale, then read Ludlow's lectures on India with great interest[52] & also *Richard II* & among

[51] The *Homer* was Gladstone's *Studies on Homer and the Homeric Age*, 3 vols. (Oxford, 1858); *Greeks* was Sir James Donaldson's *Lyra Græca: Specimens of the Greek Lyric Poets from Callinus to Soutsos* (Edinburgh, 1854).

[52] Thorndale may have been a slip for Edward Thornton's *Gazetteer of the Territories under the Government of the East-India Company* (London, 1857).

John Malcolm Ludlow's *British India: Its Races and its History* (Cambridge, 1858) was a gift to the Tennysons from Thomas Woolner.

other things I play Welsh airs to the boys & sing "Too Late" to them. It is wonderful to see their faces of awe and sadness listening Hallam by my side, Lionel on the oak chair near the Piano.

Play at "Earth, Air & Water," a great favourite with them especially as it ends in a great romp & laughter.[53] They bring me word that a very large Eagle looking almost a man on the down has been seen. Every day letters from A. reporting progress of Moxon business which is we hope satisfactorily settled. Miss Gordon & Mdlle. Zeschau, of whom I have seen a good deal & like much, come to say farewell (19th).

20th. A. arrives to-day and brings Mrs. Gatty with him, reads "The Grandmother" to her, goes to the shore with her to look for sea Anemones of which she leaves some with a Chiton when she herself leaves on the 24th.[54] A. has read "Maud," "Nimuë" & "Locksley Hall" to her. He reads some of Ludlow's *India* to me.

27th. We get news of the settlement of the Moxon affair, thanks to Charles Weld's energetic kindness. A.'s cold so bad we have to betake ourselves to our own books in the evening. He is reading Huc's *China*[55] & tells me about it. Mrs. Gatty has already kindly sent us her "Poor Incumbent" which touched us both. She now sends her *Legendary Tales* & Mr. Gatty a volume of Sermons. The Chiton has taken to walking about the finger glass, we find, but no one sees that mysterious beastie in the act.

[53] A Victorian parlor game. "Earth, Air, and Water" may begin with one player throwing a handkerchief at another and calling out, "Air!" The person hit with the handkerchief must respond with the name of some bird, i.e., a creature belonging to the air, before the first player can count to ten. A forfeit must be paid if the player names a creature that does not live in the air, or if he fails to speak quickly enough. The second player then throws the handkerchief at another and calls out, "Earth!" or "Water!" The game then proceeds in similar fashion.

[54] Mrs. Gatty was Margaret Gatty (1809–73), Emily Tennyson's friend and correspondent from the time of her first visit to Farringford in November 1858 until her death fifteen years later. The youngest daughter of the Rev. Alexander John Scott, D.D., Lord Nelson's chaplain in the *Victory*, Mrs. Gatty is best remembered for her popular children's books. Her husband, the Rev. Alfred Gatty, was also an author and a Tennyson enthusiast. On December 6, 1859, he delivered a lecture entitled "The Poetical Character," illustrated from the work of the poet laureate, which was published in 1860, and he later wrote *A Key to Tennyson's In Memoriam* (1881).

[55] Evariste Régis Huc, *L'Empire Chinois*, 2 vols. (Paris, 1857).

December

1st. A. & I sufficiently recovered from our coughs to get out again. He mows, for a scythe arrives from Mrs. Gatty bright as a sword.

7th. A. reads me interesting things from the *Times* & tells me to read the Queen's "Proclamation to India."[56] Deeply interesting of course to us both. Hallam reads to him & A. reads me what he has written of "The Maid of Astolat" & Huc & begins *Frederic the Great* to me.[57] Mrs. Cameron's gift & a great deal of letter writing lately. I play a little at battledore & shuttlecock with A.

20th. Mr. Palgrave after A. has taken me into Maiden's Croft & brings a most welcome gift from Sir Francis & himself, Milman's *Latin Christianity*,[58] a book I had just been saying we ought to have, and all kinds of presents for the children. Our mask of Dante comes which Mrs. Prinsep has kindly had mounted for us & we put it up in the lobby. A. reads some *Frederic*.

24th. Mr. Woolner comes. The boys wild with excitement at seeing him.

25th. The Gentlemen blow bubbles for the boys the day being rainy. Mr. Masson sends his *Life of Milton* & *Essays*.[59] A. reads some *Samson Agonistes*. The boys rejoice in the glorious sunrise after the rainy days. The boys & I see Mr. Palgrave off. A. & Mr. Woolner take me out after Mr. Woolner has in the morning worked hard at my Medallion as he did yesterday and for all these days. We have now made the Dining-room his studio where he finds the light better. A. reads a little of *Comus*. He tells the boys stories at luncheon.

[56]On November 1, 1858, Lord Canning announced Queen Victoria's proclamation to "The Princes, Chiefs and Peoples of India," which unveiled a new British policy of perpetual support for "native princes" and nonintervention in matters of religious belief or worship within British India.

[57]Thomas Carlyle, *History of Frederick the Great*, 6 vols. (London, 1858–65).

[58]Henry Hart Milman, *History of Latin Christianity*, 6 vols. (London, 1854–55).

[59]David Masson, *The Life of John Milton* (Cambridge, 1859); idem, *Essays Biographical and Critical, Chiefly on the English Poets* (Cambridge, 1856).

1859

January

1st. Letters from the dear ones at Grasby. Mr. Woolner still hard at work. A. reads some Milton to us.

4th. A., Emily,[1] & Mr. Woolner take me to the beacon. A. covers me with his great cloak & leaves me only a peephole but I enjoy my outing very much on this bright party day. He reads part of "Enid" to us. Next day Mr. Woolner finishes the medallion & A. finishes reading "Enid" to us & I rejoice that it seems to me so beautiful.

The day after this Mr. Jowett arrives & the boys hail him as if they had only parted from him yesterday. The day after this Mr. Woolner goes. The freshness & imaginativeness of his talk have struck me this time more than ever.

18th. Julia Cameron's wedding day. Mr. Jowett goes. We have had very interesting conversations with him, & A. & he have had long walks & A. has read on different evenings "The Grandmother," "The Maid of Astolat," part of the *Two Noble Kinsmen*, a scene from Thiery where he sees Ordetta going to the Temple,[2] some of Shakespeare's sonnets, Gray's "Elegy," Crabbe's "Parting Hour," the Song of the Maid of Astolat[3] & some of Goethe's Poems. One evening Hallam was promoted to the honour of reading "The Lad who went to the North Wind" & one evening Sir John Simeon & his brother Cornwall dined with us, & tho' I have not been able to go on the down with them, A. tells me of the magic lights. Mr. Parker sends us *Man & His Dwelling Place*[4] & A. reads me a little of it two evenings & he & Hallam take me to see the first snowdrops.

20th. We read from cantos of the *Purgatorio* together.

Next day we have worse news of Mr. Hallam. He is taken

[1]Possibly Emily Ritchie ("Pinkie"), who was Anne Thackeray's cousin and a frequent guest of the Tennysons, as were her sisters, Augusta and Eleanor.

[2]Possibly Emily Tennyson had been reading the *Mémoires de H. Masers de Latude* . . . Nouvelle edition . . . augmentée par la citoyen Thiery (Paris, 1793).

[3]"The Song of Love and Death," "Lancelot and Elaine," ll. 1000–1011.

[4]James Hinton, *Man and His Dwelling Place* (London, 1859). Parker published the volume, and he obviously sent the Tennysons an advance copy.

from us the day after & the world is the poorer.[5] Rainy & stormy. Hallam reads all but the Absolution of the service. One Sunday before he volunteered to read the Litany and he took the clergyman's part, Lionel the clerk's most devoutly.

Next day A. takes me to see a fallen tree. The hole it has left is nearly filled with water. Two then fallen in the belt & one broken. A. picks up a poor little dove which is walking feebly along. I take it on my knee but it dies in the afternoon which makes us as well as the boys sad.

25th. We hear particulars of Mr. Hallam's death. Hallam asks if he may wear mourning for him. He helps A. now with my little carriage. Both boys seem much interested in Kingsley's *Heroes of Greece*[6] which I am reading to them.

February

1st. Every evening we read the *Purgatorio* & one night a bit of the "Maid of Astolat" to me.

8th. He has quite finished writing it down now all but a little bit at the end & brings it to me for I want to read it to myself. It is well to read things to oneself without the glamour of his reading which may beguile one.

Next day "Old England" & Liddell's *Dictionary*[7] come from Mr. Jowett. A. reads to me some of *In Memoriam* & talks about it. Very delightful. The day after Mr. Gatty comes. He interests us by telling us of Dr. Hook[8] & of his own curate who has made forty youths deemed untameable obedient to him in all things. . . . A. reads "Locksley Hall" & "The Grandmother" to him & when he leaves on the 12th he takes "The Grandmother"[9] with him to be printed with "The May Queen" for the people.

[5]Henry Hallam died on January 21.

[6]Charles Kingsley, *The Heroes; or Greek Fairy Tales* (Cambridge, 1856).

[7]Henry George Liddell and Robert Scott, *A Greek-English Lexicon* (London, 1843).

[8]The Rev. Walter Farquhar Hook (1798–1875), the dean of Chichester from 1859 until his death.

[9]Printed under the title "The Grandmother's Apology," this poem first appeared in *Once a Week* on July 16, 1859.

14th. Happy evening among happy evenings. He reads me "Boädicea" & part of "Maid of Astolat."

21st. We finish the *Purgatorio* & A. to-night & other nights after this reads me some Burns & he & the boys bring me violets, primroses, daffodils, lovely nosegays day by day. I begin *Robinson Crusoe* to the children, Hallam highly delighted. Next day we mark the places for the trees & shrubs which we have got from Williams & the days following look to the planting & send for more.

23rd. Sir John Simeon, Captain Bonvene, & Mr. Eyre Powell dine with us. A. reads me the VIII Chapter of *Romans* in Greek with Mr. Jowett's commentary. Another evening some of the *Times* Leaders & I read Sir J. Pakington's speech on the Navy Estimates with great interest.[10] The boys most careful over me because of my cough. Hallam keeping me from draughts and from talking & reading, & prescribing medicine & plaster, dear little Lionel applying his remedy of pats on the back. . . . A. brings me a hyacinth in a pot & a beautiful nosegay. He reads me the 2nd Chapter of *Colossians* with the Greek. Other nights we have had Backgammon. He has walked by starlight on the Down.

Tina Garden[11] & Matilde arrive & walk with Mr. Eyre Powell & his friend VanderKisten who want A. to dine with them on St. Patrick's day but he declines. We put up the Roman Photographs of the Sybils & Modesty & Vanity given us by Mr. Arthur Butler, also the *Edinburgh* & Louy Lushington[12] & Henry Hallam's portraits.

[*March*]

16th. Our Lionel's birthday. He is pleased with his flowers. Matilde gives him a little music & A. & I have a little Blindman's buff with the boys. Hallam looks on Lionel with a kind of awe to-day & asks me if I order dinner on his birthday, knowing that I order Sunday's dinner on Saturday & thinks this day sa-

[10]In his speech on February 26, 1859, Sir John Pakington informed the House of Commons that a budget of £9,813,181 would be needed to provide proper naval defense for Great Britain during the year 1859–60.

[11]Either the wife or the daughter of Francis Garden (1810–84), the theologian; subdean of the Chapel Royal from 1859 until his death.

[12]Lucia Maria Lushington (d. 1873), the daughter of Edmund and Cecilia Lushington.

cred too & so it is to us. A. reads some of Shakespeare's Sonnets. Next day Mr. Garden arrives.

19th. The Gardens go. Next day A. too languid to read. We look at the Physical Atlas. A. reads "Guinevere" to us & the next day, the 22nd, Hallam & I take him to the Ferry for London to look after the publication of the four *Idylls.* A magic music with the boys.

Matilde most kind in taking care of me. In the evenings she reads me some of the *Morte d'Arthur* & one of Robertson's Sermons on Sunday & the Falcon.

April

2nd. Matilde goes on the 2nd & I am sorry to lose her. Daily letters from A. He cannot return before Monday because Mr. Watts is too ill to finish his second portrait which every one pronounces better than the first good as that is considered. He returns looking well & cheerful & he brings Nimuë[13] with him. He has seen a great many people in Town. He dines with Mr. Chapman at his club, is introduced to Mr. Tom Hughes[14] who delights him, sees Mr. Ruskin for the first time. He reads his "Guinevere" to the Duke & Duchess of Argyll at Argyll Lodge. Reads *Idylls* at Little Holland House and to many others. He reads one or both *Idylls* to the Somerses & all at Little H. House, to Mr. Venables, Mr. Hughes, Mr. Woolner, Mr. Patmore, Charles Weld, Mrs. Norton & Mr. Norton (her son).[15] He sees Mr. Palgrave, Mr. Barrett, the Proctors, Lady Ripon.[16] He dines with Mr. Owen, meets Dr. Farre.[17] He is

[13]First published in the 1859 *Idylls*, this idyll had been printed in the summer of 1857 as the second part of *Enid and Nimuë: The True and the False*. Although the idyll was then entitled *Nimuë*, the main character was named Vivien.

[14]Tom Hughes (1822–96), the author of *Tom Brown's School Days*.

[15]The Nortons are Caroline Sheridan Norton (1809–77), the novelist, poet, and intimate friend of Melbourne, and her second son, Brinsley.

[16]The Procters are Bryan Waller Procter (1789–1874), the poet, and his wife, the former Miss Skepper, the stepdaughter of Basil Montagu. The intimate friend of Dickens, Leigh Hunt, and Charles Lamb, Procter is best remembered for his multifarious literary efforts, including his tragedy *Mirandola* (1821) and his 1864 biography of Charles Lamb. Procter wrote under the name of "Barry Cornwall."

Lady Ripon (1793–1867), was the former Sarah Albinia Louisa Hobart, daughter of the 4th earl of Buckinghamshire and wife of Frederick John Robinson, first earl of Ripon (1782–1859).

[17]Arthur Farre (1811–87), the obstetric physician. Dr. Farre was professor of

touched by Lord Lansdowne's,[18] at his age, coming to call on him. He is introduced to the Duc d'Aumale[19] who comes to Little H[olland] H[ouse] to have his portrait taken. He likes HRH & means to send him some of the Tobacco which Aunt Franklin brought for himself from the East. Mr. Woolner brings Mr. Novello[20] to see him. Very pleasant that he should get to know these great practical men.

8th. Rather a wild night & day of pain but it is almost worth while to have the pain to be so tenderly nursed as I am by A. "Nimuë," some of *Don Juan* these two evenings. Mr. Warburton dines & stays the night.

Mr. Dodgson comes in the morning & to tea in the evening. Mr. Lear's six songs come, "The time draws near," "Come not when I am dead" seem to us the best & wonderfully beautiful. Sir John Simeon & Mr. Dodgson dine with us & Mr. Dodgson shows his photographs. A. & I read a little of the *Gododin*[21] another evening some of *The Tempest* & the Balcony scene in *Romeo & Juliet*. The Welds & Mr. Barrett come. One night when Mr. Barrett has left A. reads the Flight in Carlyle's *French Revolution*.[22] Mr. & Mrs. Butler & Mr. Galton[23] here. Arnold

---

obstetric medicine at King's College and physician-accoucheur to King's College Hospital from 1841 until 1862. He was also an examiner in midwifery at the Royal College of Surgeons, 1852–75, and for some years he served as physician extraordinary to Queen Victoria.

[18] Henry Petty-Fitzmaurice, 3d marquess of Lansdowne (1780–1863), a Whig mainstay during the twenty years of Tory ascendency following the death of Charles James Fox.

[19] Henri Eugène Philippe Louis D'Orleans, duc d'Aumale (1822–97), son of Louis Phillippe, king of the French, 1830–48. The duc d'Aumale resided in England from 1848 until 1871, when he returned to France to take his seat in the National Assembly.

[20] Vincent Novello (1781–1861), the organist and composer. Novello was one of the thirty original members of the Philharmonic Society, and he was acquainted with many of the leading literary figures of the day, including Charles and Mary Lamb, Leigh Hunt, Keats, Shelley, Hazlitt, and Charles Cowden Clarke.

[21] *Y. Gododin: A Poem on the Battle of Cattraeth*, with an English translation by the Rev. John Williams ab lthel (Llandovey, 1852).

[22] Thomas Carlyle, *The French Revolution* (New York: AMS Press, 1969), II, 156–85.

[23] Douglas Strutt Galton (later Sir, 1822–99), assistant permanent under-secretary for war, 1862–69; director of public works and buildings, 1869–75; K.G.B., 1887; and president of the British Association, 1895.

calls to see about the Oriel windows in the Attics suggested by Charles Weld & the vaulting of the ceilings.

May

1st. The Welds go. Very pleasant has their visit been. Charles takes "Guinevere" up with him & also "Riflemen."[24] I have a happy evening with my A. correcting the proofs of "The Maid of Astolat." Mr. Peel comes.

8th. Proofs of "Guinevere" come.

10th. Arnold & his men begin the alterations in the Attics.[25] We all go up, A. & I & the boys to see the work of destruction begin. Poor little room it is sad for A. & me when we see its barn-like rafters & we grow quite sentimental over it when A. talks of all the pleasant evenings spent under its low ceiling, all the thoughts & all the feelings thought & felt there.

12th. Sir John sings old English airs to Mr. Peel & A. upstairs. We have heard that Sir Alexander Grant's brother is killed in action in India.

14th. Mr. Peel takes a stanza of "Up, Jack Tar" for Balfe[26] to set.

15th. A great putting out of Greenhouse flowers. I fix the places, Hallam carries out some plants, & A. digs the holes. The following days we are busy with the Attics & A. takes Hallam & me up to the platform as best he can in its unfinished state.

23rd. We hear of his bust having gone to Trinity, Cambridge. The next day the last pane of the new window in his study is put in & he calls me to hear a nightingale from it when open. A delightful inauguration. The Duke & Duchess of Argyll walk with A. & dine with us. A. reads his Poems of '52.[27] A very

[24]Published as "The War" in the *Times* on May 9, 1859, this poem did much to rouse England to the needs of national defence. The poem was not reprinted until restored in 1892 as "Riflemen Form!"

[25]This reconstruction of the poet's attic study was the first major alteration which the Tennysons undertook at Farringford. At this time a platform was also added atop the house from which Tennyson could see both Freshwater Bay and Alum Bay, some two miles west.

[26]Michael William Balfe (1808–70), the composer. He produced the *Siege of Rochelle* at Drury Lane in 1835, the *Sicilian Bride* at Drury Lane in 1852, and the *Bohemian Girl* in Paris in 1869.

[27]When invasion from France seemed imminent in January 1852, Tennyson

pleasant evening. Next day they all three go geologizing to Brook. I not strong enough yet. The Duke & Duchess dine with us. A. reads "Maud" afterwards. We must part from them to-night as they go early tomorrow. One does not like to think of their working so hard.

For some days we take his proofs to the Summer House to correct. Sir John comes and he likes our alterations in A.'s study very much. A. wishes me to play my settings of "Hands all Round" & "Riflemen Form!" to him. I am glad that he likes them & much more than glad that he himself does. He reads me the 1st Act of *Macbeth* & next night some of the *Morte d'Arthur* where Launcelot behaves so courteously & Sir Palomides so uncourteously & where Arthur goes to see La Beale Isoude.[28]

29th. Mrs. Norton & Mr. & Mrs. Brinsley Norton come in the evening after having called in the morning. Mrs. Norton very gentle & kind.

31st. I am called up by A. to see the view from the attic window before the sash is put in. It is really enchanting. We are told that the wretched farmers poison the birds here. If the dear things must be killed let it be mercifully & so that they may serve for food.

June

2nd. Mr. & Mrs. Theodore Martin call and dine with us next day. After dinner we discover that she is the famous Helen Faucit.[29] She interests me much. Both are very agreeable. Another day Giotto's Chapel at Padua & Perugino's St. Sebastian chromographs come to us from Mr. Prinsep. All these days we take the proofs up to the Summer House.

---

wrote two songs called "Rifle-Clubs!!!" One of these is the original version of "Riflemen Form!"

[28] See Thomas Malory, *Morte d'Arthur*, ed. Thomas Wright, 3 vols. (London: John Russell Smith, 1866), II, chaps. 155–56 and chap. 158.

[29] Theodore Martin (1816–1909; knighted 1880) is best remembered for his *Life of Prince Albert*, 5 vols. (1874–80).

Helena Saville Faucit (1817–98), better known as Helen Faucit, afterwards Lady Martin, first appeared in London in 1836 in Sheridan Knowles's *Hunchback*. Subsequently she often played opposite William Mulready, her parts including Constance in *King John* and Queen Katherine in *Henry VIII*, as well as Desdemona, Cordelia, Miranda, Rosalind, and Lady Macbeth.

6th. Merwood tells us of bees in the roof of the stable. Mr. Lear comes to us in the Summer House. A great pleasure to see him looking so well and cheerful. A. & he walk & he sings in the evenings & A. reads to him "The Maid of Astolat" with which he is delighted as he is with "Guinevere" which he reads to himself. Mr. Evans arrives. Mr. Lear sings. A. reads "The Grandmother" & next day they walk & Mr. Lear sings to us & we square words. A. tells me not to look at the window until its crown is on.

10th. He has to go to London about the Proofs & to the Dentist. I ask Captain & Mrs. Bonvene to dinner because Mr. Lear knows so many of his friends & relations & the Miss Oldershaws in the evening. Mr. Lear sings & the Captain & he talk much together. Next day I get up early to breakfast with Mr. Lear. When he goes Lionel looking out of the window says, "How I like him," & one echoes the words in ones heart. . . .

13th. Hallam draws rose trees & myrtle & orange trees for A. & I send him myrtle & seringa flower. Letters as usual from A. I am very venturesome. I have opened a door into the greenhouse during his absence.

Mr. Rawnsley & Drummond arrive unexpectedly. They go next day in a boat to the Needles & are charmed especially with the arched rock at Scratchell's Bay. They go after luncheon. Most kind they have been. My A. writes to me that both sights & sounds were magnificent at the Handel Festival to which he has been. It has been one of the desires of my life to hear *The Messiah* grandly performed. Delight that it should have been fulfilled in him. One day he went to the British Museum with Frank. Another he was at Stafford House.[30]

The tailor puts up the bed, all the workmen & many besides work with might & main but the house is not made beautiful as I had wished for A.

27th. He comes. Never I think so happy a meeting for me of all the happy meetings. He likes all that is done. I have warned him beforehand how much was undone. I let the boys show him the new door from the study to the Greenhouse according to my promise to them, and he is pleased with everything. The view from the new windows is a kind of drunkenness of de-

[30] The massive palace built by Benjamin Wyatt in 1825–27 for the duke of York (d. 1827) and enlarged by Barry and Smike c. 1842 for the 1st duke of Sutherland, earlier marquess of Stafford. Known as Stafford House from 1842 until 1912, the palace was renamed Lancaster House when it was presented to the nation by Lord Leverhulme.

light. Mrs. Cameron has come with him & also likes the alterations.

28th. Sir Pelleas and Ettarre[31] to us after our pleasant talk. Next day Frederic arrives. He & A. walk on the down. A. kicks against a hedgehog & brings it in. We feed it with bread and milk which it takes & rolls itself up.

July

1st. Mrs. Cameron goes. Frederic crosses with her. Meanwhile Hallam & I call on Captain & Mrs. Hamond in their new house. Very charming it is. A. will delight in the lawn. Their little Carry says "Break, Break" to me in such a touching sweet voice. While the Grants & Mr. Ferrier[32] are dining with us there is a fearful thunder storm, hailstones as big as Walnuts, the kitchen two or three inches deep in water which comes into nearly every bedroom. Merwood pierces holes in the bathroom ceiling to let the water off & so preserve the ceiling. Just before the storm begins Mrs. Cameron's Ellen[33] arrives to our astonishment. She is sent to ask for the manuscript of "Guinevere." A. does not care about his manuscripts. He gives them to anyone who asks. To me they are more precious than words can say. Every page almost a memory. He is so good as to say that if I do not like to part from it and he has promised it, he will copy it out rather than that I should have to part from it. Mrs. Cameron thought the Grants were to have "Guinevere." A. says she shall have it if anyone has it. One does not like to refuse kind & energetic Mrs. Cameron anything.

3rd. Sir Alexander & Lady Grant leave. There are few we should so unwillingly lose. Sir John comes.

Next day Frederic leaves us for Jersey & the next the poor James Whites who have lost their daughter come to stay with us. Dear & good people, how bravely they bear up under their great loss.

10th. The *Idylls* come. Splendid weather this week since the storm.

11th. The Whites leave us. Next day Sir John dines with us. The

[31] See *Morte d'Arthur*, I, chaps. 80–82.

[32] Lady Grant's father.

[33] A maid of Mrs. Cameron's.

Bradleys & Mr. Duckworth[34] come in the evening & he sings to us.

14th. The Fields from Boston, USA come to us. She with a face like the old Italian Masters' faces. Very attractive.[35] Next day the Bradleys also dine with us. We have news of the Peace which we fear bodes no good for England.[36]

27th. We go to Park House & then to the Camerons at Ashburton Cottage.

August

3rd. We see Frederic, the Prescotts, & Mr. Stephen Spring-Rice and his daughter Mary.

On the 16th we part from A. at the Waterloo Station. He goes with Mr. Palgrave & Mr. Grove[37] to Lisbon. Mr. Brookfield with him to Southampton. He writes me three letters before he sails next day. I write but he does not get my letter, & by every mail, but he gets no letter & when he returns on the 12th of Sepb without having seen Seville, Malaga, Granada & Gibralter as he had intended he writes to know where we are & stays in the New Forest to learn. As he has returned earlier than he had intended he has promised to stay with Mr. Palgrave until Sir Francis comes back. They go to Cambridge. The apprentice at the Tobacconist's where A. lodged recognizes him & puts a paper in his hand. A. spends an evening with him and one with Mr. Macmillan[38] with whom he is much pleased. The

[34] Perhaps a relative of Sir John Thomas Butler Duckworth, 2d baronet (1809–87), M.P. for Exeter, 1845–57.

[35] After the first visit of Mr. and Mrs. James T. Fields to Farringford, Annie Fields noted that Emily Tennyson was "intellectually and morally strong, and with a direct personal influence about her such as Shakespeare has in some ways contrived to express most remarkably in his female delineations" (quoted in M. A. DeWolfe Howe, "The Tennysons at Farringford: A Victorian Vista," *Cornhill Magazine*, 63 [October 1927], 450).

[36] On June 11, 1859, in spite of his promise to Count Cavour to fight until Italy should be free from the Alps to the Adriatic, Napoleon III met Francis Joseph at Villafranca and agreed to a peace which marked the end of the Franco-Austrian War.

[37] F. C. Grove, the eldest son of Judge Sir William Robert Grove (1811–96).

[38] Alexander Macmillan (1818–96), the publisher. Tennyson first negotiated with Macmillan in 1861, but he decided to continue with Moxon's at that time. Macmillan finally became Tennyson's publisher with the publication of the 1884 *Collected Edition*.

boys & I go to Town on the 27th from Park House. A. meets us at the Station. He goes to Frank's room, I & the boys to Draper's Hotel. We go home next day. Nanny & Agnes arrive in the evening & leave on Oct. 18th. I have been too ill to keep a journal and I am still. On this account one visit from Sir John, one from Mr. Macmillan & Mr. Masson,[39] is all the change A. has had. He has read me some Juvenal some evenings.

October

27th. Mr. Charles Sumner from America dines with us and is very agreeable. When he leaves next day Lionel, as if he had foreboded his fate, said, "If a naughty comes and hurts Mr. Sumner, I will fight him and die myself for him."[40]

31st. A. sends "Sea Dreams" to Macmillan for his Magazine.[41] Next day Frank is prevented from crossing by the storm & goes again next day. A drearily short visit. Mr. & Mrs. Lewis & Mr. & Mrs. Gatty. He has been lecturing at Barnesley & Chichester on A.'s poems & has found warm response especially at Barnesley. "Sea Dreams," "Guinevere," some of Shakespeare's sonnets, "The Vision of Sin," & talk.

November

5th. Mr. & Mrs. Gatty go. We have had many trees blown down. Notwithstanding the storm, A. & boys go out to see the splendid bonfire which by A.'s care has been kept smouldering for days, Frank helping while here.

8th. Mr. & Mrs. Kingsley come.[42] Miss Heathcote came yesterday. The boys very happy with Mr. Kingsley. . . . Miss Heathcote goes, very kind & amusing she has been. The Kingsleys

[39] David Masson (1822–1907), the first editor of *Macmillan's Magazine*, which began publication in November 1859.

[40] Charles Sumner (1811–74), the senator from Massachusetts, is best remembered for his long and laborious support of slave emancipation. In May 1856 Sumner's opposition to the Fugitive Slave Law and the Kansas-Nebraska Act provoked an assault and brutal beating by Representative Preston S. Brooks, whose attack nearly proved fatal.

[41] "Sea Dreams" was first published in *Macmillan's Magazine* in January 1860.

[42] Mrs. Charles Kingsley, who married in 1844, was the former Fanny Grenfell.

leave us on the 10th. Very much have we liked having them. They have been delighted with Alum Bay & have I hope enjoyed the down up which she went on the donkey. Mr. Parker arrived yesterday & A. read "Maud." A. goes to Alum Bay with him to-day after having picked up sticks with the boys. Next day Mr. Parker goes to Mr. Helps. We go to look at the grave of Hallam's poor canary found dead in its cage on my Father's birthday. Its poor little companion made mournful cries. We see two swallows while in the garden to-day. A. reads *Richard II* magnificently to me. Another day *Henry IV*.

19th. Hallam & I go with A. to the Ferry on his way to see Mr. Cameron off for Ceylon. He brings back Mrs. Cameron & Charlie & Henry & Ellen with him next day.

Sir John Simeon dines with us one evening, he and Mr. Charles Wynne[43] another. A. reads "Guinevere" to them. Mr. Kingsley sends Hallam "The Good-natured Bear." Mr. Estcourt comes to see what can be done about purchasing these houses which may spoil our view of the sea. Mrs. Cameron has an agreement with Ling giving her the option of purchasing Linglands. She and Charlie & Henry go to-day (30th), most kind as usual she has been. A. much interested by Darwin's book[44] which Mr. Palgrave is so good as to send him, not knowing we have already a copy.

December

The Illustrated Princess comes. Beautifully got up but the Illustrations we cannot admire. A. has mounds raised & trees planted to hide Knight's house[45] & we look after them. In the evenings when we are alone he reads me some of the "Arthur & Merlin"[46] lent us by Sir John. On the 14th he brings me down his "Tithonus." Snow two feet thick, but the sun warm, perfect winter day. He takes me out & sweeps a path for me and we have "Tithonus" in the evenings. Our globes arrive. Sir John

[43] Charles Wynne Griffith Wynne, the Simeons' friend.

[44] Charles R. Darwin, *On the Origin of Species by Means of Natural Selection* (London, 1859).

[45] Probably the house of William Knight, the Farringford coachman. Knight first came to work for the Tennysons as a stableboy in 1853, and he remained with the family until his death in the 1920s.

[46] Most likely the Middle English *Arthour and Merlin: A Metrical Romance*.

dines with us & brings the boys White's *Natural History*,[47] recommended by Owen as the best first-book, as a gift. They delighted.

Mr. Ellis sends a sumptuous present of choice wines which everyone admires even Mr. Novello when he comes some days later. A. reads me part of the journal in the Cornhill written by one of the officers of the *Fox*.[48] Mr. Palgrave arrives & he and A. play with the boys after dinner on Christmas day & the Christmas Tree which Elizabeth has kindly prepared as a surprise looks rather magical in the Antiroom when we open the drawing room doors. One evening they have Magic Lantern. Charles Weld, Mr. Woolner, Mr. Jowett arrive. Sir John & Mr. Charles Wynne come to luncheon & bring an engraving from the English Cenci supposed to be the original Guido,[49] Mr. Wynne's gift to A.

[47] Gilbert White, *The Natural History and Antiquities of Selborne* (London, 1789).

[48] See "The Search for Sir John Franklin, from the Private Journal of an Officer of the *Fox*," *Cornhill Magazine*, 1 (January 1860), 96–121.

[49] *Beatrice* by the Italian painter Guido Reni (1575–1642), a portrait of the ill-fated Beatrice Cenci; now located in the Galleria Nazionale d'Arte Antica.

1860

January

2nd. Mr. & Mrs. Bradley dine with us. A cheerful evening. Next day Mr. Palgrave goes & one feels that a friend has gone. Mr. Woolner delights the boys with his stories for which he has wonderful faculty of invention.

One evening reads "Revelation" thro' to us. Very glad we are that A. has been able to persuade Mr. Jowett to stay longer on condition that he may breakfast early alone so as to get to work in good time. They walk together. In the evening Maken, the young soldier who had stopt them to ask where A. lived, came by appointment. Very intelligent he seemed. A. gave him a copy of *The Poems* & *The Princess* & wrote their names in them. Mr. Jowett translates some of *The Apology*. Very delightful to us both & for two more evenings we have it. The evening after A. reads some old Ballads to us after we have all been to Jane's room to listen to some mysterious sounds in the wall. Next evening A. reads the Balcony scene in *Romeo & Juliet*. The boys dine at our luncheon time. Mr. Jowett tells them the story of Ulysses. They listen entranced. Mr. & Mrs. A. Court Holmes call just as Mr. Jowett is going. Sorry indeed we are to say good bye to him. A. reads me some Keats.

Next day he walks with Mr. Bradley & says that he has never been out on a more delightful day on the down. The sunset gorgeous & the stars at night splendid. The Bonvenes go. A pity that one cannot keep pleasant neighbours. A. reads me some MacKintosh.[1]

February

1st. Mrs. Cameron arrives with two legs of Welsh mutton from Eastnor. We say that it is against our rule to receive gifts from her, dear, generous creature that she is, but she persists. Sir John Simeon & Sir James & Lady Carmichael call[2] A. reads me some of Victor Hugo's "[Les] Petites Epopées" lent us by Sir John.

[1]Undoubtedly a work by Sir James Mackintosh (1765–1832).

[2]Sir James Robert Carmichael, 2d baronet (1817–83), was chairman of the Submarine and the Mediterranean extension telegraph companies.

The Bradleys call to take leave. Sorry are we. Another delightful evening reading. A. reads "Amos" to me.

The poor little Squirrel given to the boys by Afton escapes while Henry is cleaning the cage. He throws a stick up at it to bring it down from a tree which kills [it] and makes us all sad. It had such pretty ways. We were all fond of it.

13th. Heard[3] arrives & we engage him. Glad to have a first-rate gardener. A. & I look to pulling down part of the sheep pen & cutting down trees. We make a door from our bedroom to the bathroom. A. goes on with the "Epopées" to me these evenings. I read *Pilgrim's Progress* to the boys which delights them.

March

1st. Mrs. Cameron brings a vivid blue paper with a border from the Elgin Marbles. The vivid blue neither she nor we like. We as usual protest against her prodigal kindness.

6th. The foundations of the Lodge in the Orchard begun to be dug. Boswell's *Johnson*, Froissart, Clarke's *Homer*, Smith's *Dictionary* arrive from Mr. Jowett.[4] The Froissart he most kindly gives. The loan of the rest right welcome. "Epopées," "Adam Adair" and other small poems.

14th We choose the [*illegible*] for the Lodge & after the next day I do not leave my room for more than a month.

16th. On our Lionel's birthday the boys bring me the flags we have given them by us & all their other gifts. The Camerons spent the day with him, and tho' Lionel has longed for the day for months he said that it had not disappointed him.

Unknown to me A. sends for the Newport doctor. In time we are told that we have whooping cough. The boys take it about a fortnight after me & Elizabeth[5] about a fortnight after them. We are shut up in three separate rooms. Fortunately the boys' opens into mine. Their nurse & I have had the cough before & I have never been beyond our own grounds. It is supposed to have come from the beautiful paper with which I papered our room knowing that he would like it. On trial it was

[3]For many years the gardener and then farm manager at Farringford.

[4]Froissart was probably *Chroniques de Jean Froissart* (Paris, 1826); Sir William Smith, *Dictionary of Greek and Roman Biography and Mythology*, 3 vols. (London, 1844–49).

[5]Elizabeth Cole, one of the Farringford servants.

found to contain a great quantity of Arsenic. A. puts off all the guests he can from staying in the house but I am glad that Mr. W. Clark from Cambridge, Mr. Woolner, Mr. Crowe, and Mr. Venables do venture to come and that the Duke and Duchess of Argyll who stay at the Hotel spend three evenings with him. Lord Lorne one & Mrs. Cameron & Mrs. Bailey many.

A. often brings me flowers and one day digs up a large root of primroses and plants them in the big Terra Cotta vase which was tumbled on my arm from its stand before my marriage & has made [it] I fear less useful for life. Now I have the happy primrose memory instead of the unhappy accident one. Mrs. Cameron & Mrs. Bailey are so kind as to bring the boys all sorts of things to amuse them & all our friends around are most kind & two of those who have to work in the day sit up with the boys at night.

April

16th. A. brings me down into the drawing room & then Hallam unexpectedly to me & . . . our Lionel comes, so here we all are once more, thank God. How beautiful everything looks. There is enchantment about all. I dine with A. & have tea & the boys come down after dinner. Tomorrow A. has to to go to his dentist.

25th. He returns & brings Hine with him about furniture for Brights' House (The Terrace).[6]

27th. He reads me "Boädicea." He digs a good deal in the garden & we look after what Heard is doing in the Terrace grounds & the making of the Terrace & about the furnishing & fitting of it. Mrs. Cameron coming from Town rushes in with a catalogue which she thinks will be helpful even before she has seen her children.

30th. Mr. Scoones our Twickenham clergyman comes.

May

2nd. Mr. Fellowes calls & afterwards Lord Dufferin who interests us extremely by telling us of Cyril Graham's discoveries of the

[6] A house adjacent to the Farringford estate where the Tennysons at times entertained long-term guests and which they bought in 1864. The Horatio Tennysons occupied the Terrace during the late 1860s.

87? White marble cities in the black basaltic land with their inscriptions in an unknown tongue.[7]

A. reads to me very interesting things from the *Quarterly*. The poor boys wild with delight at getting out again. Mrs. Cameron takes A. into her house where he finds the officers of the Fort drawn up to be introduced.[8] He offers the Major our stables & begs that he will put a married sergeant whom he does not well know what to do with in the rooms over.

Mr. Chapman & Mr. Garden come to stay & Mrs. Cameron in the evening. A pleasant heart-warming evening. They go next day.

13th. Mrs. Cameron wants to give us one of her lucky purchases of pictures, but we will not take it. These days he takes me out & mows. Next day Mr. Dempster arrives & sings. He goes next day. The draft of the Terrace road which Mr. Chapman has kindly drawn comes to-day & his gift of Thackeray's Christmas stories. A. reads some Froissart to me.

19th. A very pleasant surprise this morning. A most kind letter to A. from the Prince Consort with a request that he will write his name in HRM's copy of the *Idylls*.

20th. Henry Taylor comes. A. goes to see him at the Camerons. He comes up to Farringford with Mrs. Cameron. . . . A. takes me into Maiden's Croft & they go with us. The delight of our beautiful home is as great to-day as on the day he first brought me to it.

[7]Frederick Temple Hamilton-Temple Blackwood, marquis of Dufferin and Ava (1826–1902), was the famous diplomat who distinguished himself in a number of important posts, including those of governor general of Canada, 1872–78, and viceroy of India, a position to which he was appointed in 1884. Dufferin and Tennyson were friends and occasional correspondents, and it was at Dufferin's invitation that Lionel Tennyson went to India in 1885. In 1858, before they had ever met, Dufferin wrote to Tennyson that it was through the laureate's verse that he had first learned to appreciate poetry. As a youth, wrote Dufferin, he had positively disliked poetry, but then "I fell in with a volume of yours, and suddenly felt such an sensation of delight, as I never experienced before. A new world seemed open to me, and from that day [*illegible*]a constant study of your works. . . . Naturally enough I could not help feeling very grateful to the Orpheus whose music had made the gates of poet-land fly open" (February 20, 1858, T.R.C.).

Sir Cyril Clerke Graham (1834–95), 5th baronet, was attached to Lord Dufferin's mission to Syria in 1860–61; later he was secretary of state for colonies, 1866–67, and lieutenant governor of Grenada, 1875–77. I am unable to identify the discoveries Emily Tennyson mentions.

[8]The Golden Hill Fort was located approximately a mile northeast of Farringford.

25th. The photographs of Mr. Woolner's Llandaff statues[9] come & the casts of Michael Angelo's last work & the Phidian Victory fastening her Sandal. I rejoice to think that the children will become early familiar with these wonderful works. Mr. Woolner's must, I should think, be a great statue and also his St. Paul tho' he is not quite my St. Paul.

28th. Dr. Thompson[10] comes. Very glad to see A.'s old friend & delighted to have the James G. Marshalls next day. We gather a new white flower in the wilderness which neither we nor our guests know & the boys very excited at the idea of seeing God-mama & spend the day in gathering flowers & arranging them. Cast of the Venus of Milo comes. Charles Weld arrives.

June

2nd. We made arrangements with Keeping to go geologizing with the gentlemen to Brook next day. Mrs. Marshall & I meet them on Afton Down. They go on the 3rd. I fear that their visit has not been so enjoyable as we would fain have made. There are none to whom we would more willingly give pleasure. The white & red thorn & Laburnums in full beauty. A. flies Hallam's kite with him from the top of the house. A. reads some "Elaine" to me & next day flies kites with the boys on the Down.

7th. Dr. Wolff comes. A wonderful inspiration in some of his stories. He looks mild & kind and is very courteous to us & very thoughtful for us.

10th He preaches in the church in the morning & reads prayers to us in the afternoon & expounds a part of the 51st Psalm. Very interesting. The boys most attentive. He addresses himself a good deal to them. Some of the servants also present.

13th. Hallam says you must go out with us to Maiden's Croft and see our kites fly for you are a bride & Papa a bridegroom. Mr. & Mrs. Isaacson, Mr. Filton, & Mrs. Cameron dine with us and all except myself go to hear Dr. Wolff's lecture in the schoolroom which Mr. Isaacson has kindly lent us. A. walks with Mrs. Cameron & so is later than the rest of the party who

[9] Woolner's figures (1858) carved on the pulpit of Llandaff Cathedral.

[10] Dr. William Hepworth Thompson (1810–86), the former Apostle who became master of Trinity College, Cambridge, in 1866, after the death of Dr. William Whewell.

drive. Mr. Isaacson tells the assembly that he only waits for A. & they cheer. Six pounds are collected for Dr. Wolff's church & the boys, when they hear of the church building, rush off to their purses & give all they have except Grandpapa's sovereign. Poor Lionel has lost his & Hallam gives his money every week till it is restored to him.

14th. Frank & Mr. Lear come. Mrs. Cameron, Mr. Arthur Prinsep, Miss Kate Perry in the evening. I hear a tramping on the drive when I am resting after dinner and think it is Americans coming as seven did the other day to ask for admittance but find that it is Mrs. Cameron's Grand piano which she has most kindly sent for Mr. Lear. It is pleasant to see the surprise of each one coming in & seeing it. The Camerons in the evening. Mr. Lear sings a long time.

Next day I get up early to see him & Frank off for they must go to-day.

We are busy looking to the furnishing of the Terrace which we have bought to save the view of the sea as much as possible & to the building of the Lodge in the orchard. Arthur Tennyson with his bride, Arthur Wright & his Mary Ker & Aunt Mary Anne all visit us & at the Camerons, Lady Somers & Henry Taylor, but they are afraid of our whooping cough so we see them in the garden.[11] We have pleasant friends among the soldiers, Major Edwards & others & we see Mr. Ward sometimes & Captain & Mrs. Bonvene.

On the 18th an eclipse of the sun. The light very fine. The sky blackish like a clear moonlight sky. The clouds wonderfully beautiful, dark towards the horizon, white higher except that now & then about the sun they are amber. The gulls fly slowly & heavily & there is a sleepy light over down & sea & cape.

28th. Ally reads me the greater part of a most interesting article in the *Quarterly* on The Book & its Mission.[12] The Bradleys are here. After Edith & the boys' tea they play at the Emperor of Morocco & A. generally succeeds in making them laugh. They insist that Mr. Bradley & myself should play too. . . .

[11] Arthur Tennyson's bride was the former Harriet West, sister of Catherine West, who in 1870 became the second wife of Horatio Tennyson. Arthur and Harriet were married on May 22, 1860.

Mary Ker was the poet's sister who on July 7, 1851, married Alan Ker (1810–84), the prominent barrister.

Aunt Mary Anne was the sister of Tennyson's mother.

[12] "The Missing Link and the London Poor," *Quarterly Review*, 108 (July 1860), 1–18.

29th. We write about the Franklin Epitaph. Aunt Franklin is about to sail for America.

August

5th. A. & the boys take me in my little carriage by the Wilderness, Abraham's Mead & Hill Close, up the Down by the green road & home by the steps A. made for me. They go over the stile & gather wild flowers with which I make a glorious bowl on our return. A delightful day—once more our wild gallop on the down but not alone this time for the boys are with us.

A. reads me some of Smiles' *Self-Help*[13] & we resolve to get it for the boys.

6th. We put the beautiful Briary wreath which A. gathered for me yesterday on his chair & flowers around him with our little gifts—the boys' all—their sovereigns each in a purse. A peaceful day. A. in good spirits. Mrs. Cameron sends a copy of the beautiful Florentine Dante. Mr. White kindly comes from Bonchurch . . . on some business matter.

9th We go to Burlington House, the Welds having lent us their rooms. The quiet very pleasant to me but it is somewhat oppressed by the dismantled state of the rooms. He & Mr. Woolner take the boys to Westminster Abbey. Mr. Woolner & Mr. Palgrave dine with us these days.

11th. We keep Hallam's birthday as best we can. A. & Mr. Woolner take them to St. Paul's & after their dinner we go with them to the Alhambra. Only one of the brothers Berri there. His flying attitude magnificent. A beautiful horse. His high knightly face very grand. Mr. Woolner says that this in former days was taught by riding the horse over furze-bushes.
A. takes Hallam to the Panorama of Venice.

12th. I take the boys to Westminster Abbey for the service. Ally dines at Little Holland House.

13th. Little Holland House. Horatio, the Boynes, the Monckton Milnes, Proctors, Forsters & Pollocks. I knocked up on our return & to my regret have to go to bed & leave A. to entertain Mr. Spedding, the Brookfields, Mr. Lear, & Mrs. & Miss Bailey alone.

[13]Samuel Smiles, *Self-Help* (London, 1859).

15th. We . . . see Mr. Clough, Mr. Palgrave, & Mr. Holman Hunt. A. goes to the Foreign Office for his passport & then to Thresher & Glenny's[14] for travelling suits & a white hat in memory of the white hat he so often wore at Somersby.

Then A. takes the boys to Hampstead to see Mother & the sisters & brothers. Afterwards A. dines at Argyll Lodge. I decline all dining out. He meets the Duchess of Sutherland there & in the evening Mr. Holman Hunt. He reads "The Ode on the Duke of Wellington." Next day takes Charlie's sonnets to Stafford House but only stays a minute with the Duchess & Lady Constance Grosvenor[15] as the Duchess is going off to Paris immediately.

A. goes to the Gladstones & then to the House. We call at the Monteagles.[16] He at his office, but Lady Monteagle sends for him & very pleasant it is to have [her] affectionate greeting. Mr. Woolner tells the story of the old man who charmed with the reclining statue by Baily,[17] now in Lord Monteagle's drawing-room, then in the Exhibition, kept approaching it & saying, "I must, I must, indeed I must," and at last falling on his knees he snatched a kiss & rushed away. The statue was made from Baily's daughter, who tired by a walk had put a sofa cushion on the floor & thrown herself down upon it.

The Duchess of Argyll comes to afternoon tea & after it takes us to see the sick child & the Sisters of Charity by H. Browne.[18] A very truthful picture but one I would not have for my room. We go to the National Gallery to see the new Titian & Veronese & the Portrait of Ariosto.[19] The Mother & Child of

[14] A popular haberdashery located at 152 Strand.

[15] The Duchess of Sutherland, the queen's mistress of the robes until April 1861, and Lady Constance Gertrude Sutherland-Leveson-Gower Grosvenor, daughter of George Granville, 2d duke of Sutherland, and wife of Hugh Lupus Grosvenor, 1st duke of Westminster (1825–99).

[16] Thomas Spring-Rice and his wife, Marianne.

[17] Edward Hodges Baily (1788–1867), the sculptor. Among Baily's most notable sculptures are his *Apollo* (1815), *Eve at the Fountain* (1818), and *The Graces Seated* (1849).

[18] Hallot Knight Browne (1815–82), "Phiz," the watercolorist and book illustrator. Browne illustrated *Pickwick Papers*, taking the pseudonym "Phiz" to match Dickens's "Boz."

[19] Titian's *Madonna and Child with Saints John and Catherine* and Veronese's *Darius and His Family before Alexander*. The Ariosto is Vecchio Palma's untitled portrait of a poet, probably Ariosto, which the National Gallery purchased in 1860.

the Titian very lovely. Ariosto very fine, beautiful colouring.

17th. Fine morning. Mr. Woolner most kindly meets us at the station in spite of the early hour. I will not let A. go knowing that it would knock him up. We having been misinformed as to trains, the boys & myself end our railway journey by coat train much to their delight. They are much excited about getting to Grasby when Lionel remembers the road. I find my Father bowed & his sight less good. The boys have Backgammon with him in the evenings. So good & gentle & loving he is to them! Mr. Gifford Palgrave arrives from Syria so that his brother cannot go with A. to Cornwall as arranged. Mr. Woolner takes pity on him & goes to Oxford with him. Mr. Palgrave is to join him in a week. A. as usual very good in writing.

From one of the Scilly Isles he tells of hedges of scarlet Geranium, a delight to the eye & of Indian Aloes thirty feet high in flower which stand out all the winter & yet neither peach nor mulberry will ripen there.

September

16th. A sad parting. We go to Wrangle. The boys delighted with their visit. We go home on the 22nd after having rested at Burlington House. The boys very pleased to get home in spite of all their late pleasures & indulgences. We see all our pleasant neighbours.

26th. A. arrives unexpectedly as I am dressing for dinner. He looks well & is very cheerful.

October

3rd. Poor Sir John Simeon's first visit after his wife's death. A sad day. He gives me her little garden chair. Edmund Lushington, Nanny & Agnes staying with us & Enid & Constance Guest often with us.[20] Edmund & A. have good walks. We resume our old ways much to the boys' delight. I read about Galileo to them. A. reads me bits from the Laws of Howel Dda.[21]

[20] Enid and Constance Guest were daughters of Lady Charlotte Schreiber, formerly Lady Charlotte Guest.

[21] The Welsh Dimetian Code, which is comprised of ancient laws supposed to have been enacted by Howel the Good, modified by subsequent regulations under the native princes before the conquest of Edward I.

Mr. Cameron signs the agreement for Long's house the lease of which he buys.

Ally & the boys take me out in my little carriage & after dinner & tea he and I have long talks. Sir John & Louy Simeon come to dinner. Pleasant to see him more himself & to have the old companionship with Louy. Madame Ernestina begs to read Ally's poems to him that she may have his opinion of her reading. She reads to him & he to her. I note she invents wonderful stories of her visit of three hours.

October. This month we are very busy heating the bath & the green house, settling about alterations in the Farm cottage, making the road of the hollow way, there being a right of foot path past our garden & park. We are thankful to have been allowed to put the road further off, we making it rather shorter than before. We see a good deal of Lady Charlotte & Mr. Schreiber & of Enid & Constance. Lady Charlotte tells me that of Cobden which makes me feel that I have misjudged him.[22] The clergyman living near him says that he is a very good religious man, very sad from the loss of his sister.

November

1st. We hear of the wreck of a French sloop under our down. Ally takes me up the down, all the rest helping. Mr. Patmore who, poor man, is worn out by six months of night watching over his wife is with us.

Frederic & Guilio come.[23] Captain Hamond tells us that Government is going to adopt his plan for the fortification of the Needles' end of the Island. He gives us an air plant brought by himself from America.

6th. A. reads "Guinevere" to the Schreibers & Enid & Constance.

7th. Mr. Patmore goes, the better we hope for his visit. Mrs. Fox gives the boys Rifle caps & haversacks. We have them drilled by a soldier from the Fort. Happy days. A. wraps me in his waterproof & three doubles of fur besides & draws me about in my little carriage day by day, the boys helping.

[22]Richard Cobden (1804–65), M.P., Stockport, 1841–47, West Riding of Yorkshire, 1847–57, is best remembered as a foremost leader of the Anti-Cornlaw League, 1838–46.

[23]Guilio was Julius Tennyson, later a captain in the army, the elder son of Frederick Tennyson.

22nd. The first trees felled for the road. We go to look at them. We pick the places for the bridge & the back gate. We look at the men sawing in a pit made of four grates, also at the wood fire in which the piles for the bridge are charred.

December

5th. I go thro' the new Back entrance, A. taking me in my little carriage with Heard's help. A. & I both think the road very picturesque. I go on the bridge which is almost finished, I believe, except the railings.

A poor ilex cut down. Necessary as its removal is if we would have sun one cannot but regret it.

19th. Mr. Palgrave comes. The road is opened. Mr. White & Mr. Joliffe here. Mr. Schreiber, Lady Charlotte, Miss Collyer, Mrs. Fox, Mr. Cotton & his sister in the evening. We play at "Coach"[24] & "Earth, air & water." Mr. Schreiber tells us of the quiet pony he has bought for us. This is their last evening. We could scarcely have had pleasanter neighbours. The boys write their thanks to Mr. Schreiber. We plan about the Coach house & cottages.

22nd. A. reads the poems to us chosen by Mr. Palgrave for his "Golden Treasury." I go out with A. to see which trees are to be cut down. A delightful gush of sunshine, when the tree whose shadow trembles on the wall, falls. "Golden Treasury" these evenings.

29th. Mr. Palgrave goes. Charles Weld still with us.

[24] Another parlor game.

1861

January

1st. The day saddened by news of the death of the poor coast-guard who trying to save something from a wreck was killed by a stone falling on his head while mounting one of the cliffs. But for this the day is happy & peaceful with A. & the children. The boys are enchanted with their pony. They take it out walking with them & feed it. In the evening "The Magic Lantern" delights them.

3rd. The servants have a little dance. Their guests have not left before five & they say that they have been very happy, a pleasant thought for us. Weather cold & bright. The Bradleys here.

10th. Miss Watson, the old Somersby Governess, comes.

15th. Mr. Jowett comes having had to sleep at Lymington. When Miss Watson crossed the boat had to be cut out of the ice.

18th. Mr. Benson, the future Archbishop & his wife, come in the evening; Mr. & Mrs. Dobell & their friend Miss Jolly.[1] The Bradleys & Miss Collyers dine with us. All our kind neighbours call. Mrs. Grosvenor Hood makes her little dog perform for the boys.

24th. Sir John Simeon, Louy & Dr. Logan[2] meet the Bensons & Bradleys at dinner. . . . A very pleasant evening.

29th. The Bradleys & Mr. Philpott, Mrs. Bradley's Father, dine with us.

31st. They go. A. & the boys help to make a window in the wall & A. takes me to see all that has been done & I like it much. We

[1]The Bensons are Edward White Benson (1829–96) and his wife, the former Mary Sedgwick, sister of Henry Sedgwick, the philosopher. Benson was first master of Wellington College from 1859 until 1872, when he became chancellor of Lincoln Minster. In 1877 he was made first bishop of Truro, and in 1882 he became archbishop of Canterbury.

The Dobells are Sydney Thompson Dobell and his wife, a daughter of George Fordham of Odsey House, Cambridge.

Miss Jolly = unidentified.

[2]Sir Thomas Galbraith Logan (1808–96; knighted 1869), honorary physician to the queen from 1859 until his death.

fix the line of the sunk fence. He reads to me "The Ode on the Duke" & "The Brook."

February

2nd. Louy Simeon has been staying with us but leaves to-day. A. & the boys go with me to look at the work. I delighted with all that has been done.

4th, 5th, 6th. We still looking after the work & finding it very satisfactory.

7th. I go out with A. before he leaves for Town about his teeth. We decide to have the Stables & Brew House pulled down, good tho' they are, but too near the house. . . . The house desolate as usual without him.

11th. The boys & I look after the works—the poor Brew House nearly down.

12th. Hallam & I watch the undermining of the Coach House wall with levers.

13th. A. returns so now we have him with us to watch the work.

17th. He tells me about his "Northern Farmer."

18th. He brings me down a blue-red book (welcome sight!) with part of it written down after he & the boys have worked at the bank of the hollow way, I putting a few spades full of sand on it.

19th. The boys watch our game of Backgammon & ask me to teach them. I read some of "Sir Gareth"[3] to the boys. Mr. Dakyns comes. Lionel wild with excitement. Delightful to find Mr. Dakyns so kind & pleasant & so intelligent looking. (Lionel makes what he calls a welcome to the Tutor which he means to sing, flag in hand, but his courage fails & he only puts snowdrops into Mr. Dakyns's room. He most kind in working with us at digging sand. He takes the hardest part.)

The boys walk with him & romp with him & on the 25th begin Lessons. I cannot but miss the life we have hitherto had however good I hope the change is in some way.

27th. Mr. Dakyns helps Ally & the boys with my little carriage & they rush along the road with me, a wild part, to call on the

[3]See the *Morte d'Arthur.*

Cloughs & the Collyers. We generally have a little bit of Homer from A. in the evening and occasionally some of the Bible. Very delightful.

March

1st. The crocuses planted at last so we may hope for our golden ring. A. & I go round with Heard to see what shrubs can be moved to the bank. We have lost so many this winter that it is somewhat difficult to cover it even with help of a good many new ones. We watch the work unloading of the wagon which has brought them. Mr. Dakyns most unselfish & thoughtful for others. He helps us to plant the great Portugal laurel in the bank, the first tree there. Very pleasant to see the bank being clothed day by day more & more.

10th. A grand hailstorm. The boys watch it coming down with black fingers over the sea. A bright light behind. Something like that storm which A. & I saw over York plain as we stood on Richmond hill.

The Dean of Chichester[4] arrives. The Cloughs come to us in the day time, he not being well enough to go out in the evening but he romps with the boys in honour of our Lionel's birthday & before ours they & their children leave. Good indeed to have had such people as they & the Dean.

15th. The first flower on the bank to-day—a rose-coloured Rhododendron. Turfing begins on the lawn.

19th. Mr. Lear comes. He dines with us but too sad at the loss of the sister who has brought him up from his birth to stay with us altogether, so takes rooms at Murrow's, but he finds the society of the place too much for him & walks to Cowes on the 24th.[5]

25th. Mr. Jowett comes. I ill in my room.

28th. A. takes me down for an hour after tea.

April

1st. Franklin Lushington comes. Always welcome. Mr. Clark arrives unexpectedly. Both pleased with the changes. The Feres

[4]The Rev. Walter Farquhar Hook.

[5]Lear's sister Ann died on March 11, 1861.

& the Coltmans here & the Cloughs. The gentlemen dine with us, the ladies come in the evening.

8th. A. puts me in a warm seat under the hedge that was, the mound belt that is & we watch the planting. Mr. Dakyns goes with him to Rogers's nursery gardens at Lymington for more plants. Heard with them. Day by day we watch the planting A. & I.

15th. Matilde[6] arrives. A. reads "Locksley Hall."

18th. Some Hamlet and gets Matilde to read some Goethe & he reads some to her & she praises his reading very much & she is a lady of Saxony.

19th. He reads some of Shakespeare's sonnets. Our neighbours are so friendly as to take interest in the changes we have made & come to see them. Mr. Cotton says it is Fairyland. He has been so good as to send us things from Afton. Happy readings at night & pleasant talks.

No reading, we talk of Darwin.

23rd. Horatio & Charlie & their little Cecilia & Maud cross in a thunderstorm. A. & I superintend the planting of Butcher's broom & lilies. He & Mr. Dakyns go to hear a nightingale. . . . Sergeant Keowen has been drilling the boys for some time past & they beg us to go & see their review. To our astonishment we find the Miss Collyers' carriage drawn up in Maiden's Croft & the Miss Collyers, the Miss Feres & Mrs. Cameron all gaily dressed. Charlie & Horatio also join us. In the afternoon A. takes me into the Conservatory & bids me ask Charles & Nanny & Agnes to come here until their new home Aubrey is ready.[7] A moment not to be forgotten since I know that he longs to be alone. He & I out most days still looking after alterations in the garden. He finds the Butcher's cart overturned & the horse down, the horse having overreached itself in trying to get at grass on the bank. Mr. Isaacson helps to get them up.

May

9th. Kind letters about our going to Cambridge for his D.C.L. A. has had palpitation of the heart which prevents him from

[6]Mdlle Von Zeschau.

[7]Aubrey was the Charles Welds' home near Lymington, which they shared with Henry Sellwood from 1864 until his death in 1867. The Welds continued to live at Aubrey House until Charles Weld's death in January 1869.

accepting it at once. We have been making the experiment of "meaty tea" lately. Mr. Jowett kindly comes to it from time to time. He & Horatio teach the boys chess.

13th. Horatio & his go.

15th. It is decided that we do go to Cambridge & that we start to-morrow for Oatlands Park Hotel. Mr. Dakyns having kindly preceded us to find whether there are rooms. The situation of the Hotel delightful. A.'s heart is so bad when we are there that we telegraph to give up Cambridge. He takes me into the garden to see the beautiful banks of the river. In the evening he tells me that he is convinced smoking is the cause of the palpitation & that he resolved to leave it off. He takes his pipe up to the Belvedere, smokes it & breaks it & scatters the tobacco to the winds.[8] We drive to St. George's Hill. A. & the boys walk over it & I wait for them. They return with handfuls of beautiful white narcissus with crimson-ringed caps. The boys take me to a great oak which A. has admired. A. walks to Hampton Court.

22nd. He takes the boys & myself to Winchester on our way home. The boat aground at Lymington but after some delay we get off. A letter from A. telling of his walk to the million butter-cupped churchyard where the faithful servants lie.

27th. He returns & tells me of the glowing feelings of health he has had in the mornings since he left off smoking & of his having been so hungry. We are out nearly all day looking after flower-beds. He takes my chair from place to place. I persuade him to go to Lyndhurst for walks in the forest,[9] palpitation having somewhat returned.

The Welds & Edmund come.

June

4th. Edmund joins A. in the New Forest.

6th. They return.

8th. Edmund goes. We see two stange birds dark with light feathery tufts & a proud walk (probably Hoopoes).

[8] Tennyson's resolution was short-lived as it had been at least once previously when he had attempted to give up smoking.

[9] The New Forest. The best headquarters for visitors, Lyndhurst is commonly known as the "capital of the New Forest."

Mr. Dakyns meets his friend Mr. Sedgewick who comes to tea.

12th. A swarm of bees in & about A.'s study window which we all go to watch.

13th. A. has hay fever or our wedding day would have been a happy one. Glorious sunshine. All this while whooping-cough has never left us. The doctor who sees Hallam says the cough is only from weakness & that the best possible thing will be to take him to the Pyrenees.

27th. We started out with our two young children on our over-venturesome journey to the Pyrenees by Auvergne. Anne Weld & Agnes going as far as Royat with us. Some things one could not but rejoice to have seen but the difficulty of getting rooms, carriage, or even donkeys in those days & the impossibility of finding proper food for children took away most of the pleasure. The Cathedral at Bourges[10] was perhaps the first thing that struck one. Its great pillars so beautiful in their simplicity almost took away one's breath with awe on first seeing them. The roof was flushed by the colours of the fine old windows.

At Clermont in the marketplace we saw the Comet & but for bad drains we could have been well content there, where we were hospitably received. Looking afterwards over its grass plain could not but be striking in itself & historically interesting. The Sexton took great care of me in the Cathedral[11] with which we were all charmed & he was very anxious that the boys should see Mars & Pan beating poor Time when the clock struck twelve. We have to divide into three parties at Royat. Poor little Lionel suffers most. Fortunately his good & clever nurse makes bread & beef tea for him one day. A. takes me to what he calls his Homeric Cave where beautiful springs gush from the cave [and] women wash their clothes.

Mr. Dakyns, one of the most unselfish of mortals, tries to get rooms for us at Mont Dore. Our drive there was the first we really enjoyed on this journey. The weather delightful, the air so delicate, warm lights & shadows on mountains & plains. Sometimes the mountains looked as one fancies the mountains of Judea must have looked with innumerable white stone cities on their terraced sides.

Only a bed for A. at Mont Dore. We must go on to La Bourboule. At Mont Dore a great crowd assembled at the Hotel

[10] The fourteenth-century St. Stephen's Cathedral.

[11] La Cathédrale Notre-Dame, the chancel of which dates from 1292.

door. The English excite curiosity in a place where there is only one English maid. I ask for tea; it is promised but none comes. At last I waylay a waiter & beg a little soup for a sick child & he brings a small plate of Potage. A. tells me afterwards that the people here hate the English. The boys in the streets sing songs against him. We all go out into the Place which is charming. We sit in the delightful shade of trees & see the graceful waterfall come down over the mountain wall. Another day when we go to Mont Dore A. brings in Mr. Clough, a most welcome guest whom we now are so happy as to see often on our way.[12] He makes excursions up the mountains with A. & Mr. Dakyns, he on his pony, they walking. A. brings me back beautiful wild flowers. He says that the Forget-me-nots are the bluest he ever saw. Our first view of the Pyrenees glorious with a sort of spiritual clearness & distinctness. We have very kind travelling companions, a Comte & Comtesse who are much excited pointing out the mountains. They give us the address of proprietors at Luchon where the Comte himself has been.

August

1st. At Bagnères-de-Bigorre we get pleasant rooms & stay a little. A. & Mr. Dakyns have walks & A. says that he finds the air among the heath & the hazel very [*illegible*]. Here the people say a kind "good night" as we pass their doors. Our peep at the mountains near Eaux-Bonnes very fine. An aerial wall with watchtowers. A pleasant fruitful country almost all the way. Sometimes plain, sometimes high wooded hills with mountains & the Pic du Midi looking very lordly. Vain to hope that words of mind can recall the glories of the mountains, the delicious smell of the fir trees clothing them, their lawns, their foaming rivers & streams, nor the light stiller than other light of their glaciers, nor the sunset splendour of the mountains, nor the smile after death when this had left, and memory sufficiently records the anxieties of the days. But very pleasant it is to see Ally absorbed as he is by the beauty of the scene where the green Gave de Pau dashes by, breaking continually into little joyous looking fountains seeming fuller of life than any river I ever saw. Beautiful groups of mountains between the great stormy hills in the foreground, old castles [*illegible*] & these on small hills [*illegible*] silky black goats. The fifth time

[12] Arthur Hugh Clough traveled with the Tennyson party periodically during the next month and a half. Clough died in Florence on November 13, 1861.

A. had been this road. He seems as if possessed by the spirit of delight.

Mr. Clough & Mr. Dakyns are always doing kind helpful work for us looking after houses & carriages.

September

1st. I go with Mr. Clough & A. to see the Templar Church at Barèges all fortified forcibly bringing back the days that are gone. From Barèges we drive one day to Gèdre & I am glad to have seen the Brèche de Roland & the towers of Marboré[13] tho' at a distance. The gentlemen go to Gavarnie. While they are there I send Elizabeth up the Pic de Bergons with Mr. Clough's guide. She hears the Shepherds calling home their sheep & sees one little shepherd boy almost thrown down by the sheep which throng round him & kiss his hands & his face. A. says that his impression of Gavarnie is not so fine this time as the last. Quite different but still fine.

5th. The gentlemen go up the Pic du Midi, Mr. Clough riding, A. & Mr. Dakyns walking. Mr. Clough notices as I have done how absorbed A. seems by the beauty of the mountains. While they are away I send Hallam up part of the Pic de Bergons & a kind old man warns him to take care that he does not fall but the boys seem born mountaineers. We go to Cauteretz, Mr. Clough in the carriage with the boys & myself. A. walks with Mr. Dakyns wishing to go on the old road by which he went with Arthur Hallam. A beautiful view over the valley of Argelez. The gorge beautiful too, not so stern & overpowering as that of Gèdre. Cauteretz pleases us all as far as scenery goes more than any of the other places we have stayed in. Before our windows we have the stream rushing in its rocky bed from far away among the mountains & falling in a cataract with dark pines for a setting. Patches of snow lie on the peaks above and nearer are great wooded heights glorious with autumnal colours, bare rocks here & there among them & fields below. A. seems quite glad to be here again. He goes to his Fir island & finds more firs than when he was there years ago. Mr. Clough goes with him.

The poor bonne loves so to talk that she always lingers about one. She says that in the summer they have generally only two hours sleep from two till four, sometimes till five. Ten francs a month & what strangers give them. In the winter they work in

[13] The Pic du Marboré.

the fields and knit. This evening A. & Mr. Dakyns tell me that they have seen Eagles & Vulture Eagles. A. says that when they were on the Pic du Midi three eagles sailed about in the Valley beneath them and never but once moved their wings and this when one of them wheeled round suddenly & then it moved one wing a little. Near Bigorre Vulture Eagles swept up the mountain when A. & Mr. Dakyns were together there. Mr. Dakyns said he was quite frightened for it seemed as if the monstrous bare-necked birds were going to attack them.

The three gentlemen walk to the Lac de Gaube & A. tells me on his return how blue the lake was & how the shadow of the mountains made it purple. The Vignemale rises finely there he says.

8th. A. writes down the two stanzas of "All along the Valley" & reads them to me. We had noticed the deepening of the Voice in the night.[14]

9th. Mr. Clough tells us that he will very likely have to be in Paris on the 18th or 19th as there is a probable escort for his wife thither. We shall indeed be sorry if he cannot return with us. A. buys a photograph of the "Cirque"[15] & Mr. Clough says that it must be his gift to us.

After three thunder storms when the thunder seems to shake the ground, a rock falls which sounds like thunder in the earth. Mr. Dakyns goes to Sarbe to study French. Very sorry to lose him. We lunch . . . hear the horn sounding to summon the pigs for their afternoon daily walk & then bathe in the river. In the morning from five till nine, in the afternoon from three to six.

We hear also the man sounding his drum & the little boy after him crying the news. We meet troops of men & women chiefly young women & girls some singing probably on their way from the shrine at Bétharram. At Bétharram we see pale wretched looking faces peeping between the iron bars of the Priests' seminary. At Pau Mr. Clough leaves us. A sad parting. There could not have been a kinder or unselfish or more thoughtful companion than he. After he is gone we buy a Corneille & go with the boys to the castle.[16] One feels almost

[14]See "In the Valley of Cauteretz": "All along the valley, stream that flashest white,/Deepening thy voice with the deepening of the night" (ll. 1–2).

[15]The famous *cirque* at Gavarni, crowned with snowfields and glaciers.

[16]Pau sprang up around this castle of the viscounts of Béarn, dating originally from about the tenth century and rebuilt in the fourteenth by Gaston Phoebus. The castle is built in the form of an irregular pentagon with six square towers.

French while looking at the carved oak bed of the brave Jeanne.[17] It was interesting to us to show the boys the beautiful azure blue bed embroidered by the ladies of St. Cyr & presented by Mde. de Maintenon to the King because of the relationship to her.[18] One feels that it would not be unpleasant to live in the old castle looking over the river to the noble range of mountains beyond. A. reads to us of the Lake houses found in Switzerland said to be of a date 2000 years BC & of the relics of the great race on the hills. We lunch at Orthez & look out eagerly for the battlefield.

At Dax we liked to see women drawing out large earthern pots of water from the boiling, bubbling water in the centre of the Town for household purposes. Near was a market of splendid vegetables, boys & girls carrying baskets of grapes on their heads. The semi-circular remains of the old wall of the Town with the twelve towers we counted looks very fine. . . . The great church there,[19] carved in the 10th & begun it is said by the followers of the saint in the 8th century & finished by those who succeeded, very interesting. A very pleasant General, Aide de Camps to Ney[20] & other French Marshalls, who has had charge of Abdel Kadir at Pau, was our companion in the train to Angoulême & Tours. He seemed amused by the boys' dinner & their fight with newspaper swords against a bundle of coats. He told us that he had been in Algeria four years & that the Moors are so brave he has seen them throw themselves with their wives & children down a precipice rather than yield. He kindly secured us a railway Salon. By way of curiosity we go to the Hôtel du Louvre at Paris but like it not. At Amiens we were delighted with the glorious windows telling the stories of St. Firmin & Faustina. The expressions of the Saint with the sword over the head as divinely beautiful & holy as can well be conceived. We were sorry not to know which of the two

[17]Jeanne d'Albret, the mother of Henri IV of France. An extraordinary woman in many ways, Jeanne supposedly sang a Béarnaise song while giving birth to her son in order, as his father, Antoine de Bourbon, said, that he might "ni pleureur ni rechigné."

[18]Françoise d' Aubigné, marquise de Maintenon (1635–1719), secretly educated the illegitimate children of King Louis XIV; following the death of the queen, she was secretly wed to the king in late 1684 or in 1685. In 1685 she founded the royal house of Saint-Cyr, designed for the education of young ladies, well-to-do and poor alike, and after the death of the king she retired to that house where she remained until her death.

[19]La cathédrale Notre-Dame de Dax, remodeled in the seventeenth century, with some portions reconstructed as early as 1647.

[20]Michel Ney, duc D'Elchingen, maréchal de France (1769–1815).

windmills on two hills, one on the right, the other on the left of the sands left by the tide-river Somme, was Crecy. The sea is rough & the boat so crammed that the boys & myself lie on the lower deck. A very good place only two gentlemenly men there. Ally walks & stands about near us & glories in thus riding the waves. The boys wild with delight when we arrive at Winchester. We go to the Cathedral & look with veneration on the chests containing the bones of the Saxon kings and at the Saxon Crypt & the early Norman arches. We see the Granite Slab of St. Swithin among other interesting tombs & that of Rufus.[21]

How delightful to be at home once more. How beautiful it looks. It loses nothing in comparison with all we have seen. If A. were but well there would be nothing to be desired, but we suffer still from the chill nights in the Pyrenees.

We find Mrs. Magendio[?] here & Lady Charlotte Schreiber, Enid & Constance & Blanche Guest with Miss Kemble besides all the dear old friends of the neighbourhood. We take to our new occupation of inspecting cows & horses & carts bought by the bailiff Heard in our absence as well as to the old ways.

October

11th. The tenant Merwood sends in the keys before twelve. The boys see the cows & sheep driven off the farm, the mast of the ship preceding. It makes one sad. Most changes do, I suppose. . . .

17th. Mr. Cotton calls about Shakespeare's "New Place"[22] to be in the market to-morrow. Pleasant to see so thorough a country squire of the old stamp anxious to save it from desecrating hands. Mr. Peel with us these days.

19th. A happy old home day. A. & the boys take me about the fields in my little carriage. Mr. Dakyns with them. A. tells us his Ode for the Exhibition[23] and reads us many Poems from the *Golden Treasury* in the evening.

[21] The presbytery is enclosed at the sides by stone screens (1500–1525), upon which lie six wooden mortuary chests containing the remains of Ethelwolf, Egbert, Canute, William Rufus, and other kings, preserved from the old cathedral of the tenth century.

[22] The Stratford house, the second largest in the town, which Shakespeare bought from William Underhill for £60 on May 4, 1597.

[23] The "Ode Sung at the Opening of the International Exhibition," which was written by request and was sung at the opening of the exhibition on May 1,

20th. The boys take me to Maiden's Croft & we go to meet A. & Mr. Dakyns who are returning from the Needles. They tell me of the Military road which is being made to the old Light House. So the beautiful lonely down we shall see no more. I tell A. how much I have been interested by passages in Stanley's *Council of Nice.*[24] He reads them to us & is as delighted as I was.

21st. A. tells me his "Ode on the Exhibition" that I may write it down.

22nd. He reads to us the IVth Book of *Paradise Lost.*

28th. A. goes to Town for a doctor not having been well since our journey. I go to the boat with him. The ropes of boats get entangled in the wheel of the steamer. The Governor of the castle & the sailors are very kind in telling me about it & assuring me there is no danger. The sea is rough & I wait until the steamer appears well on its way. Franklin Lushington has been so kind as to lend A. his Chambers in the Temple & when he returns to them Mr. Venables lends his. The doctor says A. is below par. During his absence the boys sometimes amuse themselves with riding home on the Farm horses after their day's work and in driving home cows & in milking them. I read them Mr. Knowles's King Arthur stories[25] in the evening which delight them greatly, also stories of India. Constance & Blanche Guest are often with the boys. I make manuscript books for A. & arrange his study. A weary while A.'s absence has been. He returns on the 23rd of November, but he does not look as I would have him. He is pleased with all that has been done indoors & out of doors. A. reads some of Mr. Woolner's Journal to me.

November

28th. Dr. Acworth[26] comes, talks about Homeopathy.

1862. Though the poem was written in October 1861, Tennyson added three lines of reference to the Prince Consort (ll. 7–10), as the originator of international exhibitions, after the first draft.

[24] "The Council of Nicaea," lecture II in Arthur Penrhyn Stanley's *Lectures on the History of the Eastern Church* (London, 1861).

[25] James Thomas Knowles, *The Story of King Arthur and His Knights of the Round Table* (London, 1862). The volume was dedicated to Tennyson.

[26] James Acworth (1798–1883), president of Baptist College from 1835 until 1863 and author of *The Internal Witness to Christianity* (1856).

December

6th. He goes. A. has read to us these evenings. Dr. Acworth brought the account of the American insult making us of course extremely angry & Mr. Dakyns walks to Yarmouth for Papers.[27]

11th. A. reads me what he has done of "Enoch Arden." Very fine & very beautiful it seems to me.

13th. Mr. Dakyns goes because his Father is so ill & A. helps me with the boys.

15th. A note from Blanche with Lady Charlotte's photograph. In it she tells the most sad news of the Prince Consort's death.[28] A terrible blow. One fears for the Queen, for the nation, the loss is so unspeakable.

16th. We send for News from Yarmouth, we are so anxious about the Queen.

17th. A grand & touching account of the Queen.

20th. We learn to-day that the Queen arrived at Osborne yesterday. Not one even of her own servants on the platform only her children & Lord Alfred Paget.[29]

22nd. A letter from Osborne.

23rd. The Prince's funeral day. A bitter east wind & dull sky.

24th. We go to Osborne, A., myself & the boys. We have a good report of the dear Queen & Princess Alice. A beautiful day. We find Mr. Palgrave arrived on our return.

27th. Kind Mr. Cotton offers to give £50 of the hundred which Starks asks for the road rather than have The Terrace spoilt. A. has walks with me or with Mr. Palgrave & the Bradleys & our boys.

[27] This was the *Trent* incident. An American warship stopped the *Trent* in order to seize James H. Mason and John Slidell, envoys from Jefferson Davis to the British government. The American captain, Commodore Wilkes, acted without orders, and as a result of public outcry in England the envoys were subsequently returned.

[28] Prince Albert died on December 14, 1861.

[29] Lord Alfred Henry Paget (1816–88), liberal M.P. for Lichfield, 1837–65; chief equerry to the Queen and clerk-marshall from 1846 until 1874, when he resigned the office of chief equerry only.

1862

January

1st. A. walks with Mr. Palgrave & the boys and as Hallam says skips about like a young man.

2nd. Sir John Simeon brings his new wife.[1]

7th. A. sends his "Dedication" of his *Idylls* to the Duchess of Argyll & the Duchess of Sutherland. I think it magnificent. The boys busy writing what they call poems about the Prince.

9th. Mr. Bradley brings Mr. [*illegible*]'s interesting account of the Samaritan Day of Atonement. The boys listen with great pleasure to all of it that I have time to read to them. The boys delighted to hear that Mr. Dakyns will probably return to-day. They put up their flags & put on their rifle caps & receive him with military honours. A. reads to us at night. We learn that Lord Granville[2] took the Ode on the Exhibition to the Queen when he went to Osborne for that first sad Privy Council & that the lines in it to the memory of the Prince should stand.

13th. A letter from the Duchess of Sutherland saying how much she likes the Dedication. We send it with a letter from A. to the Princess Alice. Also we send what, I suppose, will be the final form of the Ode to Sterndale Bennett.[3]

16th. A day to be remembered by us. A letter of thanks to A. from Princess Alice telling us that his lines have soothed our Queen.[4] Thank God! Also a very nice letter from Sir Charles Phipps. The guns firing this morning for the first time since the

[1]Catherine Dorothea Colville had married Sir John Simeon on October 2, 1861.

[2]Granville George Leveson-Gower, 2d Earl Granville (1815–91), the statesman. Granville was minister for foreign affairs under Russell, 1851–52, and Gladstone, 1870–74 and 1880–85. He served as chancellor of the University of London from 1856 until his death and as secretary of state for the colonies from 1868 until 1870 and again in 1886.

[3]The "Ode Sung at the Opening of the International Exhibition" was published with music by W. Sterndale Bennett on April 12, 1862.

[4]See Hope Dyson and Charles Tennyson, *Dear and Honoured Lady* (London: Macmillan, 1969), p. 65, for the princess's letter to Tennyson.

Queen said that they were not to fire again till further orders. Mr. Woolner comes.

17th. A. brings me violets, primroses, anemones.

25th. Snow gone. A. & I walk these days & to-day I walk up the down with him, for the first time for years. Very beautiful. Mr. Dakyns kindly runs back for the little carriage & they take me to the beacon.

27th. Dr. Sterndale Bennett comes.

28th. He goes & Mr. Jowett arrives. The boys delighted [to] drive to meet him. His cough too bad to read them Homer as usual but he plays at chess with them & we played "Proverbs" in the evening. Jeffrey's photographs come.

31st. To-day he must go. Every day I have had interesting talks with him.

February

1st. A. reads us what he has done of "Enoch Arden." Very beautiful & heroic, I think it. A. reads us some of Jacob & Esau & other parts of the Old Testament & the boys interested by the death of Polycarp in Miss Sewell's *Church History*. . . .[5]

4th. He takes me to see the snowdrops which seem to us to have a peculiar beauty & whiteness this year.

6th. Parliament meets. Lord Dufferin quotes the end of A.'s "Dedication." Dr. Latham[6] comes. His talk very clever & learned moreover. A. looks for an umbrella to shelter me from the East wind & paints the gate green to please me.

7th. We are unexpressibly vexed to see a paragraph in the *Daily Telegraph* speaking of the letter from Princess Alice & cannot think who has been so ill-judged as to put it in. A. writes to Mr. Dasent to prevent it from slipping into the *Times*.

21st. A. & Mr. Dakyns have played several evenings at Backgammon & sometimes I play meanwhile on the piano.

[5]For Jacob and Esau, see Genesis 27–33; Elizabeth Missing Sewell, *History of the Early Church from the First Preaching of the Gospel to the Council of Nicea* (London, 1859).

[6]Probably Dr. Robert Gordon Latham (1812–88), the enthnologist and philologist. Among Latham's most important works were *Varieties of the Human Race* (1854), *Descriptive Ethnology* (1859), and *Two Dissertations on the Hamlet of Saxo Grammaticus and of Shakespeare* (1872).

23rd. A. reads us some of "Enoch Arden" to my delight & begins writing it down regularly to-day.

24th. We were to have gone to Shiplake to-day to have said good-bye to the place where we were married, but East wind & mist & rain prevented us. An extremely interesting letter from the Duke of Argyll with a most touching message from the Queen. Also a deeply moving half letter, half thinking on paper, from the Princess Royal. One cannot but feel an added glow of devotion to them seeing how anxious they are to thank A. A day I would fain remember for more even than that or even this—that I have read what A. has written of "Enoch Arden" this morning.

25th. Sir John Simeon calls. A. writes to the Princess & copies for her "The Passing of Arthur."

26th. He goes to Shiplake. I read some Mill & Sir Alexander Grant's Lecture on the Roman colonies.[7]

March

1st. A few lines from Kate telling that A. is coming home. She thinks him looking as young or younger than when we married. He looks well on his return. Another extremely interesting letter from the Duke of Argyll.

2nd. A. reads "The Parting Hour" to us.[8]

4th. We meet Sir A. Sterling & Mr. Stirling of Kier at Swainston.[9] All very kind & pleasant but I find it hard work to leave home even for a night.

5th. See the dear little faces watching the return.

9th. A. walks for a hour with Mr. Dakyns.

[7]Sir Alexander Grant, *How the Ancient Romans Delivered Their Provinces, a Lecture Delivered before the Bombay Mechanics' Institution, 17th January, 1862* (Bombay: Privately printed, 1862).

[8]Tale 2 of Crabbe's *Tales* (1812), "The Parting Hour," was Tennyson's source for "Enoch Arden."

[9]Sir Anthony Coningham Sterling (1805–71) was brigade-major and assistant-adjutant-general to the highland division in the Crimea, 1854–55; raised to colonel, 1857; military secretary to Colin Campbell in India, 1858–59.

William Stirling, of Kier, M.P., was the nephew of Sir John Maxwell (d. 1865), from whom he inherited the Pollock and other estates.

13th. The Duke & Duchess of Argyll come to us. Lord Dufferin does not arrive. A. reads "Enoch Arden" to us.

14th. The poor Duke & Duchess kept in doors from bad colds. Lord Dufferin arrives after an adventurous journey accomplished as far as Cowes before breakfast. A. reads "Enoch Arden" to him.

15th. They must all leave to-day. One has learned to love the Duke & Duchess & Lord Dufferin is delightful.

16th. Our Lionel's birthday. He delighted with a knife & both boys very pleased with their Peter the Whaler, Parker's Church stories, African Wanderers, Mère Angelique.[10]

The most absolute regularity & quiet home ways seem necessary to A. now. Read Lord Dufferin's very interesting book.[11]

25th. A letter from the Duke & Duchess of Argyll giving A. the Queen's Command to go to Osborne.

31st. Mr. Spedding sends us his *Bacon's Life & Letters.*[12]

April

9th. Sir John Simeon comes from Town, dines & sleeps here. Wins Mr. Atkinson's[13] heart as he does most hearts.

10th. Mr. Warburton arrives. . . .

12th. Mr. Dakyns & the boys meet Mr. Jowett.

[10] William Henry Giles Kingston, *Peter the Whaler* (London, 1851); Parker's church stories are undoubtedly Mrs. Jenny Marsh Parker's six small volumes of religious stories published together by the Little Church Library (New York, 1858): *Around the Manger, The Light of the World, Seeds for the Spring-Time, The Soldier of the Cross, Frank Earnest,* and *What a Little Child Should Know*; Sarah Bowdich Lee, *The African Wanderers, or the Adventures of Carlos and Antonio* (London, 1847); Mère Angélique may be Arnauld d'Andilly, Mère Angélique de Saint-Jean (1624–84), whose *Discours* (Paris, 1736) is possibly the work Emily Tennyson means to indicate.

[11] Frederick Temple Hamilton-Temple Blackwood, marquis of Dufferin and Ava, *Letters from High Latitudes* (London, 1857).

[12] James Spedding, *The Letters and Life of Francis Bacon*, 7 vols. (London, 1861–72).

[13] The Rev. Francis H. Atkinson, the Freshwater curate. Mr. Atkinson was a dear friend of the Tennysons and a frequent visitor at Farringford where he from time to time assisted Emily Tennyson with paperwork and with other business matters.

14th. Mr. Jowett kindly accompanies A. in his drive to Osborne, my cough being bad. A. affected even to tears by the Queen, who stood pale & statue-like, speaking in a quiet, sweet, sad voice. She looked very pretty and had a stately innocence about her different from other women. She said many kind things to him, for he remembers thanking her & saying that it made him very happy, but he does not remember what she said. She talked of the Prince & of Hallam & Macaulay & Goëthe & Schiller in connection with him and said that the Prince was so like the picture of Arthur Hallam in *In Memoriam* even to his blue eyes, and when A. said he would have made a great King, she said, "He always said it did not signify whether He did the right thing or did not so long as the right thing was done." Ally said we all grieved with your Majesty & the Queen replied: "The country has been kind to me & I am thankful." Princess Alice came in with Princess Beatrice when the Queen had withdrawn and was very kind "true natural & true mannered" as A. says.

The Henry Taylors & their daughters & Mr. Dodgson here at this time & we see them often.[14]

16th. Mr. Dakyns goes. A sorrowful parting for all.

17th. Mr. Atkinson arrives. Mr. Jowett goes to the Terrace, three young friends with him.

21st. Nanny & Agnes arrive while the boys are walking with Mr. Jowett. Infinite joy at the meeting. The three young creatures give us Tableaux Vivants from Shakespeare & the Sleeping Beauty & Hallam gives up his part to Lionel in the sleepwalking scene in *Macbeth.*

23rd. Sterndale Bennett's setting of the "Ode" arrives & Nanny gives it to us.

24th. I [play?] a little of it to Mr. Jowett.

25th. I go with A. to Yarmouth on his way to London. Lionel quite indignant with Nanny when she spoke of Mr. Jowett's "pupils." "They are not his pupils at all. Mr. Jowett is a young lad. They are all just the same, just entering life together." Mr. Jowett reads Homer to the boys & Agnes.

[14]Lewis Carroll was often a resident at Plumbley's Hotel in Freshwater.

May

1st. A splendid day for the opening of the Exhibition.[15] I am sorry A. is not there but he would not, of course, join the Procession, nor did I wish him.

2nd. A. goes to Cliveden to-day.

3rd. Keeping shows his fossils to Nanny & the children. They are highly delighted. I buy one of the Collections he had made of the rocks of this part. The children very anxious to hear the "Ode." It is promised them after dinner. When we arrive in the drawing room, the shutters are drawn & the curtains. When undrawn they appear, the boys in nightdresses, Agnes also in white, over their dresses, they thinking so to do honour to the "Ode" as "choristers." We do not know what to do for laughter.

7th. A. returns to-day. He has enjoyed his visit at Cliveden very much. He is very pleased to have met Mr. Charles Howard again & to have seen so much of Mr. Gladstone. He admires Lady Constance Grosvenor extremely & likes Lady Taunton[16] very much. He brings a Wellingtonia, the gift of the Duchess.[17] The seed was shot from a tree in Caufordray at two hundred feet from the ground. A. looks thin, but well & cheerful tho' he says he has had a touch of hay-fever. He & I look about the progress made in out of doors work & rejoice in the blossoming trees & flowery fields.

13th. A. brings down "A Dedication."[18] I send it to the Publishers. These days he takes me delightful rounds in my little carriage.

14th. A letter from Mr. Jowett full of affectionate warning about my health to which A. bids me attend. He has for some time been talking of trying France & Germany again.

[15] Although the 1862 Exhibition flourished during the spring and early summer, it was ultimately far less successful than the 1851 Exhibition.

[16] Lady Mary Matilda Georgiana Howard, the youngest daughter of George, 6th earl of Carlisle, and the second wife of Henry Labouchere, Baron Taunton (1798–1869).

[17] The duchess of Argyll.

[18] First published in *Enoch Arden, Etc.* (1864), this poem of thirteen lines in blank verse was dedicated to Emily Tennyson. "June Bracken and Heather," the dedicatory lines which preface Tennyson's final volume, is also dedicated to Lady Tennyson.

18th. He reads me one of Robertson's Sermons, "Thus saith the High God."

20th. A. mows, the boys sweep & I help a little.

23rd. We show Heard where we wish the Greenhouse flowers to be planted.

31st. A very interesting letter from Lady Augusta Bruce saying that she was commanded by the Queen to send A. two volumes of Poems by Zeller & another in which HM had found comfort.[19] They are marked by herself. A precious gift. We finished *Robinson Crusoe*. Homages from Frenchmen to-day & four or five times lately. One is glad to have them.

June

5th. An Illustrated Edition of Gray from Lady Taunton.

11th. I begin my rides on Fanny, A. walking by my side.[20] Very pleasant.

12th. A. calls on Henry Taylor & Mrs. Cameron makes him read "The Vision of Sin."

13th. We keep our wedding secretly. A. does not like anniversaries & this one seems too sacred to keep openly.

14th. Henry Taylor, Mrs. Cameron & the Jacksons[21] dine with us. A. reads "Enoch Arden." A very pleasant evening but that Mrs. Jackson was overpowered by "Enoch Arden." Her two dream girls haunt one. They seem to come out of some Niebelungenlied.

17th. A magnificent Blotting book from the manufacturers at Coventry with The Lady Godiva woven in silk.

[19] Lady Augusta Bruce (1822–76) was lady-in-waiting to the queen; in 1863 she married Arthur Penrhyn Stanley.

Heinrich Zeller's most notable works are his *Gedichte in Oberbayerischer Mundart* and *Gedichte in Altbayerischer Mundart*.

[20] Fanny was the Tennyson children's pony which their mother sometimes rode but which more often pulled her in her wheeled garden chair. Fanny was remembered by Edith Ellison, the Granville Bradleys' daughter, as "one of the fattest of white ponies" (*A Child's Recollections of Tennyson* [New York: J. M. Dent, 1906], p. 65).

[21] Dr. and Mrs. John Jackson, Mrs. Cameron's sister Maria and her husband, the famous Calcutta physician.

18th. Mrs. Norton & Mr. Stirling of Kier call & walk with me & then call on Henry Taylor & Mrs. Cameron to return to dinner & drive back to Cowes after. Both very agreeable.

21st. Mr. Woolner comes. A. makes hay. I help a little.

30th. A. again out in the hay field at work nearly all day.

July

1st. The last load home to-night. A. helps to the last. Mrs. Cameron comes across the Park looking gorgeous in her violet dress & red cloak walking over the newly mown grass. Pleasant to hear the men cheering.

2nd. The Men's Festival Day.

3rd. Very sad account of the Patmores. The boys drill continually sometimes on foot, sometimes on pony back & on great days have reviews.

10th. Mr. Warburton dines with us.

12th. Frederick comes. Very pleased with what we have done in the grounds.

18th. Mr. & Mrs. Cameron have kindly lent us Ashburton Cottage & we go there with our boys.

20th. Mrs. Clough & Mrs. Coltman dine with us. Very sad to see Mrs. Clough. A. & the boys go to see the shooting for Lord Elcho's[22] prize. Go to Coombe Hurst & find Mrs. Clough. A beautiful day & a lovely place. We see the Miniatures at Kensington, very interesting. Mr. Spedding dines with us & we see Lord & Lady Monteagle & Sir Vere de Vere[23] & Lady de Vere. A great please [*sic*] to A. to see Sir Vere after so many years. The Duke & Duchess of Argyll, Mr. Vernon Lushington, Mr. Chapman, Mr. Brookfield & Weld, Mr. Palgrave. Mr. Woolner has kindly got Mr. Fairbairn to have our names put down for a private view of the pictures.[24] The Norwegian pictures extremely interesting. One sees in them the Sea Kings of old &

[22] Francis Richard, Lord Elcho, 10th earl of Wemyss (1818–1914).

[23] Sir Vere Edmond De Vere, 3d baronet (1808–80), first child of Sir Aubrey Thomas De Vere; sheriff of Limerick, 1836; succeeded to the baronetcy, 1846.

[24] Sir William Fairbairn arranged for the Tennysons to see the pictures at the International Exhibition. Fairbairn served as a juror at the London exhibitions of 1851 and 1862 and at the Paris exhibition of 1855.

feels one's relationship. We go to Hampstead & find Mother looking sweet & beautiful as ever.[25] Cissy & Septimus[26] there.

29th. Mrs. Clough & Florence lunch with us & we all go to Kew Gardens afterwards.

30th. A. lunches at Argyll Lodge to meet Mr. Gladstone & afterwards joins Mr. Atkinson & the boys at the Zoological gardens.

31st. We go to Jeffreys & are all photographed. Mr. Woolner goes with us, then we call on Mr. Maurice. His welcome delightful. We buy the children watches.

August

1st. We tell our friends that we are glad to see any who will dine with us any day at half past six. We lunch with the Simeons & call on Clara Palmer[27] & have a most affectionate welcome. Franklin Lushington & his wife, Mr. Venables & Mr. Brookfield. Surely there was never a more freely flowing wit & humour than his. Mr. Lear also with us.

2nd. Charles Weld kindly gets us into the Exhibition early & we see the jewels & other things.

5th. We set off for Newcastle. A. & the boys go to see the ruins of the Castle. The beautiful church near the market place gives the look of a foreign town.[28]

6th. A. takes the boys to Lincoln Cathedral on our way to Grasby. Aunt Fytche gives us a most kind reception. We find a letter making it expedient for poor A. to return to Town.

8th. I take A. to Barnetby. He leaves his Mackintosh. I write A. Tennyson & ask the Book-keeper to pack it for me. He sees the

[25] Mrs. Elizabeth Tennyson lived at Hampstead until her death in February 1865.

[26] Tennyson's sister Cecilia Lushington and his brother Septimus.

[27] Tennyson's cousin, the former Clara d'Eyncourt, who had married an eminent Queen's Counsel, John Hinde Palmer (1808–84), M.P. for Lincoln, 1868–74.

[28] The founding of the city of Newcastle resulted from the building there of a castle by Robert Curthose (eldest son of William the Conqueror) on his return from his incursion into Scotland in 1080. Newcastle Cathedral, formerly one of the largest parish churches in England, is noted for its west tower, crowned by its famous 194-foot spire.

Alfred Lord Tennyson with Hallam (left) *and Lionel. Photograph (circa 1862) by O. G. Rejlander. (Tennyson Research Centre Collection, Lincoln, courtesy of Lord Tennyson and the Lincolnshire Library Service)*

address & says what! the great Poet Alfred Tennyson. A peaceful, happy time with my Father were it not for A.'s absence. Hallam reads Washington Irving's *Conquest of Grenada*[29] which delights us all. Grandpapa & I are much amused at the heroic-style in which Hallam gives the charges & the speeches. The one event during our visit was the death of a villager Lawy[?] by name. He had feared death, feared to meet the Judge, as he said, but the day he died, the 20th, he said all fear of death was gone. "We have never been happy like this." He lifted up his hands with the look of an angel. The boys call on some of the villagers. At two houses they are asked to go every day & find chairs placed for them like expected guests.

10th. We had given up seeing A. to-day when he looked in at the drawing-room window.

September

His tour in Derbyshire & Yorkshire on the whole successful notwithstanding bad weather. Mr. Palgrave as usual most kind. A. much interested in Dr. Lushington[30] whom he met with his son, Godfrey, at Bolton Abbey. He liked Sir Charles & Lady Trevelyan[31] whom he met at Buxton & was very glad to see something of Monckton Milnes there.

13th. The roughest crossing we ever had. The old life, drills, walks, letters innumerable, & farm accounts. We look at pretty "Nelly" with the Deer-like head, down sheep & a great many things besides. The boys like to read all about Garibaldi & Lionel wants to write to him & ask him here. A great noise among the Rooks. Mr. Atkinson & the boys have seen them chasing a Hawk these two or three days.

28th. A letter from Mr. Palgrave telling of his engagement.[32] We are delighted to receive it.

[29] *A Chronicle of the Conquest of Granada*, 2 vols. (London, 1829).

[30] Dr. Stephen Lushington (1782–1873), the famed barrister. It was to Lushington that Lady Byron first revealed her suspicion of her husband's incestuous relationship with Mrs. Augusta Leigh. With Lords Brougham and Denman, Lushington was also retained as counsel for Queen Caroline in her 1820 divorce trial.

[31] Sir Charles Edward Trevelyan (1807–86), assistant-secretary to the Treasury, London, 1840–59; governor of Madras, 1859. Lady Trevelyan was the former Hannah More, the sister of Lord Macaulay.

[32] In December 1862 Francis Turner Palgrave married Cecil Gaskell (d. 1890),

29th. A. comes to show me a glorious rainbow. The whole arch, part of it is afterwards in a red sky, a sort of glorified rainbow, & then purple clouds float over it.

October

A. goes to Swainston, returns on the 16th with Mr. Woolner.

18th. Edmund comes. Very stormy. Two shipwrecks to-night. Edmund leaves on the 22nd in spite of storm & wind, the boatmen foretelling still worse to-morrow.

26th. A. calls on Mr. Ward at night. One day A. goes with me to see sheep marked. One he piles up maubeerwurzel.

30th. A. so good as to write to Mr. Gladstone & send what I want to have shown to him.

31st. A. on the platform watching the stars.

November

1st. Mr. Atkinson walks to Ventnor to see his friend Mr. Lubbock having heard of the death of his daughter.

7th. A very kind letter from Mr. Gladstone.

8th. Dr. Ogle[33] dines with us.

9th. Rainy. We cannot go to church. A. reads the Bible to us in the evening.

10th. The boys make a bonfire in honour of Grandpapa's birthday. Hallam goes to the Ford with *In Memoriam* & the *Idylls* as a gift to him. . . .

13th. A calm, bright frost, air delicious. At night A. goes out on the platform to see if there are any shooting stars & has just said to himself, I must take care I do not fall, it is so dark, when he did fall over & cracked one of the glasses of his spectacles but did no harm to himself except a little scratch on his nose.

14th. We go to Coomb Bute where they are ploughing.

---

the daughter of James Milnes Gaskell, the close friend of Arthur Henry Hallam.

[33]Perhaps the son of Dr. James Ogle (1792–1857), the Oxford professor and physician.

17th. A. has to go to Town to have a tooth stopt.

21st. Mr. Watts kindly begins a portrait of me to surprise A. Mr. Watts so pleasant that the time does not seem long.

22nd. The boys so much interested in watching him that they beg not to go out. A. has to land in a little boat. A large Conger Eel at the landing place. I send the boys to look at it. A. brings me two Pompeian vases & one with a lizard. From Mr. Woolner a Fern dish.

27th. A. writes to thank Mr. Keeping for the curious Pewter fork & spoon which he found embedded in sand & shingle at Asherfield point & which he has given to A.

29th. Mr. Watts finishes my portrait to-day & begins one of A. Mr. Watts lunches with us & praises our bread. After luncheon Hallam takes a big loaf to him. Miss Thackeray[34] is at the Camerons these days & we see her from time to time. A. has walked along the shore to Brixton.

December

1st. His portrait grows very grand to-day. Mr. Watts takes his little bit of bread & cheese with us again to-day. A. writes to Sir Redmond Barry[35] to thank him for the Exhibition catalogue & the seeds of Wattle & the magnificent maize & the Victorian wheat & oats beautiful to behold. A. says that the shapes are so beautiful. We go to see the wheat sown.

3rd. Prince Alfred proclaimed King of Greece.[36] Lionel has begun to learn Greek every day for most days.

4th. A. walks with Mr. Atkinson on Afton Down & reads in the moonlight.

[34] "Annie" Thackeray (1837–1919). The daughter of William Makepeace Thackeray, Annie during the 1860s became one of Emily Tennyson's most intimate friends, and she was a frequent visitor in the Tennyson home throughout the remainder of Lady Tennyson's life. In 1877 Annie married her cousin Richmond Thackeray Ritchie (1854–1912; knighted 1898), the statesman and private secretary to Lord George Hamilton from 1895 until 1902.

[35] Sir Redmond Barry (1813–80), solicitor-general of the colony of Victoria, 1850; first chancellor of Melbourne University, 1855; commissioner for Queen Victoria at the International Exhibition, 1862.

[36] Prince Alfred, the second son of Queen Victoria, was officially elected king by the Greek Assembly on February 3, 1863, but the British government subsequently rejected the decision.

16th. We plant roses. Mr. Routledge[37] comes about the *Illustrated Edition* of the Poems.

18th. To my great delight A. begins reading Carlyle's 3rd vol. of *Frederich* & says he will read it to me. A return to our dear old ways most welcome to me.

19th. We are all out transplanting Rhododendrons, we choosing places, the boys helping to dig.

21st. A. reads me some of Horte's Thomas à Becket.

24th. Hallam puts up A.'s Holly wreath while we are at dinner. The boys have the Magic Lantern after having been to the accustomed house with gifts. I have a pleasant evening A. reading to me part of *King Lear* & put the gifts from Uncle & Aunt Charley & Grandpapa & ourselves by the sides of the boy's beds.

25th. A. reads me what he has done of the New Poem.[38]

26th. Sir Graham Hamond's funeral day.

31st. All these days we have been planting.

[37] George Routledge (1812–88), the publisher. Routledge's career as a publisher of inexpensive literature, on which his reputation largely depends, opened in 1848 with his publication of James Fenimore Cooper's *Pilot*, the first volume of a mammoth series entitled *The Railway Library*.

[38] "Aylmer's Field."

1863

January

1st. Old Brian lunches here. Yesterday he walked from Newport, to-day he is going to Yarmouth & to-morrow back to Newport. He was ninety last Easter. Almost every evening A. reads *Friedrich* to me & everyday we are planting.

On the 3rd Euonymous[1] in the glen.

4th. Every night A. reads to me. In the morning we go out to look after the work going on in the grounds. In the afternoons letters & bills.

9th. Mr. & Mrs. Palgrave come to-day.

10th. Mr. Clark to-day. Mrs. Palgrave gives us Mozart & Beethoven in the evenings.

13th. All our pleasant guests go. We rejoice that Mr. Palgrave has a wife who seems so well fitted to make him happy.

14th. A beautiful day. Lady Augusta Bruce comes to luncheon & brings with her what is to us beyond price *The Prince Consort*, a gift from the Queen with kind words written by H.M.'s own hand,[2] also a beautiful photograph of herself & three of her children with A.'s lines under it "May all love etc."[3] Also the prayers used at the Anniversary & the Sermon preached.[4] I feel to know & to trust Lady Augusta at once. She promises to come & sleep here next week if she can.

15th. Rogers brings us two wonderfully beautiful numbers of Gould's *British Birds.*[5]

[1] *Euonymus europaeus*, or the spindle tree, the fruit of which is alluded to in the final two lines of "A Dedication" to the *Enoch Arden* volume.

[2] Lady Augusta brought to the Tennysons a specially bound volume of *The Principal Speeches and Addresses of His Royal Highness the Prince Consort with an Introduction Giving Some Outlines of His Character* (London, 1862). The Queen's inscription reads as follows: "To Alfred Tennyson Esquire/who so truly appreciated/This greatest purest and best of men/from/the beloved Prince's/ broken-hearted widow/Victoria/Osborne Dec. 9, 1862."

[3] See the "Dedication" (of the *Idylls* to the memory of the Prince Consort), ll. 50 ff.

[4] The monthly anniversary of Prince Philip's death on December 14, 1861.

[5] John Gould, *The Birds of Great Britain*, 5 vols. (London, 1862–73).

17th. The boys go to meet Mr. Jowett.

19th. A delightful talk with him.

20th. He & A. walk and the boys & I go to meet Mr. Dakyns. A. reads "Enoch Arden" one evening and "The Tapestried Chamber." Mrs. Brookfield & Arthur here, also Sir Charles Darling.[6]

February

13th. All this time planting goes on & alteration in the grounds & filling up the space left by the great Elm Tree . . . which we had to cut down, dear as it was, sunshine being dearer. To-day A. & the boys take me to the Terrace that we may plan the grounds there. Heard's brother who has been a sailor for twenty years says that he has never known so stormy a time as two months of this winter.

15th. A. brings me *The Times* to see the article on Mr. Jowett.[7] Such a one as should be.

17th. A splendid day. A. went with Mr. Estcourt, Mr. Bird, Farmer Lane & Heard to walk the bounds of our Manor. A. reads me a little of Russell's Diary[8] & one night he reads Virgil with me. Mr. Atkinson very kind in bringing barrows full of Ferns & primroses. The boys help, A. & I help them to plant.

24th. Mr. Cotton calls to make arrangements about the celebration of the Prince's Wedding day.[9] We joyfully consent to having a Bonfire on our Down.

[6]Arthur Montagu Brookfield (b. 1853) was the son of William Henry and Jane Octavia Brookfield.

Sir Charles Henry Darling (1809–70) was a colonial administrator. Darling was appointed captain-general of Jamaica in 1857 and governor of Victoria in 1863.

[7]There were short pieces on the heresy action brought against Jowett in the vice-chancellor's court by Dr. Pusey and his other opponents at Oxford in the *Times* on February 12 and 16.

[8]Possibly the *Private Journal of John, Duke of Bedford, 1766–1770* (London, 1841).

[9]On March 5, 1863, the Prince of Wales (later King Edward VII) was wed to Princess Alexandra of Denmark. At the queen's request Tennyson composed "A Welcome to Alexandra" which was sent to the queen on March 6, published by Edward Moxon in a four-page sheet on March 7, and published in the *Times* on March 10.

March

3rd. A. & Mr. Atkinson go with Keeping to Hampstead. The boys much interested by the specimens they bring home.

6th. We send off the final copy of "A Welcome."

7th. This has been a very busy week of preparations for the 10th even in this little place, making flags, planting flags, making favours, puddings, cakes & not only in our house but others also.

10th. A fine morning. A letter from Lady Augusta with a very kind message from the Queen about the "Welcome" which arrived just after the Princess.[10] We thought it would have arrived before. Poor A.'s ticket for the Chapel only arrives this morning having been missent so he misses the glorious pageant. I go with the boys & Mr. Atkinson to see the dinner. The sight of so many dear old gray heads is touching. The boys bring their beautiful Danish & English flags & walk in procession with the school children. The poor little fellows very much excited. Mr. Atkinson makes the flower vases beautiful. We dine in the nursery, all the down-stairs rooms being prepared for the evening. The Cake is lovely thanks to Andrews & Acott & Matilda.[11] The supper too all we could wish adorned with flowers & the little flags painted by Mr. Atkinson & the boys. All our friends go on the Down with A. in spite of rain except Mr. & Mrs. Isaacson & Croziers. I go to the summer house in the kitchen garden with Mr. & Mrs. Isaacson & am joined by others.

A. tells me that the bonfire is very grand, great green tongues of flame dart out along the ground, curling & licking. The torchlight procession, too, very fine. The boys wait on us at supper. They want to stay up & drink the Queen's health & that of the Prince & Princess. Of the Queen A. says the simple words "The Queen & God bless her" very grandly & very impressively. There is a little dance after supper. The house looks very pretty with all the lamps & candles.

[10]On March 8 the queen sent a message of appreciation to Tennyson through Lady Augusta, who wrote: "Her Majesty desires me to thank you very warmly and to tell you with how much pleasure she had read the lines and how much she rejoices that the sweet and charming Princess should be thus greeted" (Dyson and Tennyson, *Dear and Honoured Lady*, p. 74).

[11]Farringford cooks and maids. Mrs. Andrews was the chief cook for the Tennysons for many years.

11th. Mrs. Gatty & her son Stephen come.

12th, 13th, 14th. They gather sea-weed.

16th. A. & I go to Osborne & write our names. We are much amused on returning to find that our neighbours have been drawn up in their carriages at our gate insisting that the Prince & Princess had promised a visit to-day or to-morrow & would not go until Mr. Atkinson assured them he knew nothing of it.

18th. Ellen & Zilly Lushington[12] come. They have expeditions with A. & the boys.

27th. Nelly & Zilly go. Most glad we are to have had them. A. reads me some Comte. Dreary reading.

28th. Carpenter & Westley send us the account of their birthday Illuminations which excited so much interest especially that of The Prince Consort with A.'s lines "O silent father of our Kings to be, Mourned in this [golden] hour of jubilee" on a blue ground with gold & white clouds & a starry crown.[13] A. reads me some *Othello.*

29th. To-day his own beautiful poem.[14] A great refreshment.

30th. More *Othello.* Delightful to have our readings again.

31st. The boys go with me to meet Mr. Jowett. A. goes on with *Othello.*

April

1st. Charles Weld comes with the beautiful Urn & Salver graceful in form & design, we think, with a very kind inscription presented to A. in acknowledgement of the Ode on the Exhibition.

[12] Ellen Elizabeth Lushington ("Nelly," 1821–86) was the sister of Edmund, Tom, Henry, and Franklin Lushington.
Cecilia ("Zilly") Lushington was the Edmund Lushingtons' second daughter.

[13] Located at 24 Regent Street, Messrs. Carpenter and Westley were well-established London opticians who gained notoriety in the early 1860s for their strange and ingenious slide shows. With the aid of their assistant, J. Manning, Carpenter and Westley staged several optical experiments using a Phantasmagoria Lantern which enabled them to produce a variety of mysterious and seemingly inexplicable illusions. Apparently in honor of Queen Victoria's birthday (May 24), Carpenter and Westley presented a slide show which they subsequently described to the Tennysons.

[14] Probably "Aylmer's Field."

2nd. Mr. Jowett goes to the Terrace. Mr. Clark is with the Bradleys & they all dine with us.

10th. A. reads "Aylmer's Field" to Mr. Jowett & me. . . .

18th. Mr. Atkinson returns from his holiday & A. takes him at night to the rooms we have furnished for him [at] the Lodge. A. says that they look so delightfully comfortable, he would like to live there himself.

20th. A. & I find a person dressed as a gentleman squatting on the top of the bank & peering into our lawn. He says "I hope you will forgive me, Mr. Tennyson." A. replies, "It is not pretty" & turns his back on him.

22nd. The Peregrine Falcons taken from our cliff have grown so tame that they will feed from Mr. Rogers' hand. At first the male used to stamp with rage & the female kept up a melancholy flapping of the wings & trod to death her little one hatched in captivity. The boys want to pay their five guineas for them & set them free. A. says it is useless, they would be taken again immediately or shot. Afterwards agrees to buy if the Maharajah to whom they are going finds them too much injured for use.

23rd. A Roman Urn found in the Terrace grounds when they were digging out earth for a mound. A. & I make out some of the thirty tyrants in Gaul of whose date the coins are. Near them was the skeleton of a horse's head in a circle of stones.

24th. Lord & Lady Lilford[15] call with Mrs. Cameron, their little boy with them.

25th. They dine with us and Lord Lilford sings some very pretty Spanish and Greek songs.

May

1st. It is settled that Lord Lilford & A. go to the New Forest together. Meanwhile Rejlander, the Swedish photographer, has been making photographs of some of us.[16] Lionel's very fine,

[15]Thomas Littleton Powys, 4th Baron Lilford (1833–96), and his first wife, Emma Elizabeth (d. 1884), youngest daughter of Robert William Brandling of Low Gosforth, Northumberland. Lilford was one of the founders of the British Ornithologists' Union (1858) and its president from 1867.

[16]Oscar Gustav Rejlander (1813–75) was a Swedish art photographer.

A.'s profile good. He is still at his work when the gentlemen return from the Forest on the 5th, Kate & Drummond with them. The boys like his Norse tales.

9th. They go by the early [*sic*] & A. & the boys & myself to Osborne. We lunch with Lady Augusta Bruce & afterwards drive with her in the grounds. We see the dairy. Very pretty it is lined with white Dutch tiles with a wreath of convolvulus round & a fountain in the middle, then the kitchen where the princesses amuse themselves with cooking, also lined with white tiles, the little garden, the fort which Prince Arthur has made, the pet donkey that draws the Gun carriage, the Swiss Cottage where they have their Museum and another where they come to tea. Soon after we return Lady Augusta is sent for & she comes to fetch us to the Queen. We wait in the Drawing-room & after a very little time we heard a quiet, shy opening of the door & the Queen came in & I kissed her hand. She shook hands with the boys & made a very low reverence to A. All the Princesses came in by turns. Prince Leopold also. All shook hands very kindly with us all. We had met Prince Alfred before in one of the corridors with Prince Louis of Hesse[17] & he had shaken hands with A. & talked to him.

The Queen's face is beautiful. Not the least like her portraits but small & child-like, full of intelligence & ineffably sweet & of a sad sympathy.

A. was delighted with the breadth & freedom & penetration of her mind. One felt that no false thing could stand before her. We talked of all things in heaven & earth it seemed to me. I never met a Lady with whom I could talk so easily & never felt so little shy with any stranger after the first few minutes.

She laughed heartily at many things that were said but shades of pain & sadness passed over a face that seemed sometimes all one smile. Princess Alice joined pleasantly in the conversation. Prince Leopold & Lady Augusta talked with the boys.

One feels that the Queen is a woman to live and die for.

I am sorry that A. might not have a warm shake of the hand such as the boys & myself had when the Queen retired. I gave Princess Beatrice A.'s poems because she had said to Lady Augusta that she wished A. would write her some "poetries" that she might learn when she was a big girl. A. wrote his name in the book & the Princess's. He & the boys had some tea & Lady Augusta went off with the Queen & Princess Alice to Newport. We saw them from a balcony when they drove away. A

[17] The husband of Princess Alice since July 1, 1862.

footman came to take us on the Terrace. As A. said the grounds looked sad, the hands that had laid them out being gone.

10th. Lord Lilford calls to say good bye.

11th. A Queen's messenger comes with Guizot's translation (made by order) of Prince Albert's speeches & *The Meditations*[18] with an Album of the Queen's in which A. is to write something. He writes "All along the Valley."

Letters from Lady Augusta to us both.

12th. A. finds me with a volume of Goëthe looking for "Edel sei der Mensch"[19] & he reads this & other things to me.

13th. He tells me what Tyndall says of the sun as the fountain of our heat & motion. We see Lady Lilford these days.

18th. On the 18th she goes & Mr. Spring-Rice & Ailene[20] come. Mr. Venables expected but does not arrive.

19th. We are all vaccinated including Ailene. She sings Hayden's beautiful Cazonet of "Good Morrow."

21st. A.'s dear old friend Spring-Rice & his Ailene go to-day. They have had rainy, stormy weather while with us, alas!

22nd. The butterfly which Rogers sent in the chrysalis that A. might see it emerge comes out unperceived. A. fetches me that I may see it. I find it standing on the chrysalis.

25th. Mr. Venables comes.

27th. Mr. Lefroy & Emma & Nanny & Agnes also come & Sir John & Louy Simeon. We have a very pleasant evening.

29th. Mr. Venables goes. Mr. Lefroy & Emma next day.

31st. Lord Somers dines with us and interests us much by his talk of many lands & many things.

Mr. & Mrs. Pike[21] call in the morning. He is United States minister at the Hague.

[18] François Guizot, *Le Prince Albert, Son Caractère, Ses Discours* (Paris, 1863) and idem, *Meditations and Moral Sketches*, translated from the French by J. Butler, marquis of Ormonde (Dublin, 1855).

[19] "Das Göttliche" (written in 1783) was always one of the Tennysons' favorite Goethe poems.

[20] Aileen Spring-Rice was Stephen Spring-Rice's daughter.

[21] James Shepherd Pike (1811–82), the American journalist, diplomat, and author, and his second wife, the former Elizabeth Ellicott.

June

11th. Mr. Moncure Conway[22] comes on a mission from America.

12th. He lunches with us. He interests us. He has released his Father's slaves & tells us that in no instance have they failed, but have uniformly turned out well, working well & making for themselves a good position tho' he could only afford to give them a roof over their heads & a very little to start with. He says that not one of the West Indian islands accepted the Government offer except Antigua & that this is why emancipation has failed in all the other islands, the slaves not having been freed at once as in Antigua. . . .

22nd. The Duke & Duchess of Argyll come. They admire the gardens & the farm. A. reads "Aylmer's Field."

23rd. They go with A. to Hampstead. . . . A. reads "Boädicea" & "The Bugle Song."[23]

24th. The Duke & Duchess with A. & the boys who bring back the Duchess as she cannot go up the Down. The Duke delighted with it. We all sit in the new lawn & then they must go. Very good in them to have come so far for such a little time. The Duke sees a Kestrel fly past with a bird & finds the nest of a golden crested wren in the Arbor Vitae. While they are with us Watts's portrait of me comes. They all say it is a Gainsborough.

25th. A. was to have gone to Little Holland House, breakfasted at Argyll Lodge to-morrow to meet Sir John Lawrence[24] & Mr. Clark but Edmund writes to say that he is coming so A. stays to see him & goes on the 27th. He sees doctors for a gouty affection.

Paget[25] says it only needs patience cure.

[22]Moncure Daniel Conway (1832–1907), the American clergyman and abolitionist. During the Civil War, Conway went to England to lecture on behalf of the Union and remained there as minister to a liberal London congregation until 1884.

[23]"The Bugle Song" ("The splendour falls on castle walls") is a song in *The Princess*.

[24]John Laird Mair Lawrence, 1st Baron Lawrence (1811–79), created baronet, 1858; viceroy of India, 1863–69; created Baron Lawrence of the Punjaub and of Grately, 1869.

[25]Sir James Paget (1814–99), surgeon-general to the queen and the most renowned English pathologist of his day. Paget periodically treated Tennyson for gout, eczema, and other afflictions.

July

11th. Cissy & Lucy come & Edmund walks to meet them.

12th. A. goes to Mr. Palgrave's. Every one most kind to him. The weather sunny & beautiful & Edmund, Cissy say that they enjoy themselves.

23rd, 24th, 25th, 26th. Days of trouble & anxiety & preparation. A. is advised by the doctors not to return home at present. We go to join him in Town & travel with Edmund & Cissy. We stay at Lansdowne Crescent & see A. from time to time.

29th. We meet A. at King's Court & all go to York. It is a great delight to hear him say that the air is sweet to him & at York that he feels much better. We all go to the Cathedral & after luncheon to Harrogate. We go to Knaresborough while there & to Fountains Abbey.[26] How beautiful it is! I heard singing in the dining hall. It seems as if the Monks were there once more. Mr. Eyre Powell, Mr. Jowett & Mr. Lyulph Stanley come to us. The Ingilbys also.[27]

31st. We have a very kind welcome to Ripley Castle.[28] A beautiful place.

September

7th. We have a kind invitation from Lord & Lady de Grey[29] but we do not go. A. is not yet well enough.

[26] A Cistercian house founded in 1132 by monks from St. Mary's Abbey at York, Fountains Abbey is perhaps the most extensive and most picturesque monastic ruin in Europe.

[27] Eyre Burton Powell (1819–1904) was director of public instruction in Madras from 1862 until 1875.

Edward Lyulph Stanley (b. 1839), the third son of Edward John, Baron Stanley of Alderley, was a fellow of Balliol College, Oxford, 1862–69, and an M.P. for Oldham, 1880–85. Stanley supported Jowett in 1863 when he was tried for heresy at Oxford.

The Ingilbys were the family of the Rev. Henry John Ingilby (1790–1870), who took an M.A. at University College, Oxford, in 1816 and was created a baronet in 1866.

[28] Located in Ripley, three and one half miles northwest of Harrogate, Ripley Castle has been the home of the Ingilbys since the fourteenth century. James I stayed at the castle, and Cromwell passed the night there after Marston Moor.

[29] George Frederick Samuel Robinson, Earl De Grey of Wrest, later 1st mar-

10th. The boys have had long walks with Mr. Butterworth & his store of books has been invaluable to us. He sees us off glad indeed are we to go. . . . I advise A. to go straight to Town. I go with the boys to Grasby tho' but for a night. Still we see them all.

11th. They are all up to see us off. A. meets us at the Station. The Cabman in spite of our entreaties would put all the luggage in one Cab. He took us in a wrong direction, made a sudden turn & overturned us. The poor horse was perfectly quiet or we must have been smashed to pieces. A crowd gathered round us. People were very kind. They took out the horse & they lifted up the Cab & we got out having, thank God, escaped with a few scratches & bruises & a shaking.

12th. We drove to Hampstead, found Mother, Aunt Mary Anne,[30] Tilly & Cissy all well.

14th. We set off home & reached it after a good journey. To my great delight & thankfulness, A. is pleased with the alterations I have had made during his absence and immediately orders the completion of my plan. I find a beautiful oak desk, Edmund's birthday gift to me made by Frank's direction & suggested by my Hallam.

16th. Frank & Kate & their baby are also here. The Pollocks, Mrs. Clough & the Coltmans here. We see all from time to time.

We have had earth from the Prince's Bonfire put in the yard that flowers may grow!

October

We have been watching the growth of the Fernery which we are putting just beyond where the great black wooden doors into the yard used to be. The soil is from Headon Hill. A box from Coniston with Stag's Horn moss & grass of Parnassus for which we have asked. We go on with planting different things as usual.

---

quess of Ripon (1827–1909), and his wife, Henrietta Anne Theodosia (1833–1907).

[30] Mary Anne Fytche, Tennyson's maternal aunt. Like her sister, Elizabeth Tennyson, Miss Fytche lived at Rosemount, Hampstead, from 1856 until her death in the winter of 1865.

10th. Mr. Butterworth goes. Miss Perry, Mr. Donne, Mr. & Mrs. King.[31] She very charming. She tells me of the letter she has had from Garibaldi in consequence of her poem on Aspromonte.[32]

17th. The boys go to Colwell Bay to wave a flag as the *Tasmania* passes; William Seaton having left us to be Steward on board. They see two pocket handkerchiefs waving on deck. A. is reading me some of Stanley's *Jewish Church.*[33] A. very successful in mending a broken vase & other things with Underwood's cement. He & the boys & Henry Cameron take me up the down in my little [carriage] & come by the green road, then walk up the steps with Ally which he has made for me.

A. reads some Virgil with me. Hallam enjoys translating his Virgil & Lionel his Horace. They are reading Cave Brown's *Siege of Delhi* which I have just read with great interest & they both enjoy Agnes Strickland in the evening reading. I am happy teaching them.[34] (What a pity this cannot last). Hallam finishes the end book of the *Aeneid.* Lionel likes learning these Odes of Horace.

28th. A. reads me his magnificent sermon in "Aylmer's Field."[35]

November

2nd. A. reads me some of Coleridge's poems.

6th. Some of his (Dry Bones poem).[36]

[31] Miss Perry = unidentified.

Mr. Donne is probably William Bodham Donne (1807–82), the friend of James Spedding, Edward FitzGerald, and John Kemble.

The Kings are Mr. and Mrs. Henry Samuel King of Cornhill. King became Tennyson's publisher in 1873, and Henry S. King and Co. published the *Cabinet Edition* (1874), the *Author's Edition* (1874), *Queen Mary* (1875), and *Harold* (1877). In 1877 King sold his publishing business to C. Kegan Paul.

[32] A mountain ridge of the Southern Apennines, Aspromonte was the scene of a skirmish in 1862 in which Garibaldi was wounded and taken prisoner by troops of Victor Emmanuel II under the command of Pallavicini.

[33] Arthur Stanley, *Lectures on the History of the Jewish Church*, 2 vols. (London, 1863–65).

[34] John Cave-Browne, *The Punjab and Delhi in 1857* (Edinburgh and London, 1861); probably Agnes Strickland's *Tales and Stories from History* (London, 1855), which Hallam Tennyson received for his birthday in 1858.

[35] See "Aylmer's Field," ll. 644–721, 735–97.

[36] Probably "Aylmer's Field."

7th. Some of Edward's Captivity in Poland.[37] Extremely interesting.

8th. We read Manzoni's magnificent ode "Egli fù"[38] & Gladstone's & Goethe's translation. A. walks most mornings with both the boys now & they all take me in my little carriage as usual.

11th & 14th. A. busy with his translation of Homer.[39]

16th. A. shows me his Alcaics.[40]

17th. He helps me with Hallam's lessons because he saw I was so tired yesterday. While we are planting trees we hear almost daily of other people building houses here.[41]

25th. A. reads his "Aylmer's Field" to me which seems to me very beautiful tho' we neither of us much like the story.

26th. Mr. Wilson recommended by Mr. Clark comes.[42] A. reads something from the *Cornhill* to us. They with the boys take me to the Beacon in my little carriage & run all the way from the beacon to the ledge back.

30th. A photograph from Cincinnati of Donaldson's Lotos Eaters comes.[43] A pleasant picture but not A.'s.

December

1st. We hear that Mr. Bradley is very pleased with A.'s "bits of Homer, the only perfect reproduction of the passage," to which A. replies "not perfect."

[37] Henry Sutherland Edwards, *The Polish Captivity*, 2 vols. (London, 1863).

[38] Undoubtedly "Il cinque maggio," first published in 1823.

[39] "Specimen of a Translation of the Iliad in Blank Verse," first published in the *Cornhill Magazine*, December 1863. Tennyson's poem is a translation of the *Iliad* VIII.542–61.

[40] "Milton, Alcaics" was also first published in the *Cornhill Magazine*, December 1863.

[41] Tennyson deeply regreted the loss of privacy through the years as the Freshwater area steadily grew in population. It was partly in order to shut out the unpleasant sight of the new houses around him that the poet constantly worked at planting trees and shrubberies on his Farringford estate.

[42] Henry Dakyns began teaching at Clifton College in September 1863 and was replaced by Mr. Wilson, who tutored the Tennyson boys until late 1864.

[43] Emily is referring to Sir James Donaldson's *Lyra Graeca*.

2nd. Sir John & Lady Simeon dine with us. A. reads his "Northern Farmer" & that wonderful prophecy in the Polish Captivity.

5th. I busy copying out the first word of every line of "Enoch Arden" because A. thinks of sending it to be published for a Christmas book, & he has no other copy, and we fear that this may be lost.

8th. A. reads some of the Cabbala to us.

17th. A. reads to me "Edel sei der Mensch" & other poems of Goethe & FitzGerald's translation of *Omar Khayam*.

21st. A. reads Milton & some of the Bible to us.

22nd. Lady Augusta's wedding day. The boys hoist flags & fire caps in honour. From the Bradleys we have an interesting account of the wedding which was by torchlight in Westminster Abbey & very imposing.

Mr. Palgrave is with us. Mr. & Mrs. Butler[44] in lodgings.

25th. Today we hear of Mr. Thackeray's death.[45] A great shock.

26th. Mr. Allingham[46] comes so we have a pleasant party & A. has good walks with Mr. Bradley & Mr. Butler. One day Mr. Butler brings his big dog Nelson [which] puts his paws round me & fondles my arm & is most affectionate to Lionel.

[44]Henry Montague Butler and his first wife, the former Georgina Isabella Elliot.

[45]Thackeray died on December 24, 1863.

[46]William Allingham (1824–89), the poet, a close friend of the Tennysons and a frequent guest in their homes. Allingham is best remembered for *Day and Night Songs* (1854), for "Lawrence Bloomfield in Ireland" (1864), and for his *Diary* (ed. Helen Allingham and D. Radford, 1908).

1864

January

4th. A. & I call on the Miss Thackerays.[1] Hallam takes me in the little carriage.

13th. Mr. Dakyns arrives. The boys wild with delight tumbling over one another all the afternoon.

17th. A. & I walk thro' Maiden's Croft to Hill Close to see it now that the hedge is thrown down. . . . We like it. We never tire of the fields. . . .

20th. The Bradleys go but Mr. Philpott remains & A. has some walks with him.

February

2nd. A. reads me some of his little poem. A meteor falls & bursts into sparks midway from the zenith just over the wreath of elms.

3rd. A. is writing out his small poems. A letter from the Dean of Windsor[2] saying that the Queen would be very much pleased if A. would write four lines to be put on the statue of the Duchess of Kent in the Frogmore Mausoleum. A. sends four lines.

A letter from Mrs. Bruce[3] saying that beautiful as they are they are not what the Queen wants.

A. sends several forms of lines. The Dean had not explained the Queen's idea. Most gracious & kind thanks from the Queen thro' Mrs. Bruce who tells us that one form is already in the sculptor's hands.[4]

[1] Almost immediately after their father's death, Anne Thackeray and her sister Harriet ("Minnie"; later Mrs. Leslie Stephen) came to Freshwater to live in a cottage provided by Julia Margaret Cameron. Later they rented "The Porch," a small house located in Freshwater Bay which was periodically used as a holiday home by the Thackerays and their friends and relations in the years to come.

[2] Gerald Valerian Wellesley (1809–82), dean of Windsor, 1854 to death; domestic chaplain to the queen, 1849 to death; lord high almoner, 1870 to death.

[3] Katherine M. Bruce, one of the queen's ladies.

[4] According to Sir Charles Tennyson and Hope Dyson in *Dear and Honoured*

7th. A. scrambles with the boys & Mr. Wilson by the cliffs from Watcombe Bay to Freshwater. He reads a sermon to us in the evening.

8th. Goes to town to-day.

10th. A letter telling that he is all safe at Mr. Spedding's rooms.

13th. A letter from A. with "Enoch Arden" printed.

14th. To-day his letter comes with "Aylmer's Field," "Sea Dreams," & "The Grandmother."

March

1st. We all go to meet A. How long it seems since he left me! He interests us all very much in the evening. He shows me his sheets and reads the "Northern Farmer" to Nanny & wants her to stay longer but she must not disappoint the sisters at Bath. Heard & Mr. Wilson look about Aubrey[5] for her.

2nd. A. & I talk about the poems in the evening after Hallam has read one of the leading articles of the day to us.

5th. Plays a little at football.

9th, 10th, 11th, 12th. Mr. Wilson & I play at Backgammon in the evenings with A.

15th. A. laying down turf. Mr. Wilson helps.

16th. Lionel gets up at half past twelve to look at his birthday gifts. He rides with his gifts to different cottages on the down, his cap blows off & frightens Fanny & he is thrown & dragged in the stirrup but not hurt thank God. A grand football match. Many officers & many ladies in the field which looks gay with

Lady (pp. 79–80), the request from the dean of Windsor was received by Tennyson on January 3, 1864, not February 3, as the Journal indicates. The commission must in fact have come in January, since Katherine Bruce's letters concerning Tennyson's first and second attempts are dated January 21 and 27 (*Dear and Honoured Lady*, pp. 79–80). Possibly Emily Tennyson unintentionally set down her January 3 entry under February 3 when she transferred that entry from one of her earlier notebooks into the final Journal. The four lines the queen chose were printed in the *Court Journal*, March 19, 1864, and later in the *Memoir* (II, 17): "Long as the heart beats life within her breast, / Thy child will bless thee, guardian-mother mild, / And far away thy memory will be bless'd / By children of the children of thy child."

[5]Aubrey House.

its flags. Great excitement about the charades. Lionel recites the Thisbe part of one very prettily. Besides ourselves only Mrs. Cameron & the servants as spectators.

18th. Mr. Lawrence comes to make a portrait of A. for some American gentleman.[6]

19th. Mr. Jowett's four friends come to the Terrace.

21st. Mr. Jowett himself comes. I leave his friends at the Football match & go myself to meet him. He takes the proceedings about himself so meekly & sweetly. He says he thinks that the vote is owing to the decree & if so there is ample compensation.[7]

22nd. Mr. Clark comes.

23rd. He & A. go to look at the football match a little.

25th. Mr. White comes.

28th. We are fourteen to luncheon. Mr. & Mrs. Worsley, Mr. Edmund Venables, the son of Mr. Robertson of Brighton, Mr. Simcocks, Mr. Jebb, Mr. Allingham among our guests.[8] Mr.

[6]Samuel Laurence (1812–84), the portrait painter, was a close friend of James Spedding and G. H. Lewes.

[7]At Oxford in early spring 1864, Dr. E. B. Pusey proposed a statute according to which the salary of the Greek professor (Benjamin Jowett) was to be made up to £400 from the University Chest, until such time as other provision should be made. The statute, which reserved judgment on Jowett's theological opinions, was defeated in Convocation on March 8 by a vote of 467 to 395. When Jowett's essay on atonement in his *Epistles of St. Paul* (1855) had been attacked as unorthodox, and again when his contribution to *Essays and Reviews* (1860) had prompted his opponents at Oxford to accuse him of heresy before the vice-chancellor's court, the Tennysons gave him their unflinching support. Throughout his long friendship with the poet and his family Jowett corresponded primarily with Emily Tennyson. And after Tennyson's death he wrote to her, "You have the satisfaction of knowing that you have contributed to that great life in a manner that no one else could . . . and that he has the simple and absolute love of you; and that you have never been for an hour parted in sorrow or in joy" (October 4, 1892, Evelyn Abbott, *The Life and Letters of Benjamin Jowett* [London: John Murray, 1897], II, 457).

[8]The Worsleys = unidentified.

Edmund Venables (1819–95), the antiquary and divine, was curate at Bonchurch, Isle of Wight, 1853–55, and for some years after 1855 he remained there taking pupils. In 1867 Venables became precentor of Lincoln, and he held that position until his death.

The son of Mr. Robertson of Brighton = unidentified.

George Stauton Simcockes was vicar of Hankerton, Wiltshire, from 1855 until 1864.

Richard Claverhouse Jebb (later Sir; 1841–1905), the Greek scholar and

Henry Taylor calls, also Mr. Latham.[9]

29th. Mr. Lawrence goes. Mr. Jowett reads me some of his Plato which of course we like very much. . . .

April

A. & Mr. Wilson planting primroses these days.

[*Page cut*]

5th. We go to Brook to pay our respects to Garibaldi, A. having refused an invitation to dine there. Mrs. Seely takes us into his bedroom.[10] He meets us at the door. A most striking figure in his picturesque white Poncha lined with red, his embroidered red shirt & a coloured tie over it. His face very noble powerful & sweet, his forehead high & square. Altogether he looks one of the great men of our Elizabethan age. His manner simple and kind.

[*Page cut*]

He stroked Hallam's head. We all talked together a little, then Mrs. Seely fetched the boys, myself, & Mr. Wilson away & A. was left alone with him. After dinner Hallam read Garibaldi's Life . . . & A. came in to listen. A very touching life.

[8th. A glorious sunshine to-day. A.T. and the boys planted the flags, two at the front door, the rest opposite the drawing-room window, for Garibaldi had announced his intention of coming. A.T. and I went out to fix a spot where the Wellingtonia should be planted (given A.T. by the Duchess of Sutherland, and raised by her from a cone that had been shot from a tree three hundred feet high in California). Poor Philip Worsley's poems had just arrived—the thought of him dying of consumption mingled strangely with the feeling of the moment and the shouts at the front gate as Garibaldi passed thro'. People on foot and on horseback and in carriages had waited these two hours for him. Some rushed forward to shake hands

---

fellow of Trinity College, was a friend of the Tennysons from the mid-1860s. Jebb was especially devoted to Emily Tennyson, in whom he found "something of the sweet queenliness of a French mistress of the manor of the old *regime*—helped by some quaint felicity in her dress, which would evaporate under male analysis." "If I had to say what is distinctive in her," he wrote, "I should say—the gift of making one feel that goodness, intelligence and good breeding are a Trinity, of which, in her, we can worship the Unity" (*AT*, p. 408).

[9]Mr. Latham is evidently Henry Latham, the vicar and occasional writer.

[10]Garibaldi stayed at the Seelys' home during his visit to the Isle of Wight in the spring of 1864.

with him. He stood up and bowed. A.T. and I and the boys were in the portico, awaiting his arrival. I could not prevail on Mrs. Seely, at whose house Garibaldi was staying, to come in herself, or to allow any one else to come in, for she thought the General and ourselves would be much more comfortable alone. Garibaldi admired the primroses with which the rooms were decked, and liked the view, and said to A.T., "I wish I had your trees in Caprera." A.T. and Garibaldi went up to A.T.'s study together and they talked on politics, and A.T. advised the General not to talk politics in England. They repeated Italian poetry to each other. A.T. said some of Manzoni's *Cinque Maggio*, and Garibaldi repeated and wrote out eleven lines of Ugo Foscolo for A.T. beginning 'Il navigante che veleggio"[11] and signed—to my friend Alfred Tennyson, G. Garibaldi.][12]

[*Page cut*]

a few steps but I would not go to A.'s room thinking that the General would be more at ease without me. A. said he wished that I had gone. Garibaldi repeated Italian poetry & wrote out some lines of Ugo Foscolo for A. & told him that he was his favorite poet. Mr. Wilson rode off with letters which I had forgotten to give to Mrs. Seely.

[We introduced Garibaldi to Sir Henry Taylor and to some of our other friends. It was pleasant to see how his face lighted up when he recognized his old acquaintance Mrs. Franklin (wife of Colonel Franklin[13] stationed here): and he greeted the Colonel warmly too. Mrs. Cameron wanted to photograph Garibaldi, and dropped down on her knees before him, and held up her black hands, covered with chemicals. He evidently thought that she was a beggar and turned away, until we explained who she was.

Then we went to plant the Wellingtonia. A.T. had the large screen made of old *Punches* put up to protect Garibaldi from the cold east wind. Several strangers were there, and when the tree was planted, they gave a shout. "Garibaldi must go now," Mrs. Seely said.][14]

I had committed Pietro[15] to the care of the Housekeeper's

[11] See Ugo Foscolo's "Dei Sepolcri, carme a Ippolito Pindemonte" (1807), ll. 201 ff. "Dei Sepolcri" was Garibaldi's favorite poem.

[12] *Materials*, II, 394–95.

[13] Col. Charles Trigance Franklin (1822–95), of the Royal Artillery.

[14] *Materials*, II, 395–96.

[15] Possibly Pietro Ripari, the surgeon-general who sometimes attended Garibaldi.

room for refreshment but . . . no one could make him understand for he could not speak a word of English. Finally I sent him out with Acott for a walk and tho' one talked English & the other Italian, he seemed well pleased and at the end said "Zoo Zoo" which was supposed to mean "Thank you, Miss." I sat with the Franklins until Mr. Seely arrived as they kindly did not wish to disturb the two so I sent the boys up with coffee and cake & oranges & raisins & when Mr. Seely came we all went up.

[*Page cut*]

He shook hands with all & kissed the boys. We went with him to the door & he bowed & waved. The boys followed him to the Bay where Flags were flying. Hallam raised an Hurrah & the people followed him. He ran after the carriage almost to Afton. Garibaldi got up & waved to him. Our friends soon went after his departure & so ended the memorable afternoon.

[A.T. was charmed with his simplicity but thought that he had the "divine stupidity of a hero" in worldly matters. A.T. also saw Mazzini and was struck with his keen intellectual face, and quoted with approval what he said, "nothing in this world is so contemptible as a literary coterie."

(After Garibaldi left some reckless strangers broke into the grounds and plucked branches off the Wellingtonia and carried them away as souvenirs. Happily the tree recovered.)][16]

Mr. Henry Taylor & Ida & Tina here.[17] We see Mrs. Taylor occasionally. Mr. Allingham here.

14th. Mayall[18] photographs A. & the boys. They take me out in the little carriage day by day on every possible day. Sometimes I ride on the pony, they walking. The Rhododendrons where the big Elm stood splendid, rose red & crimson Anemones in the kitchen garden make it very brilliant. A branch broken from the Garibaldi Wellingtonia & carried away.

19th. We hear that Garibaldi is overdone & returns to Cos & next day we receive from him a copy of Ugo Foscolo's *Poesie*. A. takes me to see the Marsh Marigolds gorgeous in the withy. We have pleasant talks with Mrs. Taylor. She is delighted with the kitchen garden now bright with flowers & well cultivated, the only garden she has seen which reminds her of her Father's. . . . A letter of thanks from Garibaldi. We all wrote to him.

[16] *Materials*, II, 396.

[17] Ida and Tina were daughters of Henry and Theodosia Alice Taylor.

[18] John Edwin Mayall.

23rd. A. & the boys & Mr. Wilson take me up the down. We see the drilling in Easton Field & then go to the upper corner of it & lie by the sea. The first time I have been there since it was ours. Afterwards they take me to the beacon. There is no keeping of Shakespeare's day unless remembering him thankfully is to keep it.[19] A. & the boys take me into the fields or the garden & stay with me under a hedge. A. reads me one day a story from Henry Taylor's note-book which he has been so good as to lend him. He calls & talks about A.'s "Aylmer's Field" which [he] likes much. The Bradleys come. We go to the Pritchards & see their beautiful greenhouse & hot house & the gentlemen go to the Observatory. I do not like to give Mrs. Pritchard the trouble of taking me.

The boys ride or climb trees or bathe & one day A. plays croquet with them & Ida & Tina.

May

The Taylors go & soon after the Bradleys. Hallam makes an appointment with Rogers to show me the beautiful birds & butterflies from Egypt & the interesting things he has brought for us. Our own garden beautiful with blossoms of Fruit trees & flowers, the air of the down delicious, the green of the young leaves lovely among the pines crowned by the Solent. A. & the boys take me to look at all beautiful things & to hear the nightingales. One rainy day when there was not riding or running up, down green slopes or sitting under hedges, A. & the boys fought each other with rolls of newspaper by way of exercise.

9th. Professor Blackie[20] comes. We like the good, kind, mild man. They all go to the Needles together. The Professor sings "The Genie with Crooked Horn" and approves of our new crimson carpet with its silver stars. He leaves us for Ventnor. Archbishop Trench has sent his sermon on Shakespeare which I have read.[21]

[19] Shakespeare was baptized on April 26, 1564; April 23 was perhaps the birthday.

[20] John Stuart Blackie (1809–95), Scottish professor and man of letters. He was professor of Greek at Edinburgh University from 1852 until 1882; among many works in verse and prose, his publications include *Faust . . . Translated into English Verse* (1834) and *Lays and Legends of Ancient Greece* (1857).

[21] Richard Chenevix Trench (1807–86) was a Cambridge Apostle and the close friend of F. D. Maurice, John Sterling, and John Mitchell Kemble, as well as Tennyson. Trench was professor of divinity at King's College, London, from

A. reads me Gladstone's speech on the six pound voters—We are afraid.[22]

Mr. Wilson & Hallam have been so good as to give up their ride that they may help A. & our Lionel to take me to the Beacon so we have tea & dinner kept for them that they may go to the Needles. They clean their own horses afterwards. A. fetches me to hear the Nightingale.

Mr. Warburton[23] & Mr. & Mrs. Garden. It is pleasant to see how much the Gardens enjoy the country. The air is delicious, the sunshine (20th) glorious. Mr. Warburton must go. The rest of the party except Lionel & Hardinge, who return when I return, go on to Brook where A. & Hallam & Mr. Garden splash in the water & enjoy themselves much. The Franklins dine with us and are very pleasant & so passes Louy's[24] birthday.

A. & the boys go again to splash.

24th. The boys put up flags & we have plum pudding in honour of the Queen & of Charlie & Louy. A. & the boys take me up the down. I walk up the steps that were & they race me home in the little carriage down the green road. A. reads some Shakespeare to me.

28th. Mr. Martin Farquhar Tupper calls, gives me a copy of his works, writes his name & mine in it & says that he knows Aunt Franklin.[25] A. & the boys & Mr. Wilson have archery sometimes in Maiden's Croft & I watch them. I see Lionel riding the white pony on the down & he looks a spirit creature.

June

1st. Edmund comes. He has had to cross in a sailing boat because the steamer has run aground. Mr. Allingham comes. All except

---

1846 until 1858; he became dean of Westminster in 1856 and archbishop of Dublin in 1863.

[22] Gladstone's speech was in support of the then pending Bill for the Extension of the Suffrage.

[23] William Warburton (1806–1900), B.D. and D.D., 1853, dean of Elphin from 1848 until 1894.

[24] Louisa Turner.

[25] Martin Tupper (1810–89) is best remembered for his enormously popular *Proverbial Philosophy* (1838), which for twenty-five years sold no fewer than five thousand copies annually in England alone but which also made his name a synonym for contemptible commonplace.

Aunt Franklin was the widow of Sir John Franklin.

myself go with him to Beaulieu & enjoy themselves very much. Hallam wants to stay with me. I will not, of course, hear of it. A. has insisted on my driving in his absence & Hallam also insists. They walk & take me out. A. reads "My Last Duchess" & others of Browning's Poems.

Catherine Rawnsley & Margaret arrive. The beautiful Mary does not come.[26] Her lover Captain Percy Chaplin who had met her five weeks ago at his brother's wedding heard when in Paris that she was to be at a certain ball & rushes home to dance with her & does dance with her. A. says he is glad that there are still some people young.

13th. Presents from the boys & ourselves to our three years old bridesmaid Margaret. . . . Walks and drives on the Down & to Alum Bay. A. stays with me. People stand in the drive staring at us & one gentleman actually in the Portico.

We see the old Shepherd fondling his sheep. They lift up their faces in the prettiest way to him. When I said your sheep are very fond of you, Shepherd, he replied, "Two ladies were on the down & they ran up & kissed me & they said they had never seen such a thing in their lives." A. takes him to mean the ladies which makes the old Shepherd shake with laughter. Mr. Valentine Prinsep comes in the evening and tells us of the intended purchase of Riter's little property. A. goes to Town on business. Dreary work when he goes. Mr. Prinsep goes with him. I have my boys to cheer me & Mr. Wilson is very kind. One day they walk to the Needles with the "Love stories" for which the poor lonely soldiers at the Fort have asked. They say it is so dull there.

25th. To-day A.'s poems are to be all printed.[27] Charlie [supposed to ?] come next day. I do not think I ever remember the air so divinely sweet for so long together as this year.

27th. We go to Aubrey near Lymington which my Father has bought in order to be within easy reach of us. We are delighted with it. Lionel has taken possession of Uncle Charlie's sonnets & says that he must read them to me himself.[28] He likes so much reading them to me & reads them so beautifully that I

[26] Margaret and Mary Rawnsley, daughters of Drummond and Catherine Rawnsley, served as bridesmaids at the Tennysons' wedding.

[27] These were the poems for *Enoch Arden, Etc.*

[28] Charles Turner's 342 sonnets were published by C. Kegan Paul in a collected edition in 1880, the year after Turner's death.

Lady Tennyson with Hallam (left) *and Lionel. Photograph (circa 1864) by W. Jeffrey. (Tennyson Research Centre Collection, Lincoln, courtesy of Lord Tennyson and the Lincolnshire Library Service)*

cannot refuse tho' I get but slowly thro' them in consequence. . . . Mr. Wilson is so kind as to look after our people at Aubrey for me.

July

6th. My A. returns. The boys & I go to meet him. I am very glad that he likes the alterations I have made in the hall. He tells me how eloquent Gladstone was on Monday. The Speaker was so good as to make an exception in A.'s favour & let him in tho' all seats were supposed to be full and the Speaker winked hard at his using opera glass. A privilege Mr. Merivale[29] says "not allowed to ordinary mortals but an honour we pay the Immortal Bard." The opposition too had their joke, seeing him sit on their side they said, "We have the Poet Laureate on our side at all events." A. says that Gladstone's voice trembled when he began speaking & then when he answered Disraeli the whole tide of oratory flowed forth in invective.

9th. Letters from my dearest Father & Louy with good wishes. A. does not like keeping birthdays so I do not tell him or the boys that it is mine. Very pleasant to have our boys & the little Bradleys & Henry Cameron in the Hayfield.[30] We have had on the whole beautiful weather. A. takes me there and all the hay is got in. At the sheep-shearing the Shepherd tells me that the "Old Lady" meaning his wife sat by him an hour two days following a compliment to our skill as doctors. Day by day the same happy outings for me.

12th. A. & Mr. Wilson go across to Aubrey with Nanny & Agnes in a rowing boat.[31] A noble view of five stalwart soldiers rowing. A. & Mr. Wilson bring back a splendid Salmon Peel, Nanny's gift. A letter from a Liberian Negro. Very interesting.

Our kitchen garden rich with the breath of lilies & I do not think that in any spot on earth the air could be sweeter & more

[29] Charles Merivale (1808–93), chaplain to the speaker of the House of Commons, 1863–69; dean of Ely, 1863.

[30] Henry Herschel Hay Cameron ("Punch") was the Charles Camerons' youngest son. Although he intended a career on the stage, Henry Cameron eventually became a professional photographer with a studio in London near Cavendish Square.

[31] The daughter of Charles and Anne Weld, Agnes was to become Tennyson's favorite walking companion during the years when his sons were away at school.

delicate than at the beacon where they take me. We find Mr. Archibald Peel on our return. He recognizes the little pony carriage he chose for us. Mr. Barrett also here. Colonel & Mrs. Franklin dine with us.

17th. The Simeons, Mr. Parlby & Mrs. Franklin. He alas has gone. Louy Simeon says she must see me alone. She tells me that she is going into a convent. This makes me very sad. I tell her that I cannot part from her thus & I beg Sir John to let her stay all night to which he kindly consents. Next day he fetches her & Mr. Wilson bids us farewell. A sad day. I find poor Lionel kneeling by the sofa in the Study fondling Tiny[32] & weeping.

20th. A., Mr. Peel & the boys go out fishing. They take their luncheon with them and come home very bright. Hallam has caught his first fish. They bring a Rock fish with them, a beautiful creature pale green, gold & a little red. A. takes me into Maiden's Croft. We examine a thistledown, teagel flower, beautiful both & the teagel very fragrant, and we gather a lovely bunch of different grapes in the Wilderness.

25th. The Commissioners come to decide the Eastern field question. Our flags up to show how we may be built out of the view for which we have fought so hard and paid so much but the Commissioners are inexorable. Three volumes of Rawlinson[33] arrive from Mr. Wilson. We hear of that most sad event at Yarmouth yesterday evening. Miss T.F. out in a sailing boat with her brother & her lover drowned. She has floated away & cannot be found. The poor lover dived three times. He was taken up by a schooner nearly dead, the brother has also been taken up. It is supposed that she must have been stunned. We are told that they had this morning received her father's consent to their marriage. The body of the poor girl found by a Southampton bargeman just where she had gone down. The Master of the Barge takes her into the little cove near her father's house, lowers his mast & goes to tell the parents.

July. We are busy looking to the furnishings of The Terrace which we have bought to save our view of the sea.

[32] Tiny Cotton.

[33] *Herodotus: The History*, ed. George Rawlinson, assisted by Sir Henry C. Rawlinson and Sir J. G. Wilkinson, 4 vols. (London, 1858–60).

August

We made our farewell calls on our friends in the neighbourhood & set off for Town on the 3rd where we are most hospitably received by Mr. Barrett. We go to Aunt Franklin's & find that she left yesterday for Headingham. Sophy[34] shows us the Japan collection & the Arctic portraits which, of course, interest us much. A. takes the boys to St. Paul's & to the Tower & says that he thinks the Tower the most interesting thing in London. Old Gore Lodge is a place one might live in very happily but we leave it for Hampstead. It is sad to see Mother & Aunt Mary Anne.

6th. We leave for Boulogne. A gentleman, a stranger to us, leaves his daughter in our care & we take charge of her to Boulogne. A beautiful day & a splendid passage & we enjoy ourselves in the paddle box until a sailor tells us we must not stay there it is so dangerous.

Boulogne looks like a painted city. We go to the beautiful Cathedral.[35] A. & the boys go up to the Triforium. The kind concierge puts me where I can watch them for he says that he has a little boy himself. They look like angels passing along. The concierge asks me of what country we are. We are seldom taken for English when on the Continent. It is rather striking to see the Choristers cast their red caps down when they make prostrations. Our coachman takes pleasure in showing us things. A. admires the lights among the trees of the public walk. Our coachman stops before the prisons where prisoners imprisoned for a long time are. It is very touching to hear them singing as we do.

8th. We go to the Windsor Hotel Paris. It is so full that we have to go to the highest story but one. However, we are very well waited on.

Drove to Notre Dame & thro' Luxembourg go to Versailles. I extremely disappointed that the Oeil de Boeuf & Louis XIV apartments are not shown because of the approaching fêtes in honour of the King of Spain. I had set my heart on A. & the boys seeing them. A. admires the Old Red Court. We go over the Trianon.

Another day to the Chapelle Ardente of Louis XVI. It is an

[34] Sophy Cracroft.

[35] Probably the Church of Notre-Dame, a building in the degraded Italian style, erected in 1827–66 on the site of a Gothic church destroyed in 1793.

affecting sight that avenue of tombs of the Swiss Guard. The boys are very much interested in seeing them & the Sarcophagus where the dust of Louis XVI & Marie Antoinette still remains tho' the bodies are removed to Saint Denis.

We then go to see Napoleon's Tomb. The yellow glass make a perpetual Chapelle Ardente. There is a kind of barbarous splendour about the whole. An old solider of Napoleon's opened the carriage door with manners like a king. I said to him you have seen great battles whereupon he showed me his medal with St. Helena on it and when I said jusqu' à la fin tears came into his eyes.

We see immense preparations for the Emperor's fête & A. says stay if you [*sic*] & I feel rather tempted but he does not want to stay, so we go to Chartres. It has been one of my wishes that he should see the Cathedral[36] which I admired so much when there with my father & I am glad that he should see it on our Hallam's birthday & he & Lionel with us. A. gave me a pretty little true lover's knot in green & white before leaving Paris. Lionel gives Hallam a seal and we promise a Shakespeare, the gift he chooses. They go twice again to the Cathedral. Le Mans is our next halting place. We are all charmed by the Cathedral.[37] The jeweled splendour of the windows in the gloom of the high springing pointed arches [*illegible*] by the lower round arches in front.

The Lady Chapel not only with stained windows but with painted pillars & roof. We see the strange block of stone built into the church & supposed to be Druidic, also Notre Dame du Pré & Notre Dame de la Couture. We like Le Mans so much that we are tempted to stay. However we keep our purpose of going on to Angers. We go to the Castle.[38] A young officer courteously tells that we may go in. We are much interested by what remains of this once grand castle. One of the dungeons very sad. Rings still in the walls & the guide tells us also [*illegible*] prisoners' shoulders. We see also a spoon drawn by a poor

[36] The grand Gothic Cathedral of Notre-Dame. Tradition has it that the cathedral is built above a grotto where the Druids celebrated the worship of a "maiden who should bear a child."

[37] One of the noblest French churches, the Cathedral of Le Mans is dedicated to St. Julian, the first bishop of Le Mans. The building consists of two distinct parts which differ widely: the nave of the 11th–12th century, with some modifications in the Transitional style, and the choir and transept rebuilt on an ampler scale after 1217.

[38] The Castle of Angers was once a powerful feudal stronghold and remains one of the most imposing edifices of the kind in existence. It was built in the form of a pentagon and dates chiefly from the thirteenth century.

Vendean while there. We are shown the school where Wellington & Pitt were for a time & the house where Rabelais lived. We see the statues of the Dukes of Anjou, René & others, & then we go to the cathedral.[39]

Our journey to Nantes very pleasant by the banks of the Loire. We see the remains of the true Blue Beard's castle at Champtocé, Gilles de Retz, Sieur of Laval in Charles VII's time, & we pass the pillar St. Florent where the 100,000 Vendeans crossed the Loire after the battle and rout at Cholet, men, women, and children leaving nothing but their smoking homes & their dead behind, such a scene Madame de la Rochejacqueline says as the world must see on the day of Judgment.[40]

At Nantes we find the Cathedral[41] full of peasants in their beautifully starched caps with blue & white banners inscribed to "chaire." A huge image of Mother & Child raised high over the high altar. We see the tomb of the last Duke of Brittany raised to his memory & that of his wife, Marguerite de Foix, by his daughter Anne of Brittany. Very fine it is. Very fine too the Cathedral, rather Egyptian looking. We go to the gloomy Salorges, the driver knows nothing of its awful story.[42] I speak to a soldier-like looking man near and ask him where the bridge of the Noyades is. He says he does not know, thinks it is outside the Town. He comes up to me afterwards & says that "les anciens" have told him of the Salorges but it was a long

[39]René I of Anjou (1409–80) was a French prince who was titular king of Naples from 1435 to 1442 and duke consort of Lorraine from 1431 to 1453 but whose more permanent authority was confined to Bar, Anjou, and Provence.

The Cathedral of St. Maurice, a Romanesque and Gothic building dating from the twelfth and thirteenth centuries, is particularly noted for its stained glass windows, magnificent works of the twelfth, thirteen, and fifteenth centuries, and for a calvary by David d'Angers in a chapel to the left of the nave.

[40]Cholet was the site of a major battle in the War of Vendée, part of the civil war between the royalists and the republicans of which France was the theater from 1792 to 1796.

Marie-Louise-Victoire De Donnissan, marquise De La Rochejaquelein (1772–1857), was the wife of Henri Du Verger, comte De La Rochejaquelein (1772–94), the commander of the Vendean insurgents in the War of Vendée; he was killed on January 28, 1794, not far from Cholet.

[41]The Romanesque Cathedral of St. Pierre. The chief object of interest in the interior of the cathedral is the tomb of François II, last duke of Brittany, and his wife, Marguerite de Foix, an elaborate work in the Renaissance style, executed in 1507 by Michel Colomb.

[42]On December 14, 1793, by the order of Jean-Baptiste Carrier, all the prisoners of La Bouffay prison were taken to the front of the Salorges (the bonding-house for salts) at the far end of the quay of La Fosse, whence they were shipped to the island of Belle Îsle and almost certain death.

time ago. He is very kind, regrets that it is a jour de fête.[43] Says that if we will come again to-morrow, all will be open & he is sure we may go in.

Singing multitudes in the streets. We meet little girls in white with wreaths dressed like brides. Soon after half past ten in the evening, the procession comes in sight. Soldiers on prancing horses first (always a beautiful sight), chanting boys, chanting girls, some in white with white garlands some with red, banners innumerable, chanting men & women, priests in costly robes, cannon firing, trumpets & many other instruments. The great Image of the Mother & Child from the Cathedral. Soldiers on prancing horses bringing up the rear. . . . One of the attendants in the hotel is anxious we should go out to see all the fire-works but we go to bed instead.

Next day we proceed to Vannes, find on the way an official who remembers having seen us at the Rouen station four years ago. We talk to him a long time at Redon & give him half a franc for each of his six children. Before Redon the country is rather dull, there we get a glimpse of a fine old convent & church & the country of heath & rocks & trees & broom very pleasant to us. The hotel at Vannes only tolerable, we are glad to go on to Auray where we find fresher rooms. The same sort of country. A. settles with Joseph to go to the Morbihan. He takes the boys. I not quite well enough to accompany them. They jogged uphill to the old gateway & some Churches. They see a dolmen engraved & a tumulus & poor darlings come in all overheated fearing to frighten me by being late.

18th. We set out for Carnac. One feels excited being so near the fulfillment of the chief object of our journey. We get out of the carriage to look at Dolmens on the road. We like our drive over the wild heath which is here & there still in flower. We gather some [*sic*] & some blue gentians. The view from the Tourbelle de Saint Michel [Tumulus Saint-Michel] very fine & wide & wild, but the Druid stones by no means so prominent a feature as we had expected. Before going there we went to the Inn at Plouharnel & saw the Tongue & the bracelets & the hatchets & the hammers which had been taken from one of the Dolmens that we have seen.

A great deal of low furze all in flower all around. Our stately, kindly hostess took my fancy. Tears came into her eyes while I was speaking. I felt that she had some great sorrow in her heart which looking on "mes anges" she had fain have told me. She

[43] Throughout France, August 15 is a church holiday celebrating the Assumption of the Virgin Mary.

had with her a beautiful hound with loving eyes and a graceful arched neck. She told me that the country was very wholesome & the people on the whole temperate, that the women never took anything but water nor the men neither as a general rule except the sailors. The people live she said on rye bread & boiled millet & curds. But she gives us a very good shoulder of mutton & white bread & butter.

It rains as soon as we get in. We wait & it clears a little but the rain comes on again. . . . We are not prepared for the rain. I cannot go but I give A. my wadded coat & Hallam who has his own overcoat my parasol. They are of course much interested by what they see but A. says it is "not nearly so fine as Stonehenge."[44] Our coachman is very good-natured in driving us as near as he can. I ask him whether the old songs about King Arthur are sung now. Not now he said—such things used to be sung but people are too wise now to sing forbidden things.

19th. We drive to Locmariaquer. It is very cold but we all love the wild heath. A. and the boys go to the Mayor's, buy books, pay the fees & get a guide to the newly discovered Dolmen. All the treasures found in it have been transported to the Museum at Vannes which for such things, they say, stands alone in the world. What a pity we did not find out this when we were there!

The engraved entrance stone is very curious & interesting, so is the great fallen Menhir broken in three pieces & the Table des Marchands & the Dolmen of Caesar some of the stones of which are engraved. Our wild looking guide whom we brought with us from the Inn helped the boys to go up it & come down. We ascended a height for the view. Viewed lights over the sea & the little ports came out here & there very brightly & we saw many tumuli on the island of the Morbihan. They showed me Gavr'inis & altogether the scene was very impressive & I am glad to have seen it. Hallam took his Father's place outside in returning, the coachman expressed his fear of the cold for the "Petit." However, the "Petit" managed to talk to him & to understand him.

20th. We come to Quimper. The country more wooded, streams here & there with rather steep wooded banks. . . . We see several of the old Breton dresses in the market. The long hair & the blue dresses & embroidered shirts & trunk hose. We go to

[44]Tennyson and Hallam viewed the prehistoric Alignements of Carnac, 3,000-odd standing stones arranged in the form of a quincunx, on the moor half a mile north of the town.

the Cathedral.[45] A man praying in a white woollen dress & long hair makes a beautiful picture as Hallam says.

21st. We spent a quiet Sunday. I walk up to the old walls with A. & the boys & they have other little walks alone about the town & on the fine wooded heights opposite our hôtel de l'Epée. Next day we leave at nine in a little close carriage for Morlaix. A fine country, well wooded with a great deal of Bracken & more Broom than we have ever seen in our whole life before almost. We lunch at Pleyben. We go to the church & admire the fine Calvaire on a great Archway of meeting arches at the entrance of the churchyard.[46] The Church is the keel of a boat, each beam ending in a fish's head, all the beams painted with small rows & squares in red white & green, I think.

The effect is very good. There are many skulls sculptured in white on a black ground & what looks like a black & white marble coffin with death's heads about it & candlesticks.

The pleasant Bonne said to us of course you would have understood me better if I had spoken Welsh. It had been raining all the morning a little & soon it came down in torrents, so a drive over the savage moorland with its bowery lanes at the entrance was continued, heath, jagged rocks crowning the heights. . . . At last our good driver & his willing horses brought us safely to the Hôtel de France.[47] The rain continues all night & the next day, the day after we go to Guingamp. At first the road wound round hills as it did from Quimper to Morlaix but hills not so high & wild, then over wide hills thro' a well-wooded country. Our driver told us that there are many wolves in the woods. At Guingamp to the Church, & to Notre Dame de Grâce.[48] The Church looked like some strange dream so little was there of any perceptible plan. Next day we drive to Lannion to see King Arthur's country, the road dull. One great convent half way & there was a kind of romance about the road as we approached Lannion. The Hôtel de L'Europe excellent,

[45]The Cathedral of St. Corentin (13th–15th cent.), one of the finest Gothic edifices in Brittany.

[46]Like so many Breton villages, Pleyben is remarkable for its church, a Gothic building with a curious calvary resembling that at Plougastel.

[47]Emily Tennyson probably meant the Hôtel de l'Europe, which she mistakenly places in Lannion (see below). *Baedeker's Northern France* (1905) lists no Hôtel de France in Morlaix.

[48]Guingamp is noted for its church of Notre-Dame-de-Bon-Secours (13th–16th cent.), one of the chief pilgrim resorts in Brittany. The Gothic chapel at Grâces, one and one-fourth miles to the west, dates from 1507–21.

the salle hung with Gobelin Tapestry. The story of Alexander. We drove to Keldthuen but the family was at home & finding that it was not generally shown we did not like to intrude tho' the servant said he thought we might go in.[49] The place which looked like the remains of King Arthur's palace only a Château of perhaps 150 years old partly surrounded by a moat and standing in a [*illegible*] wooded ground. After leaving it we saw what our coachman said was the Isle of Avalon but we thought it was probably the Isle Domet.

We found none of the great rocks & wild coast which we had been led to expect at Péran only some rocky islands near the shore. The hostess some way found out who A. was & wished us to stay that we might see the other part of the coast which she said was much finer. I told her that A. had written about their roi Arthur.

We ought to have come by the coast road from Morlaix it seems but we did not know that there was such a road & now we were afraid of running short of money before we reached Avranches.

At St. Brieuc we found a Conseil General proceeding so we could not have any of the good bedrooms but the hostess & her daughter kindly gave up their own pretty sitting room to us & the daughter said that if there were anything there which would give us pleasure she hoped we would use it. Next morning the hostess gave Lionel some cakes. Fine country again, hills & woods. We passed Broons where Du Guesclin[50] was born. A beautiful view when St. Michel first came in sight the sea crowning an immense stretch of woodland.[51] At Dinan the old gateway very fine & while we were looking about for Du Guesclin's a man in a blouse came up to us & asked if we wanted a carriage, "Yes a calèche for Avranches to-morrow." He & his Bourgeoise took us to their stables by the rampart & he said to her, "Ma fille show the lady & gentlemen all that is most [*illegible*] that will be a little walk for thee." She held up my train coming down the steep & took us to the English Church. The simple service was impressive in this land. The carriage we had ordered was ready & our Bonne Bourgeoise drove with us to the rampart & showed us the splendid view

[49] The Tennysons went to Lannion principally to see Keldthuen, where, according to Breton legend, King Arthur held his court.

[50] Bertrand Du Guesclin (1315 or 1320–80), the popular French soldier and high constable under Charles V.

[51] Mont-St.-Michel is a village which clings to a curiously isolated rock, rising 160 feet above the "Grève," or sands, at the end of the bay of the same name.

over the castle & the bridges.[52] A. & the boys went down the castle mound over the bridge & great was the excitement among some French boys smoking their cigars. "Le petit ne Viendra pas" "Mais le voilà qui vient." Then we went to the Cathedral[53] & saw the place where Du Guesclin's heart was buried.

At Combourg we just saw the great salle & the salle à manager & the salle des Oiseaux where birds are painted in shields on the ceiling & there is rather a fine old chimney piece. We saw also the rooms where Chateaubriand slept & studied.[54] Very little rooms. A weary afternoon, we had continually to intercede for one poor horse which the driver beat unmercifully so at last we slept [at] Pontorson. I too tired to go over St. Michel myself but I begged that we might drive there & very glad I was that A. & the boys saw what interested them so much ascending the Mount while I rested below. The kind driver went gently over the rough road crossing sands of the approach. The view from the hill near Avranches very fine. An immense stretch of wooded country with water winding thro'. Mount St. Michel grand & dark [in] the distance.

September

1st. We go to the beautiful Vire & see the model of the Cathedral which once stood on that glorious site. We see also the poor little remains left by the Revolution. One of them the stone where Henry II knelt to receive Absolution from the Pope after the murder of Becket.

We go for some distance along a fine wooded hill & then up & down fine wooded hills to St. Loo with many apple trees, finely situated on a rock.[55] We meet in the train to Caen a pleasant French lady who tells us of the great quantity of butter

[52]The fourteenth century Dinan castle, now a prison, is noted for its *donjon*, 112 feet in height.

[53]Tbe church of St. Sauveur, the right side of which is Romanesque, the left Gothic. A stone in the north transept marks the spot where the heart of Guesclin is buried.

[54]The Tennysons visited the château (14th–15th cent.) belonging to the Chateaubriand family, in which the famous author spent part of his childhood.

[55]A very ancient place and the chief town of the department of the Manche, St.-Lô is situated on a slope on the right bank of the Vire about thirty miles from Coutances.

made in the country, that sent to the Tuileries from cream of the first night, that for other people from the cream which rises after. The cattle have very few roots & only beef-root when they have any.

The Bayeaux tapestry[56] extremely interesting. It gives one a feeling of perfect truthfulness. The horses very spirited many of them. The houses great & small with the rounded arches such as we saw in Brittany. The object of the piece seemed to us the justification of William. A good wife's deed. The Cathedral very fine—A. is, I hope, glad to have been here.[57]

3rd. Caen. We are delighted with the Cathedral St. Pierre & with the Abbaye aux Hommes & the aux Femmes.[58] This last we agree looks just like the wife of the other, the same rounded arches but smaller. We stay a long time in the Abbaye aux Hommes, the music extremely beautiful. The voices so sweet I wish the Queen could hear it & see the church so noble & simple. The thought so solemn that the office has been going on ever since the death of William, however mistaken we may deem it. The Beadle (an enormous man & very courteous) took us to see the portrait of William & is reproved by the priests. We beg him not to let us intrude but he says that it is no intrusion. After "office" is finished he shows us the slab over William's tomb & we hear the sweet voices of girls sounding angel-like while we look. The Nuns asked of the boys are they English? & with a longing tone are they Catholics? & I seemed to see a shudder come over them when I said "No."

We go to Honfleur & find that no boat is crossing because of the tide.

[56]The 230-foot-long Bayeux tapestry illustrating the events that led to the conquest of England by William in 1066. A favorite opinion of the origin of the tapestry ascribes it to Matilda, wife of the Conqueror.

[57]The Cathedral of Notre-Dame is a striking Gothic building of the 12th–15th centuries, built on the site of an earlier church founded in the 11th century by Bishop Odo of Bayeux, half brother of William the Conqueror.

[58]Dating from various epochs from the thirteenth to the sixteenth centuries, the Cathedral of St. Pierre is remarkable for its Tower (255 ft.), to the right of the main portal, a masterpiece of the bold and graceful style of the early fourteenth century. La Trinité, the church of the Abbaye-aux-Dames, was founded in 1066 by Matilda, wife of William the Conqueror, while William at the same time founded St. Etienne, the church of the Abbaye-aux-Hommes. Matilda and the Conqueror undertook the establishment of the two churches as an expiation of the sin they had committed in marrying within the forbidden degrees of consanguinity.

6th. To Rouen by boat. This very same voyage made by A. with Arthur Hallam. We go to beautiful St. Ouen[59] & A. & Hallam to the Musée d'Antiquités which interests them much.

We go to Dieppe. We find that there are no beds in the boat only sofas. A. objects to this & [*illegible*] dreads the night for me so we stay at the Hotel & cross next day, the Waves washing over us, but we all prefer this to the cabin. The boys positively enjoy it in spite of the drenching & A. is an excellent sailor. He sends Lionel & me to bed between the blankets at the Hotel.

9th. A pleasant journey home. We cross by Ryde. The sea rough but green & beautiful. Right glad are we to get home. Everything looks clean inside and beautiful outside. We go all of us to look at the new rooms in the Gould Cottage & to call on Shepherd Paul's wife & A. takes me over the Park. The Camerons, Pollocks, Croziers, Mrs. Franklin, Mr. Isaacson, The Dean of Chichester, Enid Guest, Mrs. Dulane, Mr. Allingham call, also Sir John & Lady Simeon & to our surprise Louy with them. She has not been able to bear the Convent life.

22nd. Aunt Franklin & Sophy Cracroft arrive. They have had to sleep at Lymington. Lady Charlotte Schreiber, Enid & Blanche Guest, & Mrs. Alderson call. We walk about the grounds with Aunt Franklin & in the evening A. reads her "The Grandmother" which is a great favourite of hers & she of his. He says she is charming, so clever yet so gentle & such a lady.

Next day she & Sophy leave. We cannot go with them to Portsmouth tho' we are all invited by Sir Sherard Osborne to see the "Royal Sovereign."[60] Lady Charlotte & Mr. Schreiber come to say goodbye. A. reads "The Farmer"[61] to them.

The day after Col. & Mrs. Franklin & Mr. & Mrs. Frederick Pollock. Mr. & Mrs. Dulane, Enid & Blanche Guest, Mr. Cameron & Ewen[62] & Mr. Neil in the evening.

[59] Most of the Gothic church of St.-Ouen was built in 1318–39 by Alexander Berneval. Particularly notable features are the south Portail des Marmousets, so called from the heads with which it is adorned, and the statue of St.-Ouen, archbishop of Rouen, which crowns the portal.

[60] Sherard Osborn (1822–75), the rear admiral and author. Osborn commanded the *Vesuvius* in the Black Sea, 1855; commanded the *Furious* in the Chinese War, 1857; and was managing director of the Telegraph Construction and Maintenance Company, 1867–71. In 1865 Osborn published the *Last Voyage and Fate of Sir John Franklin.*

[61] "Northern Farmer: Old Style."

[62] Ewen Cameron was one of the Charles Camerons' older children. In 1862

Our Charlie & Louy arrive. They have crossed in a boat & walked from the Fort & soldiers bring their luggage. Franklin Lushington & Kate & their children come to-morrow.[63]

The day after Frank lunches with us. Sir John & Lady Simeon & Louy dine. Charles & our Louy much pleased with them & they with the Simeons.

We all go to lunch at Swainston & A. & I like the alterations they have made. We call at the Seelys, & see their orchard house & they give us grapes & a golden pippin rather sacred fruits with me for I have seen the old kind in Berkshire held by my Father as best of apples.

Mayall comes to photograph. Lady Charlotte, Mr. Schreiber, & Constance Guest came to stay with us, & there are walks on the down & then to Brook & Donkey Taredowns & more sober drives. Col. & Mrs. Franklin come to say goodbye. We are sorry to part from them.

30th. Day of days to me. My Father comes, but he is very tired. The Schreibers go. Poor Lady Charlotte has not recovered the death of her son Augustus. Constance stays with us.

October

1st. My Father & Charlie & Louy go. It seems like some [*illegible*] dream that they have been here. Before they go Mr. Cameron & Sir Henry Taylor call & he carries off my Father to photograph him. Mr. Worsely & his brother have arrived on the place. One feels a great interest in them. Poor Mr. Worsley is so very ill. . . . At Mr. Dulane's earnest entreaty made to A. thro' me he reads "Guinevere" to them in the evening. Mr. Macmillan & Mr. Allingham & Mr. & Mrs. Prinsep & Mr. Watts who have come to look at their newly purchased fields.[64]

Mr. Lear arrives. A most beautiful day & he is charmed & makes a sketch on the South side. We see the Worsleys from

---

Henry Taylor described Ewen as "the most agreeable of youths, gay, easy, and sweet-tempered, with a good word for every man, woman, girl, baby, or dog" (*Autobiography of Henry Taylor* [New York: Harper & Brothers, 1885], II, 162).

[63] The Franklin Lushingtons' children were Henry, Gertrude, and Mildred.

[64] Although they purchased the land in 1864, it was not until a full decade later that the Henry Thoby Prinseps and G. F. Watts abandoned Little Holland House and moved into "The Briary," their new home adjoining the Farringford estate.

time to time & one day Mr. Philip & the boys pelt each other with chestnuts which looks as if he were better. A. & they all call on the Shepherd who has been. It is very pleasant to see Mr. Lear so well & cheerful. He interests A. & me much by his talk of Crete & other countries & other things. Very busy planning the "Selections" for the People.[65] Mr. Payne is here.[66]

Among the various walks & drives & games A. has a game at football with the boys. . . .

31st. Another game to-day after A. & Frank have looked about a site for the new coach house.

November

Baron Bernhard Von Tauchnitz comes.[67] Pleasant & unpretending.

A. reads to me Allingham's Ballads.[68]

8th. He writes his little dedication for the *Selections.*

11th. Mr. Lipscombe comes & next [day] Mr. Wilson leaves us.[69]

[65] In 1865 Edward Moxon published a one-volume selection from Tennyson's poetry entitled *A Selection from the Works of Alfred Tennyson* (Moxon's Miniature Poets Edition).

[66] J. Bertrand Payne was a longtime employee of Moxon and Company. In the spring of 1868 the Tennysons became highly irritated with Payne because of what they considered his extravagant and flamboyant plans for advertising the proposed edition of the laureate's collected works. In all likelihood dissatisfaction with Payne influenced Tennyson's ultimate rejection of that proposed Moxon edition. In 1869 Payne again distressed the Tennysons when he sanctioned the inclusion of Tennyson's privately printed "The Window" in D. Barron Brightwell's *A Concordance to the Entire Works of Tennyson* (London, 1869), which Moxon's published without Tennyson's knowledge.

[67] Christian Bernhard, baron von Tauchnitz was founder of the Tauchnitz publishing firm, which made its name chiefly through the *Collection of British and American Authors*, a series introduced in 1841. The inexpensive "Tauchnitz Edition" of Tennyson (1860) was particularly popular in Germany and among English travelers on the Continent. Tennyson made what he termed "rather a bad bargain" with Tauchnitz, and when in 1868 the baron offered him an increased royalty, he gratefully accepted (Tennyson to Tauchnitz, April 29, 1868, *Memoir*, II, 54).

[68] In 1864 William Allingham edited *The Ballad Book* for the *Golden Treasury* series.

[69] Lipscombe was the tutor for Hallam and Lionel Tennyson from late 1864 until shortly before they left home to attend C. Kegan Paul's school in May 1865.

He has [been] most kind to all & is most anxious to do everything possible for the boys & we are very sorry to lose him.

Busy days about the *Selections*.

16th. Mrs. Cameron comes to hear "The Captain."[70] We send it to be published.

A. has another game of football with the boys. He goes to Town. Poor Lionel has had a bad fall jumping. I bandage him & sleep in his room. He is very tired going only to Grover's to see the cider made! Five hogsheads we have it seems. Thankful indeed am I when the Doctor says that there is no displacement in the arm. A letter every day from my A.

We go to Aubrey. Delighted to find Father so comfortable & happy in his new home. All in it very pretty. The drawing room lovely. C.R.W.[71] hoists his Flag to welcome us. All most loving in their care. Crossing to obey A. I went down to the Cabin. Mr. Pritchard[72] came to me & told me of the work he has in hand making the object glass for his telescope, a work of trade not of art generally.

December

1st. The air delicious & delicate. We meet Mr. Eliot Yorke[73] on our return.

3rd. A. arrives rather hoarse but very cheerful tho' with a bad head-ache.

5th. We go to the belt to see if anything can be done to hide Spencer's hideous house. Afterwards we look at the mound being reared to hide the new stables.

A kind letter from Mrs. Gilchrist asking us to stay with her when we go to see "The Jumps."[74] I liked the country so much

[70] "The Captain: A Legend of the Navy," first published in *A Selection from the Works of Alfred Tennyson* (1865).

[71] Charles Richard Weld.

[72] Charles Pritchard (1808–93), the astronomer. Pritchard became Savilian professor of astronomy at Oxford in 1870. He joined the Royal Astronomical Society in 1849 and was chosen president in 1866.

[73] Eliot Thomas Yorke (1805–85), the prominent barrister. Yorke was M. P. for Cambridgeshire from 1835 until 1865, and he served as chairman of the Cambridgeshire quarter sessions from 1839 until 1873.

[74] The widow of Blake's biographer and a close friend of the Carlyles, Mrs. Alexander Gilchrist did entertain the Tennysons in the fall of 1866 when they

when living with my father at Hale that I think A. will like it too for a second home.

We go to the belt to see how we can block out the dreadful red houses.[75]

The *Selections* both in its plain & ornamented form came. We much prefer the plain but decide on the other not to disappoint the Publishers who have set their heart on it.

Mr. Bird[76] comes about the railways & is glad to get A.'s vote against them. The Bradleys arrive. Mr. Bradley & A. have a game at football with Arthur Bradley,[77] Mr. Lipscombe, & our boys.

28th. Mr. Jowett comes.[78] The boys rush out as usual with the greatest glee to meet him & as usual the chessboard is brought out at once. Mr. Jowett says that Hallam is very much improved in chess & plays a real game now. The Worsleys come & Mr. Butler.

A. reads the "Cinque Maggio" & his translation of "Achilles over the Trench."[79]

Mr. Jowett & A. play at football with the boys & Mr. Lipscombe. Mr. & Mrs. Bradley & Mr. & Mrs. Butler dine with us. Poor Mr. Bradley is very unwell from a chill after his football. The [Wednesday?] of walks & football & chess & poor little Lionel tormented by chessmen spearing his eyes.

---

finally visited the "Devil's Jumps," Haslemere, where they had heard of a possible site for a summer home.

[75] As early as January 1860 Emily Tennyson had complained of the "ugly brick houses" that had begun to block the view from Farringford to the sea (Lady Tennyson to Frederick Goddard Tuckerman, January 12, 1860, *Letters of E. T.*, p. 146).

[76] Henry Edward Bird (1830–1908), the famous chess player. Bird wrote an *Analysis of Railways in the United Kingdom* (1868), and he devoted much attention to railway finance and management. In 1868 he gave evidence before the parliamentary committee on amalgamations of home railways, and he framed the statistical tables that still govern the Great Eastern Railway.

[77] A son of the George Granville Bradleys.

[78] Jowett was a regular Christmas guest at Farringford for nearly forty years.

[79] First published in the *Nineteenth Century*, August 1877.

1865

January

5th. Mr. Jowett goes. We are all very sorry. He has been particularly delightful this time & he seems better, his throat stronger but he acknowledged that he overworks his brain. The *Selections* come while Mr. & Mrs. Bradley & Mr. & Mrs. Butler are dining with us. Mrs. Cameron comes & puts photographs on the stair-case wall.

Mr. Philip Worsley & his good Canadian brother, who gave up bright prospects in Canada to come & help him when he became so ill, [are] here.

A. writes to Debrett to contradict the rumour about the baronetcy saying it is wholly unfounded.[1] We fear that the Queen may have heard it & been annoyed & we would not for the world that this should be, H.M. has been so good to us.

18th. A. & I go to see the servants' room decorated for their bath. The long wished for people's number comes to-day. Mr. Allingham & Mr. Philpott here in addition to our other friends.

Mr. Pritchard dines with us [*illegible*]. Mr. Bradley last night. We are always sorry when this ceases. The Worsleys go also.

February

I am reading St. Augustine's *Confessions* & some of Renan's things[2] A. takes me to see the planting of Crimson Rhododendrons in front of the Anteroom & study windows.

The Pollocks come with Mrs. Cameron. Charles Weld arrives & interests me much by reading the introduction of his lecture about Rome[3] & telling us of the under church of St. Clement & other things.

[1]Tennyson had recently been approached, through Frederick Locker (later Locker-Lampson), Lady Augusta Bruce's brother-in-law, on the possibility of a baronetcy being conferred on him. Emily Tennyson strongly opposed the idea, and after some indecision the laureate indicated that he would not feel able to accept the honor. Debrett's *Peerage of England, Scotland, and Ireland* was first published in 1802.

[2]Joseph Ernest Renan (1823–92) is best known as the author of the series *Histoire des origines du christianisme* (1863–83).

[3]Charles Weld, *Last Winter in Rome* (London, 1865).

I have been reading some Scherer.[4] Cold comfortless reading these Renans & Scherers tho' Scherer seems to me clear & powerful.

A. & Hallam saw up trees. I dare not [let] Lionel go to them much as he wishes to help. It is so cold.

16th. We write to-day agreeing to buy Mr. Plumbley's land. A letter from the Duke of Argyll asking in the kindest way if he may propose A. for "The Club."[5] Mr. Bulfinch sends A. his legends of Charlemagne[6] which enchant Hallam. They bring me snowdrops & violets. Lovely spring-like morning.

21st. News of Mother's illness.

22nd. Worse news to-day. A. goes by the four o'clock boat, the boys & Mr. Lipscombe with him to Yarmouth.

Next day I learn that my A. was too late.[7] This will be a great shock to him. A few sad lines from him to-day. There could not have been a more graceful end. On Tuesday morning she gave one sigh and was at rest. We send snowdrops & myrtle to be put in the coffin. Some of the snowdrops from the boys' gardens. They go to Cowes to be measured for mourning suits. As Grandpapa says it is sad that this first change in their dress should be for mourning.

The Tailor fits out many for Eton & Harrow but he says that they are the tallest of their age he has measured, & Hallam the broadest but both are broad. They ought to be. Both their grandfathers about six feet two & their Father six feet.

24th. Our Mother's funeral day. By a touching chance Lionel put snowdrops into the tall glass she gave us when we were married. I look upon snowdrops as especially her flower. This year the snowdrops are sweet, other years I have only smelt them fresh. A solemn gathering of the Family. One feels a feeling that it is some high & holy bridal. The view has its most spiritual lights.

[4]Undoubtedly some work by Edmond Henri Adolphe Sherer, perhaps *Mélanges d'Histoire religieuse* (Paris, 1864).

[5]The celebrated club founded by Johnson, Reynolds, Gibbon, Burke, Langton, Beauclerk, and Goldsmith in 1764. In Tennyson's day "The Club" consisted of thirty-five members, most of them distinguished in the literary world, the church, the law, or politics, who met to dine once in every fortnight during the session of Parliament.

[6]Thomas Bulfinch, *Legends of Charlemagne* (Boston, 1864).

[7]Apparently Mrs. Elizabeth Tennyson died on February 21, 1865, before Tennyson even left for London.

28th. Two letters to-day from my A. One before one after the funeral. He says that they all hate the pompous funeral & feel that they ought rather to go in white & gold so blessed a being was she.

March

1st. I drive out for the first time to meet my Ally. He looks sad & worn but not ill. Mr. Allingham has crossed with him.

4th. Frederic comes before breakfast looking young & well. The next morning he talks Swedenborgianism to me all the morning. Mr. Woolner has been here some days.

6th. Frederick says he must leave us to see Guilio who has arrived some days ago for his fortnight's leave. I am sorry that Mr. Woolner must go. His bright spirits cheer A. His stories of life are wonderful, so vivid & dramatic.

Two wagon loads of trees arrive for the bank but there is snow. Next day however all are planted.

11th. To-day we hear that yesterday at one o'clock in the morning our dear Aunt Mary Anne followed her sister.

14th. Her funeral day. We sent daffodils & Laurustinus yesterday. My A. brings me violets.

16th. The great Battledore & Shuttlecock games begin. The battledore & shuttlecock Mrs. Cameron's gift to our Lionel on his birthday. A. likes the game & plays sometimes.

We hear from Mr. Estcourt that the threatened railway with a terminal at the Bay is to be stopt at Hook Hill or Pound Green. Not welcome to us even then.

Day by day we have a little snow. Sir Alexander & Lady Grant return. Delightful to see them again. This year the Daffodils have quite short stems. They cannot get up out of the ground.

When Sir Alexander & A. return from one of their walks on the Down they find Mr. Jowett has arrived & on his shaking hands with Sir Alexander A. says, "East & West shake hands."

The Grants go after a very short stay at Afton but we have Mr. Jowett & his friends at the Terrace & cannot but enjoy our frequent intercourse.

Mr. Allingham arrives & gives A. his book.[8]

[Photographs of great Wellingtonias in California have been

[8] William Allingham, *Fifty Modern Poems* (London, 1865).

sent A.T. by Captain Fearn,[9] also photographs of various objects found in the lake dwellings.

About Mrs. Marsden, who was staying here, A.T. recalled the story of how through his mesmerism before her marriage she had recovered her health. He and my mother were staying at Malvern,[10] Dr. Marsden was attending my mother and said to my father, "Instead of paying me my fee, I wish you would grant me a favour. Come and mesmerize a young lady who is very ill." My father said, "I can't mesmerize, I never mesmerized any one in my life." But the doctor would take no refusal and said, "Pooh! look at your powerful frame!" So he mesmerized her according to the doctor's instructions. The first day it took him about an hour to send her to sleep; afterwards only a few seconds. Once she had a pain over her eye and the doctor said, "Breath upon her eye!" My father did so, then begged her pardon, saying that he had forgotten he had been smoking. Dr. Marsden said, "She cannot hear you, that one breath has sent her off into the deepest of slumbers." In a little while the lady grew better and my father and mother moved to Cheltenham. A week or two afterwards he returned to Malvern for a few hours, but had not thought of telling anyone that he was coming. He met Marsden in the street, who then went and told the lady. Before the doctor had said more to her than "I have good news for you;" the lady said, "I know what you have come to tell me. I have felt Mr. Tennyson here for half an hour." This lady eventually married Dr. Marsden.][11]

April

1st. Our dear good Andrews says she thinks that her health will not allow her to stay. Bad news for us. I had not courage to tell A. yesterday but I have told him to-day. He & the boys take me to see the lambs.

Tilly & Horatio come, too. Mr. Allingham & Anne Thackeray, the Prinseps, & Mr. Watts arrive. The boys go to Mr.

[9] J. Eaton Fearn, author of *Modern Photography for Amateurs* (London, 1890). Wellingtonia is the popular name in England for *Sequoia gigantea*.

[10] During the spring of 1852 the Tennysons spent some time with John Rashdall at his Malvern vicarage. Emily Tennyson was pregnant with Hallam at the time.

[11] *Materials*, III, 10–11. Obviously Hallam Tennyson has recast this portion of his mother's Journal, setting down her entry in the third person and narrating from his own perspective.

Watts on the 10th & we hear that there is a good beginning of their portraits tho' poor Lionel nearly faints, he is so overdone with yesterday's jumping. Hallam sits up at Mr. Lipscombe's. . . .

A pleasant evening for us at all events. The widening of the Lawn is completed. A. takes me out to give my opinion about it in my little carriage.

Yesterday while we were there looking at the trees which are coming now for this, the last load having already arrived for the bank, an Italian solider came to us who said that he had been Master of Frederick's children in Florence. He had deserted rather [than] serve against Garibaldi but that the King had now pardoned him & he wanted to return to Italy. Poor man he lost his Father & two brothers in the war & himself an eye & all his wordly goods. We brought him into the Study & gave him food & did what we could for him in other ways.

Horatio I think takes interest in our tree planting. He looks better & it shocked me to see him when he came to us quite hollow chested & hollow cheeked & with a short cough overworn by district visiting & Bible reading. . . .

13th. The men work very late at the trees. The beautiful photographs of the Wellingtonias sent by Captain Fearn arrived today. Mr. Lee & his son call & then come to tea & bring us photographs of things found in Lake buildings. A. takes me to look at the transplanting of the trees.

Dean Liddell, Mr. Wilson, Mr. Watts call & afterward Miss Thackeray & her cousin St. John & Mr. Paul lunch & go with A. & Mr. Lipscombe to Brook.[12] A. very merry.

25th. Horatio & Matilda go. No two nobler or better ever came or went.

Small-pox in the village. Vaccination of the household. The doctor says that the boys must not go to Church, people in the village are so reckless about infection. One man on being reproved for going from house to house while still infectious said

[12]Henry George Liddell (1811–98) was domestic chaplain to Prince Albert from 1846 until the prince's death; vice chancellor of Oxford, 1870–74; professor of ancient history at the Royal Academy, 1882 until his death; and compiler, with Robert Scott, of *Liddell and Scott's Greek-English Lexicon.*

C. Kegan Paul (1828–1902), the author and publisher, became vicar of an Eton living at Sturminster Marshall, Dorsetshire, in 1862, and for some years while there he took pupils. He took over Henry Samuel King's publishing business in 1877 and inaugurated the house of C. Kegan Paul and Co. Paul thus succeeded King as Tennyson's publisher. Hallam and Lionel Tennyson became Paul's private pupils in May 1864. The following May, Hallam enrolled at Marlborough College, but Lionel remained with Paul until 1868.

someone gave it to me why should not I give it to someone or something to this effect.

In addition to friends & an acquaintance already here Mrs. & Miss Marsden & Mr. Henry Prinsep.

A. & the boys take me to see our tenants' wives, Mrs. Paul, Mrs. Larkham, Mrs. George Smith.

May

2nd. Mr. Lipscombe goes to a mastership at Winchester. I am happy with my boys at their lessons on each side of me as in the old days. . . .

7th. Last evening in answer to a letter from Florence asking for lines of Dante, he made six and sent them off to-day in honour of Dante's six hundredth centenary.[13]

9th. A grand thunderstorm last night. The Barch[?] Dagger arrives from Mr. Charles Cameron. A tremendous looking weapon. Also Tobacco the choicest in the world from Captain Fearn.

I cut off part of the boys beautiful golden hair preparatory to sending them to Mr. Paul.

We look at our new purchase of Plumbley's fields. A. finds a mouse's nest in a Butcher's broom. None of the men know what sort of mouse it is. It has a very long taper snout which it moves about continually.

Henry Cameron & our boys run & jump & hop & A. joins a little.

15th. A letter from Aubrey de Vere telling of Stephen Spring-Rice's death at sea. We look at coins found in a Terra Cotta vase in the Terrace Grounds near the skull of a horse's head in a circle of stones. They are coins of the thirty tyrants in Roman Gaul & A. reads about them to us. Day by day A. & the boys take me out in my little carriage.

To-day (18th) I have to be left in the Hundred acres because the wheel is unsafe. Lionel stays with me & runs to fetch the *Conquest of Mexico*[14] which enchants both boys. Sir John dines

[13] "To Dante," first published in 1880. The long delay in publication seems to have occurred simply because Tennyson forgot about the little poem, which he described as "something like a Greek epigram," after he sent it off to Florence (*Poems of Tennyson*, ed. Ricks, p. 1191).

[14] William Hickling Prescott, *History of the Conquest of Mexico*, 3 vols. (London, 1852–55).

with us. Mr. Warburton comes in the evening. A. & I get up about half past five & go to his dressing-room to look at the delicate brilliance of the morning & breathe the pure air.

Annie Thackeray & her sister lunch here & we all watch Beach cutting our boys' hair, the first time that a barber's scissors has touched it.

We go by Old House field to Papa's field & call on Shepherd Paul & his wife & find them a[t] tea. We take the sisters to our cottages because they think they would like one here. Charles Weld kindly comes to take the boys with him to fish.

22nd. [We started with the boys for their private tutor's, Mr. Paul, at Baillie in Dorsetshire. We visited the Minster at Wimborne on the way. A monument of Margaret Beaufort with her hand in her husband's.[15] A sorrowful sight to us both, our two boys on the Baillie platform, alone, for the first time in their lives as our train left.][16]

He takes me out into the Dean's garden to see the fine view of the Cathedral & the wonderfully clear stream. He gives me a flower from a Tulip tree. We return by the late boat but the time of our return having been uncertain we have no carriage to meet us. Having ensconced ourselves in the coach we hear a jingling & we see first our man then a wagon all gay with flags & banners & Jackman in a scarlet shirt & lilac gray trousers on our beautiful Prince making his white coat look very splendid & himself very grand & a great many [Entry breaks off]

June

8th. A. told a story of his driving into Winchester on the coach when a young man and asking the watchman, "What can you tell me about Winchester," his answer—"Debauched, sir, like all cathedral cities." He and Mr. Warburton compared notes, for A. had been reading *Job* in Hebrew, a book in which he had always rejoiced.

12th. Mrs. Woolner speaking of a party at Oxford at which A. had been expected wrote, "Everyone was regretting Mr. Tennyson's absence from the party, above the rest Bishop Colenso who had been very desirous to meet him.[17] Indeed he said that

[15] Margaret of Beaufort, countess of Richmond and Derby (1443–1509), was mother of Henry VII. In the list of her many benefactions is included a school and chantry at Wimborne Minster.

[16] *Materials*, III, 13.

[17] John William Colenso (1814–83) was bishop of Natal. Colenso evoked great

your husband was the only man he had wanted to see before leaving England, as he thought him the man who was doing more than any other to frame the Church of the future."

As we drive to our door we see the flag gleaming thro' the trees from where the tent has been pitched & made very fairy-like with greenery we are told. . . . We find my Father looking well & happy tho' a little tired of his solitude since May 29th. When on being delayed in Town, I telegraphed to stop his coming but too late. Miss Laudry tells me of Sir John Richardson's sudden death.[18] A good and true and devoted soul such as the world can ill spare.

All except my Father leave after luncheon next day. Short walks with him. I read a little to him & A. plays Backgammon with him.

15th. My Father must go having to find documents for the settlement of some business. He travels with a lady who asks if it is that [Tennyson] is "high" that he will not see people or because he likes to be quiet. No need to give his answer. Then she asks questions about me but of course he keeps his counsel as to who he is. Constance Guest, Mr. Alderson.[19]

22nd. We have this one day alone except that Mr. Cameron comes in the evening. Mrs. Cameron brings her photographing apparatus to photograph the hay-field. It sounds very sad when she not knowing that Poor old Arthur[20] has just told me of the death of his son bids him look merry for her group. Mr. & Mrs. King & Mr. Allingham, Harriet & Richard Wright.[21]

---

opposition with the publication of his 1861 "Commentary on the Epistle to the Romans," which attacked the sacramental system, and he subsequently issued serially his "Critical Examination of the Pentateuch," 1862–79, concluding that these books were postexile forgeries.

[18] Sir John Richardson (1787–1865) was the Arctic explorer and naturalist. Richardson traveled with Sir John Franklin on his 1819 polar expedition, and he later accompanied Franklin on his second expedition to the mouth of the MacKenzie.

[19] The Rev. Frederick Cecil Alderson (1836–1907), curate of Hursley, Hampshire, 1863–65; rector of Holdenby, Northampton, 1865–93; chaplain-in-ordinary to Queen Victoria, 1899–1901; and honorary chaplain to King Edward VII. Mrs. Alderson was also an occasional vistor at Farringford.

[20] One of the Farringford hired men.

[21] Mr. and Mrs. King were the Henry Samuel Kings.

Richard Pears Wright (d. 1892) was a mathematical master at University College school for some years, and he published *The Elements of Plane Geometry for the Use of Schools and Colleges* in 1868. Wright committed suicide by taking chloroform.

We walk & talk & write & read and have Backgammon occasionally. . . .

July

13th. A. with Mr. Locker arrives to-day.[22] A. better. He brings many photographs of himself & the weird picture of the Lady of Shalott. The gift of Mr. Hughes. A. leaves his card on Prince Jérôme Buonaparte.[23] We take Mr. Locker to Swainston. So warm a reception pleasant especially from them.

17th. Mr. Locker leaves. We have had long talks. Very kind & pleasant he has been.

Mr. Plumptre calls with an introduction from Mr. Maurice, his wife's brother. We can only see them in the morning, as we go to Cheltenham next morning. We got lodgings near Aunt Russell's.[24] She looks peaceful & beautiful in spite of a painful kind of paralysis. A. & I have each long talks alone with her & one day he refreshed her spirit by telling her of Primeval Dragons & particularly of that found not far from Farringford which Professor Owen is coming to see.[25] A. & Arthur call on Mr. Dolson.

21st. We set off for Axminster. Thence we drive to St. Mary's.[26] A very fine country all the way uphill. Within St. Mary's gates

[22] Locker was Frederick Locker-Lampson (1821–95), more commonly known as Frederick Locker, the author of *London Lyrics* (1857), the particular friend of Thackeray, George Eliot, Dickens, and Dean Stanley, and the father of Eleanor Locker, who in 1878 married Lionel Tennyson. Locker was a favorite traveling companion of Tennyson's; they visited Paris together in December 1868 and toured Switzerland in the summer of 1869.

[23] Napoleon's youngest brother (1784–1860). Apparently Emily Tennyson originally made this entry in one of the early diaries during the summer of 1860 (Prince Jérôme died on June 24) and placed it here in the Journal by mistake.

[24] Elizabeth Russell, Tennyson's aunt; the widow of Maj. Matthew Russell and mistress of Brancepeth Castle.

[25] Professor Richard Owen (1804–92), the famed naturalist and anatomist, did visit the Tennysons during the last week in July. The poet took Owen to Brightstone to see the fossilized remains he had told Mrs. Russell about, and Owen fitted the bones together to simulate the original animal.

[26] A house near Seaton that Woolner had suggested in March 1865 as a possible summer home for the Tennysons. Emily Tennyson always yearned for a home in Surrey, where she had lived with her father from 1848 until her marriage in June 1850. Blackdown, the site eventually chosen, is located near Surrey in the Sussex North Downs.

wild heath & ferns. The house paneled throughout even to the scullery, slanting on a terrace with a stone balustrade on one side of the ravine leading to Lyme. The sides are clothed with wood and in clear weather the sea is seen thro' the Lyme opening. We did not see it but we went down to the streams below. For part of the year it would be very pleasant but mist so often enfolds the hills it would not do for a permanent residence.

23rd. At Church for the greater part of the morning service but we find we must travel a little this Sunday in order to be at home to receive Prof. Owen.

For about two hours' journey we have to spend nine or ten on the road. So much waiting is there. At Templecombe A. could get nothing but cold ham & boiled eggs for dinner. I had lunched at Axminster so I wanted nothing. Luckily for us a Mr. and Mrs. Clarke had a private omnibus coming for them & courteously offered us seats or I do not know what we would have done. At Axminster a little girl dressed in white (I think) with a beautiful nosegay was led up & presented it to me as a "token of respect." Had I not known that it was meant for A. the glance at him would have told me. I passed it on to him but he returned it. I kissed the little girl & thanked her & took her up to A. who shook hands with her.

As we passed Baillie station we looked out for the platform where we last saw our boys. Little pleasant as the travelling had been it was pleasant to see the holiday look of the people. None drunken. All well dressed & cheerful, some passing to & fro by train, some lounging on the pleasant hills or walking in the fields.

Next day we hear a carriage full of happy school boys hurrahing and see happy Mothers with these boys.

The sea lovely. I never saw our island look more of a summer isle but when we have reached it a good deal is shrouded in mist.

Professor Owen arrived. A. & Professor Owen enjoyed their trip & return in high spirits. They spread out their luncheon on Mr. Fox's lawn they looked at the great dragon which is quite new to the world & quite answers expectations.[27] He never saw one so sheathed in armour and thought of calling it Euacanthus

[27] Mr. Fox was for many years the curate at Brixton, Isle of Wight. On August 17, 1869, Tennyson wrote to the duke of Argyll in behalf of Fox, whom he described as "a very worthy man, and poor," praising him as both a dutiful clergyman and a learned amateur geologist. Tennyson requested that Argyll use his influence to secure a permanent living for Fox at Brixton (see *Memoir*, II, 81–82).

Vectianus. Most interesting he was. [The story of his medical student days, of the negro's head slipping from under his arm, bounding down the hill and bursting through a window into the midst of a quiet family at tea—their horror—his rushing in after the head without a word, and clutching at it and "bolting" was very ghastly.][28] We watch the boat & he looks thro' the glass to try & see the boys. I don't know whether I have had such a moment since I first welcomed my little Hallam into this world as this moment when I have them again. We stay with the Professor till the second bell rings. . . . Outing around home. Ally & Hallam bring me a beautiful nosegay of Meadow Sweet, Willow Herb, Valerian, & Heath from the Plumbley wood and now ours.

August

1st. A. & I play at Backgammon with our boys & they stay up till past ten to hear "The Northern Farmer" and "The Voyage."

A. is so good to me, he has put me to sleep or rather made me quiet enough to sleep every night lately.

9th. We drive to Ryde. A most lovely day. It is worthwhile to be so unwell, A. & the boys are so good to me. A prosperous journey to Dover by the Mid Sussex. . . .

Next day to Brussels. There were no comfortable rooms in the Hotel de l'Europe so we went to the Grande Bretagne. We had hoped to take our Hallam to Waterloo on his birthday but the morning was raining till too late so we drove about Brussels after luncheon instead & saw the Chamber of Representatives, the Pillar in the Place du Congrès, the Cathedral with its wonderful picture-windows and best of all the Old Square where are the Hôtel de Ville, the Maison du Roi . . . & the Statues of Egmont & Hoorne on the spot of their executions.[29]

The Hôtel de Ville very fine with its Gothic pictures & tapestried rooms. We did not see the banqueting hall which was undergoing repair.

[28] *Materials*, III, 15.

[29] The cathedral is an imposing Gothic church which was begun about 1220. The beautiful stained glass dates from different periods (13th century down to modern times); the finest glass is that in the Chapel of the Sacrament with its five windows presented in 1540–47.

Lamoral, comte D'Egmont, prince de Gavre (1522–68), and Filips van Montmorency, graaf van Hoorne (1524?–68), were condemned as rebels and heretics because of their part in the Netherlands' revolt against Spain and were executed by the duke of Alba at the express command of Philip II.

12th. We drove through the Forest of Soigny to Waterloo. The high pillared beeches delighted A., "making a grand aisle, their leaves dappled with sunlight, a wonderful fawn-colored carpet of sward beneath." At one spot they were burning charcoal: there was a clearing in the wood, and the seed of innumerable willow-herbs made a silver mist. At Waterloo we lunched at the top of the Lion Mound, which has spoilt the field. A. and the boys went to Hougoumont, looked at the red wall that the French charged, mist along it for our redcoats, and saw the famous gateway. They took a bullet out of the wall. We stayed at the Hôtel du Musée, and made a careful tour of the whole field with maps and Sibourne's volumes.[30]

Next day we accomplished the circuit of the field, going over the French position. A. was impressed with the "wailing of the wind" at night, as if the dead were lamenting; and with the solemn feeling that all around us were the graves of so many thousand men. We saw the bank behind which our guards lay when the last French attack was made by the "Old Guards." Sergeant Mundy, who showed us round Hougoumont, assured us that the Duke of Wellington did not say "Up, guards, and at them," but merely put his hand to his head and said "Ready." As A. observed, "that is infinitely more like him." One of the old French imperial Guard visited the place afterwards, and said that it seemed on that day and at that hour as if our men had "risen out of the earth." The sergeant told A. a striking fact, that he had sat all night on horseback in rain and thunder and lightning without anything to eat, not even tasting food till next night, yet so great was the excitement that he neither felt wet nor hunger, but that the whole time seemed to him five minutes.

We spent a week at the Hotel, A. enjoying his study of the battlefield and his long walks.

Thence we went to Luxembourg and Trèves. The last is an enchanting place—the Cathedral, the river, the Porta Nigra, the Basilica and the Palace of Constantine, and the Amphitheatre, where so many thousands of Christians have fought with beasts, or have been bidden to slay each other.[31] A. called

[30]William Siborne's *History of the War in France and Belgium in 1815, Containing Minute Details of the Battles of Quatre-Bras, Ligny, Wavra, and Waterloo*, 2 vols. (London, 1844).

[31]The cathedral is one of the oldest churches in Germany, the nucleus of which consists of a quadrangular basilica erected by the emperor Valentinian I (364–375), probably for a court of law.

Most likely built in the reign of Constantine, the Basilica served originally

the Basilica "The ideal Methodist Chapel"; outside the proportions are grand and simple. There are fine old MSS in the Museum.

We drove to Mülheim and rowed down the Moselle in a little boat by Berncastel and Zell to Coblentz. A lovely row between hills of all shapes, sometimes clothed with vines, sometimes with forest.

A. disliked Coblentz as much as ever; we left this (going by Eisenach and seeing the Wartburg) for Weimar. The people there seemed to be rather stupid about Goethe and Schiller, and in vain we tried to impress upon our driver that we wanted to see all which concerned them. Thanks to the kindness of a soldier we got inside the palace, and saw the rooms where Goethe lived so much with the Grand Duke and Duchess.[32] Next morning we secured a commissionaire, who took A. and the boys inside the Fürstengruft, where they saw Goethe's and Schiller's coffins lying beside those of the Royal Family. Lionel had a leaf of bay given him for A. from Goethe's coffin. We were very much pleased by the cheerfulness and simplicity of Goethe's gartenhaus, which we visited. Afterwards we drove to Schiller's house, three rooms pleasant enough in spite of their bareness. His wife's guitar lay near his bed; on it a portrait of himself, said to be good, taken soon after death. The "other-world" peace of it struck A. and me. Then we went to the Church to see Lucas van Cranach's altar-piece, so interesting from the portraits of Luther and himself.[33] The portrait of Luther as a monk I liked best. We drove to Tréport, charmingly situated on the Ilm which babbles pleasantly along.

September

1st. Went with Mr. Marshall—secretary to the Grand Duchess—to Goethe's town-house. No key there for the rooms. The old woman said that she was alone in the house, and could not possibly go and fetch it. A. was touched by seeing the "salve" on the door-mat, and all Goethe's old boots at the entrance.

---

for the administration of justice and for commercial purposes, like the similar ancient Roman structures at Rome itself. It was restored after 1846 by order of Frederick William IV, and in 1856 it was consecrated as a Protestant church.

[32] Karl August (Charles Augustus), grand duke of Weimar (d. 1828) and his duchess Luise (d. 1830).

[33] Weimar's Stadt-Kirche possesses one of Cranach's largest and finest pictures, a Crucifixion containing portraits of Luther and the artist himself.

Mr. Marshall brought the Herr Direktor, for eight years Goethe's secretary, who courteously left his dinner to come. Mr. Marshall expressed his regret that there was no time to write to Madame von Goethe for an order to see the study. The Director made no remark at the time, but when he had shown us the busts and gems and statuettes, and Goethe's own drawings, he took us into the sacred study. One cannot explain in words the awe and sadness with which this long dark room filled A. The study is narrow, and in proportion long. In the middle was a table with a cushion on it where Goethe would lean his arms and a chair with a cushion where he sometimes sat, but his habit was to pace up and down and dictate to his secretary. On one side of the room was a bookcase about two-thirds up the wall, with boxes for his manuscripts. There were also visiting cards, strung like bills together, and Goethe's old, empty, wine bottles, in which the wine had left patterns like frost patterns. On the other side of the room was a calendar of things that had struck him in newspapers. Here a door opened to his bedroom. Such a melancholy little place! By the bed was an arm chair, to which at last he used to move from his bed for a little change. All round the wall, by the bed and the chair, a dark green leafy carpet or tapestry was fastened half-way up the wall of the room. On the washing stand was some of the last medicine he took. The one window at the foot of the bed was partly boarded up. It looked I think into the garden.

After seeing Goethe's house Mr. Marshall met us at the station, and saw us off for Leipzig. Next day we left Leipzig for Dresden. On our arrival at Dresden we went to the gallery. The Madonna and Child by Raffaelle struck A. and me as wonderfully "human and Divine."[34] We seemed to see the trouble of the world in the Virgin's eyes, and the child made A. "marvel at His majesty." Indeed there is a still majesty in the whole picture. Afterwards A. and the boys visited the Zoological Gardens and A. saw the great aurochs which interested him. Next day to the gallery, to see the Raffaelle Madonna again; we also looked at the Holbein Holy Family, which is very great, Titian's Tribute-money, and Correggio's Magdalene, etc.[35] The

[34] Located in the Dresden picture gallery, essentially the creation of Augustus III (1733–63), Raphael's *Sistine Madonna* was acquired from Piacenza in 1753.

[35] The "Holbein Holy Family" is the Madonna of Burgomaster Meyer, long ascribed to Holbein but only an admirable copy of the Darmstadt original. *The Tribute Money* is one of three Titians in the Dresden gallery. Supposedly a Correggio, the famous little picture of the Magdalen has been pronounced a copy.

day after A. and the boys went to the Green Vaults, and the splendour of the diamonds struck A. much. A German professor suddenly discovered A. and made him a long complimentary speech, which was trying. A. took us to the gallery again, and showed us the Titians, also Correggio's Virgin, La Notte, and the Spanish pictures, and again the two great Madonnas.[36]

6th. A. and the boys went to the armoury, to the picture-gallery once more, and then to Saxon Switzerland.

7th. After a very pleasant walk at Dresden, we went by train to Brunswick. At night we heard tremendous crashing, as if all the windows in the house were being smashed. We asked what it meant, and were told that to-morrow a very rich young lady was to be married, and that it was the custom on the eve of the marriage to break all sorts of dishes and bottles against the bride's door. Was this the Polternacht for good luck? The houses are quaint.

9th. A. [&] the boys [go?] into the Crypt to see the coffins of the nine Dukes of Brunswick who fell in battle buried there.[37] Then we see the Lion which Henry brought from Constantinople.[38] The old Town Hall & the Church of St. Jean, very fine.[39] Houses too fine & quaint. Sorry to leave our comfortable hotel & to travel on Sunday but we must hurry home. Next day by far the most intelligent Commissionaire we have had shows us where our Guelph sovereigns & their ancestors lived & where the present king of Hanover holds his court & on rising ground an Old Castle of the Guelphs where he will live some day, it is said. The Stadthaus of Red-moulded brick wonderful, something like the Palaces at Modena but much more quaint. The Churches too very interesting to look at. We have

[36]Besides *The Tribute Money* the Dresden gallery has Titian's portrait of his daughter Lavinia (*Lady with the Fan*) and that of an unknown person, formerly supposed to be Aretino. Correggio's early *Madonna Enthroned* shows the strong influence of the example of the master of chiaroscuro at his best. The most noteworthy works of the Spanish School are the portrait of an elderly man by Velazquez (no. 697) and the *Madonna and Child* of Murillo.

[37]Nine dukes of the last branch of the elder Brunswick line are buried in the crypt of the Cathedral of St. Blasius, which was begun in 1172 in the Romanesque style by Henry the Lion and completed in 1194.

[38]In the Burg-Platz, on the north side of the Cathedral of St. Blasius, rises a bronze lion erected there in 1166 by Henry the Lion as a symbol of his supremacy and restored in 1616 and in 1858.

[39]Emily Tennyson perhaps had in mind the Church of St. Catherine, which was begun by Henry the Lion and continued in 1252. There is no Church of St. Jean in Brunswick.

not time to go inside. The Leibnitz house beautiful & in beautiful order bought by the King & kept by him in repair. To Hanover & then to Aix-la-Chapelle. See the banks of [*illegible*] and the saltworks on which the salt crystallizes & the great Iron foundery for Cannons & the many coal pits.

Next morning we drive to the Church where Charlemagne was found sitting in regal state in his tomb in that Church he himself had built after the model of that.[40] Mass is going on. Very impressive as we stand in the great crossplate bearing his name & just over the spot where he was found. We cannot see the chair on which he was seated & crowned. Ferdinand the last also we see . . . , the remains of the old Carolingian palaces & the statue of Charlemagne standing in the market place with flowers & fruit piled at his feet. The coronation hall striking inside & out. Underneath is the Municipal Hall.

Aix La Chapelle looked very wonderful as we swept thro' the old gates last evening & saw the domes set in hills gold & blue in the sunset. A trying journey to Ostend, the carriages are so full.

12th. That day faultless. Sky & sea bright & calm as can be. Next day by the Portsmouth direct [?] to Ryde. The lovely country makes A. think of the jumps again. We arrive home between two & three. A. & I go to look at the Trees & Shrubs & [*sic*] have prospered & to call at Heard's; pile of letters alarming.

Our friends call. Also Baronne Von Bülow, Matilde Von Zeschau's friend. Strange just when we have been vainly hunting for her in Dresden & she there all the while. The Baronne very simple & charming.

21st. The day cold & dreary & to us sad for our darlings go to Mr. Paul's.

22nd. A. reads to me "Edel sei der Mensch," one of our great favorites. . . .

Next day Mrs. Cameron calls with the Misses Gladstone (nieces of our friend.) Mr. Schreiber & Enid & Blanche Guest come to luncheon. A. reads Egmont & Hoorne to me & in the day takes me out in the little carriage. I have to arrange about Queen Emma's visit.[41] A. reads me some of Tyndall's "Heat as

[40] The Aix-la-Chapelle (present-day Aachen) Cathedral, or Münster, was erected in part by Charlemagne in 796–804 and consecrated by Leo III. The Hochmünster, or gallery, of the octagon built by Charlemagne contains the Imperial Throne, on which the remains of Charlemagne (d. 814) reposed for more than 350 years.

[41] Queen Emma of the Sandwich Islands and her late husband, King Kameha-

Cause of Motion"[42] & always he takes me out in the day when fine.

28th. Beautiful morning. A. & I watch Heard & Mr. Walton[43] weaving the small Dahlias into an "Aloha" on a background of ivy over the portico & A. takes me down to see the arch over the entrance. A flowery wreath with the Union Jack. The Hawaiians' flag waves over the portico near the Queen's bedroom.

Joyful sight our boys drive up. We were not sure if Mr. Paul would think it right they should come. Aunt Franklin, Sophy, Nanny . . . come. The Seelys most kind in sending beautiful flowers & fruits. We wait for the Queen. . . . [Queen Emma of the Sandwich Islands arrived, Major Hopkins and a huge native Mr. Hoapili in attendance. Aunt Franklin came. The Queen's maid and her luggage lost on the road. They arrived at midnight. We had a throne chair made out of our Ilex wood, and it was first used by the Queen. She, poor lady, wanted to stay quietly here, but she must go to banquets, etc. about the Island. I collected money for the projected cathedral in Honolulu.[44]

30th. A.T. took the Queen up the Down. A meeting was held at the school. Endless guests came in to tea. John Welsh, the Queen's servant, said nothing would induce him to leave her for she was so good. There was a wailing thro' the seven Sandwich Islands for the Queen when she left because the natives thought she never would return. A.T. took her out that she might read her letters; and hid her from the guests in the summer house in the kitchen garden ("among the cabbages" she said). A.T. and I were pleased with her sweet dignity of manner and calmness that made one think of an Egyptian statue; her voice was musical. Mr. and Mrs. Hoapili sang some Hawaiian songs. They sat on the ground and acted the song while they sang. They then chanted an Ode to the young Prince, a wild monotonous chant. All great people's children in Hawaii have odes made to them on the day of their birth, a kind of

---

meha IV, had planned a trip to England before his death in 1863, and the young dowager subsequently made the intended visit without him. Queen Emma and her attendants were guests at Farringford from September 28 to October 2.

[42] John Tyndall, *Heat Considered as a Mode of Motion* (London, 1863).

[43] A Freshwater neighbor.

[44] While in England, Queen Emma sought assistance for the recently established Episcopal Mission in the Sandwich Islands.

foreshadowing of their lives. When a bard meets the hero of any ode so made, he has to sing it to him.

October

1st. The Queen went to see a Mrs. Currie here, 100 years old who had dined with Captain Cook's widow. The old lady *would* be dressed and put into her chair, and greeted each of us appropriately in the same words when we came and when we went.

The Queen was anxious to drive to the Needles so A.T. drove with her. She ran down like a child with delight on the downs, and said that the view near the Needles reminded her of her own country, the air also.

2nd. Queen Emma walked up the Down with Hallam before breakfast and wondered at the snail shells which she said were bigger than those in her own land.][45] A. gave her two large magnolia blossoms on her leaving. She has an affectionate nature; something very pathetic about her.

3rd. Our boys go by the early boat. Dreary enough for us all. A. takes me out in the little carriage.

Next day the Hamonds come & the Simeons & their friend Allingham. Before they arrive we have called on the Henry Taylors.

6th. A. read me some Lucretius and the 1st Epistle of St. Peter. At work at his new poem of "Lucretius."

8th. Mr. Henry Taylor & Mr. Cameron before [*illegible*]. A thunderstorm, Fine zig-zags of bright light & once a great part of a circle a kind of half coronet. A. reads me the 1st Epistle of St. Peter.

10th. A. is going to have some large Laurustinus planted in the glade & is preparing for them by digging up what was the old road. Tilly arrives with Cole to make this her home. May it be a happy one to her, dear soul!

Mr. Henry Taylor, Mrs. Cameron, Mrs. Prinsep dine here. All kind & pleasant. Conversation never commonplace where he is.

12th. Mr. Allingham comes to luncheon. A. reads Captain Hall's wonderful letter about Captain Crozier & two others.

[45] *Materials*, III, 21–22.

13th. A. reads me some Lucretius.

14th. He busy again with Laurustinus. I go to look at them. Today Mr. Dalrymple brings Mr. Watts's picture of our boys.[46] Very beautiful but not so beautiful as they. Like them but not their very selves.

15th. A. takes me to look at his lordly wreath of Laurustinus & then to Maiden's Croft where I sit in the seat he puts outside the summer-house.

16th. A. & I busy putting up pictures in the Anti-room & pasting frames. The Magdalen & the Venetian Lady we brought from Dresden. A. pleased to see the beautiful old China vases from his Father's house which Tilly has brought with her. Still busy planting.

19th. Lady Simeon arrives. Mr. Allingham comes to luncheon. Mr. Leach[47] an American calls in the morning. Mr. Winthrop Sargent,[48] also American, in the afternoon. Both modest men. Mr. Winthrop will not dine with us but comes in the evening bringing with him some of those horrible Pharaoh's serpents.[49] We have the servants in to look at them.

Next day Mr. Allingham goes & Lady Simeon & Tilly call with the Harrisons for me. He was the clergyman who married my father.

22nd. Louy . . . walks with A. to our boundary on the downs. I have interesting talks with her this day & other days.

24th. She goes, Simeons and Bakers coming for her.

27th. A. gets the bank finished. I have happy talks with him after dinner.

[46] Mr. Dalrymple was a London friend of G. F. Watts. At the time Watts wrote to Tennyson of the boys' picture, "If there had been any correspondence between my will and power, the picture would have been worth acceptance for itself, but I can only hope that it may have some small value as a token of friendship and an expression of profound admiration and respect" (*Materials*, III, 24). Watts's portrait of Hallam and Lionel is now in the Usher Art Gallery, Lincoln.

[47] Possibly Daniel Dyer Leach (1806–91), the Episcopal clergyman, educator, and author of *Directions to Teachers* (1873), among other textbooks.

[48] Winthrop Sargent (1825–70) is the Philadelphia writer, the author of the *Life and Career of Major John André* (1861). In 1865 Sargent began a law practice in New York City, but soon thereafter he gave up the law to seek rest in Europe.

[49] The Pharaoh's serpent was a popular mid-nineteenth-century chemical toy composed of sulfocyanide of mercury, which fuses in a serpentine form.

28th. He takes me out to see the planting.

Mr. Francisque Michel[50] & Mr. Payne arrive. The torrent of wit & puns almost overpowering. They overtire the poor man walking on the Down. He interests us much. A. says that he has a free Shakespearian wit. He tells him about the Capets too into whose history he has ingrained & hardened for himself that they are remains of the Goths.

31st. He & Mr. Payne go to-day. A. reads me the Abstract of Dean Stanley's sermon on Lord Palmerston. Even in this form it is very fine.

November

1st. Mr. Barnes the Dorsetshire Poet[51] and Mr. Allingham come to dinner. Mrs. Cameron, Ewen, & Mr. Dalrymple in the evening. Mr. Barnes seems to us very good & simple. His conversation interests us much. He & Mr. Allingham leave next day.

Little George (one of ploughman's (Hiscock) sons) shows me his new shoes & his mother tells me how with the three pounds she has bought winter shoes for Hiscock & all the children.[52] He is working in the garden & we go to congratulate him. We go then into several fields. We love our picturesque fields. Each would have had its own little romance had we been born among them.

7th. We have been seeing Mr. Watts, the Prinseps & Mr. Dalrymple these last days. Mr. Watts & Mr. Dalrymple call to-day to say good-bye. . . .

We had expected Sir John but he could not stay. In the morning he went over our new fields with A. & admired them much. In him we have a real friend one interested in all that concerns us. He & Lady Simeon dine with us on the 16th. A. has been busy planting Barberries & Euonymus.

15th. Mayall comes with the Photographs. That of A. very fine. It gained a prize in Dublin. Mr. Mayall's father knew nothing

[50] Michel (1809–87) was a French antiquary, a professor at Bordeaux from 1839. He earned a substantial reputation for his researches in Norman history, French *chansons*, argot, and the Basques.

[51] William Barnes (1800–1886), the pastoral poet, known for his idylls in the Dorset dialect and for his somewhat fanatical attempts to Saxonize English.

[52] On November 2 Mr. Hiscock won a community plowing competition and was awarded £3 (Lady Tennyson to Hallam and Lionel Tennyson, November 4, 1865, *Letters of E. T.*, p. 196).

of his having been here nor of the experiments in enlarging photographs which he had made. He had said that they had nothing worth sending to Dublin, so would send nothing. The son arranged seven photographs of A. arranged in different degrees & brought his Father in to see them saying I think I have found something for Dublin. The Father was delighted & all Photographers admitted that the son had done a new thing in Photography. A. reads to us as usual almost every evening & takes me out in my little carriage when it is fine weather.

C.R.W., Mr. Allingham, Mr. Woolner. C.R.W. helps A. to take me to Haynes' Cottage which we want to look at.

24th. Mr. Woolner goes with A. to the Bay where the great waves are breaking over the road. Some of our trees blown down & a bit of the wall near A.'s room. They have walks most days. Mrs. Gatty & her daughters. A. at Mrs. Gatty's request reads "Locksley Hall" & "Too Late."[53]

29th. They go.

December

1st. A. goes to town with Mr. Woolner. Very dreary to lose him. During his absence a very graceful & kind letter comes from Queen Emma with the Prayerbook & Preface.

8th. Our Lionel comes home quite knocked up. Hallam kind boy has written beforehand to qualify Mr. Paul's report that I may not be too alarmed.

To-day A. is to be formally introduced to the Royal Society. He is staying at Mr. Palgrave's & writes to me every day. I am very glad that he is seeing those he loves to see, Carlyles, Froudes,[54] & others.

15th. Our Hallam arrives. The Pauls with him. The Butlers are also here. We see all from time to time.

18th. I go with the boys to meet A. He not there. He said he was afraid he should not be on time to come. The mist was too thick.

19th. The boys & I have the joy of seeing him land. Our boys

[53]For "Too Late" see "Guinevere," ll. 166–77.

[54]James Anthony Froude (1818–94), the historian, Carlyle biographer, and editor of *Fraser's Magazine*, 1860–74, and his second wife, the former Henrietta Elizabeth Warre.

ride often, play at whist, backgammon & chess. A. sometimes plays at whist with them. We have ordered *British Butterflies* & Arnold's *Physics* for their Christmas gifts but have to substitute money, Mr. Payne insisting on making the gifts his.[55] C.R.W. here.

24th. Mr. Jowett arrives.

30th. C.R.W. leaves for Florence. Both very kind in playing at chess with the boys.

Mr. & Miss Elliot[56] also here. Mr. Elliott & Dr. Butler help with my carriage which A. has not been able to get to Glenbrook that we might pay our intended visit. The road is so broken up.

[55] John Obediah Westwood, *The Butterflies of Great Britain* (London, 1860); Neil Arnold, *Elements of Physics* (London, n.d.).

[56] Mr. Elliot is perhaps a son of Hugh Elliot (1752–1830), the diplomat, Henry Montagu Butler's father-in-law.

1866

January

1st. On Saturday evening A. reads us some Lucretius. On Sunday Mr. Jowett reads us some of the Revelations of *Daniel* & *Isaiah* 53. On Monday his *Visions of Ur.* Refreshing evenings.

2nd. Poor Mr. Worsley goes.

3rd. Mr. Jowett & Tilly go. Seldom can two so good go from any house. A happy evening. Hallam reads some of Prescott's *Ferdinand & Isabella* to Lionel & me.[1] They have been reading his *Peru* themselves.[2] A. reads me private letters from Honolulu which have come to me thro' Mrs. Grosvenor Hood. Very interesting.

5th. A. goes to meet Mr. Dakyns. We are all delighted to have him again with us. Poor Mr. Worsley in great danger this week. Dr. & Mrs. Butler, Mr. Arthur Butler in the evening. They get me to ask A. to read "Guinevere." The boys stay up to hear it. A happy evening for us all. Mr. Browning of Eton.[3]

12th. Sorry to part from Mr. Dakyns. No one is exactly what he is to us. Mr. Worsley's brother telegraphed. His brother Edward calls. Mr. Clark comes to-day. Sir John summoned to his sister's death.

20th. A sad day for us. Our Hallam leaves for Marlborough. Professor Owen, Mr. & Mrs. Fowler, Mr. Vernon Harcourt lunch with us.[4] Mr. Harcourt has just applied for Aunt Franklin's house. They are all very kind & pleasant.

[1] William Hickling Prescott, *History of Ferdinand and Isabella* (London, 1838).

[2] William Hickling Prescott, *Conquest of Peru* (London, 1847).

[3] Oscar Browning (1837–1923), master at Eton, 1860–75; examiner, University of London, 1899; author of the *Life of Peter the Great* (1898) and the *History of the Modern World, 1815–1910* (1912), among other works.

[4] Robert Nicholas Fowler (1828–91), the conservative politician, was M.P. for Penryn and Falmouth, 1868–74, and for London, 1880 to death. In 1883 Fowler was chosen lord mayor of London, and in 1885 he was created a baronet. His wife was the daughter of Mr. Alfred Fox.

The Rev. William Venables Vernon Harcourt (1789–1871) was prebendary of North Newbald, York, 1821 to death, rector of Whildrake, 1824–33, and rector of Bolton Percy, 1837–65. He was the founder and general secretary of the British Association, 1831, and later its president, 1839.

22nd. Mr. Clark has been so kind in trying to cheer Lionel. One likes him more & more the more one sees of him. He leaves us to-day. Mr. & Mrs. Bradley & Mr. Grove[5] came. We have great talks about Eton & Marlborough. Mr. Bradley kind & generous as ever. A. reads the *Morte d'Arthur* in the evening. They have been walking a good deal in the morning.

25th. Mr. & Mrs. Bradley, Mr. Grove, & Mr. Phelps[?] all go to-day. A. busy planting & transplanting. A. reads some of the "Conscrit"[?] to me.

February

2nd. We go to Aubrey & next day to Aunt Franklin's House (Gore Lodge), Kensington.

4th. We find an invitation to luncheon at the Deanery, Westminster for to-morrow. We go there, Lionel with us. It does one's heart good to have so warm a reception from such people. Mr. Vaughan came in & we had a delightful talk before luncheon & also at luncheon when the Carlyles joined us. [The Dean took us into the Abbey, and the Jerusalem Chamber, and the Westminster schoolroom the tables of which were made from oak of the Spanish Armada. A.T. is fond of the Abbey and of strolling about it by himself. "How dream-like it looked," he said. We went to see Thackeray's bust. The Dean said at luncheon, "having to do with artists and sculptors about statues and busts of great men gave fresh cause to lament their death."][6] Lady Augusta made me rest in Mr. Vaughan's room & just as we were leaving the Dean ran upstairs to show Lionel the secret door in the library. Then we went to Lord Boyne's & had a kind reception there also. Lady Boyne seemed especially glad to see her godson Lionel. Her husband showed us his beautiful Hogarths which A. knew before. . . . At our door we found a carriage & the servant said to Lionel a lady wants to see you. He went to the carriage & found Mrs. James Marshall & Julia in it & presently they came in, a welcome sight. A. and Lionel lunch at the Palgraves'.

A. takes Lionel to Mr. Forster's. Mr. Payne lunches with us & we go afterwards to Little Holland House & see Mr. Watts, then to Argyll Lodge. The Duke & Duchess out. Afterwards to

[5]George Grove (1820–1900; knighted, 1883), editor of *Macmillan's Magazine* and author of the four-volume *Dictionary of Music and Musicians*, 1878–89.

[6]*Materials*, III, 32.

the Maurices, find them & their soldier son. A pleasant fresh young soldier.

Mr. Garden, Franklin Lushington, Mr. Clough call while we are out. A. goes to Lord Russell's, sees Mr. Gladstone & Lord Houghton.[7] At the Marshalls' door we learn the death of dear old Lord Monteagle of which they have just heard. . . .

The Boynes, Duke & Duchess of Argyll, & Mr. Forster come while we are out. We find the Dixons[8] on our return. A. takes Lionel this morning & every morning to his riding lessons. . . . While they are away Mr. Locker, Lady Charlotte, Mr. Seely call, Louisa Dixon.

A. dines at Brookfields. Mr. Grove sends us beautiful Ferns, Camellias, Rhododendrons & other flowers. A. asked by Mr. Pritchard to dine at the Astronomical Society. A. takes Lionel to the Zoological Gardens & Mr. Seely takes me for a drive.

10th. Mr. & Mrs. Palgrave, Mr. Woolner, Mr. Browning, Mr. Barrett[9] dine with us. Mr. Browning gives me an affectionate greeting after all these years (asks if he may be excused if he looks at me a little more). In the evening the Brookfields, Magdalene with her white dress, gold-bordered, looking as if she had come out of a Fairy story. A quiet talk with Mr. Jowett & Mr. Bowen.[10] Mr. Locker, Lady Charlotte, & their Eleanor also come. Sir Francis Doyle.[11] I talk to him of Arthur Hallam & old

[7]Lord John Russell, 1st Earl Russell (1792–1878), was twice prime minister, 1846–52 and 1865–66. Russell introduced the 1832 Reform Bill the second time, in June, and the third time, in December, when it was passed. He served as home secretary in Melbourne's administration, 1835, and as foreign secretary under Palmerston.

Lord Houghton, of course, is Richard Monckton Milnes.

[8]William Hepworth Dixon (1821–79), the historian and world traveler, and his wife, Louisa. Dixon was editor of the *Athenæum* from 1853 until 1869, and in 1862 he published *The Story of Lord Bacon's Life*. His other works include the *History of Two Queens* (1873–74) and two works of fiction, *Diana, Lady Lyle* (1877) and *Ruby Grey* (1878).

[9]George Goodin Barrett was Elizabeth Barrett Browning's favorite brother and her closest family counselor.

[10]Charles Synge Christopher, Baron Bowen (1835–94). Bowen was appointed judge of the queen's bench and knighted in 1879; he received a life peerage in 1893. Benjamin Jowett once described Bowen as the greatest English lawyer of his day.

[11]Sir Francis Hastings Charles Doyle, 2d baronet (1810–88), the poet. Doyle was professor of poetry at Oxford, 1867–77, and commissioner of customs, 1869–83. He was an intimate friend of Arthur Henry Hallam, through whom he first became acquainted with Tennyson. Doyle's modest poetic fame rests

days. Lord Dufferin calls. Mr. Tyndall lunches. Mr. Marshall brings the young Lord Monteagle.[12]

Lady Simeon takes me for a drive. A. is going but Mr. Carlyle & his brother call so he walks with them instead. . . .

13th. The Duke of Argyll comes early to ask if A. will dine at the Club. Hitherto we have missed each other. Mr. Browning comes as we are dressed for the wedding breakfast at the Boynes. All very beautiful at the breakfast as flowers & silver vases & gold pitchers & a much adorned bride-cake & a bride in Satin & Brussels lace & ladies in gay dresses could make it. Lady Boyne very kind to all. No stiffness. All went off well & the old satin shoe was not forgotten so all that could be done was done for Mr. & Mrs. Banbury & Captain Hutton took me in to breakfast & kindly took Lionel afterwards to see fencing & boxing & broad sword exercise.[13] Then after a short rest at home A. & I went to Mr. Gladstone's five o'clock tea. My wedding garb made me feel shy among so many strangers. Glad was I to welcome the Dean & Lady Augusta's friendly faces & to see Mr. Woolner. Many that were very kind to me. Lady de Grey, Mr. Hughes, Mr. Woolner, Mr. Holman Hunt come while A. is at the Froudes, Lionel with him.[14] They also go to the Strangfords.[15]

Mr. & Mrs. Brookfield, the Pollocks, Mr. Spedding dine with us. In the evening the Duke & Duchess of Argyll, Lady

---

chiefly on his ballads, which include "The Red Thread of Honour," "The Private of the Buffs," and "Mehrab Khan."

[12]Thomas Spring-Rice, 2d Baron Monteagle of Brandon (1849–1926), grandson of the 1st Baron Monteagle.

[13]The Banburys are probably Henry William St. Pierre Banbury (1812–75) and his wife. A career soldier, Banbury was raised to the rank of lieutenant colonel in 1855.

Capt. Frederick Wollaston Hutton (1836–1905) served in the Crimea, 1855–56, and at the relief of Lucknow under Lord Clyde. In 1866 he left the army and emigrated to New Zealand where he was Professor of Biology at the University of New Zealand from 1880 until 1893.

[14]Lady de Grey was Henrietta Anne Theodosia, Lady De Grey of Wrest, wife of George Frederick Samuel Robinson, Earl De Grey of Wrest.

Mr. Hughes was Thomas Hughes (1822–96).

[15]Percy Ellen Frederick William Smythe, 8th Viscount Strangford and 3d Baron Penshurst (1826–89), the philologist, and his wife, Emily Anne, youngest daughter of Adm. Sir Francis Beaufort. Strangford wrote extensively on topics of the Near East, mainly for the *Pall Mall* and was oriental secretary in Constantinople in 1857–58.

Boyne, . . . the Simpkinsons, Dixons, Ettisons, . . . Mr. Locker & Lady Charlotte, Mrs. Gladstone & her daughters, Lady Gertrude Talbot, Franklin Lushington, the two young Maurices, Mr. Wilson.[16] Mr. & Mrs. Gladstone & Lady Gertrude Talbot dine with us. Lionel's two wishes for London were that he might see Mr. Browning & Mr. Gladstone. He has had the first & now we cannot refuse letting him dine with us that he may have the second. Mr. Gladstone's talk full of interest. A glow and intensity in his whole being.

March

5th. Another little party, Mr. Locker, Mr. Baker (a Japanese noble with him who sang), Miss Eden, Mr. Woolner, Lady Florence Cowper.[17] I was too ill to appear.

Another evening when A. read "Maud" to the Lilfords, Airlies, Brookfields, Mr. Julian Fane. . . .[18] I did appear but my cough obliged me to leave several times.

For nearly three weeks out of the seven A. has been shut up by Influenza & Lumbago & I six weeks.

22nd. I send A. with Miss Eden & drive myself with Mrs. Carlyle. Little did I think that I saw her then for the last time. Her

[16]The Simpkinsons are possibly John Nassau Simpkinson (1817–94), the dear friend of Arthur Hugh Clough and his wife. Simpkinson was assistant master at Harrow, 1845–55; rector of Brington, Northamptonshire, 1855–68; and rector of North Creake, Norfolk, 1868 to death.

The Ettisons = unidentified.

Lady Gertrude Talbot is the wife of Gladstone's friend, Edward Talbot, bishop of Rochester, 1895–1905.

Mr. Wilson is the former tutor to Hallam and Lionel.

[17]Emily Eden (1797–1869), daughter of William Eden, 1st Baron Auckland, was the author of several books, including two popular novels, *The Semi-detached House* (1859) and *The Semi-attached Couple* (1860). Miss Eden was a prominent figure among London's social elite, and her home, Eden Lodge, in Kensington, was frequented by all the notable people of the day.

Lady Anne Florence Cowper (1806–80) was the widow of George Augustus Frederick Cowper, Earl Cowper (1806–56).

[18]The Airlies were David Graham Drummond Ogilvy, 5th earl of Airlie (1826–81), and his wife, the former Henrietta Blanche Stanley (b. 1830).

Julian Henry Charles Fane (1827–70), the diplomat and poet, was secretary of legation at St. Petersburg, 1856–58, and he served as first secretary and acting chargé d'affaires at Paris, 1865–67 and 1868.

little dog was with her. The fatal little dog.[19] Lionel fondled the timid little creature with the fine black coat.

Ill as we have been I have notwithstanding pleasant recollections of our visit. People have been so very kind. The Stanleys kind as kind can be, so also Miss Eden, Mr. Seely,[20] Louisa Dixon. We are much interested by Lady Lothian.[21] It is sad to see that lovely young creature look so worn as she does from constant attendance on her husband. A. went two or three times to see him & would have gone oftener but for his illness. Lady de Grey has been so very kind about Lionel & strongly recommends Dr. Hunt.[22]

23rd. We go home. The Marshalls' carriage takes us to the Station. How thoughtful & kind they are. Next day our Hallam comes.

26th. Lady Florence Cowper & her sister Arline call in the evening with their brother Henry. They stay after but I too ill to go down.

April

1st. Easter Sunday. I was to have taken our Hallam to his first Communion today but this is not possible. Very happy holidays with him.

May

1st. Today I was to have gone with A. to take our Hallam to Marlborough but could not. My cough is so bad & the weather so bitterly cold that A. will not let me go. They write to me from Reading. The Bradleys most kind. A. & Hallam pleased

[19]Jane Welsh Carlyle died on April 21, 1866. Mrs. Carlyle apparently overexerted herself that afternoon rescuing her little dog from the street after it had been hit by a carriage, for she died shortly thereafter.

[20]John Robert Seeley, author of *Ecce Homo: A Survey of the Life and Works of Jesus Christ* (1866).

[21]Lady Constance Lothian (1836–1901), the former Constance Harriet Mahonese, wife of William Schomberg Robert Kerr, 8th marquis of Lothian (1832–70).

[22]Lionel stuttered. On August 20, 1866, the Tennysons took him to Hastings to place him under the tutelage of Dr. Hunt, who was widely known for his success in helping children with speech difficulties.

with Marlborough & the Forest. Poor A. two days on the road home because of changes of which he was not made aware & Sunday rains & no boat from Lymington.

A. takes me to London about my health.

12th. We return home. We are cheered by happy letters of our Hallam & good news of him from Mrs. Bradley. We travel with Mr. Aldis Wright.[23] Miss Collier & poor Mr. Godfrey Worsley who comes to his brother's funeral with us in the boat.

15th. Mr. Philip Worsley laid in our church yard. His sister & his brother Godfrey come to us after the funeral. He looking pale & worn & anxious tho' less than one could have hoped after his devoted nursing & watching day & night for four months. They leave next day. Mrs. Cameron who has suffered from having been so much in Mr. Worsley's room goes to Town.

We see Mr. Wright most days but I not well enough to have him to dinner. He reads Miss Austin because "The Master" (Whewell)[24] admired her so much that he had her read to him even on his deathbed & he knew her so well that he corrected the Reader when he made an error.

23rd. Mr. Manochjee Cursetjee[25] comes to luncheon & stays till four, then A. goes with him to Mrs. Cameron & afterwards to see his daughter ill with rheumatism.

In the evening took an illustrated "Enoch Arden" (unfortunately rather spoilt one for we had no other) & presented it to her. Here we talked of his religion & ours, of free-will, evil & suffering. Tho' seeming a religious theist who might shame oneself, many a Christian besides, he did not appear to see the distinction between sin & evil in the form of suffering, nor conversely between the different goods. Therefore, I suppose he does not care to believe in free-will as we do. He said that one of the grand rules of duty to each other is "Do unto each other as ye would they should do unto you." He said also that he believed in the One Great Being who orders all for good.

31st. The Cursetjees call to take Leave. I have a nosegay ready for the daughter & put on my fur cloak to shake hands with her at the door. Her Father takes Lionel also to see her & A. wears the

[23] William Aldis Wright (1831–1914), the Shakespearean and biblical scholar. Wright was joint editor, with William George Clark, of the *Cambridge Shakespeare* (1863–66).

[24] Dr. William Whewell.

[25] Manakji Khurshedji, the Indian writer, best remembered for *A Few Passing Ideas for the Benefit of India and the Indians* (1852–53).

silver ring with the chapter from the Koran on it which Mr. Cursetjee gave him last night. He wants A. to correspond with him when he returns to Bombay. I am lying in my little carriage by the crimson Rhododendrons when Mr. Peel comes. He sits on the lawn & talks to me & the boys sweep the lawn made untidy by the ilex & the men too busy in the hay field to attend to it.

I in great pain from my teeth. A. wants to take me to London but I will not let him go because of his hay-fever but I go alone & leave him & Mrs. Woolner & her baby.

June

On my return I look over *Ecce Homo* again & mark those passages which I want A. to see, for Mrs. Woolner is very kind & leaves me time to read & write. Letter-writing I have as much as I can manage. Mr. Woolner, Mr. Allingham, Mr. Henry Taylor in addition to Tilly & Mr. Reginal Gatty. A. reads the Sea-Cavern from "Les travailleurs de la Mer."[26]

13th. My Father arrives looking well & cheerful. Delighted to see him. He walks generally twice a day while here, reads & writes morning & afternoons & plays at Backgammon with Lionel in the evening & sometimes also reads the newspaper to us. Our Hallam arrives late from Marlborough. A happy supper. He so free & cheerful, not shy as he has been before on coming home. A. much interested to hear all about the school & Hallam enthusiastic in praise of the Master's kindness & of their interest in the boys. Of the Bradleys' goodness to him he cannot say too much.

29th. He has his first swimming. Next day Mr. Archibald Peel, Mr. Payne, & Mr. Thompson[27] the Confederate. He, poor man, looks very sad and well he may having lost his all in the war including the finest Library in the South. One cannot but feel very sorry for him.

[26] The Victor Hugo novel (1866).

[27] Waddy Thompson (1798–1868), the South Carolina Whig congressman and diplomat.

July

Lessons sometimes with the boys and very happy we are. But on the 7th Lionel becomes so unwell that I have to sleep in his room three nights. At last Chloride of Potash Chloridine & Tincture of Orange stop the sickness caused, I think, by a slight sunstroke.

Archibald Peel wishes us to call on Lord & Lady Durham.[28] We find them only just arrived. They were to have come the day before, but they kindly receive us. We only call to say that we leave home to-morrow.

13th. We come to the Crown Hotel, Lyndhurst. Next day we have a delightful drive to Boulder woods & Rufus Stone where we lunch under the trees. A. & Hallam go afterwards to Knightwood Oak. Mr. Allingham in answer to a telegram kindly comes to us in the evening. He & A. walk. An enchanting drive thro' glades & lawns, grand groups of trees & ferns & a rich smell of heath (Even the forest flies and the stints[?] are welcome), the wild ponies.

[We] go thro' a young plantation & a baby wood & an old woods. Then we came suddenly on a scene of desolation. Many huge trees torn up by the roots. I get out & stand in the gloom of the forest. We go on we know not whither but at last come out on the Christchurch road. The driver is so lost that but for A. he would have driven us away from Lyndhurst.

Two mornings A. wanders alone & returns for us in the afternoon. One day the forest grand & sad in mist. The next we go up Emery down & return by the Royal Oak. In rather marshy places we find lovely fairy wreaths of little pink & blue flowers strange to us. The day after our excursion was spoilt by rain. The day after (July 18th) A. & Hallam set out to walk to Romsey Church.[29] [A.T. thought that it was one of the simplest and finest churches in England; it reminded us of William's church at Caen. Lionel and I followed driving, and found them as I thought we should, near the river Test. Some parts of it higher up "every square inch a ripple," and here A.T. was charmed with the swift clear stream gliding over its rushy bed.][30]

[28] George Frederick D'Arcy Lambton, 2d earl of Durham (1828–79), and his wife, the former Beatrix Frances Hamilton (1835–71).

[29] Founded in the tenth century, the Romsey Abbey Church is a massive cruciform edifice which dates in its present form mainly from the twelfth century.

[30] *Materials*, III, 47.

We all drive back to within two miles of Lyndhurst when A. & Lionel get out & walk. A very pleasant day we have all had. The next A. & Hallam walked to Beaulieu thro' the woods. Lionel & I drive over the heath. The house shut up. The lodge keeper & his wife very kind. He shows us the garden the flowers of which he tends as his wife tells with pride (as well she may) tho' never having been taught to garden. Then he shows us the ruins & the Dormitory & fetches the clerk to show us the church, once the Refectory.

25th. We go to Aubrey. Next day all except my Father go to Christchurch Bay. A. & Hallam walking, the others driving. Very pleasant. The bay is so fine & the Cliffs so interesting. Standing on the cliff we see [*illegible*] passing on the sands below. We call but of course the noise of the waves prevents him from hearing. The coast-guard shows us a fossil Nautilus he has found & gives us fossil shells.

The day after the boys go out fishing. Then we all go in a boat to Hurst Castle, except Grandpapa. I have an interesting talk with him on our return and the day after this we go home.

August

1st. A. & the boys take me to see the reapers reaping winter barley & oats at Middleton—these pleasant breezy fields of ours. The day after they take me to look in at the drilling of turnips in the Withy field. The horses look fine drilling & harrowing. We are rather proud of our horses. We have lessons in the mornings. A peaceful happy time.

6th. I find the boys making a Parody of God save the Queen in honour of the day but as A. does not like having birthdays kept we have our plum-pudding & health drinking unnoticed & unnoticeable. They go out in the rain to throw down the banks between St. George's Field & Abraham's Mead. I watch them working at it next day. . . .

7th. Our Hallam leaves us for Marlboro', dreary day. Aubrey de Vere here. Busy getting A.'s books in order ready for our return.

We took our Lionel to School at Hastings. Dr. Hunt confirms Dr. Johnston's opinion that his stammering is only from weakness & will with care be quite cured. A very sad parting. Dr. Hunt sends his carriage for him. I watch the little face & then the hand & then the top of his hat. A.T.[31] walked twice

[31] Here Emily Tennyson refers to the poet by both his initials, as is Hallam Tennyson's habit in *Materials*.

back along the road with him to comfort him at parting. Then they part, he a little consoled. A. & I go to Park House by Battle & Tunbridge.[32] Beautiful country, one continued Park almost with here & there a fine old house. Fine England. As ever here a loving welcome. Pleasant drives & walks. One day we go to what was mother's house at Boxley. I have been there before but not to A.'s room. A delightful room looking upon the bright garden with its fir trees & its crystal stream.

A. reads the "Norse Queen," "The Voyage," "All Along the Valley." A dinner party which I enjoy because Frank[33] takes me out. A. talks a good deal. Another evening he reads "Enoch Arden."

A. & Edmund talk metaphysics in the Bow-room. They have engrossed A. much of late. The materialism of the day has revived his interest in them. He has almost lived in the summerhouse till the rain drives him into the Greenhouse.

10th. A. tells me that Septimus is gone.

Edmund kindly takes A. one day to Luce. Another to the Druid Stones in the Staffore's Park, thinking it will be good for him. He enjoys his day in the Park.

14th. We go. How good they have all been. It is sad to leave them. At Haslemere we find the best rooms taken at the Blue Bell but we sleep there. Rush bottomed chairs in our sitting room but everything clean & the food well cooked. Mrs. Gilchrist kindly goes to Mrs. Simmons who orders another pony carriage to take Mrs. Gilchrist to Churt that she may ask Mr. Simmons about the Devil's Jumps and all other land to be sold in the neighbourhood. We wait in his little room at Churt while a storm lasts. Then he mounts his horse & we all drive to the Devil's Jumps. A magnificient storm towers over the purple distance. A grand view. If it were not looking north we should buy the place forthwith. We go to the Devil's Punch Bowl after having taken shelter from a storm at the Huts. A. no longer laughs at me for my love of this wild region. We take leave of Mrs. Gilchrist & Mr. Simmons who have been most kind & go to Petersfield.

16th. A rainy Sunday at the Red Lion as one is very tired & has not energy to think much. Next day we go to Mr. Cobb's house, taking our luncheon. The house might do very well with its Fir Knoll & its little glen & its heath & wood close by but it is only to be let not sold.

[32] Battle Abbey and Tunbridge Wells.

[33] Franklin Lushington.

The hills on both sides lovely. Those on inside as one goes from Petersfield chiefly wooded with wavy outline, those on the other scarped. We call on Mr. Stowe whom Mr. Bradley had recommended as Lionel's tutor. Charming old oak-wainscoted house, flat lawn flower bordered, & delightful glimpses of hills beyond. Mr. Bonham Carter kindly offers to take A. in his carriage in the direction of White's Selborne.[34] Very pleasant drive to Uppark[35] by Harting with Mr. Stowe. A. much delighted with the Park. Its great wooded slopes are very fine & so are the views of the hills from them. The story of the lady of the place romantic.

21st. Very glad that the day for our return home has come. Frank & Katie have been there some days & everything bright & pretty to welcome us. Next day my Father and Charles Weld arrive.

October

1st. Days generally rainy & misty & dark. A. & Frank work at the bank & take me out to see their work. My days spent chiefly with my Father. A. & Frank play at Backgammon. Sir John & Lady Simeon call & ask us all to Swainston. Frank rides over there.

6th. He & his have to leave us & return to Park House. Very glad we have been to have them. A. walks to Swainston. I play & sing old airs to my Father. Simeons, Henry Taylor, & Mrs. Cameron see him. She brings him a violet poncha of Mr. Henry Taylor's invention to wear in bed & he looks very grand in it.

8th. A. returns from Swainston. Louy brings him. I am shocked to hear of Mr. Estcourt's death.

9th. I go to the boat with my Father. I see him seated on deck in his great cloak looking like a pale king. The boat looks majestic as it moves away. I never saw it look so before. In the evening A. reads me some of Heine's songs.

13th. A. reads what interests us both much. A working man's

[34] About two and a half miles to the east of Tisted lies Selborne, the home of Gilbert White.

[35] One and a half miles south of Harting, Uppark is particularly notable for its fine eighteenth-century furnishings.

idea of what education for the people should be. A paper in the *Cornhill*, also a leading article on Bright's speech which I liked in the morning.

He reads some of the Maccabees. Continued news that our Lionel is very weak. Day & night the thought possesses one. A. takes me into the fields in the day & reads to me in the evening.

16th. Mr. Knowles[36] calls to return our Layamon's *Brut.* Some little time ago he kindly sent A. his delightful book of Stories from the *Morte d'Arthur* for children. In acknowledging this A. said that he wished he would write a similar book from Layamon's *Brut.* On the plea of borrowing it he introduced himself personally to us the other day & so began our personal acquaintance. We hear from Albert Fytche that he is going to be married & that he is appointed Chief Commissioner or virtually Governor of British Burmah.[37] Mr. Grove & Mr. Sullivan come. Mrs. Cameron & Lady Manners[38] join us in the evening when Mr. Sullivan sings his "O mistress mine" & "Sweet day." Both beautiful I think. A. reads.

The gentlemen go, Mr. Grove having to receive the Prince of Wales. A happy day with my A. He reads me his "Song of the Wrens" which he has written for Sullivan.[39] He subscribes to the Eyre fund.[40]

The Longs & Maiden's Croft. Happy days but for anxiety about our Lionel. Mr. Valentine Prinsep comes in the evening.

[36]James Thomas Knowles (1831–1908), editor of the *Contemporary Review*, 1870–77, founder and editor of the *Nineteenth Century*, 1877, and editor until his death, and the architect who designed Aldworth. From the late 1860s until his death the laureate often went to London with Knowles, and occasionally Tennyson accompanied him to meetings of the Metaphysical Society of which Knowles was founder.

[37]Albert Fytche (1820–92) was chief commander of British Burma and agent to the viceroy from 1867 until 1871.

[38]Lady Lydia Manners (d. 1916), the former Lydia Sophia Dashwood, wife of John Thomas Manners Sutton, 2d Baron Manners (1818–64).

[39]Alexander Strahan published Tennyson's "The Window; or the Song of the Wrens" with music by Arthur Sullivan in December 1870.

[40]Both the poet and Mrs. Tennyson expressed a somewhat reluctant approval of the severe measures taken by Col. Edward Eyre (1815–1901), the governor of Jamaica, 1862–66, in suppressing the native rebellion of October 1865. Tennyson sent a subscription to the fund for Eyre's defense against the prosecution for murder pressed by John Stuart Mill's Jamaica Committee. And later when Gladstone attacked Eyre's actions, Tennyson let it be known that he thought Eyre justified in the steps he had taken.

21st. A. finishes the Songs & reads them to me. Next day Mrs. Cameron brings two Irish Yews, coming thro' the rain. She goes out with A. to plant them when he has read the Songs to her. He takes me to see the trees planted in the mound in the Park and reads to me some of Lady Duff Gordon's Letters from the East.[41] Very graphic. Happy days of solitude for us. One much like another.

A. anxious about the facts in Jamaica not knowing whether to accede to the request of the Committee that he would place his name on it. (It seems enough that he has done so in the subscription list.) As he cannot approve of all the late proceedings there the question of course was could Governor Eyre have prevented the revolution & massacre otherwise?

24th. Busy with "Hands all around" this week. A. takes me to watch the planting again this time in the sunny little nursery. He brings me the Golden Euonymus to look at & shows me the Yews & the Scarlet Rhododendrons. Mrs. Cameron brings a variegated laurel. Generous creature, how hard it is to stay her hands from gifts! She brings us what she has copied about Governor Eyre before we go to Town on Nov. 1st. Mr. Barrett with his accustomed hospitality insists on our staying with him. Mr. Prinsep & Mr. Watts call & we have an interesting talk about India.

November

3rd. We go to Guildford. A. enjoys his walk of fourteen miles, passes Ockham but forgets that Dr. Lushington lives there or he would have called on him. Next day we go to the White Hart, Haslemere, & take rooms & order dinner but Mrs. Gilchrist has been so good as to prepare everything for us at her house so we countermand all at our Inn & go there.

5th. Mr. Simmons comes in the morning. He is so thoroughly kind & simple that A. takes much to him.

7th. We drive to a rivulet & there come to Stoaltey farm. Mr. Newman very kind & attentive & a good cook but the rooms smokey & the fires obstinately bent on not burning.

9th. We roam about the country to look at this piece of land & that. The donkey from the chair which Mrs. Gilchrist has procured for me from Guildford has one day to be taken out & the

[41] Lucie, Lady Duff-Gordon, *Letters from Egypt, 1863–65* (1865).

chair bodily lifted over some very bad ruts. Fortunately we meet a carter boy who helps. One ought to be the better for knowing Mrs. Gilchrist & seeing her so beautifully contented under her great sorrow. She thinks that she owes her life to the quiet of her cottage & the beauty of the neighbourhood. For four or five months during the fever which carried off her husband she never was in bed but twelve nights. The children fell ill of it & recovered. He took it from them & died. I never before saw any one so really convinced apparently of the good of poverty.

We go to Grayshott Hall.[42] We do not absolutely take the rooms there but nearly resolve on doing so. A. enjoys his walks & at dinner says I do not eat in this way at home.

13th. Unfortunately he forgets the day of the month & I had not heard of the glorious sight expected to-night & so we miss the great fall of meteors.

14th. Mrs. Gilchrist comes with Mr. Simmons in her carriage to take me to the Station. Surely never were there kinder people than we have met here. One of my eyes has been very bad lately. A. leads me about. We sleep at Winchester & have the sitting-room we had with our boys when we returned from the Pyrenees.

15th. Very thankful to be back in my own delightful home. The Fields, Gattys, Louy Simeon, Mr. Allingham. Louy, good & kind to me almost as a daughter, helps with the Gattys. Tilly & Cole come. . . .

December

3rd. Sir John dines with us, a pleasant evening as usual with him. A letter from Mr. Michel saying that he has not waited for the proofs of "Elaine" over which I spent so many hours last week. Vexatious as these many things we would not have [the poems] go as they are in his prose rendering.

[42]The Tennysons leased Grayshott Farm for short stays during the summer of 1867 while they continued their search for a desirable location for a permanent summer home. The poet was especially eager to escape the Isle of Wight summer tourists. As Emily Tennyson wrote to Margaret Gatty at the time, she and her husband were "trying to find a plot whereas to build a few rooms to come to when the cockneys are insupportable" (November 9, 1866, T.R.C.). Tennyson and his family returned to Grayshott for a short stay in the summer of 1868.

A. reads some of the Duke of Argyll's *Reign of Law* to us on the flight of birds. Very interesting.

13th. Our Lionel comes looking rosy & happy, thank God, & his stammering nearly cured. He is his Father's walking companion until our Hallam arrives on the 18th & they both walk with him. French Proofs. Very hard to alter them to one's mind. Hallam helps me. How thankful I ought to be for such a Father & sisters & husband & sons as I have. The boys wonderfully tender & thoughtful, so different from what one often hears of boys.

1867

January

1st. Hallam reads Molière with me & very well. He & Lionel go to meet Mr. Tuson, Lionel's Australian friend. Chess & Charades & not much going out these days because of frost & snow.

Mr. Tuson goes & next day (the 6th) Mr. Jowett arrives and as usual the boys go out to meet him. Mr. Bennett comes & both walk with A.

Mr. Warre comes with Lord Francis Hervey in the evening.[1] Mrs. Cameron & Hardinge the life of the party. Mr. Warre dines with us next day after a walk with Mr. Jowett. Mr. Lacy de Lacy,[2] Mrs. Cameron & her three sons & Mr. Atkinson come to act charades. Our boys acting very natural. Mr. de Lacy sings some songs.

14th. Mr. Jowett goes—a good friend goes, one of our truest.

15th. "Ici on parle Francais" acted by Mde. de Lacy, the Camerons, & our boys. The Camerons act admirably. Skating, sledding, shooting, walking.

20th. I hear that my Father taking off his hat in the cold while speaking to a lady, has had a partial stroke of paralysis. Mrs. Cameron most kind about him. Charlie & Louy go. I have better news. The [*illegible*] reports favorably but very anxiously.

23rd. A. brings me my first snowdrop. Hallam finishes "Les fourberies de Scapin"[3] with me.

[1]Julian Henry Charles Warre (1827–70), the diplomat and poet, served as first secretary and acting chargé d'affaires at Paris, 1865–67, and again in 1868. He issued his *Poems* in 1852 and a translation of Heine two years later.

Lord Hervey is Arthur Charles Hervey (1808–94), fourth son of Frederick William Hervey, 1st marquess of Bristol. A contemporary of Tennyson at Cambridge, Hervey was bishop of Bath and Wells from 1869 until his death.

[2]Willam Lacy (1788–1871), the famous singer, widely considered the finest bass voice in England in the nineteenth century.

[3]The Molière play (1671).

February

8th. A dreary day of wind & rain & a dreary parting from our boys. But it is for their good as Hallam says. Thankful for a very favourable report of my Father from the doctor. Louy Simeon comes & Mr. Sullivan. He sings his "O Mistress mine" & his "Sweet Day" which Louy likes as well as I do. Next day he plays us some exquisite bits from Bach. Talk much to Louy. I can talk to her. She leaves in the afternoon. A. is reading me Disraeli's speech but we are interrupted. He goes on with his two hours' walk every day. He reads from the Bible to me. Amongst other portions the 15th of the first of *Corinthians*. We talk of the subject that most fills his life, the immortality of man.

15th. Ally goes to Osborne. My cough bad & I not equal to so long a drive & have to excuse myself & I am sorry. A. glad to find Mrs. Gordon there.[4] The Queen looking well & being merry. Kind & gracious to him. H.M. is always.

16th. Fine illustrations of "Guinevere" & "Vivien" from Doré[5] to-day. A sprig of myrtle from the tomb of Keats sent us by Mr. Clark. A. reads to me the Tubingen school commentary on the keeping of Easter. We compare the different accounts of the Passion & the Crucifixion. Much cheered by a letter from our Hallam. He seems to breathe more freely in a higher form.

A. takes me out in the little carriage over the prostrate rails which are being moved further back, the growth of the trees making this necessary. Some Daffodils in the Park. Those of Doré's Illustrations of "Guinevere" arrive.

21st. Mr. & Mrs. Bayard Taylor come. A. gives them some of Mr. Ellis's (sherry made in 1815) Waterloo sherry & some of his yet more gorgeous wines. He reads "Guinevere" to them.[6] She

[4]Other visitors at Osborne on February 15 included Caroline Gordon and Caroline Herschel, daughter of Sir John Frederick William Herschel. It was while Tennyson and Caroline Gordon were alone with Queen Victoria that the poet made the queen laugh by talking about his continual frustration with "the Cockneys" who spied on him and trespassed on his property. "But we are not much troubled here by them," commented the Queen—to which Tennyson responded, "Perhaps I should not be either, Your Majesty, if I could stick a sentry at my gates" (*Letters of E. T.*, p. 208).

[5]Gustave Doré (1833–83), the French artist who illustrated works by Dante, Rabelais, Balzac, and La Fontaine, as well as Tennyson's *Idylls*.

[6]Bayard Taylor (1825–78), the American traveler, translator, and man of letters, best remembered for his translation of Goethe's *Faust* (1870–71). Tenny-

is a charming German lady & I have very interesting conversations with her. A. tells me the striking story of Mr. Bayard Taylor's uncle now an old man of 70 or 80, the son of the late Duke of Saxe-Gotha's chief huntsmen. He was at the time of Napoleon's greatest power about fifteen & was so wrought upon by hearing Napoleon continually called the enemy of the human race that he determined to shoot him (the general) while passing alone thro' one of the long corridors of the palace as he often did when he visited the Duke, of whom he was very fond. One day accordingly the youth posted himself in a corner of a corridor, rifle in hand. He heard the Emperor's footstep in the distance, coming nearer and nearer. [He] put his hand to the trigger as he approached. But Napoleon fixed his great eyes upon him in such a terrible manner that he was paralized (with fear) & trembled from head to foot (all but surrendered & let his rifle drop). The Emperor did not swerve an inch from his course, or quicker or slower but the boy felt that he knew what he was about to do & his legs could scarcely bear him from the spot. The rifle fell from his hand. No notice was ever taken of the circumstance.

25th. A. takes me out in my little carriage & we plan about the small terrace where the white gate, "Mama's Gate," used to be. . . .

March

1st. A telegram telling of our boy's serious attack in his lungs. We go off by the next boat to Marlboro'. At first they say that there is no fresh telegram but when we are in the cabin they bring us a very comforting [one]. Still we determine to go on. Still another at Reading & better. Here we sleep as we cannot reach Marlboro' to-night unless we rest. We start by the first train the next day. Dear Mr. Bradley meets us next day at Savernake with "all-right." Mrs. Bradley has beef tea ready for me. How can we ever forget all their goodness & tenderness to us!

This [is] all I can record about this terrible time. A. was very

---

son thought the wines sent him by the poetic wine dealer Ellis so superb as to be fit "to be drunk by Cleopatra or Catherine of Russia." Tennyson read the description of Arthur's forgiveness of Guinevere with such emotion that the Taylors wept. "How can you say that you have no surety of permanent fame?" asked Taylor when the poet had finished. "This poem will only die with the language in which it is written." Emily Tennyson at once voiced her agreement: "It is true!" she cried, "I have told Alfred the same thing" (*AT*, p. 366).

calm but deeply moved. At the crisis he said, "I have made up my mind to lose him. God will take him pure & good, straight from his mother's lessons, he is very simple & religious. Surely it would be better for him than to grow up such a one as I am." But he is wrapped up in the boy. He talked a great deal about "our all being gathered up somehow into the all-absorbing love of God, into a state infinitely higher than we can now conceive of."

[We telegraphed for Dr. Symonds at Bristol.][7] [Great] comfort his visit gives & his exceeding goodness to us & the kindness & affection of friends & the blessed feeling that our boy is in the Hands of One who loves him better than we can. I get up again at the same time to breakfast with the doctor. Now we are allowed to go every day twice to the Sanatorium. Two days we are preceded by a snowplough. The snow being otherwise impassable. Our boy has an airy room & a doctor & a nurse unwearied. Very touching to us showing how much they care for Hallam. Perhaps even more touching is the fact that there is a general feeling in the school about him as Mr. Bradley tells us. We quiet our poor Lionel as best we can by telegram & letter, not of course letting him know the danger. We see our Hallam's little cheery [face?] at present.

25th. One long farewell to our dear friends. It is much to have seen a life so devoted to others as that of Mr. Bradley. Mrs. Bradley too does very much in spite of great suffering. Their servants too have done everything possible for us. Before leaving Mrs. Bradley shows us her Arthur's room which she most kindly says Hallam shall share if he returns.[8] It rains & the driver does not know his way so I have an anxious time with my Hallam before we meet A. & Mr. Bradley at the train. Our

[7] *Materials*, III, 54. By the time Dr. Symonds, Jowett's "Beloved Physician," arrived at Marlborough, the crisis had already passed. Although Hallam Tennyson's lung congestion was quite serious, indeed critical, for a time, his illness was brief, and he returned to Farringford with his parents on March 26.

[8] Marian and George Bradley were especially fond of Hallam Tennyson, and during his tenure at Marlborough from 1865 until 1872 the Bradleys treated him like their own son. In the autumn of 1868 Mrs. Bradley wrote to Emily Tennyson in praise of Hallam: "He really is a very dear boy," she said. "I find home influences tell remarkably in his case—he has all the marks of a carefully cultivated childhood acting on an originally thoughtful and uncommon nature. I find him a delightful companion and enjoy many talks with him—There is an amazing charm in that mixture of childish simplicity and confidingness, with thoughtful manliness" (October 3, 1868, T.R.C.).

good William[9] meets us at Reading & says that he has been used to carry sick people. He carries Hallam from train to train. . . . Thank God we reach home safely. Hallam none the worse.

The Bradleys say they never knew how great A. was until they saw him under this great trial. So calm, so kind, so thoughtful for everyone. By degrees our Hallam gains flesh & strength & rides & drives most of the day. He has been very good & patient & cheerful throughout.

April

25th. Mr. Blumenthal[10] comes.

27th. Very busy preparing for Grayshott.

29th. We arrive at Grayshott farm where we were to spend the early summer. In the copses the nightingales were singing; the anemones were out in all the woods. [The] Pony carriage too late for the horse-boat so Hallam & I get the little omnibus in which we came here yesterday & drive to Guildford to meet our Lionel. The fifteen miles do not seem long the drive is so beautiful. We have forgotten to bring my luncheon but get some light thing at the station & in about half an hour have the delight of welcoming our Lionel. He looks thinner & less well than at Christmas. We look for Cabinets and other things at Rimm's & Williamson's. The day stormy with sleet.

1st. Better day. A & the boys go to call on Mrs. Gilchrist. A. delighted with the drive & the air. She is very thankful. The cellar at Grayshott alas! proves rather a receptacle of drains than a cellar but we all enjoy the pure air & the views of the neighbourhood & the freedom of A.'s walks rejoices him.

6th. We go to Haslemere after to take A.'s portmanteau & see him off.

18th. They all go to Selbourne. The Bells very kind. A. admires

[9] William Knight.

[10] Jacob Blumenthal (1829–1908), the German pianist and composer who took up residence in London in 1848 and subsequently became pianist to the queen. While at Farringford, Blumenthal sang several songs for the Tennysons, including his "The Days That Are No More," and he was photographed by Julia Margaret Cameron.

the place very much. Mr. Simmons kindly gives our boys fishing in some of his ponds.

22nd. Frost in the night, snow-showers in the day. . . .

24th. Drummond Rawnsley comes. Next day Mr. Palgrave. Both welcome guests.

26th. Mr. Palgrave has been to Lord Craneborne's[11] & we have all been wandering when near our gate we are surprised by Mr. Allingham's running after us. He had found his way from Liphook.

27th. A. reads me a new Version of one of the Songs[12] which I like better than the old. He reads Heine to me at night. A piano & a larger library are sadly wanted for the boys. One feels that even this little time may have a large influence & one is anxious notwithstanding continual rides & drives & walks.

June

1st. They drive to meet Mr. Jowett but return without him. He however arrives later. Sir John & Louy come. He looks sad & ill from the loss of his brother.[13] One feels that it is exceedingly kind in our friends coming so far to see us.

4th. I finish the *Reign of Law* which seems to me a really fine book in more senses than one. The Chapter on Law in Politics interests me specially. The book it seems to me might have for one of its objects the glorification of my A., so concisely, so beautifully do the quotations from him express some of its deeper truths. Seeing this I feel that perhaps I have been wrong in not having fulfilled my half formed purpose of making a book of the great thoughts & sayings of Tennyson. Perhaps not for great thoughts & sayings lose so much of their life when given [apart] from their natural place.

5th. Mrs. Gilchrist & Mr. Simmons having taken no end of trouble in communicating with Mr. Lucas [about Blackhorse Copse on Blackdown we went there in an odd procession, Lio-

[11] Robert Arthur Talbot Gascoym-Cecil was 3d marquis of Salisbury; he succeeded his brother as Viscount Craneborne in 1865.

[12] "Take My Love," later titled "No Answer," from "The Window; or the Song of the Wrens."

[13] Capt. Charles Simeon (1816–67), the second son of the 2d baronet.

nel on a donkey with a lady's saddle, I driving in the basket-carriage, the rest walking. The wheels spun round on the axles without touching ground in some of the deep ruts and the carriage had to be lifted over, William leading the pony carefully. At last we reached the charming ledge on the heathery down, looking over an immense view bounded by the south-downs on the South, by Leith Hill on the North. Copse wood surrounds the ledge, and the hill protects it from the north-west. The fox-glove was in full bloom. A. T. helped me down the mountain-path. We all enjoyed the day thoroughly.

Mr. Lear came from Liphook, he liked our neighbourhood so much that he said we were to look out for more land for him hereabouts.][14]

While we are at luncheon Lionel drives up with a big letter which he waves in triumph. This is the agreement which Mr. Simmons has had made with Mr. Lucas for Greenhill. How good he is! Yesterday he rode over to Mr. Lucas for the third time & settled the matter. A. went yesterday to Mr. Simmons to know the event of his third ride but he had not returned.

16th. A. met Mr. Knowles at the Station. When he was at Farringford A. had said to him as he does to most strangers, "I am so short-sighted that I shall not know you if I meet you unless you speak to me." Mr. Knowles accordingly spoke to him, reminding him of this. Having then been told A's errand [he] said I am an architect. A. replied, you had better build me a house, & Mr. Knowles said "On one condition that you take my services freely only paying the journeys." Afterwards this was agreed upon.

A. calls at Argyll Lodge to receive Longfellow's Pipe Brace brought for him by Lord Lorne & lunches there.[15] He also goes to Eden Lodge & sees Miss Lena Eden, her aunt not well.

20th. Delightful drive with A. nearly to Liphook.

23rd. A beautiful morning for our Picnic at Greenhill. I ride part of the way on Mrs. Simmons's donkey which she kindly sends down the steep for me. A. & Hallam nearly carry me & once we all come down softly together & sit laughing. A. & the

[14] *Materials*, III, 57–58.

[15] Longfellow had sent Lord Lorne two pipes to present to Tennyson as a gift. Shortly thereafter the laureate mentioned the gift, rather unappreciatively, in a letter to the duke of Argyll: "It is odd that the Americans always send me pipes, or tobacco, as if I cared for nothing else in this world; and their tobacco is not my tobacco, nor their pipes my pipes: bird's-eye and a Milo-cutty being more according to my fancy than costlier things" (*Memoir*, II, 46).

boys take me to our wood & we bring home the fairy white bell, some insect nest hung on a spray of heath. Mr. Knowles lunches with us & drives with A. to see Mr. Buchton's[?] house.

24th. Our Hallam very unwell with feverish sore throat. We have to send for Dr. Hammond who sees him again on the 27th. Mr. Locker leaves us, most kind he is.

Thankful are we for a fine day on the 29th to take him home tho' yet by no means well.

Two small Flys convey us to Farnham but we have to leave part of our luggage to come in the washerwoman's cart if it is to be had. I seize upon a butcher's cart & send Andrews back in it. Thankful indeed to reach home. No carriage comes for us but Mrs. Cameron kind as ever takes A. & Hallam & myself in her fly. The boys (Hardinge, Charlie, & Lionel) come after us.[16] Fortunately Dr. Hollis is in the Village & he puts our Hallam on a totally different system.

A. fetches me up to his study to see the Glades from his window. He says that he wonders at the beauty of the place. . . .

11th. Our dear Charlie & Louy come with Frederic's Elise & Emilia.[17] Walks on the down & drives & croquet. The Camerons, Mr. Charteris (a young Paladin we say) & Mr. Muir here. They & Hardinge drive with us.

16th. Tilly arrives. All except myself go to the Review. We take an Omnibus & Mr. Atkinson & his brother accompany them. They take luncheon & go to Bembridge down.

A. & the boys who have not been ill have enjoyed the day in spite of storm & rain. The illuminations & the salute fine.

Mr. & Mrs. Simmons come. They are most kind & like Farringford. Edmund comes. The Simeons & Mr. Henry Cowper.[18]

Mr. & Mrs. Knowles arrive. I spend a long time with him making a measured plan of Aldworth. We arrange together what the modifications of the plan are to be.

[16] Charles and Hardinge Cameron were the elder two of the Camerons' four sons.

[17] Elise & Emilia were Frederick Tennyson's daughters.

[18] Henry Frederick Cowper (1836–87), M.P. for Hertfordshire, 1865–85.

August

1st. Mary Ryan's[19] wedding day. All our party go to Church. Lionel not allowed to officiate as Bridesman so he dons his new gray suit & borrows white gloves from me & mounts the carriage as page. The boys & girls from Farringford go to luncheon & our own boys on their carriage which takes the Bride & Bridegroom to the boat as it did the Bride to Church.

The Bradleys, Mr. Lacy, Mr. Allingham.

6th. A.'s birthday. He does not like to have it kept so we say nothing about it.

16th. Our boy so anxious to return to Marlboro' for the quarter at least that we yield. To-day he leaves. Frederic is here and one cannot but be touched by his kindness to him. A. very anxious to go away the place is getting so full. Mrs. Grosvenor Hood & the Hamonds most kind about Elise & Emilia. . . .

23rd. A. goes with Frederic & the girls. They to Grasby, he to Lyme Regis.[20] Letters nearly everyday from him. Mr. Waldrin has been frequently coming since he introduced himself to Lionel by talking of King Arthur.[21]

September

6th. Notice of Scarletina at Marlboro'. We telegraph to beg that on account of his recent illness he may be sent home at once. Next day I have the blessing of seeing him look more himself than when he left.

10th. The boys and myself wait on the Quay for the boat, A.

[19] Mrs. Cameron's maid and model who married Henry Cotton, only son of Sir Arthur Thomas Cotton.

[20] When he learned that Francis Turner Palgrave and his family were spending their holidays at Lyme Regis, Tennyson determined to take his usual summer journey in that direction. The poet and his traveling companion, William Allingham, arrived in Lyme Regis in late July, and, having viewed the Cobb where Jane Austen's unfortunate Louisa Musgrove had her fall, they proceeded on a walking tour to Exeter, then across Dartmoor to Dartmouth, thence to Salcombe, Kingsbridge and Thirlestone, and finally through Ivybridge back to Lyme.

[21] When he met Lionel Tennyson a month earlier, Mr. Waldrin had identified himself as a King Arthur devotee, and he had talked to Lionel about the historical accuracy of the Arthurian legend, Ossian, and other literary matters.

having said he may come. He is not there. The Dowager Lady Hamond & Mr. Hamond kindly invite our boys for tomorrow, Larry's birthday. We drive to the Lodge & leave the boys. Mrs. Grosvenor Hood takes me. Miss Hamond shows Hallam the tablecloth made for her sister by the soldiers out of scraps of their companions' coats & other interesting things. They have supper in Colonel Grosvenor Hood's tent. Mrs. Grosvener says, that the account in Kinglake[22] of her husband's part in the Alma charge is admirable.

12th. The boys go to their dancing lesson in the morning. The ponies are tired so only Hallam & I meet A. at the boat afterwards. He is not looking well & has not been well. On his way home he lunched at Canford & saw the Assyrian Bulls given by Mr. Layard to his cousin & admired extremely the books printed by the Guests themselves on their own press.[23] Our former servant William Seaton who went out as Steward returns a ghost having got a chill waiting on sick people. He is an orphan. We take him in. Of the crew he alone remains except one other. A fine eclipse of the moon.

14th. Enid Guest comes.

19th. We are summoned by telegrams to my Father. Thank God that it is granted me to see his beloved face once more in life. Our poor Charley & Louy travel all night but are too late. I am made to go to bed the doctor saying that my Father may last at this state for many days. I sleep a little but at the first glimmering of light I cannot rest having heard that the spirit so often departs as night & morning meet.

Nanny & Agnes & myself watch for half an hour, then there was a deeper breath & then a pause & a few fainter breathings & all was over. A little bird sang at the window. Two of the deepest desires of my heart granted. I have seen him again & he knew A. & me & he has passed away in sleep. God alone knows of the noble self-denying love, the beautiful simplicity & cheerfulness of him whom we shall see no more in this world.

25th. We put Farringford roses on his coffin in the beautiful

[22] Alexander William Kinglake, *The Invasion of the Crimea*, 8 vols. (1863–87).

[23] Canford School (Manor), Dorsetshire, was formerly the seat of Lord Wimborne. Sir Ivor Guest, the son of Lady Charlotte Guest, printed "The Window" on the Canford Manor Press in late 1867.

Sir Austen Henry Layard (1817–94) was a politician and excavator of Nineveh.

cemetery, he having so often spoken of the last roses of summer which he had placed on our mother's.

26th. A. & I go to Salisbury on our way home. The return to everyday life very difficult.

29th. Mr. Lear comes, he is so good & kind & gentle that he helps not harms one.

October

1st. He goes to Swainston.

2nd. We read Norman Macleod's *Reminiscences of a Highland Parish.*[24] A. & the boys play at battledore & shuttlecock, walk, & take me out driving.

16th. Mr. Mornington[25] leaves us. Kind & pleasant he has been. The interest he took in all that was greatly good & that with which from early days he strove to inspire his children. One of the great blessings of my life is that he & A. have cared so much for each other. Of the three little birds Agnes & he petted one flew away before that day, the other dies of grief, & no one knew how the third went. He would get up from his bed early in the morning to put the little bird he called Captain in the sunshine.

November

2nd. Nanny, Agnes, & Horatio come.

17th. The Queen's Book arrived for A. with an inscription in her own hand.[26] The second precious heirloom of the kind. . . .

25th. Horatio goes, very glad we are to have had him. Mrs. Clough & her little Theresa & their maid come. Pleasant talks

[24]Norman Macleod (1812–72), *Reminiscences of a Highland Parish* (London and Edinburgh, 1867).

[25]Probably a younger son of William Wesley-Pole, 4th earl of Mornington (1788–1857). For a short time Mornington tutored Hallam and Lionel.

[26]*Leaves from the Journal of Our Life in the Highlands* was the queen's first publication. The poet's copy, now at the Tennyson Research Centre, is inscribed: "Alfred Tennyson Esquire,/Trusting he will/not criticise too severely/from/Victoria R. Osborne, January 18, 1868." Apparently this entry is dated incorrectly; it should be joined with the record of the arrival of the queen's book in the entry for January 20, 1868.

with Mrs. Clough. Mrs. Cameron brings a photograph of Horatio. He looks in it like one of Landseer's Stags, not one of the "King's Sons."[27] We have had a beautiful November dry tho' cold with a great deal of sunshine. One of our dear evenings.

December

1st. The Songs received from Sir Ivor Guest. A. talks with me of Hebrew these evenings & of Matter & Spirit.

5th. By A.'s desire I send "The Victim" off to *Good Words.*[28] Happy evenings with him. He reads Hebrew to me, brings me down his Psalm-like poems.

10th. Nanny & Agnes come to us again.

28th. Mr. Clark & Mr. Woolner come in spite of Scarlet Fever at the Farm. Mr. Allingham also. Very pleasant.

[27] Although a number of Edwin Landseer's paintings contain stags, Emily may have in mind either *The Stag at Bay* (1849) or his better-known *Monarch of the Glen*, which was first exhibited in 1851 at the Royal Academy, a majestic picture of a single stag represented before the merest suggestion of distant mountain scenery in the background.

[28] *Good Words* paid Tennyson £700 for "The Victim," which it published in January 1868. Its first volume publication was in *The Holy Grail and Other Poems*.

1868

January

2nd. Our pleasant guests leave us.

7th. Mr. Digby comes.[1]

10th. Henry Cameron & our boys act *Box & Cox.*[2] Everyone marvels at the good acting especially at Lionel's intonation & perfect ease. Lord Donoughmore[3] arrives late from Cowes. All the household looking on at the play. Hallam opens the door to him in his dress.

Mr. Jowett goes to Lambert's Hotel but we see him often, have interesting talks with him. Lord Donoughmore comes with him, generally has football with Mr. Digby & the boys. Mr. Moxon comes.

20th. The Queen's Book on the Highlands comes with a very kind inscription to A. He reads some of it to me. Touching records of a simple happy life. Read the interesting article on the Talmud by Deutsch.[4]

23rd. Mr. & Mrs. Bradley. Welcome guests. Sir John & Louy Simeon. Mr. Bradley in his goodness offers to take Hallam into his house if we think it good for him to return now. More & more one feels the energy of his desire to lift his pupils up from the clod. Mrs. Bradley & Kate[5] & both read "The Lover's Tale." Allowance must be made for the redundance of youth into words, but it does seem to me the very health of young pure love which should strike a new pulse thro' the world grown rather old in love & I fear if old mean cold. But what know I

[1]Digby was tutor for Hallam and Lionel Tennyson from January 1868 until the following September, when Lionel entered Eton for his first half.

[2]*Cox and Box* (1867), a lively musical piece by Arthur Sullivan which marked his first departure from "serious" music and whereby his name first appeared on a playbill.

[3]John Luke George Hely-Hutchinson, 5th earl of Donoughmore (1848–1900).

[4]Emanuel Oscar Menahem Deutsch (1829–73), the Semitic scholar who introduced the *Talmud* to English readers virtually for the first time with his famous essay in the *Quarterly Review*, 123 (October 1867), 417–64.

[5]Katherine Rawnsley.

here?[6] Mr. Bradley tells A. that if he had searched the whole world over he could not have found a more satisfactory boy or one who promises to be a more satisfactory man.

28th. A. & the Bradleys go to Swainston for the night & bring the Simeons back with them. Our boys act *Box & Cox* with [*illegible*] Hamond[7] & are all much applauded by Mrs. Grosvenor Hood & the rest of our friends from the neighbourhood.

30th. A. goes with Mr. & Mrs. Bradley to Winchester & meets Mr. Knowles at Greenhill to fix the site for the house & dresses at his house on Clapham Common. He goes afterwards to the Deanery, Westminster, & hears the Dean preach in the Abbey and is much pleased.[8]

February

4th & 5th. These days I copy "The Lover's Tale" & send what is done to A.

8th. Franklin Lushington comes good & kind as ever. I have interesting talk with him.

9th. A. writes from Mr. Woolner's to-day. (He goes to the Lodge,[9] Trinity today), is hard at work arranging his books. The boys & I [get] A's room painted, shelves & a window put in.

15th. The boys & servants help me with right goodwill to finish A.'s sitting-room & dressing-room. The boys & Mr. Digby have a good football match. I go to meet A. There is a purple hue over all things tho' the sun does not shine. A. looks well & is cheerful. He is very much delighted with his rooms & I am very thankful. He has had a very pleasant time at the Lodge.

[6] On several occasions before 1868 Emily had urged Tennyson to perfect and publish "The Lover's Tale," which he initially prepared for publication in 1832, but neither she nor others who admired the poem, such as the Bradleys and Mrs. Rawnsley, were successful in persuading him to "pick it to pieces and make it up again" (quoted in Ricks, p. 300, from Marian Bradley's manuscript Diary). Richard Herne Shepherd's piracy of the poem in 1870, however, stirred Tennyson at last, and after extensive revision he published "The Lover's Tale," including as Part IV his previously published "The Golden Supper," in May 1879.

[7] Apparently a son of the Andrew Hamonds of nearby Afton Manor.

[8] The dean was Arthur Penrhyn Stanley.

[9] House of the master of Trinity College. Dr. William Hepworth Thompson (1810–86) became master of Trinity in 1866.

The Master & his wife having been so very kind & hospitable. He had also a very pleasant meeting with Mr. Clark & a very interesting talk with dear old Professor Sedgwick.[10] Mr. & Mrs. Knowles & the Woolners have also been extremely kind. He had met Mr. Deutsch & Sir Bartle Frere[11] among other people new to him & the Stanleys & Lockers & others whom he is always glad to see. The Sunday after that at the Abbey he was at Trinity Chapel, which could not fail as he said to arouse many old memories.

18th. The Hebrew Bible beautifully bound in four limp covers arrives from Mess. Moxon. He reads a little from it to us. Plants trees these days & transplants snowdrops helped by the boys. Hallam is reading the Dean's book on Westminster[12] to us which interests us much.

22nd. He drives to meet Mr. Venables. Pleasant talks & walks & drives with him. Louy Simeon comes to stay a few days. Reads me some of her novel & is taught football by the boys!

25th. Mr. Venables goes. We are very sorry & he is kind enough to say that he is very sorry.

March

1st. Mr. Digby, A. & Hallam read Milton to us. Afterwards A. reads some of his own things. Louy helps me with Francisque Michel's translation of "Guinevere." A rather hopeless task. Mr. Payne's new edition of A.'s works & his advertisement both hateful to us.[13]

2nd. Louy goes. I have no time to drive with her. A. reads some

[10] Adam Sedgwick (1785–1873) was a renowned geologist. He became Woodwardian professor of geology at Cambridge in 1818; he was elected president of the British Association in 1833 and of the geological section in 1837, 1845, 1853, and 1860.

[11] Sir Henry Bartle Edward Frere (1815–84), chief commissioner of Sind, 1850–59, and governor of Bombay, 1862–67. Frere returned to England as a member of the council of India in 1867, and ten years thereafter he was made governor of the Cape and first high commissioner of South Africa.

[12] Dean Stanley's *Historical Memorials of Westminster Abbey* (1868).

[13] Displeased especially with what he and Emily regarded as tasteless advertising, Tennyson soon called a halt to J. Bertrand Payne's plans for a Moxon edition of his collected works. Alexander Strahan published the six-volume *Imperial Library Edition* in 1872–73.

of his Poems from the 1830 book to us & makes merry over them.

4th. Professor Tyndall sends a note from the hotel asking the boys to walk with him. We beg him to come here. He comes in the evening but returns to the hotel to sleep but next day comes to stay with us. Pity that he must go so soon. It is so beautiful & he enjoys it so much & is so pleasant.

10th. A. reads what he has written to Mr. Digby & myself. Very fine it is. Very much annoyed by Mr. Payne who cannot understand our love of absolute simplicity in advertisement & business arrangements so that we may be free to take thankfully what comes in this way. Be it much or little. What grieves me is that his love of excitement may mislead the public as to A. who has nothing to do with these matters. For instance, the world thinks that we are enriching ourselves by Doré's editions. Whereas we have not received a penny as yet for the use of the poems tho' [he] promises something when thousands of each is [*sic*] sold. To my great satisfaction A. now works walking up & down in Maiden's Croft & writing in the Summer House. Both air & view are so fine there. The boys have frequent football matches here & a bevy of ladies to look on.

Read Lamartine's *Celebrated People*, last Sir Masingberd, & Mirabeau's Life.[14] What a tragic one!

26th. The boys like their pins with their Father's photograph burnt in glass which I have had set in gold for them & Lionel our gift of a chess board, Aunty Nanny's of a concertina. There has been a great deal of smoke in the Yew-trees this year. One day there was such a cloud of blue white smoke from that opposite my window that I thought there seemed to be a fire in the shrubbery.

28th. We drive most days. To-day the carriage stops & Minnie Stephen's face looks in.[15] Her husband is with her. They go to meet Annie Thackeray & next day they & Mrs. Grosvenor Hood lunch with us & their party & Mr. Deveril[16] are added to

[14] Lamartine, *Memoirs of Celebrated Characters* (1854–58).

The "last Sir Masingberd" undoubtedly refers to Francis Charles Masingberd's *Sermons on Unity, with an Essay on Religious Societies* (1868).

Theodor Mundt, *Count Mirabeau*, translated from the German by T. J. Radford (1868).

[15] In 1867 Thackeray's younger daughter Harriet married Leslie Stephen.

[16] Mr. Deveril may be the son of Walter Deverell (1827–54), the Pre-Raphaelite painter and friend of Rossetti's.

ours as well as Mr. Graham who is often here & the Hamonds & the Camerons in walks & games. Mr. Aidé, Mr. Parry, Mr. Allingham also with us.[17]

April

9th. Mr. Egerton & Lady Mary[18] & their daughters as well as Miss Hurt & Mr. Allingham in the evening. Mr. & Mrs. Watson & Lipscombe stay with us.[19] Mrs. Watson very charming. Mr. & Mrs. Paul come. A. in his room.

A. drives with me & Mr. Lipscombe & Mr. Digby & the boys to the wood where the Anenomes grow.

"Claribel" comes.[20] The Simeons & the Wilsons meet her at luncheon & have interesting conversation with her.[21]

17th. The Monteiths come. I very tired with this long continuance of large luncheon & dinner parties. Our friends are in raptures with our home & are all very kind & pleasant.

19th. Annie Thackeray comes with her two little cousins one on each side looking like Charity.[22] She comes to take leave.

20th. The Monteiths & their two daughters leave us. A. hears a nightingale in the Glen in the East Lawn & calls Mr. Digby to listen. I catch a note or two.

[17] Charles Hamilton Aidé (1826–1906), the author and musician, is best remembered for his *Eleanore* (1856) and his numerous society novels.

Sir Charles Hubert Hastings Parry (1848–1918), the musician, matriculated as a commoner at Exeter College in 1867.

[18] Lady Mary Frances Herbert (d. 1905), daughter of Charles Herbert, 2d Earl Manvers (1778–1806), and her husband, Edward C. Egerton (d. 1869), M.P. for Macclesfield and brother of Lord Egerton.

[19] The Watsons = unidentified.

Mr. Lipscombe had been (1864–65) the Farringford tutor for Hallam and Lionel.

[20] This possibly is the original for the Claribel of Tennyson's 1830 poem "Claribel," in the manner that Sophy Rawnsley and Tennyson's mother are the originals for "airy, fairy Lilian" and the "reverèd Isabel" in the 1830 poems bearing their names.

[21] Thomas Wilson was an Isle of Wight neighbor and a close friend of Sir John Simeon's. Excerpts from Wilson's slender "Reminiscences" of Tennyson in the years 1863 and 1864 are included as an appendix to volume one of the *Memoir*, pp. 511–12. Among other things, Wilson recalled a stern warning from little Hallam never to disturb the poet when he was smoking his first morning pipe, for that was when his best inspirations came.

[22] Possibly a Thomas Woolner statuette.

22nd. Rainy morning but it clears & A. goes to Ryde on his way to lay the foundation stone of Aldworth on Greenhill. I never heard a thrush sing as one did early this morning. The cuckoo shouts with might & main this afternoon. Mr. Digby walks to Yarmouth on his way to visit his Dorsetshire relations. The boys with him. Everything beautiful. The crimson Rhododendrons which A. moved that I might see them from the study window gorgeous. Forget-me-nots & Hyacinths in front of the Drawingroom lovely. Leaves of the Elms almost fully out.

23rd. Thankful to have a sunny day. A nightingale sings on the lawn opposite our bed-room window.

24th. Mrs. Gilchrist has seized the few minutes before post after the laying of the stone to write to me. It rather glorious. Sir John & Lady Simeon & Louy, Mr. Knowles there. Sir John said a few simple appropriate words when the stone was laid. Provisions abundant & excellent. Enough left for all the farm people & work people. A. in excellent spirits. He is pleased with the inscription on the stone "Prosper Thou the work of our hands & prosper Thou our hands' work."

27th. William goes to fetch his bride. A. confirms Mrs. Gilchrist's account of the day & in short all went off beautifully & Louy writes that they were all very pleased.

28th. William brings home his bride. We have been busy preparing their rooms. I put some Lilies of the Valley in A.'s room. Claribel told me of the notion that year by year they lose a bell & so die out dying with the last.

May

2nd. A. arrives with Mr. Seely & Mr. Digby. The boys go to Norton for Croquet. They do often with Mr. Digby. Mr. Allingham comes & he & Mr. Henry Taylor & Ida[23] dine here. Mr. Cameron & Miss Murray in the evening.

5th. Mr. Lecky[24] & Mr. Allingham leave us. We have had many interesting conversations with Mr. Lecky and I am very glad to have made his acquaintance.

Mr. Digby brings a beautiful nosegay of Bog Bean, Bog

[23] Sir Henry Taylor's daughter.

[24] William E. H. Lecky (1838–1903), the historian, essayist, and liberal Irish politician. Emily Tennyson was particularly fond of Lecky's *History of European Morals from Augustus to Charlemagne* (1869).

Fern, White Hyacinth & blue [*illegible*] & we all drive to Mrs. Prettyman's[25] & A. takes me into Mr. Wilson's garden to show me what he calls "a peep into paradise." A charming Rectory & pretty church. The very soul of peace seems to brood there. A large party at Westover. Mrs. Prettyman as usual very kind. The girls very pretty & pleasant.

19th. Mr. & Mrs. Tytler & their daughters come here & have tea on the lawn.[26]

A. & Mr. Digby bring me some of the wild white roses which grow near Totland Bay (not Eglantine). A. & I look to putting summer flowers into the beds & to planting the Fortune Palms & Indian Rubber Plant. Mr. Digby & the boys walk with Mr. Fraser Tytler & his three daughters to Compton Bay to look for the wild Stocks. All within reach gone but some higher up still flowering. They get handed Poppies & have tea with Mr. Tytler & Mr. & Mrs. Littleton. A. walks with Mr. Littleton. Kate & Drummond come.

The picnic we had planned with the Hamonds is given up (the ground being too wet). We have a dance instead. The Fraser Tytlers, the Isaacsons, Camerons, the Officers[27] & others come.

24th. All of our party & the Fraser Tytlers go to Mr. Pritchard's[28] to look at Venus & the moon thro' his telescope.

28th. Drummond & Kate leave. Very affectionate they are & very amusing with their wonderful Lincolnshire stories. Mr. Digby & Lionel go for the day to Spring Hill. Hallam not well enough.

June

6th. The carriage takes Mr. Digby & our boys to Norton for Croquet & brings back Mr. Gifford Palgrave.

[25]The Prettymans were neighbors whose family home, Westover, was located near Weston, little more than a mile west of Farringford.

[26]The Fraser-Tytlers were Freshwater neighbors whose three daughters were contemporaries of Hallam and Lionel Tennyson. In 1886 Mary Fraser-Tytler became the second wife of G. F. Watts.

[27]Soldiers from Golden Hill Fort.

[28]Charles Pritchard, the astronomer and stellar photographer. Tennyson and Pritchard saw a good deal of each other between 1862, when the astronomer moved to Freshwater, and 1870, when he became Savilian Professor at Oxford.

8th. Mrs. Prettyman & the Fraser Tytlers. In the evening Mr. Palgrave performs the Moslem service & the summons to prayer. Very solemn & imposing.

9th. Mrs. Cameron photographs him. All go to croquet at Norton except A. & myself. . . .

10th. Our brilliant & wonderfully gifted guest leaves us. He says that he "boils over with life" & we can well believe it.

12th. Mr. Mornington leaves.

13th. Our wedding-day. Mary Ker arrives.[29]

18th. She leaves us.

19th. A. & I drive to Ryde & sleep at the White Horse, Haslemere. A.'s hay-fever very bad until he gets to Blackdown. All trace of it leaves him at Greenhill. We send the carriage for Mr. Knowles & Mrs. Gilchrist. A. walks & I drive with them to Greenhill. We are charmed with the house. The big log huts for the workmen & the men at work very picturesque. We like what we see of our Builder, Mr. Duke, & the Clerk of the Works, Mr. West, & we all enjoy ourselves. Mr. Knowles kindly takes A. & me back to Clapham Common as A. feels the small hot room at Haslemere. We have a great deal to do planning the addition we wish to have made to the house. I call at the Edens & take Lena with me to the Kensington Portrait Gallery where we are to find A. & Mr. Knowles.[30] She dines with us at the Knowles. We see Mr. Macmillan & Mr. Craik, Mr. Locker & Eleanor, & Mr. Hewett, Mr. Hopgood.[31] We

[29] Mary Ker must have been pleasantly surprised at the obvious success of her brother's marriage, for at the time of his wedding she said that though she hoped he and Emily would be happy, she felt "very doubtful about it" (quoted in Willingham Rawnsley, *Tennyson, 1809–1909: A Lecture* [Ambleside: George Middleton, 1909], p. 21).

[30] Lena was Eleanor Eden (1826–79), daughter of Rt. Rev. Robert John Eden, 3d Baron Auckland, and niece of Emily Eden. She published several novels, including *False and True* (1859) and *Dumbleton Common*, 2 vols. (1867), as well as *Emily Eden's Letters from India*, 2 vols. (1872).

The Kensington is now the Victoria and Albert Museum.

[31] George Lillie Craik (d. 1905) was the manager of Macmillan's and a partner in the company from 1865 until his death.

Sir Prescott Gardner Hewett (1812–91) was the surgeon who attended Tennyson at Aldworth during his near fatal illness in the fall of 1888. In 1863 Hewett was elected president of the Pathological Society of London, in 1873 he became president of the Clinical Society, and in 1874 he was chosen a fellow of the Royal Society.

John Hopgood was Alexander Macmillan's solicitor.

have a long consultation with Mr. Arnold White[32] on our affairs.

The boys had a large party from Swainston to lunch with them on Saturday. Mr. Jowett & the Grants we expect on Tuesday. We must return. We find Mr. Jowett & the boys on the pier waiting for us. We see the Grants in the evening. Lady Grant gives me a beautifully carved Sandalwood box from Canaries.[33] She & her sister come to us.

1st. We have a dance.

2nd. Sir Alexander comes in the evening, his last time in England.

3rd. The boys take a note & magnolia flower to Lady Grant & greet them on their way to the boat.

14th. We drive to Swainston, find Sir Anthony Sterling & Mr. Wynn Finch there and learn what we can of Mr. Longfellow whom we have been expecting for some days.[34]

[15th. Mr. Longfellow arrived. They were a party of ten. Very English he is, A.T. and I thought. (A.T. thought his *Hiawatha* his most original poem and he quoted his translation "The mills of God grind slowly, tho' they grind exceeding small.")[35]

16th. The Longfellows and A.T. talked much of spiritualism. (A.T. was greatly interested in spiritualism but suspended his judgement, and thought that if in such manifestations there is anything, "Pucks, not the spirits of dead men, reveal themselves.") A.T. took Mr. Longfellow and Mr. Appleton[36] to call

[32]Arnold William White (later Sir; 1795–1893), solicitor to the queen from 1864 until his death. A partner in the firm of Arnold and Henry White of Great Marlborough Street, White was Tennyson's solicitor for many years.

[33]The Canary Islands.

[34]Sir Anthony Coningham Sterling (1805–71), the brother of John Sterling, was military secretary to Colin Campbell in India, 1858–59.

Charles Griffith Wynne-Finch (1815–74) was M.P. for the Carnarvon district from 1859 until 1863.

[35]The allusion is to Longfellow's translation of Friedrich von Logau's "Retribution," from *Poetic Aphorisms* (1654).

[36]William Henry Appleton (1814–99), the American publisher and friend of Thackeray and Thomas Moore.

on Admiral Sir Andrew Hamond who had received the latter and Mr. Longfellow's son on their last visit to England. Mr. Appleton recognized Lady Hamond as the little girl he had met years ago in Hawaii. We invited forty or fifty neighbours to tea. Mr. Longfellow spoke kindly and graciously to each guest: Mrs. Fraser-Tytler and her daughters among them and Mr. Longfellow said that "it was worth while coming to England to see such young ladies." Mrs. Cameron photographed Mr. Longfellow. A.T. went with the gentlemen of the Longfellow party to Swainston and afterwards to Mrs. Prettyman's and the Fraser-Tytler's at Westover.

The Longfellows were all charmed with our down. Indeed I believe the ladies wished to remain on the Island.

18th. Poor little Alamayu, King Theodore of Abyssinia's son, came with Captain Speedy.[37] The Captain said that Alamayu would not sleep without both his (Captain Speedy's) arms round him, lest the evil one should take him. His nerves had been greatly shaken by the seige of Magdala, and the knowledge of his father's fate. King Theodore had killed himself, when the English had sealed the rock of Magdala, and his body had been found just inside the gate of the city. Captain Speedy tried to put the boy off when he began to speak of this, but he said "Oh, I know it is so, I heard them tell all about it." He thought that our English bread was the best thing he ever tasted. When he drove past the large ilex here, he said "Take care, there will be an elephant in that jungle," and when he saw A.T. on the lawn before the drawing-room window, he clapt his hands and was much excited and called out "Papa, papa, papa."][38]

20th. Mr. Lear comes & A. goes to Greenhill. He will not let me go with him because of the torrents of rain.

21st. Mr. Digby sees an oyster-catcher in Watcombe Bay. A. has a very rough passage returning.

23rd. He reads "Guinevere" to Dr. Hook & Sir William.[39] I see a

[37]Captain Tristram Charles Sawyer Speedy served with General Napier in Magdala, Abyssinia, in 1867, and, after the death of the emperor Theodore, Speedy acquired custody of the emperor's son, Prince Alamayahu. The prince remained Speedy's ward after his marriage to Tiny Cotton in December 1868. Later he attended Cheltenham College, Rugby, and Sandhurst; he died of pleurisy in November 1879.

[38]*Materials*, III, 82–84.

[39]Sir William Page Wood, Baron Hatherley (1808–81), became lord chancellor

long course of tears on the Dean's cheeks afterwards. A. takes much to Sir William. They argue a good deal in their metaphysics. Mr. Graham kindly calls to tell us of the American Yacht race & that if Mr. Digby & Lionel will go to the Needles they will find a good many of them (the officers) there. A., Mr. Digby, Lionel, & Mrs. Cameron drive on the Down. Mr. Digby stays & they have a little drive, too. A. takes me out in my little carriage to see our avenue of Tobacco & Castor Oil plants in their glory.

Mrs. & Miss Ferrier[40] & the Rhodes call. We hear afterwards that Mrs. Ferrier says she never saw anyone so delightful as A. She amused him much with her stories.

Mrs. Cameron brings the Miss Jewells to sing. Mr. Cotton hears that "The Messiah" is to be sung & rides over & asks if he may come in. It is most touching to hear the dear old man repeating to himself "I know that my Redeemer liveth." Surely "The Messiah" must be the crown of human music. A. reads me some of Bossuet's sermon on Henriette of England.[41] We are disappointed at the entirely Grand Monarque style of the eloquent preacher. A. drives with me to the Seelys & we take Lionel. While they are with Mr. Seely in the garden, Mrs. Seely tells me the sad story of Garibaldi's second marriage. A formal marriage the bond of which was at once dissolved by the receipt of a letter telling who & what the lady was by whom he had been entrapped.[42]

Mr. Cotton comes to tell us of his daughter Tiny's engagement to Captain Speedy. Aubrey de Vere comes & Mr. Allingham.

---

in the first Gladstone administration in December 1868. Wood was as remarkable for his devout churchmanship as for his legal abilities, and he published several religious works, including *Truth and Its Counterfeits* (1857).

[40]The wife and daughter of James Frederick Ferrier (1808–64), the metaphysician, author of *Institutes of Metaphysic* (1854).

[41]Jacques Bénigne Bossuet (1627–1704), an earnest preacher of sermons, panegyrics, and other religious addresses. He was particularly eloquent in his first two major funeral orations, those of Henriette de France (1699) and Henriette d'Angleterre, duchesse D'Orléans (1670).

[42]In 1860 Garibaldi, then fifty-nine, married the eighteen-year-old eldest daughter of the Marquis Raimondi. Shortly after the wedding he discovered that his wife had previously been the mistress of several men, the first relationship dating from her eleventh year. He never spoke to her again, though a formal divorce was not granted until 1880.

September

1st. A. reads me some of St. Palaye on Chivalry. We have some Agaric Steak for one of his Fast Day dishes & he likes it. Mrs. Cameron opens her wooden room with a ball. We let Lionel go for a little while. The room overflows so much that many are alfresco under the beautiful moon. Some amusing themselves by spying the newly betrothed under a walnut tree.

Lady Strangford leaves a note at the lodge telling us that her husband had got out of his carriage yesterday on the down to speak to us but that we had driven on (thinking them in fact cockneys) so they did not push their intention. We call to explain & find them in a delightfully lonely lodging house at Alum Bay.

5th. We drive with Mr. DeVere to Swainston & find Colonel Colvile[43] & Mr. Virette there. We talk with Mr. DeVere of the sketch of the Sangrail.

7th. Lord & Lady Strangford dine with us. Mrs. Cameron & Annie Thackeray in the evening. Mrs. Cameron shows the wonderful photographs of the Miss Campbells[44] whom she brought yesterday to see us.

9th. A long visit from the Strangfords. We talk of her life. What a life of suffering & devotion it has been! but she feels it as she ought, but more than well repaid by love.

When I think what he [Tennyson] was between twenty & thirty in face & form I can scarcely imagine anything more glorious in human form. He read the Sangraal in the garden to Mr. Warre before we left.[45] I am pleased to think that the Queen & the Crown Princess wished him to write it. My own desire concerning it is more than fulfilled & I trust that theirs may be also.[46]

[43]Henry Robert Colvile (1795–1875), who was raised to the rank of colonel in 1864 and to general in late 1868.

[44]Freshwater neighbors who occasionally served as models for Julia Margaret Cameron.

[45]Edmund Warre (1837–1920) was headmaster of Eton from 1884 until 1905 and provost from 1909 until 1918, when he retired.

[46]Tennyson began writing "The Holy Grail" around September 1, 1868, and finished it by the 20th. For years Emily had urged her husband to compose on the Grail legend, as had Macaulay and others, including the duke of Argyll, who shared Macaulay's opinion that the subject was one "capable of being made much of" in Tennyson's hands (Argyll to Tennyson, September 23,

24th. We sleep at Reading. It is desolating to see our poor boy weeping alone in his garret. . . . He takes the wrong books, which spoils his Greek, but Mr. Hornby kindly promises A. to make allowance.[47] He drives with us to the station and we part there and see him alone in the Fly.

25th. A storm rises in the night & we crossed the roughest gale of the year we are told. We are tossed like shuttlecocks as A. says. He gives up his place on the steps to me & I sit crouched under the little sort of hood there. We find a large party of Farm labourers feasting at the harvest home supper in the servants' hall but the distant sounds of mirth & revelry do not take away the heart stillness of the house. A. feels it as much as I do.

We have the comfort of cheerful letters from our boys (more cheerful at least from Lionel & 28th one to-day saying that he is safely landed in the upper school). Mr. Warre very encouraging & kind about him. Delightful letter from Mr. Bradley about our Hallam.

29th. A. so very good. We have delightful talks. One's heart cannot but yearn towards one's boys but surely I, if anyone, ought to be thankful for my lot!

30th. Francisque Michel's proofs, alas!

Drives with A.

October

7th. Mr. & Mrs. Max Müller & their dear little girl dine & sleep here & drive with A. on the down.

8th. I go to Alum Bay with them. They admire both down & bay. A. takes me out in my little carriage as in old days. We look round on things.

A. has some good walks with the Miss Ritchies, the Franklins, & Prinseps.[48] One day he & his party go to Brook point.

1859, T.R.C.). Once the idyll was complete, all who saw it responded enthusiastically. In his Christmas letter to the poet, Tennyson's old friend Francis Turner Palgrave remarked on "the skill and splendour of your Graal, which grow upon me every time I read it" (Palgrave to Tennyson, December 23, 1868, T.R.C.).

[47] On September 23, 1868, the Tennysons took Lionel, who was then fourteen, to Eton for his first half.

The Rev. James J. Hornby was the new headmaster at Eton.

[48] Anne Thackeray's cousins, Augusta, Eleanor, and Emily Ritchie, were frequent guests at Farringford.

A. sees, as he thinks, one of them beckon twice in vain. The third time she comes & tumbles into the water. He picks her out but still does not discover that she does not belong to him & is not unnaturally shocked to think what the lady must have thought of him he being told that she is a stranger.

Annie Thackeray, the Ritchies, Prinseps, Mrs. Franklin, Arthur Brookfield, Mr. Allingham, Miss Irving come.[49] We have "Russian Scandal," "Earth, air, & water," "I love my love," & "We plant."[50]

21st. A. gives me his finished "Holy Grail" to read. Miss Worsley comes & [at] her request he reads "Boädicea" & some Heine & Goëthe.

24th. Annie & I show our plans & money calculations for our Ladies' house to Mr. Knowles who with Mrs. Knowles crosses in spite of stormy weather. At my request A. reads "The Holy Grail" to Annie & she is enchanted.

25th. A. makes comical lines on our Ladies' House. We say good-bye to Annie, delightful creature that she is. A. reads "The Holy Grail" to Mr. & Mrs. Knowles.

28th. I get up early to see them off. Mr. Warburton comes to luncheon. Mr. Henry Taylor calls. Mr. Warburton & Sir Hercules & Lady Robinson dine with us.[51] Their daughter & Annie & Louy Prinsep come in the evening.

31st. They & Col. & Mrs. Franklin walk with A.

The Franklins were the family of Col. Charles Trigance Franklin (1822–95), of the Royal Artillery, who served at Mhow in Central India from 1869 through 1870.

The children of Henry Thoby Prinsep, Annie, Alice, May, and Val, often visited both the Tennysons and the Charles Camerons.

[49] Miss Irving was the daughter of Sir Henry Irving, who staged *Queen Mary* in 1876 and *Becket*, with more success, in 1893.

[50] These were Victorian parlor games.

[51] Sir Hercules George Robert Robinson, 1st Baron Rosmead (1824–97), served successively as governor of Hongkong, 1859–65, Ceylon, 1865–72, New South Wales, 1872–79, and New Zealand, 1879–80. From 1880 until 1889 he was governor of Cape Colony and high commissioner of South Africa.

Lady Robinson was the former Nea Arthur Ada Rose D'Amour Rath, daughter of Arthur Annesley Rath, Viscount Valentia.

November

1st. I send off a letter to Mr. Strahan in answer to his liberal offers.[52]

3rd. We are shocked & grieved by news of dear little Charlie's sudden death.[53] Horatio & Mr. & Mrs. Field were at Woolwich & tho' they came off immediately on receipt of a telegram announcing her illness they were too late to see her alive.

5th. Charlie's funeral day.

7th. Horatio & the two little girls & Tilly & Cole come to us. Too much occupied with letter writing & the poor little children to have time for my journal.

11th. A. has to go to Town on publishing business. I drive with him to Yarmouth. Mr. & Mrs. Knowles kindly take him in again. . . . I send to meet my A. but I am really thankful he has not come. Our poor kitchenmaid has been delirious except at intervals from typhoid fever. Servants & a tenant who come to nurse very kind but it is anxious work. Letters from A. cheer me. A. tells me that on account of the uncertainty of his plans he has refused to meet the Crown Prince & Princess at the Deanery. I am sorry, for she is so well worth meeting.

One night Horatio reads "The Holy Grail" to Tilly & me which A. has sent me in print.

30th. He goes off to his Tenby home. I send children & servants away to Mrs. Cameron's cottage which we hire.

December

2nd. I should have been dreary as I have to write all day & cannot see to read by candlelight had not dear Mrs. Cameron come to me night by night for an hour. Louy Simeon & Nanny would fain have come to stay with me but of course I did not let them. I kept the trouble[54] all along from our boys until one unlucky day I forwarded a letter in which it was mentioned so I have disturbed their dear hearts.

[52]In November 1868 Tennyson reached an agreement with Alexander Strahan making Strahan and Co. his publisher for a period of five years.

[53]Horatio Tennyson's first wife died in October 1868.

[54]Emily feared the spread of typhoid fever from the kitchen maid to other members of the household.

7th. A. & Mr. Locker go to the Convent des Oiseaux by my request & see Della.[55] She begs to go again to-morrow for the Benediction as her name day, Louise Marie de la Conception. They go & are introduced to her English friends. She writes me one of her enthusiastic believing letters & sends me photographs of her Church inside & outside.

14th. To my great delight a letter which Lady Charlotte[56] has got into the Queen's bag arrives from my A. saying that he & Mr. Locker reached Victoria Street at midnight Saturday the 12th.

15th. I have had a little air hole window put into my working closet & have the light thro' it for the first time this morning. When Tiny is married to Captain Speedy little Alamayou, Henry Cameron, Johnny Simeon, & Mr. White groomsmen. Louy Simeon, Annie & Lou Prinsep, Miss Ferrier, & Miss Way bridesmaids. Louy, Annie, & Lou came to show me themselves in their bridesmaids dresses.

18th. My Lionel arrives to-day at Headon Hall which I have kindly been allowed by Mr. Bird to take for a week.[57] He has a cough & a sore throat but to my dismay comes without a great coat notwithstanding. Still he has never looked nearly so bright & well on his return as now. He is clean & rosy & taller & stronger.

19th. A. comes to-day. A most splendid day. Sea & sky glittering. I have made the bare brilliant room as comfortable as I can for him with a turkey carpet & books from home but still it is bare.

[55] Following an initial five-day delay in departure, Tennyson and Frederick Locker left London for several days in Paris on December 2, 1868. The two visited old friends and went to numerous galleries and to the theater (where they were stuffed just under the ceiling cheek by jowl with the enormous gas chandelier). By the time they returned to London on December 12, they had determined to have other similar holiday expeditions together, as indeed they did, traveling to Switzerland in the summer of 1869 and touring France and the Pyrenees in 1875.

The Convent des Oiseaux was a convent of canonesses devoted to the education of young girls. It was dissolved in 1904 and subsequently became a habitation and workshop of artists, including Matisse and Othon Friesz.

Della = unidentified.

[56] Lady Charlotte Locker (d. 1872).

[57] Emily and her sons stayed at Mr. Bird's Headon Hall near Alum Bay from the 18th until the 28th. Alarmed by the kitchen maid's typhoid fever, Tennyson had Farringford thoroughly scoured and disinfected and oversaw a close inspection of the crude drainage system for possible sources of contamination.

21st. He finds it so dreary & the entrance from out of doors thro' the kitchen so inconvenient that he says he must go home.

22nd. We drive to meet our Hallam. We take down Mr. West the Aldworth (Greenhill) clerk of the works to inspect the Farringford drains & says to our relief that he can find nothing amiss in them, nothing in the house that could cause illness. The boys drive down with me to see the children & they play with them. He reads the "San Grail" to himself & to us.

24th. We take down all the children except the little three year old Percy to meet Horatio. The four scream with delight when they see their Father on board. Many people on the pier turn round & look kindly at them.

Hallam & Lionel read some of "The Lover's Tale" to me. One day we saw a beautiful heron swoop down into the Bay & looking [for it] afterwards, it was alas! in the bird-stuffer's shop.

25th. A. reads "Michael" to us.

26th. We drive to meet Mr. Jowett. We hear from Edmund that his dear little Emmy's gone from typhoid.[58] A. has been so wearied by the tumult of storm at Headon Hall that he has gone to spend the day in his own study at Farringford.

28th. We joyfully & thankfully return home.

30th. Mr. Jowett goes. The boys to whom he is ever so very good drive with him to Yarmouth.

[58]The Edmund Lushingtons' eldest daughter, Emily, died of typhoid fever at the age of nineteen.

1869

January

2nd. Mr. & Mrs. Bradley & Mr. Clark come. The Bradleys bring us a Périgord Pie.

3rd. A rainy morning. Mr. Bradley reads the Litany to us. We have the Haunch of Venison which they have brought us. Rehearsals for the Play at Mrs. Cameron's Theatre.

4th. Horatio dines with us.

6th. Mr. Clark goes to our regret.

7th. To-day the Bradleys. No friends can be nearer to us.

8th. Good and generous Mrs. Cameron receives what with Mr. Jowett's & Mr. Henry Taylor's gifts will enable her to found the Hospital she wants to found here. A dance after the theatricals. All our neighbours there apparently. A. not there.

12th. Hallam reads "The Brothers"[1] to us. A dreadful crush at the theatricals tonight. Mr. Grosvenor Hood & the Croziers here again. Many force their way uninvited.

14th. A. has to go to Town again on this troublesome Moxon business. We drive with him to Yarmouth. A perfect morning. Hallam reads some of "The Gipsy"[2] to us.

Sad news of the death of Nea Robinson from scarlet fever after a two days illness.

A letter from poor Lady Strangford most desolate telling of her husband's death on Saturday morning. She was down stairs having breakfast, thought him too long in coming, went up & found him cold in his bath or just out of it. A devoted wife has she been.

15th. A sad parting from our good Andrews who goes to help her parents in the shop they have bought.

To-day the Moxon connection of thirty-seven years ceased.

[1] Wordsworth's narrative pastoral, written in 1800, as was the somewhat similar "Michael," which Tennyson had read aloud a fortnight earlier on Christmas Day. Although Tennyson admired Wordsworth and thought his verse the finest since Milton, he once called him a "thick-ankled" poet and criticized his prolixity (*AT*, p. 451).

[2] Undoubtedly Arnold's "The Scholar-Gypsy" (1853).

A. however anonymously still allows the widow (Mrs. Moxon) and her daughters a considerable sum a year. We would that the necessity for leaving had not arisen.

16th. This morning again brings me sad news. Charles Weld died in my sister's arms on Friday night. Agnes present. He rang for Nanny about eleven, she was with him in a moment. A quarter of an hour of terrible agony which he bore without murmuring as he had done all the suffering from the illness consequent on enlargement of the heart. He blessed them & was gone. They lay him by my Father on the 21st. . . . The dove which had come to Charles' window a little time ago was flying from window to window.

19th. A. returns to-day. Ewen Cameron has come with him & Mr. Allingham crosses with him.

20th. Our Lionel leaves us to-day. I drive with him to the boat & watch the little hand waving the little white handkerchief on the little steam-boat.

21st. A. & I go to the Terrace[3] & Hallam with us to look to the preparations there for Horatio & to see about the road for which Starks wishes.

Touching letters from Nanny & Lady Strangford.

Charles Cameron comes from India.

Dudley Elwes & Horatio arrive. They dine with us to meet the Simeons.

28th. Miss Vernon[4] comes. I drive Horatio & Mr. Elwes to Brook that they may see the raft.

February

2nd. Hallam has to spend a good deal of this week rehearsing for the performance in Mrs. Cameron's theatre. Hallam is "Marmion" in the tableau.

9th. Horatio returns & brings part of the Pedigree which we wanted drawn out by Dudley Elwes & emblazoned by him.

All at Norton are so very good to our boy.[5]

[3]The Terrace was occupied by Horatio Tennyson and his daughters during the late 1860s.

[4]The governess for Horatio's children, Maud and Violet.

[5]Both the Andrew Hamonds and the Graham Eden Hamonds lived at Norton, a village not far from Farringford.

He leaves us to-day. Wet & stormy. I have telegraphed to put off his journey but he thinks that he had better go. The Bradleys are so very good as to take him into their house this winter.

13th. I see a good deal of Miss Vernon & like her more & more & think that it is a great blessing she has come to take care of the children.

Happy evenings with A. He reads me what he had done of the birth of Arthur & his marriage.

[16th. The agreement with Mr. Strahan came for signature. Mr. Strahan had offered to publish for A.T. for nothing, but that A.T. would not allow. A letter arrived from Mr. Gladstone in answer to one about a proposal for increasing the post office saving percentage on small deposits.][6]

Nanny generously gives the boys a costly gun & a brace of pistols & lends a gold watch which she cannot give. A letter from Mr. Gladstone in answer to one I wrote. I begged him not to answer. It is very good in him to find time. A. walks about twelve miles, reads me the dreadful translations of so-called British poems in Skene,[7] afterwards some of Layamon's *Brut*. A very happy evening. He reads to me every evening, takes me to see the gap made by the two great Elm trees which have been blown down near the Farm Cottage & the beautiful Euonymous with their fresh green leaves & now grown into large shrubs. The yew tree already sending out its dust when he blows across it. He reads me "The Coming of Arthur."

I read Caponsacchi & Pompilia.[8] Both very beautiful in Browning's own peculiar style.

Mr. Grove dines with us. A. walks with him after he has looked to transplanting things.

March

1st. Mr. Gladstone's great night.[9]

2nd. I go to Yarmouth to meet my poor Nanny & Agnes. A very stormy passage they have had. The furniture cannot come.

[6] *Materials*, III, 103.

[7] William Forbes Skene, *The Four Ancient Books of Wales*, 2 vols. (Edmonston and Douglas, 1868).

[8] Books VI and VII of *The Ring and the Book* (1868–69).

[9] On March 1, 1869, Gladstone introduced the Irish church bill in a speech

3rd. It arrives but after an accident to one of the wagons. The men leave it in the dark & after having gone about a mile beyond A. said we had better return, it must be out the other road, & returning A. spied it, William Seaton being on the top with a light. At last it was all safely housed at the Terrace stables.

4th. Mr. Grove goes. A kindly & pleasant man with much to tell that interests me.

11th. A. goes to Greenhill, driving to Ryde. He returns on the 15th & I go to meet him.

25th. Enid & Mr. Layard lunch with us.[10] My first introduction to him. He seems so kindly & genial that I think dear Enid has a good chance of happiness. I go to meet our Lionel. He is so much grown & so much more manly looking that people do not recognize him at church. Only Sir Andrew & Lady Hamond speak to him. The Layards dine with us several days.

30th. The Duke & Duchess of Argyll are so good as to come all the way from Ventnor to see us tho' they have to return after luncheon. [*illegible*] glad we are to see them again here. A. read the "San Grail" to them.

The weather very bitter. Just as they are driving away Mr. Jowett drives up. Very cheerful & delightful he is. Enid & Mr. Layard dine with us. Mr. Jowett sees the seal of the Esarhaddon[11] which interested us so much. Yesterday one of Mr. Layard's gifts to Enid. It is a carnelian cylinder engraven with the figure of the King, the god Dagon,[12] the Sun, the Moon, & other things. It was rolled on the Clay books now it is enclosed in a gold bracelet.

---

which even Disraeli admitted did not contain a superfluous word. The bill, which provided for the immediate disendowment of the church and for its disestablishment as of January 1, 1871, was passed substantially as it left the House of Commons on May 31. It received the queen's assent on July 26.

[10] In 1869 Austen Henry Layard married Mary Evelyn ("Enid") Guest, daughter of Sir John Guest. Layard's most significant works include *Nineveh and Its Remains*, 2 vols. (1849) and *Discoveries in the Ruins of Nineveh and Babylon* (1853). He served as British minister at Madrid from 1869 to 1877.

[11] The cuneiform Cylinder of Esarhaddon, king of Assyria from 680 until 669 B.C.

[12] The Philistine fertility god, half man and half fish.

April

1st. Mrs. Cameron calls delighted at having made Lionel & Agnes April Fools. Sir John Simeon & Louy come to us & meet the Layards at dinner from whom we were very sorry to part. They go by the early boat to-day & Mr. Jowett also to our regret has to go to-day. Nanny & Agnes are persuaded to come down to dinner.

2nd. The Simeons go. We have enjoyed their visit very much.

3rd. Lionel & I drive thro' the rain to meet Franklin Lushington. Capt. Speedy & Alamayou call.

5th. A. & Frank have a long walk. Lionel & Agnes to Chorley with them.[13] The Speedys & Agnes & Horatio dine with us.

9th. Mr. & Mrs. Chittenden lunch with us also. Miss Fitzgerald & her little niece Julia Molyneux with her governess Miss Wiegand. Miss Fitzgerald delightful. One feels at once like an old friend to her being as she is a cousin of the Spring-Rices & De Veres. Lady Molyneux[14] not having been well enough to come they have to return after luncheon. She gives me her sister's photograph. A. & I look after the planting at the Terrace. I go with Nanny to Norton & call [on] Sir Andrew, the Lodge. Mrs. Grosvenor Hood shows us her models & her wood carvings & drawings & is delightful as usual. A., I am thankful to say, very happy with Nanny & Agnes & even proposes their living with us.

19th. We go with our Lionel to Ryde on our way to Haslemere. The time of the boat is changed & we have to wait four hours. We have Turtle soup at dinner. Strange to say the first I ever tasted.

20th. Mr. Knowles comes to breakfast. A rainy, misty morning but A. & Lionel walk to the house & we drive over the new road which Mr. Simmons with his accustomed kindness has had made passable for me. The clouds roll away grandly & there are gleams of sunshine over the house & over the landscape & we are all very much pleased with the house. We lunch in the log huts. A. & Mr. Knowles go to Town after dinner.

[13]Located in Lancashire, near Bolton, Chorley is the birthplace of Henry Tate (b. 1819), the donor of London's Tate Gallery.

[14]Lady Mary Augusta Molyneux (1814–1906), the widow of Charles William Molyneux, 3d earl of Sefton (1796–1855).

Anxiety about Horatio has made him so unwell that I am anxious he should be amused.

21st. Mr. Knowles & A. go to the first dinner of the Metaphysical Club. After dinner I take my Lionel to Clapham Junction for Eton. Mr. Knowles most kindly goes about with us to Haywards about grates & tiles & takes us to the Deanery to see a certain stone mantel-piece which he admires. It is very simple & graceful & we adopt it. Mr. Hewlett & Mr. Lambert dine with us.[15] Interesting political talk. Glad to find Mr. Lambert enthusiastic & chivalrous, not a mere utilitarian.

23rd. I tell Ally that I will not take him out shopping to-day. Mr. Knowles most kindly goes with me.

24th. A. comes also to look at Eastern carpets at Vincent Robinson's & carved furniture at Woodgate's at both which places we make purchases & at Colnaghi's.

Mr. and Mrs. Tom Taylor dine with us. She plays some Beethoven magnificently.

25th. Mr. Church[16] comes in the evening.

26th. We call at Howards'[17] & then go to Marlboro'. Our beloved one meets us at Savernake. He has a cold but what a different meeting from the last at Savernake when Mr. Bradley's "all right" only relieved some of its terrors. Mr. Bradley meets us at the Marlboro' Station. How delightful our loving welcome at the Lodge!

The next day we have all three a delightful drive in the Forest, beautiful with its trees & flowers.[18] I never saw so many wood anenomes. Mr. & Mrs. Bright[19] lunch at the Lodge. Mr. MacDonald, Mr. Store & Mr. Preston bring microscopes which interest us all very much. . . .

29th. We leave. Another delightful drive thro' the Forest & so ends our happy visit. We sleep at Reading.

[15] Mr. Hewlett was the brother of Mrs. James Knowles.

[16] Perhaps Alfred Church, who in 1891 published a topographical book entitled *Laureate's Country*.

[17] The George Howards (afterwards Lord and Lady Carlisle) of Naworth Castle.

[18] Savernake Forest, the domain of the marquess of Ailesbury, is the only great English forest not owned by the Crown.

[19] The John Brights. Bright was Lionel Tennyson's housemaster at Eton.

30th. Dreary misty morning but the sun shines on our return & the sea is calm, the coast lovely & dream-like. Mrs. Prettyman & her sister, Mrs. Wright, on board. A. cheerful in spite of trials.

May

6th. Katie comes.

7th. A. reads Leodogran's dream[20] to me, just made, giving the drift of the whole poem. The charter of Trinity offers him a Diploma which he declines (today 9th) not liking the public ceremony & having some years ago declined the honour when offered by the Duke of Devonshire.

A happy Sunday. A. reads to me bits of Italian, French, German poets & translates Latin & Greek. Delightsome bits of poets, the glory of the world.

10th & 11th. Happy days with A. reading, talking, & driving. Mr. & Mrs. Andrews of Lincolnshire have tea with us. Mr. Andrews tells the story of a Lincolnshire clergyman who praying for rain, said, O my God, send us rain & specially for John Stubbs' field in the Middle Marsh & if thou dost not know it, it has a thorn bush in the middle of it. A. reads "The Northern Farmer" to them & they promised to listen to Lincolnshire talk to test its correctness. The Duke d'Aumale sends A. his *Histoire des Princes de Condé.*[21]

12th. Mr. & Mrs. Knowles come. We take drives. [His active nature I thought sometimes spurred A.T. on to work when he might be flagging—][22]

A. reads some *In Memoriam* & some of "Sir Pelleas." Thankful to find that the children are cheerful at the Terrace. A. reads some Marcus Aurelius to us.

18th. Mr. & Mrs. Knowles go. A. brings me a beautiful bit of lilac & on Whitsunday we find a most Queenly rose of deep red on the Drawing room table. For the first time I learn that gooseberries are considered the proper thing for Whitsunday. [A. read the "San Graal." I doubt whether the "San Graal"

[20] See "The Coming of Arthur," ll. 424-45.

[21] Henri d'Orleans, duc d'Aumale, published a *Histoire des princes de Condé pendant les XVIe et XVIIe siècles*, 8 vols. (1863–96).

[22] *Materials*, III, 107.

would have been written but for my endeavour, and the Queen's wish, and that of the Crown Princess. Thank God for it. He has had the subject on his mind for years ever since he began to write about Arthur and his knights.][23]

[A. sends] the birth of King Arthur to [the Crown Princess] & she is charmed.

25th. Mr. & Mrs. Fields & Miss Lowell come. [A.T. took them to the Needles. Miss Lowell said that her grandmother Mrs. Spence used to shut her shutters and put crape on her knocker every 4th of July. Her grandfather was even banished for his love of England. A.T. said that he would drink her grandmother's health. Miss Lowell saw her first cowslips here. Very pleasant guests.][24]

I am really thankful for an opportunity of entertaining Americans for whom we can feel so kindly as for Mr. & Mrs. Fields & their pretty simple friend.

29th. Eardley calls.[25] A. half inclines to accompany him to Mürren. He is a perfect enthusiast for mountains.

June

2nd. A. is photographed by Mrs. Cameron. One of the portraits majestic but lacking delicacy.

3rd. I go with A. to Yarmouth. We cannot drive up to the boat because they are landing great guns.

8th. A. presides at "The Club" in the place of Mr. Spencer Walpole.[26] The Duke d'Aumale, the Archbishop of Canterbury,[27] Lord Salisbury, Mr. Vernon & others there.

[23] Ibid., p. 108.

[24] Ibid., p. 109. The Tennysons were very much taken with Mabel Lowell (b. 1847), the daughter of James Russell Lowell. In her letter of May 26, 1869, to Hallam Tennyson, Emily praised Miss Lowell as "a simple nice girl . . . not very American. Her great grandmother was cousin to Sir Walter Scott's Minna & Brenda & lived in the Orkneys" (T.R.C.).

[25] The Rev. Stenton Eardley (1823–83) was vicar of St. Stephen's, Birmingham, from 1849 until 1854, when he became vicar of Emmanuel Church, Streatham. Eardley traveled through France to Switzerland with Tennyson and Frederick Locker during June and July 1869.

[26] Spencer Horace Walpole served as conservative M.P. for Midhurst from 1846 until 1856, and he was home secretary in 1852, 1858–59, and 1866.

[27] Archibald Campbell Tait (1811–82) became archbishop of Canterbury in 1868.

9th. I take Mathilda[28] with me & go to Guildford & London furniture hunting.

11th. I meet A. at Haslemere, Mr. Knowles with him. Kate has kindly come also. All very pleased with the house. We lunch in one of the attics.

We find that Mr. Spenser Walpole can do more with Lord Egmont than anyone else & he has kindly promised to try & get a road for us.[29] I say good bye to A. I cannot love the farewells tho' I am glad for his own sake that he should be going.

12th. I reach home.

14th. A. leaves Folkestone [with Mr. Locker for Münich. Mr. Eardly joined them. Before starting, A.T. had written to Mr. Locker "we will go by the Brussels route, we might possibly be detained at Paris which seems ready to break out into fire. 8:45 we will meet at Charing Cross or rather at 8:30."][30]

19th. I get the side windows in the dining room put in.

22nd. Hallam goes to Eton on his way home. I go to meet him. He arrived in the evening.

26th. I drive to meet his friend Sandys & call for him at Norton Lodge; then we wait to see the boat pass where little Alamayou & the Speedys are on board. Hallam borrows the cover of Mrs. Grosvenor Hood's carriage & he & Sandys together wave it for a flag. The poor Father is watching at the pier but of course no one goes near him. We hear that he is so devoted to the poor little boy that he says he scarcely knows which he shall miss most him or his daughter. Alamayou for days has been saying "Grandpapa come, too" & now he lays his head on the dear old man's breast & sobs & weeps bitterly.

A haymaking party. The children tumbling about in the hay & the gaily dressed ladies having tea under the chestnut trees. A pretty sight. Croquet & a dance & a supper. Our friends of the neighbourhood & the officers & their wives here. Beautiful weather.

A. shivering at Mürren in a great coat. Rain or snow daily but at last it clears & he has a splendid view of the mountains &

[28] The most prominent Aldworth maid during the Tennysons' first few years there.

[29] George James, 6th earl of Egmont (1794–1874), for some time refused to allow the Tennysons to open an access road to Aldworth through his land.

[30] *Materials*, III, 108.

his vision over the Valley. He gathers blue gentian & the lovely mountain forget-me-not. One day four letters from him come to me.

July

1st. I have got half way thro' my French proofs of "Enid." Mathilda brings me A.'s curtains which she has finished. They look very grand I think. What a help she has been to me in this rather anxious work of furnishing when we are so far from everything. I not strong enough to look for the best of things as I could wish.

2nd. Aunt Tilly & Mr. Digby, a very great pleasure to have him with us again.

Mrs. Grosvenor Hood lunches & they all go to look for flowers in the marsh. . . .

11th. A. reaches England having called on Doré in Paris & dined with him & seen his Mother & been very much pleased.

13th. I go to meet him. Mr. Allingham crosses with him whom we ask to meet the Lockers next week.

17th. Lady Charlotte & Eleanor come.

20th. Mr. Locker arrives. All most kind & agreeable. Lady Charlotte quite delightful, her delicate wit which never wounds & her loving heart ready to do the humblest service for any suffering human being.

26th. We pack for Aldworth.

29th. Hallam & I go by the Portsmouth boat. Kate with us & all manner of packages, even chairs. We find Mr. Knowles there. Very kind as usual.

30th. Hallam goes to meet Lionel. Both boys very pleased with the house & furniture. Mathilda has made our rooms comfortable for us in spite of the anxious state of things. No work seems too much for her. The boys go to Farringford for Miss Crozier's dance & have a tableau at the Camerons.

August

5th. They return.

6th. I have A.'s curtains put up for his birthday.

13th. Our Hallam leaves us. Both boys most good. Never complaining for want of their home pleasures but reading to me or to themselves, taking me out or walking themselves.

September

Our neighbours all kind. Mr. & Mrs. Burdon most especially. Mr. Locker comes unexpectedly. Very affectionate he is. He writes several letters for me & offers to help me with them whenever I send them to him wishing me to do so & regularly every fortnight.

10th. A. & I awaken[ed] at night by a fearful clap of thunder. We seem in the very heart of the storm. Lionel & Mr. Strahan who is staying with us sleep thro' it. A. says he does not think that he ever saw anything more sublime than the great plain of Sussex beneath us covered with moving mist in the dim twilight & bellowing from end to end with thunder.

16th. Our Lionel leaves us. The engine breaks down & he is detained on the road. Thank God no one hurt.

20th. Charlie, Louy, & Nanny & Agnes. A sacred day to us. Louy looks thin & worn. He eats scarcely anything and is very weak. They are all pleased with our house & furniture & view & they enjoy the beautiful walks.

24th. Nanny & Agnes leave for Ireland & next Charlie & Louy must go. Their holiday for the year has ended.

26th. Mr. Lear comes, shows us his beautiful drawing, walks to Blackdown House & admires it much.

29th & 30th. I read the *Idylls* thro' in their proper sequence, also Pressensé's *Life of Christ*[31] which delights me as enabling one to live with Christ in His earthly life. To some of the Dogma one might object perhaps.

October

2nd. Mr. Knowles goes by the *Portsmouth.* We have lent them Farringford where they went on the 9th of Sept. A grand fringed

[31] Edmund de Pressensé, *The Critical School and Jesus Christ: A Reply to M. Renen's Life of Jesus,* translated by L. Corkran (London, 1865?).

ball of cloud, one head very sublime. One flash of lightning & torrents of rain.

I read Martineau's Sermon on The Peace of God & like it very much, also part of *King Alfred's Life* by Hughes.[32] A. reads me "The Old Cumberland Beggar" & "Peel Castle" & part of the Ode to Childhood. Mr. Wilson lunches with us. Mr. Allingham comes.

7th. A. & I help to lay the first turf [of the Aldworth lawn] & to plant. He gave me the beginning of "Beaumains"[33] to read, written (as was said jokingly) to describe a pattern youth for his boys.

All day long almost I sit out watching the planting. A. & I superintend the planting day after day. A. annoyed by the Concordance of his works. It seems to him that the world must think it an assumption to have one published during his lifetime but he knew nothing about it. He finds "The Window" in the Concordance published by Moxon, another breach of trust on Mr. Payne's part. Mr. Locker tells us that it is sold underhand.

14th. He goes to Mr. Locker's house where he is ever lovingly received.

16th. He returns. I have had the yard made tidy for him.

19th. We send Sophia to prepare Farringford for us thinking that the Knowleses will have left according to their arrangement. A. gave me the beginning of Beaumains (Sir Gareth) to read. I am reading Lecky's *European Morals*.[34]

It is too cold for me to go out with A. planting to-day, much as I delight in it especially when Heard is here to have our orders executed. Now he is not, the blunders are rather trying. However we persevere day by day.

Dr. & Mrs. Acworth come. A. & Tilly much amazed by raps on the table in the middle-room. In A.'s study a table heaves like the sea. Mrs. Acworth is a great medicine tho' a delicate little creature with very bright eyes. Something there must be in it. What I cannot say but it seems to me a power more liable to abuse than others. The Acworths bring us an evergreen La-

[32]James Martineau, *Essays Philosophical and Theological*, 2 vols. (London, 1869); Thomas Hughes, *Alfred the Great* (London, 1868).

[33]"Gareth and Lynette," completed in the summer of 1872 and first published in *Gareth and Lynette, Etc.* (1872).

[34]W. E. H. Lecky, *History of European Morals from Augustus to Charlemagne*.

burnum.[35] Mr. Woolner a very pretty little picture of our own Farringford down. In his picturesque nervous style he tells us many artist stories which interest us.

20th. Mr. Knowles as usual much absorbed in the Poems. I differ from him on some points & express my difference somewhat too warmly as I know & tell him so afterwards.

November

1st. A very happy day. A. & I sit reading. We talk together sitting over the fire in our room at night.

2nd, 3rd, 4th, 5th. Busy about the new Poems.[36] Heard has come & work goes on well out of doors.

Mr. Burdon when calling says that the change looked like magic since he was last here as if the house had been taken up & put down in another place.[37]

Mr. Palgrave comes & is pleased with our house & with the views from it and about it.

9th. A. goes to Town. He cannot get on with his publishing so far from the publisher. Dreary without him.

Mrs. Gilchrist calls & I show [her] over the house all except the servants' part. She says "It is all nothing else but perfect." Then Mr. Simmons who is with her takes her to see what we have done with the grounds.

Rhododendrons arrive, I look to the planting.

15th. A. arrives.

16th. Mr. Estcourt lunches with us. He is pleased with the place. He tells us that the report goes that the Queen has been here & requested to call the place Queen's Hurst. Who invents all the stories that get abroad!

We fix the terms of our agreement with Heard as tenant of the Farm. The land having improved so much under him as our Bailiff. The Farm is not the source of out of doors interest

[35]In her letter of October 15, 1869, to Hallam Tennyson, Emily remarked that the Acworths' visit was "not to my delight. . . . She is a so-called spiritualist!" (*Letters of E. T.*, p. 242).

[36]Although dated 1870, *The Holy Grail and Other Poems* was issued in early December 1869.

[37]Burdon worked for Lord Egmont, whom he represented in negotiations with the Tennysons regarding the access road through Egmont's estate.

to A. which I had hoped it might have been when we had no longer that of making new lawns & glades & otherwise altering the grounds at Farringford & the accounts proved too hard work for me with our many letters. But he did like to hear that only the Duke of Richmond's sheep could rival his & I can record as my experience that we did not lose by a home farm tho' we did not gain except by way of having everything of the best in Farm produce.

One night Mr. Knowles & myself sit up till twelve marking passages in "The Lover's Tale" hoping that A. may consent to publish them.

25th. Mr. Locker comes. No one more affectionate among A.'s friends.

26th. A. goes with him to look after his proofs. Turfing finished or nearly finished to-day.

29th. Another day of mist & rain. Tilly in the evening tells me how on an autumn evening at Somersby just before Arthur Hallam's death she and Mary saw a tall figure clothed from head to foot in white and followed it down the lane & saw it pass thro' the hedge where there was no gap & how she was so awed that on reaching home she burst into tears. Then how being at Spilsby for her dancing lesson she had brought home the letters and one among them from Clevedon. This was addressed to A. She gave it to him as he sat at dinner & went to take off her bonnet but she heard afterwards that he had suddenly left the table & that poor Emily had been summoned to have the dreadful news broken to her & of the terrible scene that followed. Then Tilly told me how she & the younger ones "roared" when Arthur Hallam went away with Charlie & A. to college & that Arthur was so delightful to them that they were all in love with him from the first when they saw him on the lawn where he & A. were playing with Billy the monkey. She added that he had always begged that the children might be of any pleasure party that was made but that A. was kindest of all to the children often taking them on his knees on the lawn & telling them ghost stories & other stories of his own invention.

A. wrote to me the thought of giving up "The Lover's Tale" and only publishing "The Golden Supper" with a preface.

December

2nd. To-day he comes. Mr. Pollock on Saturday notwithstanding snow. He gets out a little with A. & is very pleased with the place & is himself very pleasant. Terrible mists but the servants so anxious to go that I send them off on the 8th only keeping Frank & Mathilda who must stay to put things away that have to be put away.

Still too bad to travel. The cold mist seems to suck the life out of one Vampire-like.[38]

10th. Mist still but we go & find William waiting with the carriage at Ryde & we get home comfortably & thank God that we are at home.

11th. Next day brings us news that our Lionel has measles at Eton & I make all preparations for going if desirable when my telegram is answered. Thankful indeed for favourable reports of our boy. He writes that Mr. & Mrs. Stone are kindness itself to him.[39] A. reads me some of Maurice's "Social Morals."[40] "A noble book" it seems to one, as A. called it. He writes to Mr. Eddy expressing the hope always dear to us that cabinet ministers are thinking how to make England and her colonies one body & soul instead of casting them off, and he cannot & I cannot but feel that those who think otherwise must be blind to our real interest & our high calling. He also expresses his entire willingness to sign the petition.[41]

[38] Emily was quite disturbed by the bitter, damp climate at Blackdown during the Tennysons' first autumn there, and for a time she even wished they had chosen another site for their summer home. Indeed, her December 10, 1869, letter to Hallam at Marlborough is solely concerned with the subject: "The weather here has been more dreadful than anything I ever felt. Such a cold mist! It is a pity we were not told of it before we built here. . . . I mean a pity for our Lionel if he is to have this place but God knows what is to be. Perhaps he will be a rich man who will have another place to go to in winter—& in summer weather the climate is perfect—& now I am thankful if the mist makes Papa thankful for Farringford" (T.R.C.).

[39] Edward Daniel Stone (1832-1916) was assistant master at Eton from 1857 until 1884. Lionel Tennyson lived with the Stones during much of his residence at Eton.

[40] F. D. Maurice, *Social Morality* (Cambridge, 1869).

[41] Mr. Eddy is C. W. Eddy, the author of *Assisted Colonization* (1870). In late 1869 a popular petition letter in support of Britain's imperialist role was prepared for transmission to the respective governments of all the colonies and circulated in London.

Alfred Lord Tennyson in 1869. Photograph by Julia Margaret Cameron. (National Portrait Gallery)

17th. Thankful indeed are we to welcome our Lionel. Many reviews of the *Holy Grail* Volume. All more or less favourable. Almost all very favourable. A letter from the poor Duke of Argyll saying that the doctors have for two days given up hopes for the Duchess.

21st. Today our Hallam comes & our Lionel would fain have gone & A. & I go to meet him. He has traveled part of the way with Mrs. Grosvenor Hood. She is so very kind to him always.

A good deal of snow. We see Horatio every day. A. reads part of "The Holy Grail" at my request & Hallam some of *The Winter's Tale*.

1870

January

The Butlers, the Bradleys, the Cornishes, & Mr. Paul. We have noticed how pale & depressed our Hallam has been since he returned. Dr. Hollis pronounces his illness chicken-pox. He shook hands with his friend [*illegible*] on leaving who had just had it.

Hallam & I shut up alone. Tilly goes to Edinburgh & I bid her farewell from the top of the staircase.

The ladies & gentlemen walk together every day. Annie Thackeray, Pinkie Ritchie, Magdalene Brookfield,[1] Mr. Young in addition to those I have named.

Hallam well enough now for us to have friends to dinner. Many having had chicken-pox have kindly come to see him. The Bradleys stay with us. A. has games at Battledore. The boys go to dances at Miss Crozier's & to one at Norton Lodge.

25th. I go to meet Mr. Mornington & unexpectedly find Mr. Jowett who had forgotten to mention his day. A welcome find indeed.

A. reads some of *The Winter's Tale* to us at Hallam's request he having to learn 200 lines of it for his holidays task with Abbot's Grammar.

February

5th. A. has walks with Hallam. Hallam takes Miss Lane[2] to the Shepherd's to present the scarf she has made for him. Our good Andrews returns. Thankful are we.

6th. The boys go to Shepherd's that Lionel may say good bye.

7th. But to-day is so stormy that we have a respite. I telegraph to Mr. Stone. The boys & A. play Battledore. Yesterday a fragment of a Vessel bearing a Danish name & a pair of gentleman's boots floated into our Bay. Pathetic record.

[1]Magdalene was the W. H. Brookfields' daughter.

[2]A Freshwater neighbor and special friend of Mrs. Cameron's.

8th. Our Lionel goes to-day. Hallam sees him off. Bitterly cold it is.

9th. Louy Simeon comes & the Miss Bridges with her. We are to have the last scene in *Winter's Tale* acted in which she is to take part but she has a fall on the ice & is ill in bed, so it has to be given up.

Not to disappoint the officers of the Southampton ball we change the day of our dance. All seem merry except some do not dance much because of the stranger ladies among them. The Miss Herchels with us.

27th. Hard to part from our tender manly boy to-day. A sunbeam in the house. He is gone & we have just had prayers when a telegram from Mr. Bright arrives saying that we had better keep him for two or three days as there is scarletina in the house. I dispatch a boy on a pony who overtakes the carriage before it crosses the bridge. Hallam having gone to take some snowdrops to Lady Hamond & say goodbye. So we have the joy of seeing him return. A. reads to us from that delightful book Stanley's *Eastern Church.*

Hallam meets the officers in the march. They kindly press him to go to their party in the evening. (The officers very kind in their invitations to him.)

March

1st. Next day, March 1st, he helps Mrs. Cameron to prepare for her dance. He himself does not return till a quarter to five from the dance. Targett's band is there from Southampton. Hallam reads some of the 4th *Aeneid* with A. (Horatio sad for his children at the Terrace have measles but get well over it.)

9th. Our Lionel is ordered home by the doctor because of his cough.

10th. He could not have had a more lovely day for his journey. He looks thin & heavy eyed & coughs every minute. Hallam gives up the concert to welcome him.

15th. A. goes to Aldworth. Things rather wretched there from the ravages of frost among the pipes. Mr. Locker & Mr. Knowles think that A. likes his rooms in Victoria St. which Lady Charlotte has been so very good as to furnish for him.

The boys work every day at Horace or Herodotus & sometimes at both.

26th. The sorrowful news of poor little Franklin's[3] death. It was thought that he was recovering but he sank [and] died in a few minutes. What a terrible blow to his parents in India. Hallam writes to the Colonel saying what a pure innocent good little soul he was & I tell her of the nurse Clark's tenderness to Hallam of whom she was fond as she was of their dear little fellow. The Bradleys beyond measure distressed by this death & three others at Marlborough.

28th. Horatio comes most days & is very merry. He & the boys have great fun together making endless riddles.

April

A. returns by Blackdown with Mr. Knowles but has to go again about Moxon affairs.

12th. Returns in an open boat on the 14th. He is told that he will not be able to come for a week if he does not come then. The crush is so great that he has to drag his own portmanteau to a truck. He steered by moonlight seeing nothing.

20th. Cornishes & Freshfields. Mr. Freshfield interests A. by what he says of the Caucasus. . . .

May

2nd. Hallam goes to a dance at Mrs. Prettyman's.

6th. Our Lionel leaves us.

9th. A. & Hallam drive to Swainston. They come too late to see Sir John & Lady Simeon who have left for Switzerland, the last time they ever leave home together.

14th. Our Hallam goes. Sad enough to part from our boys but not so bad as to have them at home idle which one knows is so bad for them.

A. takes me into the kitchen garden & the Orchard to see the Apple blossoms. A. takes me out this week in the carriage. . . .

23rd. The terrible blow of Sir John Simeon's death fell on us just as we were starting for Aldworth, Mr. Estcourt having kindly

[3]A classmate of Hallam's at Marlborough, son of Col. Charles Trigance Franklin.

written to us. When we reach Aldworth we find a letter from dear Louy who has made the effort to write to us herself. These days A. reads to me & takes me out in my little carriage. The happiest times [we] have had here.

30th. Tilly comes.

31st. A. goes to Swainston for the funeral. All dreadfully sad & trying & seeming all the sadder that the sun shone & the roses bloomed profusely. A great many people there. A. went as a mourner. The poor heart-broken widow & Louy see him for a minute. He thought it best not to sleep there. They bear up bravely.

June

7th. I enjoy our drive to Guildford very much. We get most of the things we want at Haslemere. He is very sad. His loss haunts him.[4]

10th. Mr. Locker & Mr. Venables come. Both very kind & pleasant. Mr. Venables frightens us by falling back in a big oak chair in which he was rocking thinking it a rocking chair. The chair was broken but he not hurt to our great relief.

Mr. Knowles comes. Great trouble still with the drains. A. goes with him to a dinner at the Metaphysical Club.

We have news from Mrs. Cameron that Aubrey Taylor died on the 16th on board.[5] His Mother & Eleanor went to the London Dock & his servant met them with this sad news. He died without suffering. They had at least this comfort.

Aunt Cracroft[6] & Catherine have come with Harriet Wright to luncheon.

[4] As he so often did during times of trouble, Tennyson distracted himself with domestic chores when he returned from the funeral at Swainston. He was particularly obsessive in his desire to landscape his gardens and to encourage the new grass on his distressingly barren lawn. In her letter of June 6, 1870, to Hallam, Emily reports what "an innocent sight" it is each day to watch "Papa running up & down stairs with his two pitchers of bath water to water the lawn or making a great rain from thy bed-room window falling before that in which I sit" (T.R.C.).

[5] Aubrey Taylor (1847–70) was Sir Henry Taylor's only son. Despite various lifelong infirmities, young Taylor had shown considerable intellectual promise.

[6] Possibly Arabella Cracroft Lister (1801–73), a Lincolnshire cousin of the Henry Sellwoods. During the early nineteenth century Arabella's cousins the Robert Cracrofts owned Harrington Hall, which was leased by Arthur Eden,

Drummond & Kate come. All very charmed with the place.

22nd. A. comes to my great delight.[7]

23rd. Drummond & Kate go. For a whole fortnight I have had [men] at work on the drains & admirably have they worked even on one Sunday after having been at work till 12 the night before and one day they get up at three or four, Mr. Knowles thinking it important. No traps where traps are marked & altogether a disgraceful state of things.

27th. Nanny & Agnes come.

29th. Mr. Jowett very kind to Nanny & to us as ever most kind. It is very pleasant to see him so cheerful & to have him taking interest in our furniture with a view to his own.

5th. Poor Lady Simeon comes. A very sorrowful meeting. A deeply interesting talk with her. She goes next day.

6th. Mr. Clark comes. Very cheerful & pleasant he is. Mr. Charles arrives & on the 9th our Lionel. A basket of beautiful flowers from Mr. Burdon. Lionel leaves before six on Monday driving to Godalming. Louy Simeon comes. Mr. Knowles [comes] to settle about the Terrace Balustrade.

13th. To-day A. has to go to propose the Duke of Argyll & Lord Houghton at the Metaphysical Club.[8] He is suffering from his

---

Rosa Baring's stepfather, in 1825. Arabella's parents, John and Penelope Ann Cracroft, owned Hackthorn Hall, Hackthorn, which is presently owned by Lt. Colonel Sir Weston Cracroft-Amcotts.

[7]Shortly after her husband's return home, Emily expressed to Hallam her satisfaction that during this last visit to London more than ever before people recognized the poet and displayed their high admiration for him: "People in Town take to bowing to him now as he walks in the streets. . . . An honour I think that has befallen no man since the 'Great Duke' died. Duties come to us all from this voluntary homage to our head, do they not mine own?" (Lady Tennyson to Hallam Tennyson, June 28, 1870, T.R.C.).

[8]Richard Monckton Milnes (1st Baron Houghton) was nominated by Tennyson and seconded by Sir John Lubbock for membership in the Metaphysical Society, but he was not elected when balloted for on December 13, 1870. Later Milnes did gain membership, evidently in July 1871.

I find no evidence that the duke of Argyll was ever a member of the Metaphysical Society, though he did join two other philosophical societies, the British Association (Glasgow) in 1855 and the Royal Society of Edinburgh in 1861.

back & leg & is very sad & unwilling to leave home. Mr. Paget will keep him ten days or a fortnight. He is to lie in bed till 4 & then on the sofa for this gouty infection.

18th. Mrs. & Miss Leader[9] who had tea with him on Saturday come & good simple girls intelligent & cheerful. Mr. Burdon lunches with us & walks with them. We watch the progress of the Drawing room cornice which Broad & Fuller have come to do. Sorry that I have to settle about it without A. I am glad to have seen so much more than I have done before of Mrs. Leader, being as she is an old friend of A.'s family. They go on the 22nd.

23rd. To my great joy Hallam arrives unexpectedly about ten. He has stumbled his way over stones & sand in the dark. At first seeing him I think how ill he looks & then I learn that one of his poor eyes has been nearly put out by a cricket ball. Its deep setting saved it. He played out his game but was very unwell for two or three days after. He has also run the greatest risk of scarlet fever. A boy in his room became delirious in the night & came raving to his bed. Hallam took him on his knee to soothe him.

26th. He & I [go] to Town to fetch A. & that I may receive instructions from our kind friend Mr. Paget how to treat the leg. The Cabman at last finds Albert Mansions, Mr. Knowles kindly meets us with a chair. Mr. Paget, Mr. Bray,[10] & Mr. Locker come. I am charmed with Mr. Paget. Mr. Locker goes with Hallam to be photographed by Rejlander. They meet Lady Charlotte & Eleanor coming up the stairs. Very glad I am to see them. Lady Augusta kindly takes A. & me in her carriage to the Station. Lady Charlotte with us. Hallam following with the luggage. A. tells us that war[11] is declared.

A. much depressed very often by imprisonment because of his poor leg. Hallam & I do all the nursing & valeting for him. He lies out on the lawn & enjoys it.

29th. Our Lionel returns. The boys play at Backgammon with A.

[9] Probably the wife and daughter of John Temple Leader (1810–1903).

[10] Charles Bray (1811–84), the friend of George Eliot and the author of *On Force: Its Mental and Moral Correlates* (1866), *A Manual of Anthropology* (1869), and *Psychological and Ethical Definitions on a Physiological Basis* (1879), among other works.

[11] The Franco-Prussian War, 1870–71.

August

We rejoice to hear of the Prussian victory at Wissembourg being all of us Prussians.

5th. Hallam reads *Esmond* to me at night and in the morning the "Causeries de Lundi."[12]

7th. Charlie & Louy arrive.

10th. Mrs. Greville & Miss [*illegible*] come to luncheon & Mrs. Greville reads "The Grandmother" in a highly dramatic way.[13] We go to A.'s study & he reads a good deal.

Mr. Dakyns arrives, always welcome.

Charlie & Louy drive with me to Black Down Cottage & House and are as much charmed as I am with the old forest look of the Park with its fine trees & broken ground & lovely views of the distant hills. A. & Lionel go to meet Emily Jesse so that with Tilly we are a large family party.[14]

17th. To our great regret Charlie & Louy leave us. Their faces beam with such a heavenly light one feels there is a blessing in their presence.

20th. We hear from Franklin Lushington of the death of our good & kind friend Mr. Chapman.[15] Never could any one have lost a friend more ready to serve.

22nd. Our Lionel leaves us. Our kind friends have given him shooting to his great gratification. The train does not stop at

[12] Thackeray, *Henry Esmond*, and Charles Augustin Sainte-Beuve, *Causeries du lundi*, 15 vols. (Paris, 1849–61).

[13] Mrs. Sabine Greville was a great admirer of Tennyson's verse, which she was in the habit of reciting all over London. Though not a gifted or tactful woman, Mrs. Greville was sincerely devoted to the Tennysons, and she spread a kind of Tennyson gospel everywhere she went. Perhaps she was accurately described by Henry James, who once wrote of her "genius . . . for friendship" and added, "I can't praise her better than by saying that though she is on the whole the greatest fool I have ever known, I like her very much, and get on with her most easily" (*The Letters of Henry James*, ed. Leon Edel [Cambridge, Mass.: Harvard University Press, Belknap Press, 1975–], I, 241).

[14] Emily Jesse was Tennyson's sister. She married Capt. Richard Jesse, R.N., in 1842.

[15] Benedict Lawrence Chapman (1810–70), barrister, equity draftsman, and conveyancer, was admitted at the Inner Temple in 1833; he died on September 12, 1870. Lady Tennyson placed her reference to Chapman in the wrong spot. As it stands, her mention of his death antedates that occurrence by three weeks.

Godalming or they have gone to a wrong station. They hurry on to Guildford. Lionel describes Wellington College as looking fine as it gleams with its hundred lights, then he hears a lovely peal of bells, then at Slough he is pushed at by an Engine, the carriage near him driven off the line. One of Lord Lyttleton's sons jumps out of the window. Our Lionel sees a boy's face turn white & thinks that all is over with him but thank God no one had more than a few scratches.

A. brings me an Iron chair, one being already on the lower Terrace, & we sit side by side watching the Turfers.

The Bishop of Winchester[16] & Mr. Hook call & have a slight luncheon in spite of both saying they do not take it. Both are very agreeable. Glorious weather. Aurora blood red at night.

29th. Edmund, Cissy, & Lucy [Lushington] arrive. We are sorry to lose Emily next day. She has been very affectionate & very good company. Louy Simeon & Margaret Rawnsley come. All think Margaret very attractive, ourselves included.

September

14th. I am very thankful that the Lushingtons are the better for their visit & have enjoyed it. They have always been most true & loving friends. Louy has to go & I am sorry. No one except my very own sympathizes with me as she does.

18th. A. & I take Margaret to the train.

19th. Dr. Bray comes for the night & most kindly present is for A. A. & I have German Backgammon now in the evening. It is better for him than reading all day as he cannot get out much.

21st. He & I have a delightful drive to Maurice Young's garden. Beere goes with us. We return by dear Wild Hind Head.

23rd. A divinely happy talk alone with my A. One to be remembered as long as I live.

24th. He brings me his Preface to the Songs. He & I give away . . . buns & gingerbread to eight little girls from the Infant school. The poor little boys weep when they find they are not to come we hear.

A magnificent Aurora, Red as our curtains, in the North East. Saturn below, white light streamers shooting thro' the

[16] Samuel Wilberforce (1805–73) served as bishop of Oxford from 1845 until 1869, when he was appointed bishop of Winchester.

red. A. reads some of Kant's Prologomena to me & we discuss it. Another Aurora fainter red shooting in along the house.

27th. Louis d'Eyncourt[17] & his wife come & Mr. Garden. Mrs. Mangles lunches with us.[18] All like her. Mr. d'Eyncourt sketches & makes a very pretty drawing of the house & the hill from the wood on the promontory. All go. All have been very agreeable & A. bright so we have had a cheerful time.
Lady Georgiana & Mr. Peel[19] arrive.

30th. Very glad we are to see one old friend & happy. His thankfulness to the wife who takes such good care of his three motherless children is very touching. A. reads "The Northern Farmer" to them, "I have led her home"[20] & part of "The Passing of Arthur." They go. They have been merry & A. very merry with them so I hope they have enjoyed their visit. They say they have.

October

1st. How strange the tendency to invent stories. Emily[21] copies that passage in Miss Mitford's letters which states that A. dug the garden of Miss Repton's Father at Sevenoaks whereas A. never saw either him or his garden. Then there is an illustrated paper which states that he was at Louth School until he went to Trinity. The fact being that when about seven he was asked whether he would go to the sea or to school. School seeming a sort of Paradise to him, he said to school so he was sent to his Aunt Mary Anne Fytche's house & went thence to school daily. Many a time sitting on his bed crying at having to get up at six & go to the school he hated & at which he only remained two

[17]Louis d'Eyncourt was Tennyson's cousin, the son of Charles Tennyson d'Eyncourt (1784–1861).

[18]James Henry Mangles and his wife, Isabella, were Surrey neighors of the Tennysons, and their house Valewood was within walking distance of Aldworth. Between August 1870 and October 1872 Mangles kept a journal quoting or summarizing the poet's comments on a great variety of subjects. This unpublished manuscript journal, now owned by Mrs. J. Norman, is in the Ohio University library.

[19]Archibald Peel and his wife, Lady Georgiana Adelaide Peel, the daughter of Lord John Russell. With her sister, Lady Victoria Russell, Lady Georgiana published a verse drama entitled *Dewdrop and Glorio* (c. 1860).

[20]See *Maud* I.xviii.

[21]Emily Jesse.

or three years & was afterwards taught at home by his Father until he went to Trinity. Another story the paper gave of his having been taken into custody as a smuggler when watching a stormy sea. The only foundation for this being that one stormy night on the Farringford Down the coast-guard said "Who goes there?" "Oh, you, Sir, a stormy night" or some such word.

Excellent news of our boys who seem to be doing well. Hallam hopes to have won a silver cup in the race & is commended for his work in form. Our Lionel too seems to have awakened to a desire to be industrious. His themes & his verses have been praised. Delightful being alone with A. We drive & have Russian Backgammon. We look to the clearing of the new lawn.

4th. Mr. Knowles, Mr. Sullivan & Mr. Strahan come. Mr. Sullivan wishes to publish the Songs. We did not like it especially at such a grave crisis of affairs in Europe; but the advance of money does not satisfy Mr. Sullivan not being what he wanted. "He that sweareth unto his neighbour & disappointeth him not" determines us. So they are to be published. As they have already been pirated it does not so much matter.[22]

7th. Mr. & Mrs. Synge[23] arrive just as we start on our drive. They lunch. He tells us a story of a dinner in honour of American Independence one 4th of July. The guests were very merry drinking & singing. At last one sang a song about the glorious days when we were colonists & had a king and was rapturously applauded. He also told us of the wailing for Queen Emma how one party took it up when the other ceased. He wonders how she could have lived thro' this & the six weeks day & night in the room where her husband lay.

8th. A. drives to meet Mr. Peach whose stories of his life are very picturesque & interesting. Busy with the new lawns clearing & their planting. A. takes out my cloak to put over me as he sheltered me yesterday with his own and an umbrella. He reads to

[22] See Psalms 15.3. Tennyson thought "The Window; or, the Song of the Wrens" far below his standard and would not have permitted its publication but for Arthur Sullivan's insistence and his own feeling that he was bound by having allowed Sullivan to initiate the project four years earlier. It is said that Tennyson at the last moment offered Sullivan £500 to cancel the agreement.

[23] William Webb Follett Synge (1826–91), diplomat, author, and friend of Thackeray, was appointed secretary to Sir William Gore Ouseley's mission to Central America in 1856; he became commissioner judge in Cuba in 1865. His wife, Henrietta Mary, was the youngest daughter of Robert Dewar Wainwright, a colonel in the United States Army.

me some of Pepys' *Journal*. He talks of writing to Lord Granville to tell him how grateful he was for his spirited remonstrance.[24] How strange that ministers cannot see that our true policy lies in a close union with the colonies.

12th. A fine day. Aunt Franklin & Sophy Cracroft & Miss Grenell come from Moor Park to luncheon. All charmed with the house & the view. My Aunt very kind to us.

14th. Miss Vernon comes. I have many letters to write because of a difficulty in Horatio's marriage settlement which his second marriage makes important. Sad indeed that the children must now be divided. . . . Mr. Allingham, Mr. Knowles, Mr. Barrett, Miss MacKay. Our friends feel the cold very much.

December

5th. A. goes with Mr. Allingham & Miss MacKay after luncheon.

6th. Lionel & I hard at work arranging A.'s books & making a catalogue preparatory to our return home. Mr. Mangles most kindly gives Lionel shooting as Mr. Burdon has done.

8th. Bright fires in the hall & other rooms. The old house delightfully comfortable & homey looking. Good old Mr. Smith's gladness at seeing us very pleasant to us.[25]

11th, 12th, 13th, 14th. Very busy arranging the books in A.'s studio & his dressing room. Lionel very good company translating Virgil & Homer to me all night. He translates admirably. We have German Backgammon afterwards.

[24] Lord Granville's "Answer to the Russian Circular," which he dispatched from the foreign office on November 10, 1870, was printed in the *Times* on November 11. Granville's answer expressed Great Britain's entire dissatisfaction with the recent avowal of Prince Gorchakov that Russia now felt free to disregard certain provisions of the Treaty of 1856 regarding restraints on Russian use of the Black Sea.

[25] Emily's characteristic joy in returning to Farringford was lessened only by the discovery that the sofa and easy chair in her husband's bedroom had been ruined by moths during the summer, while some of her own clothes, including her wedding dress, had been spotted by the damp. Nevertheless, she managed to find a good omen in the ruined dress, writing to Hallam that "if luck comes only when the wedding dress is worn out mine must come now,—but what better can I have than I have had with my Husband and my boys. I ask nothing but the old days ever new, in Him who makes all things new" (December 13, 1870, T.R.C.).

16th. A. returns, is pleased with the look of the place which he says is very homey. It is a touching sight to see the old gray head of the Shepherd bared reverently to greet him. I watch them as they stand by the railings, Lionel with his father. We often see Nanny & Agnes, their house being now finished & they in it. A. likes it. I have a cold & cannot go with him to see them & it.

20th. Lionel & I go to meet our Hallam. For many a year I have not seen him look so well on his return. He brings the joyful news that he is in the sixth and that he has been publicly thanked for his services as Sergeant of Volunteers; he sings war songs. We are very quiet for several days.

A. declines going in the Cadiz ship, finding that a poem on the eclipse is expected from him. "A thing absurd of course & out of the question."[26] Likely enough that no one will go if this insolent dispatch of Gortschakoff brings war as it should do if not withdrawn. Mr. Locker comes to bring what seems to me anxious news of dear Lady Charlotte. . . .

All these days we superintend work on the lawns. I am indeed thankful for this improvement in strength since I have had the rest & refreshment of being alone with him sometimes. Scarletina [*illegible*]. Lionel returns in consequence of our telegram. He over done at football & ill, poor boy.

25th. Mayall comes to photograph A. He photographs him on the front porch. A. very anxious about this Russian affair.

27th. [Lionel] goes out shooting in all weathers cold as it is & one day near the Needles sees a cloud of Grebes over head but too high to be reached by his gun or that of Henry Cameron, his constant companion. A. agrees to join with Lord Eversley,[27] Mr. Seely, Mr. Estcourt & others to call a meeting for raising a memorial to Sir John Simeon. The Butlers, the Cornishes,[28] Mr. Oscar Browning.

[26] The Royal Society astronomers, who were planning a trip to Cadiz, wanted Tennyson to accompany them in order to write a poem on the eclipse they anticipated viewing there.

[27] Charles Shaw-Lefevre, Viscount Eversley (1794–1888), speaker of the House of Commons from 1839 until 1857.

[28] The Cornishes were Francis Warre Warre-Cornish (1839–1916), the teacher and bibliophile, who was made assistant master at Eton in 1861 and served as vice-provost and librarian from 1893 until his death, and his wife.

1871

January

The Butlers, Cornishes, Mr. Young, Mr. Oscar Browning, the Pauls, Pinkie Ritchie. All have walks with A. & we see them from time to time to luncheon or dinner. Mr. Cornish sings. . . . Pinkie plays Beethoven exquisitely. Our Lionel acts Mrs. [*illegible*] at the Camerons. The Cornishes, Pinkie, Hallam sing the Marseillaise afterwards.

8th. A., Hallam, & Pinkie read part of *Julius Caesar.*

10th. Hallam works in the morning & walks with A. in the afternoon & makes kind little visits. Never was there a more contented boy. He seems to want nothing else. A. & the boys finish *Julius Caesar* & Hallam goes to meet Mr. Jowett.

16th. The Butlers & Mr. Young go. Mr. Jowett reads us some of his *Plato* & goes next day. Most kind he is in every way.

19th. Our Lionel goes. His sweetness & simplicity are most touching. He looks strong & rosy notwithstanding his being already six feet.

February

4th. Mr. Cameron's sister, Mrs. Darling, dies. Every one in his house & on all sides of it startled by a great rattling of windows.

8th. Shepherd comes to supper & to say good-bye to Hallam. He for the first time tastes chicken & likes it very much & is greatly amused at Doré's *Don Quixote*[1] which Hallam shows him.

10th. A stormy morning. I telegraph that he cannot go. He rides with Annie Prinsep to call at Norton Lodge, walks with A. & goes on with *Philip Van Artevelde*[2] to me. Mr. Cameron sends a petition that he may stay for his birthday but the 11th is sunny tho' very cold so we have no excuse for keeping our boy &

[1] Doré's illustrated *Don Quixote* (London and New York, 1864).

[2] Sir Henry Taylor's 1834 drama.

with heavy hearts we see him go. Never had parents a better son. My A. is so good to me.

12th. He reads me some of Westcott's *Gospel of the Resurrection*[3] which Mr. Butler has sent me.

16th. A. receives Mr. Jowett's four volumes of *Plato.* A most welcome gift for itself & for the donor. I cut open the Phaedo volume for him & we talk on the subjects nearest his heart—the Resurrection of Jesus Christ and the Immortality of the Soul. He reads me a paper in the Edinburgh Royal Society Transactions.

Lord Elcho walks with A. & I talk with Lady Elcho of Mrs. Cameron's wonderful acts of love & of all the orphans & the desolate creatures she receives under her roof.[4] Surely never was there a larger heart. We talk of the Resurrection of our Lord & of the Immortality of man.

19th. Mrs. Cameron brings A. a volume of Faber[5] & he reads some to me. We talk a good deal of Romanism & hear the Ceylon letters.[6] A. begins cold milk & bread for luncheon instead of meat & wine. We drive sometimes & occasionally A. walks with Agnes & Annie & Lou Prinsep.

26th. I go with A. into Maiden's Croft. He talks despondingly of Swinburne's book[7] & (he lived long enough to rejoice in the altered spirit of his work) of the tone of literature in his set as he does now from time to time foreseeing the fiercest battle the world has yet known between good & evil, faith & unfaith. What does midnight tonight bring? Peace or war for France & Germany. Surely peace. The continuance of such a war is too dreadful to think of.

27th. Our little homage to Carlyle is presented to-day at Lady Stanley's of Alderley, who has kindly asked us to be present.[8]

[3]Brooke Foss Westcott, *The Gospel of the Resurrection* (London, 1866).

[4]Francis Richard, 10th earl of Wemyss, and his wife Anne Frederica, Lady Elcho.

[5]Probably the Rev. George Stanley's *The Difficulties of Infidelity* (London, 1833).

[6]These were letters from Charles Hay Cameron, who was periodically in Ceylon managing estates he owned there.

[7]Tennyson called Swinburne's *Songs before Sunrise* (1871) "blasphemous" and advised Mrs. Cameron against sending a copy to her husband in Ceylon (Lady Tennyson to Hallam Tennyson, February 24, 1871, *Letters of E.T.*, p. 271).

[8]A group of prominent ladies, all of them connected with the literary world in

March

3rd. I think that we finally settle to have the two new rooms built. He watches the cutting of branches from the trees. Ally's poor eyes suffer so much from the winter darkness of the dear old study.

4th. This morning the wind blows so there are clouds of dust from the Yew Tree. Agnes brings some huge barnacles to one of which a bit of wood of the unhappy ship to which they had gathered adheres. They look something between worms & seaweed with a shell helmet at one end with many feelers. A. reads to me of the departure of the Germans from Paris.

5th. In the evening he reads to me a very interesting account of what seems to one the wonderful outpouring of the Spirit on [*illegible*] flock in Calcutta. How thousands drest in white with white banners, East & West on one or more, make a procession to the Temple singing hymns to the One God & how the hundreds who cannot find room within stand without torch in hand singing so sweetly that it seemed as if Angels had come down from heaven. A. reads to me [from] Pouchet about plants. Very interesting. Next day he reads me more of Pouchet about volcanoes.[9]

8th. To-day we begin digging up the big Bay & other shrubs to make space for A.'s new room. I finish Markham's Life of the great Lord Fairfax,[10] Westcott's *Church of the Resurrection*. . . . My eyes have not been well enough to make the best use by way of reading of these precious days alone with A. The most, I think, we have had for many years. The great Poplar on the new lawn has fallen & smashed many things. . . .

---

one fashion or another, presented a little clock to Thomas Carlyle on February 27, 1871. The presentation was made at the home of Lady Henrietta Maria Stanley of Alderley (1807–95), and the "paper of signature" included the names of Louisa, Lady Ashburton, Henrietta Froude, Anne Farrar, Mrs. Oliphant, Juliet Pollock, and Anne Thackeray, as well as those of Emily Tennyson and Lady Stanley. In her letter of March 10, 1871, to Hallam Tennyson, Emily quoted Anne Thackeray's description of Carlyle's reaction to the gift: "'Dear old man he began to tremble; first he said What have I to do with time any more. Then—God be with you all & thank you many many hundred times—'" (T.R.C.).

[9]Felix Archimède Pouchet, *The Universe, or the Infinitely Great and the Infinitely Little* (London, 1870).

[10]Sir Clements Robert Markham, *The Life of the Great Lord Fairfax* (London, 1870).

14th. The contract about the rooms signed by A. & by Kenneth & witnessed by Andrews.[11]

15th. A little snow. All that has to come down of the green house is down & we shall never again see the lovely green gloom of the old long house when it was roofed in its whole length with vines. A. walks on the Newport road & bids me follow until I overtake him. I find him near Westover. We learn that poor Mrs. Prettyman is overwhelmed by news of her grandson. He took a Header bathing in Bermuda & broke his neck.

21st. The wedding day of the Princess Louise.[12] The first of the new room laid for an arch over the well to make the new rooms safe. A. takes long walks & finds that they do him great good.

24th. He goes with me to pay my first visit to Nanny in her new house. I like it very much. She has lovely hyacinths & tulips in her garden & a beautiful view. Every night we have German Backgammon to spare his poor eyes which do not see as well as they did but to-night he reads me a little of Lanfrey's *Napoleon*[13] & we talk a great deal.

26th. To-night very gravely.

27th. He has so much palpitation of the heart & fluttering of the nerves that he resolves on going to Aldworth. I would not let him go alone but that our Lionel is coming on the 28th for the confirmation on the 29th, so I go no further than Yarmouth.

28th. I hear of his safe arrival & go to fetch our Lionel from the boat.

29th. He is very devout & simple about confirmation & I have the comfort of being with him. A. & Beere give a lamentable account of the state of Aldworth. A. dines with Mr. & Mrs. Mangles & sleeps there.

30th. Mr. Knowles goes to Aldworth.

31st. A. returns. Lionel & I go to the boat to meet him. A day

[11] In early 1871 the Tennysons began construction of a large library on the second floor of Farringford, on the south side, with a playroom or ballroom under it.

[12] The fourth daughter of Queen Victoria, Princess Louise (1848–1939) married John Campbell, Lord Lorne, son and heir to the duke of Argyll, on March 21, 1871.

[13] Pierre Lanfrey, *Histoire de Napoleon Ier*, 5 vols. (Paris, 1867–75).

never to be forgotten. Surely love as one grows older has the tenderness of the eve of parting—the long parting. A. never seemed to me so beautiful & touching & I never had moments of the same sort of happiness. Thank God for ever for this time alone with him & our boys.

April

2nd. I go with Lionel to his first communion. The Bradleys are here & we see Dr. & Mrs. Jackson.[14] Horatio & Cathy,[15] Nanny & Agnes at luncheon or dinner & later the Worsleys.

7th. One day we call at Norton Lodge & the cottage & tell these kind friends who take so much interest in Hallam of the Cups won by him in the races. All these days we have cold North-East winds. Sir Alexander Grant arrives. Lionel fetches him from the boat. He is charmed with Annie Thackeray. Who but must be charmed. A delightful letter from Mr. Butler at Marlboro' Lodge telling of our Hallam's Essay on Milton & of the race & of all else that one loves to hear of one's boy.[16] A. walks & drives with Sir Alexander. Mrs. Speedy is obliged by ill health to return from India. She gives a good report of Alamayou who she says is very manly & gentle. . . .

The Watsons, Mrs. & Miss Synge, & Mr. Edward Bowen[17] arrive. There are luncheons & dinners & drives & one day as I am following the gentlemen in the carriage on their walk to

[14] Dr. Jackson was a Freshwater physician who often ministered to the Tennysons' minor complaints.

[15] Horatio Tennyson's second wife, the former Catherine West.

[16] Emily Tennyson frequently advised her sons of her thoughts regarding literature and literary figures, and her comments to Hallam on Milton while he was writing his Marlborough essay in the spring of 1871 are especially interesting. Although she confessed to a less than thorough acquaintance with some of Milton's works, she ventured the opinion that although Milton "had a sublime soul . . . it might have been wanting somewhat in tenderness and sympathy. I suppose it is next to impossible that so strong & soaring & absorbed a nature should have them. He would have been almost more than human if he had." And Emily followed this rather Blakean criticism of Milton with a final telling remark: "I fear he had only one wife who understood him & she died after a year of marriage" (Lady Tennyson to Hallam Tennyson, March 31, 1871, T.R.C.).

[17] Edward Bowen (1827–97), canon of Taughboyne, 1851–54, and rector, 1867–86. He served as archdeacon of Raphoe from 1874 until 1882 and as dean from 1882 until his death.

Calbourne Miss Lena Eden suddenly appears. Poor thing she has gone thro' a great deal since last we met. Her Father & her Aunt both dead & she herself has been in bed nearly the whole winter from bronchitis.

Mr. Digby, Mr. Charles Digby,[18] & his little niece Geraldine & Mr. Stone & Margaret Arden come by the boat. The Digbys meet Mr. Frederick Pollock & Mr. Richmond Ritchie & the Fraser-Tytlers at luncheon. Mr. Liddell & Mr. Fraser-Tytler come afterwards. They all go with A. to Watcombe Bay.

21st. The Digbys & Watsons & Mr. Buxton[19] dine with us.

23rd. The Buxton baby christened. Mr. Clifford, Annie Thackeray, & Colonel & Mrs. Field dine with us.[20]

24th. We have nineteen children including the baby. We pick Cowslips & to tea afterwards. The number of their elders I have not counted.

25th. The Digbys go. It is delightful to see a family so loving as they are.

26th. Shepherd dines here & we have the dear old man a long time in the dining-room afterwards.

1st. Mr. Knowles comes.

2nd. Mr. Strahan.

3rd. Madame Goldschmidt (Jenny Lind) calls. A. walks with her in the garden. Miss Eden & Mr. Paget lunch here. Dr. Jackson calls to say good-bye.

4th. The Jacksons & Duckworth & Mr. Knowles & Margaret go. Sorry to part from Margaret who is a charming girl. Mdme. Goldschmidt, Miss Lena Eden, & Mr. Paget dine with us. All very pleasant. Mdme. Goldschmidt sings to us. Her voice thrills one in a wonderful way. She sings the song from "Elaine" set by the Rugby organist. He likes it.

[18] Possibly Everard Charles Digby (1852–1914); later colonel.

[19] The Buxtons were Freshwater neighbors.

[20] Sir John Field (1821–99) was made a lieutenant colonel in the Bombay infantry in 1862; he was raised to general in December 1888.

5th. Miss Eden & Mr. Paget go. Mr. Ralston[21] comes, walks, & drives with him.

10th. Mr. Ralston goes.

11th. A. & I drive to Brightstone to see Mr. Fox. When I see him coming out of the cottage where he lodges I think of the fine, old, simple clergymen of long ago. He is very kind, & shows us the bones of the marvellous huge new beast pictured by Mr. Owen & other beasts. A beautiful day.

12th. Madame Goldschmidt dines with us & sang "Auld Lang Syne" & "Auld Robin Gray" for Ally, at his expressed request, two Swedish songs & another which shows her voice off wonderfully. I venture to ask the great favour of her singing to Agnes. She is most kind & offers to go & sing to her when she thinks that she is too ill to come to us.

She sings magnificently some of Handel's "Milton" & some [*illegible*].

14th. She calls to say good-bye. She is delightful, so kind, & so full of feeling & of fun & apparently so deeply religious. A. & I go to look after Mr. Heard & Mrs. Knight & the babies. We find that Madame has been charmed with Mrs. Heard's baby & with the milk of the dairy. A. & I talk after tea about St. John.

Mrs. Grosvenor Hood & Miss Hamond take endless trouble about a maid for me. We are indeed fortunate in our friends of the neighbourhood. A. & I drive & then he takes me to see the old Laburnum under the Fir Trees. It has great bunches of streamers close together instead of the usual single streamer. Almost all of the trees and shrubs are laden with flowers this year. We suppose of the quantity of sunlight they drank in last year.

24th. He reads me his "Tristram."[22] Very grand & terrible in its beauty, I think. The Whites & Sir Laurence Peel.[23]

We drive to the Needles, A. & I. A beautiful day. I enjoy it

[21] William Ralston Shedden-Ralston (1828–89), the Russian scholar and translator. A close friend and frequent companion of Turgenev's, Ralston published *Kriloff and His Fables* (1868), *Songs of the Russian People* (1873), and *Russian Folk Tales* (1873).

[22] "The Last Tournament," first published in the *Contemporary Review* in December 1871.

[23] Sir Lawrence Peel (1799–1884) served as advocate-general at Calcutta from 1840 until 1842, when he was promoted to the chief justiceship. After returning to England, Peel was made a director of the East India Company in 1857, and in 1864 he became president of Guy's Hospital, London.

much. There is the old mystic light on land & sea. He drives with me not unfrequently now & we have together such little walks as I can take.

28th. To-day we go into the kitchen garden that I may see the splendid poppies. He brings me wildflowers.

In the evening he reads some of "Proverbs." A letter comes from Miss Vernon about the living which the Lord Chancellor has been so kind to give her Father at A.'s request. Lady Simeon & Louy come to luncheon. A great pleasure tho' a sad one to have them.

June

5th. When I return I find the Dowager Lady Hamond's carriage at our door & while I am in the Green House showing Mrs. Sheddin the new rooms, Lord & Lady Lichfield[24] come.

6th. Agnes & Horatio come. There is rain but it ceases before we cross & we find all very comfortable at Aldworth. A. takes me round with Beere to look at things. The new walk marked out by A. & Mr. Knowles in the winter, charming. Another day we look where another walk shall be & next day with stick & Alpine stock follow Beere & Luff [?] as they cut it out.

12th. A letter from our Hallam saying that he goes in for the Trinity examinations.

13th. Our 21st wedding day. A rainy day but beautiful sunshine to me within doors. Mr. Macmillan has been so good as to send me Kingsley's "At last." A. reads me some of it and the Heine letter, as translated in the *Spectator*.[25]

14th. The Miss Fraser-Tytlers come.

15th. A letter from our Hallam asking whether he shall accept the prize offered him by the Governing body of Marlboro' for some "splendid lines" in his poem which being written in a wrong metre cannot have the prize tho' it is pronounced second.

[24] Thomas George, 2d earl of Lichfield (1825–92), M.P. for Lichfield, 1847–52, and his wife, the former Lady Harriett Georgiana Louisa Hamilton (d. 1913), eldest daughter of the first duke of Abercorn.

[25] Charles Kingsley's *At Last: A Christmas in the West Indies* was published in 1871. Several excerpts from Heine's correspondence are included in a piece entitled "Heine on the Commune," published in the June 10, 1871, issue of the *Spectator* (pp. 699 ff.).

Aldworth. (National Monuments Record)

16th. A. walks with them. I have pleasant talk with them. When we are all round the tea-table in the drawing room, Morgan announces our Hallam. The dear old boy set off from Cambridge immediately on coming out of examinations & there being no train to Marlboro' comes to Haslemere & walked up here. We telegraph to Mr. Farrar[26] asking him to excuse him from examination at Marlboro' thinking one examination immediately after the other will be too much for him. Our request is kindly granted. A. now has him for a companion in his walks. The Miss Tytlers go.

18th. We ask A. to read us his Ode on the Duke in honour of Waterloo.

19th. A. likes us to stay with him after dinner that we all read to ourselves. In the morning Hallam translates in a Chapter from the Greek of the 1st of *Corinthians* and at night in my room The Episode of an obscure Life.

22nd. They both go. A. & Hallam went to Town for the Academy & I drive with them to the Station. They return in the evening.

23rd. I meet Kate & Drummond at the Station. Both very affectionate, but they must go to-morrow they say. Mr. Clark comes. Kind & pleasant as ever.

27th. Mr. Turgenieff & Mr. Ralston arrived. Mr. Turgenieff a very interesting man who tells us stories of Russian life with great graphic power & vivacity. He tells how in the Cossack council they used all to stand round & talk or fight until they were unanimous, great matter or small. "Peter" or "John" it might be and they would fight till all said "Peter." He told us too of a wonderful instance of the origin of legends as he called it. After the enfranchisement of the Serfs by the Czar many became unruly & would not submit to the servitude imposed for nine years. So the Czar resolved to make a progress thro' his dominions. At each place the serfs were assembled & he made a little speech telling them that he was their Czar who had freed them & that he expected them to be obedient to their old Masters until the nine years were passed & then that [they] were to be entirely free. When the Czar came to Turgenieff's Village Turgenieff was ill & could not go with his serfs but the

[26]Frederick William Farrar (1831–1903), headmaster of Marlborough from 1871 till 1876, archdeacon of Westminster, 1883, chaplain to the House of Commons, 1890, and dean of Canterbury, 1895 till death.

Starosta[27] went. Presently he with about thirty serfs rushed into the room where Turgenieff was sitting & they all together began saying oh, we have seen such a wonderful thing. He said I cannot hear if you all talk at once. Let the Starosta speak. Accordingly he spoke & said, there came a carriage with a beautiful man in it, but he was not the Czar. Then there came another carriage with a still more beautiful man & this was the White Czar & he stood up & spread his arms & beat his breast & said do you know who I am? Do you know who I am? Do you know who I am? Then we all fell to the earth. We said nothing but he beat his breast again, & said "obey," "obey," "obey" & he stood up in his carriage as far as we could see & said "obey," "obey," "obey." While the Starosta was speaking the serfs every now & then chimed in Yes, it is all as he says. When Turgenieff was well enough he went to the Station and asked what had happened & was told that the Czar did not once get up in his carriage but made the same quiet little speech he had made all about the villages in the country.

Turgenieff plays German Backgammon with A. I talk to Mr. Ralston of the poor girls he puts to school in London. Rather a hopeless task it seems, poor man.

28th. Mr. Turgenieff has a letter about the sale of his house in Badend, to our regret has to go to-day.[28] Before he goes he plays at chess with Mr. Clark & with Hallam.

29th. Mr. Clark & Mr. Ralston go.

30th. Mrs. Greville, Lady Charlemont, Mr. Locker, & Admiral Englefield come to luncheon.[29] A. & Hallam have called on Mrs. Hodgson[30] in the morning & asked her to meet Mrs. Gre-

[27] The headman, usually elected, of a Russian village.

[28] Turgenev had taken up residence in Baden-Baden in southern Germany, to which resort Mme. Viardot, the renowned singer, whom he first met in 1843, had retired. When the Franco-Prussian War, 1870–71, forced the Viardots to leave Baden-Baden, Turgenev accompanied them to Paris.

[29] Elizabeth Jane, Lady Charlemont (d. 1882), was the wife of James Molyneux, 3d earl of Charlemont (1820–92).

Adm. Edward Augustus Inglefield (later Sir; 1820–94) accompanied Lady Franklin's private steamer in its expedition to the Arctic in 1852 and the following year published *A Summer Search for Sir John Franklin*. He served as second in command in the Mediterranean from 1872 until 1875 and was knighted in 1877.

[30] The wife of Shadworth Hollway Hodgson (1832–1912), the metaphysician and author of *Time and Space, a Metaphysical Essay* (1865) and *The Philosophy of Reflection* (1878), among other works.

ville in the afternoon. She & her sister Miss Forsyth come. A. reads "Boädicea" & part of "Maud" to them & Lady Charlemont recites or rather acts "the Sisters"[31] after A. has at her request read it & then she reads "Break, break, break." All have tea & go, except Mr. Locker, just as Mr. & Mrs. Farrar arrive.

July

1st. All except myself drive to Hind Head. Mr. Walton White[32] arrives just as Mr. Locker has dined & is going.

A. reads "Guinevere." We are very glad to have made Mr. & Mrs. Farrar's acquaintance. They are kind & gentle. He with the most richly stored memory.

4th. Mr. Knowles & Mr. Teetgen[33] come. Mr. Teetgen sings & plays his own music & goes after dinner.

5th. A. goes with Mr. Knowles.

6th. My Hallam reads to me & sings to me & walks with me.

7th. A. has kindly bought a bed for his dressing room that Hallam may if he likes go to Mr. Gladstone's garden party tomorrow. We telegraph to know if A. desires it himself or only because he thinks that Hallam will like it. A. leaves him free & he does not go. It is touching to hear that A. sees himself to the airing of the bed.

A. lunches with Annie Thackeray & the Leckys, calls on the Airlies & Argylls & dines at Little Holland House. He has also seen the Layards who spoke of coming to lunch here. Glad shall we be to have them. The Gladstones have also promised to come.

11th. We hear that A. dined & lunched with the Simeons & took Louy to the British Museum where she had never been. Hallam has long drives these days. . . .

14th. A. comes. He travels down with Mr. George Lewes who takes him to his home & introduces him to Mrs. Lewes. [A.T. thought her like the picture of Savonarola. She told him that

[31] Tennyson's "We were two daughters of one race" (1833).

[32] The son of Richard Walton White (1809–54), the rector of Up Cerne, Dorsetshire, from 1828 until his death.

[33] Alexander T. Teetgen, the occasional poet and musical critic; author of *Fruit from Devon:* (*Lyrical Vignettes of the North Coast:*) *and Other Poems* (1870) and *Beethoven's Symphonies Critically Discussed* (1879).

Professor Sylvester's laws for verse making had been useful to her. A.T. replied that he could not understand this. He liked her *Adam Bede*, *Scenes from Clerical Life*, *Silas Marner* best of her novels. *Romala* he thinks somewhat out of her depth.][34]

16th. A. walks with Sir Frederick Pollock & reads "The Holy Grail" to them (Annie Thackeray & Sir F. & Lady Pollock).

17th. The Pollocks go. A. & Hallam drive to [*illegible*].

18th. Mrs. Clough & Florence come. Mr. Wilson also. They play Whist in the evening with the famous blank seven diamonds. Independent of all liking for herself, Mrs. Clough & her children have for his sake a kind of sacredness in our eyes.

20th. A., Hallam, & I drive to Cowdray Park and home by Fernhurst.[35] A. especially admired the large Spanish chestnuts and the Templar's walk of yews at Cowdray.

22nd. A. & Hallam drive to meet Mr. & Mrs. Gladstone & their daughter Helen. A telegram comes to say they will not arrive till a later train so A. & Hallam come home by Mr. Lewes's where they call. She is delightful in a tête à tête and speaks in a soft soprano voice, which almost sounds like a fine falsetto with her strong masculine face. An interesting evening. At the Gladstone's request A. reads "The Holy Grail."

23rd. Hallam drives our guests to the school room service at Haslemere. They ask to see the church but as the key has to be fetched from the Vicarage they do not wait.

Mr. & Mrs. Burdon & Mr. & Mrs. Hodgson come to luncheon. The Mangles get wet & have to return home. Mr. Gladstone is glad to meet Mr. Hodgson whose brother he calls a princely merchant & one of the best governors the Bank of England ever had. Every one most agreeable. I talked with Mr. Gladstone of the Goschen parish plan & other things equally interesting.[36] After luncheon A., Hallam, & the Gladstones

[34]*Materials*, III, 172–73. George Eliot and G. H. Lewes resided at Shottermill, near Haslemere and the Tennysons, during the summer of 1871. Although Emily was fully aware that Lewes and "Mrs. Lewes" had been living together unmarried since 1854, she apparently had no qualms about visiting the couple. She later accompanied Tennyson to George Eliot's home in November 1880, two years after Lewes's death (*Letters of E.T.*, p. 277).

[35]Located near Midhurst, Sussex, Cowdray was an elegant sixteenth-century mansion which burned in 1793. The ruins survive in a large park notable for its avenues of Spanish chestnuts.

[36]Serving in Gladstone's first cabinet, George Joachim Goschen, 1st Viscount

walked to the end of the down & our other guests depart. The conversations at dinner & afterwards most interesting. Mr. Gladstone assures us that he is conservative & that he has been driven into measures which he deprecates for fear of more extreme measures from the opposition. It is indeed a privilege to talk to one of so much thought & feeling. One cannot but feel humbled in the presence of those whose life is one long self-sacrifice &, one would hope, quickened to more of it in one's own life. Mrs. Gladstone wears herself out, I fear, by all her hospital work in addition to the work of a prime minister's wife. Her daughter helps her & helps her brother also in his bad Lambeth parish. Mr. Gladstone kindly asks to see Hallam's poem & says that it is really very good. He praises his fine courtesy, too, & asks him to come to them whenever he is in London. Thursday a good many people were at the Station to see him.

Mr. William Lushington & Mr. Shadworth Hodgson come to luncheon.

25th. We call at Mr. Stilwell's & ask to be allowed to go into the hayfield. He misses the haymaking, the harvest here very much. So do we all. He hears enviously two rooks.

26th. Mr. & Mrs. Cracroft Wilson come. . . . He the judge who was thanked for what he did in the Indian mutiny & now he is a Patriarch in New Zealand where he seems to live in princely style with children & grandchildren.[37] Mr. C. Wilson told me that there are no jars, that they are all perfectly happy.

28th. Haslemere Church consecrated to-day.

29th. Mrs. Greville, Mrs. Fanny Kemble, & Lord Houghton with her come to luncheon. Fanny Kemble read Shakespeare magnificently, with tears streaming down her cheeks. She told us that when she was nearly drowned, she did not recall the scenes of her former life, but the terrible thing was that all her life appeared a blank. As they drove away up the hill we heard her command Lord Houghton in her tragic way, "Get down, my lord, from off the box, for you are no inconsiderable weight."

Goschen (1831–1907), led a major reform of local government in England intended to replace the chaotic system, or want of system, on the local level with a methodical system of administration.

[37] Sir John Cracroft Wilson (1808–81) entered the Bengal civil service in 1827; he was civil and sessions judge at Mordabad from 1853 until 1859 and served as special commissioner for the trial of rebels and mutineers, 1857–58.

A. is rejoiced that the National Education Bill has been passed. "No education, no franchise" is A.'s epigram.

August

4th. A. was reading some Heine to us after lunch & in Lionel walked. A lovely vision to his mother's eyes belonging to a brighter poem than any she knows of Heine's.

6th. A beautiful day & I think A. has a happy birthday tho' we do not mention it to him. We drink his health when he has left the table & send wine to the servents to drink it too.

7th. A. & Hallam set off to-day for [North Wales]. Sad to part when only just re-united but A. wants change & wants a companion. Our poor peacocks taken to Mr. Mangles' farm. Beere thinks they do so much harm. They look so beautiful on the balustrade of the Terrace that I am very unwilling to let them go.

11th. The first anniversary of our Hallam's birthday on which I have ever been separated from him. A very dear letter from them, with hexameters partly by A. partly by him describing the ascent of Snowdon. [They had arrived in Llanberis and there was a jovial party in the room above theirs in the Hotel Victoria.

Dancing above was heard, heavy feet to the sound of a light air,
Light were the feet no doubt but floors were misrepresenting.
Next morning they started early.
Walked to the Vale Gwynant, Llyn Gwynant shone very distant
Touch'd by the morning sun, great mountains glorying o'er it.
Moel Hebog loom'd out and Siabod tower'd up in aether:
Liked Beddgelert much, flat green with murmur of waters,
Bathed in a deep still pool not far from Port Aberglaslyn
Then we returned. What a day! Many more if fate will allow it!][38]

My Lionel drives me out, walks with me & reads "Il Penseroso" & "L'Allegro" & Milton's sonnets & Wordsworth's Ec-

[38] *Materials*, III, 174–75.

clesiastical sonnets & Shakespeare's sonnets. I notice that Hallam comes into a room like a spirit as A. does. Lionel with a grand step like an old Baron in his armour.

16th. A letter from our Hallam saying that they may be here to-day but more likely to-morrow, that they will write or telegraph. They do neither but to our joy walk in while fish & soup are on the table.

19th. Hallam & I look over the Essay on Greek. A. hears the end & thinks it very clever.

20th. After luncheon to our great surprise Giulio[39] drives up. He has not got leave so has to return after dinner.

We hear from Mr. Knowles that Mr. Gladstone says it is worth having been to Aldworth if only to have made Hallam's acquaintance.

25th. Our boy leaves us. We all A., Lionel, & I go to see him off. Lionel's friend Cator[40] comes & Mr. Mangles walks with A. & dines with us & interests [us] by his talk.

28th. Cator goes. Lionel reads nearly all the Pied Piper to me.

31st. He goes off to-day in the Dog-cart with his dogs happy as a king. After luncheon A. drives to the Lewes'. He reads to them & last of all at Mr. Lewes' request "Guinevere" which causes weeping.[41]

September

A. & I walk down the hill to look about the road. A. takes long walks & in the evening he is very cheerful. We have talks together very dear to me. He reads me bits about Russia. One night about those wonderful mounds & statues on the Steppes

[39] Julius Tennyson, the poet's nephew.

[40] Henry William Cator, later a priest in the oratory at Brompton and editor of *Oratorium Biographies* (1913). The day after Cator arrived at Aldworth, Emily wrote to Hallam that Lionel's Eton friend "looks a tall high-nosed Baron of old days—fair-haired & fair-skinned." A few days later she wrote that Cator reminded her of "an old Van Dyke portrait" and added that he had a beautiful touch on the piano (August 26 and 29, 1871, T.R.C.).

[41] It was George Eliot who wept, as Emily indicated the following day in her letter to Hallam: "Papa drove down in the pony-carriage after luncheon to the Lewes's & after having read other things he at his request read 'Guinevere' which reading was repaid by tears on Mrs. Lewes's part. She says Ally's reading is 'wonderful' & so it is as we all know" (September 1, 1871, T.R.C.).

from China to the Crimea. Another about the strange sects in Russia & the character of the Russian peasant and the strong feeling of unity in the nation. He gave me yesterday *Fraser*'s to read. The suggestive articles on Colonial Federations & on the Enclosing of Commons.[42] A general Colonial Council for the purposes of defence sounds to us sensible. He advocates inter-colonial conferences in England; and was of opinion that the foremost colonial ministers ought to be admitted to the Privy Council or some other Imperial Council where they could have a role in Imperial affairs.

16th. A. goes to Brancepeth.

19th. He returns unexpectedly. Mr. Mangles & Mr. Burdon have been most kind in giving Lionel shooting.

21st. Our darling leaves us to-day. Captain Jesse arrives.[43]

25th. Mary & Emily arrive.

26th, 27th, 28th. Much talking & occasional drives but the weather is bad.

29th. Mr. Carr a Yorkshire gentleman whom the President of Brasenose has asked A. to hear read.[44] I [*illegible*] with him having read in the evening.

30th. We find fault with his reading as wanting the melody of Verse. He insists that this is necessary in public reading. He evidently does not care for A.'s reading. The very first person I have known who does not.

[42] "More on Great Britain Confederated," *Fraser's*, August 1871, pp. 249–50, and "The Preservation of Commons," *Fraser's*, September 1871, pp. 293–306.

[43] Apparently Captain Jesse was somewhat more liberal than the Tennysons in his political views, and Emily therefore feared his conversation might upset her husband. "Captain Jesse arrived here yesterday by the 1.27 train," she wrote Hallam. "He is very kindly but I am in constant fear less [*sic*] his talk should overpass the measure of Papa's patience. . . . The only Republicanism I can understand is that each man should be equal in the eyes of the law & each have a chance of gaining an honest livelihood. I think that those born to wealth and station ought to have more state duties imposed on them and not merely open to them as now" (September 22, 1871, T.R.C.).

[44] Edward Hartopp Cradock (d. 1886) was president of Brasenose College, Oxford, from 1853 until his death.

October

1st. Mr. Mangles dines with us. Mr. Carr goes after dinner.

2nd. Mr. Mangles dines. Very kind & pleasant both days.

4th. Our Charlie & Louy come.

5th. Mary, Emily, & the Captain go.

10th. Lady Simeon comes, says how much Charlie's face is like the most beautiful face she knows, that of Lord Essex.[45] She likes Charlie & Louy & they her. We have learnt to feel her charm of late.

14th. Mr. Palgrave comes.

15th. Charlie enjoys his talk on Shelley, Keats, Wordsworth & other poets. A. reads Wordsworth to us at night.

16th. Mr. Palgrave goes & so do Charlie & Louy. These partings are solemn now. Charlie looks so fragile that it makes one count the days with him. Mr. Palgrave is very happy in the purchase of a country home at Lyme.

17th. Annie Thackeray comes. A pleasant evening with her.

19th & 20th. Thankful for these two days of rest. A. walks with me & we have Backgammon at night. I read Pressensé's 2nd vol., the latter half with extreme interest. For a while it lifts me above the petty cares of life. Infinite refreshment.

21st. Mr. & Mrs. Knowles come. Mrs. Gilchrist & her two daughters lunch with us. Mr. Mangles dines with us.

23rd. Mr. Knowles helps A. to arrange the scattered leaves of "Tristram" for press.

25th. Mr. & Mrs. Knowles go. Kind people. He very able, helpful, & energetic.

27th. I read the proofs of the Library Edition.

28th. Our Lionel comes for his Sunday out. Goes to church in the morning, walks with A., & reads "Tristram" to Tilly & me.

31st. A. goes to the Knowles's today in order to be near Mr. Strahan & to look after the Library Edition but Mr. Strahan has left him so little time that he cannot do much with it. A. & I have talked over the corrections of "The Last Tournament." Sad

[45] Arthur Algernon Capel (afterwards Capell), earl of Essex (1803–92).

alone. I wonder more & more at the beauty of his character. I see something of his meek dignity in Lionel.

November

3rd. I start with Mary for Oxford. A fine day. I call on Richard Sellwood. More glad am I than I can say to see the noble old man. The last of my Father's name & race as far as I know. Mr. Jowett meets me at the Station & gives me the kindest of welcomes. A. comes by a later train & finds me in my room, where I am resting after tea. To our great pleasure Mr. & Mrs. Bradley meet us at dinner.

4th. I call on Charlie & Louy. I meet A. At luncheon the Bradleys, Mr. Tyler, Mr. & Mrs. Max Müller & another gentleman lunch there. At dinner at Balliol we have Dr. Liddon, the Talbots,[46] & others to dinner & still others in the evening. Among them Mr. & Mrs. Bradley. All very pleasant. Dr. Liddon takes me down to dinner. I talk a great deal with him & he is very agreeable. The Bradleys have most kindly telegraphed to our Hallam who comes to me while I am resting in my room before dinner. He dines with the Bradleys & accompanies them to Balliol in the evening. Our poor boy has swollen lips & dark marks under his eyes from a blow at football.

5th. Our Hallam lunches with us. The Max Müllers call. We have an interesting talk. Mrs. Bradley comes. The Greens, Smiths, Lord Elgin & others unknown to me dine with us.[47] Mr. Bowen takes me in to dinner.[48] Very brilliant. Our Hallam, Mr. & Mrs. Hatch, a Siamese nobleman & others in the evening.

6th. We lunch & bid farewell to our dear host & then A., Hallam, & I go together as far as Reading. At Oxford a tall, thin man with aquiline nose & yards of white linen round his throat rushes in & says to A., "Let me shake hands with the greatest

[46] Edward and Lady Gertrude Talbot.

[47] Thomas Hill Green (1836–87), the idealist philosopher, became a fellow and tutor at Balliol College in 1860; he was Whyte Professor of Moral Philosophy from 1878 until 1882.

Henry John Stephen Smith (1826–83), the mathematician, was a tutor at Balliol for many years and was elected Savilian professor of geometry in 1860.

Lord Elgin is Victor Alexander Bruce, 9th earl of Elgin (1849–1917).

[48] Charles Synge Christopher Bowen was made a fellow at Balliol College in 1857.

poet of the day." A. says, "At least tell me your name." He replies, "You have written to me, never mind, it is a great pleasure to have seen you" & away he goes.[49]

We bid my A. good-bye at Reading. Hallam sees me into the train with Mary & then he goes to Richard's & afterwards to Marlboro'.

7th. A hard day's work & then a little rest & then Mr. Bradley comes. We walk & talk & write letters. A. is busy with the Library Edition still but he comes on the 11th with Mr. Huxley[50] & Mr. Knowles.

12th. Mr. Huxley very charming. We have a great deal of talk. He is so gentle, chivalrous, & wide & earnest that one cannot but enjoy talking with him. All except myself walk to the Summer House. Young [*illegible*] Richmond calls. Mr. Knowles goes in the evening.

13th. Mrs. Bradley after luncheon to-day having walked before with A. Very bright & delightful she has been.

14th. Alone with my A. to-day.

15th. Mr. Maclaren[51] comes with the 1st vol. of the Library Edition & sorry are A. & I that he has been persuaded to put back some of the old things. Mr. Knowles has advised it in order to vary the "Harem" as he calls it.

16th. Happy days with my A. He walks on the hill whether in sunshine or mist.

19th. He reads to me Maurice's paper on Nature & the Supernatural.[52]

[49]This passage is quoted in *Materials*, 3, 177. In a note Hallam says, "Mr. [Walter] Pater told me this was Dean Burgon." The dean was John William Burgon (1833–88); vicar of St. Mary's, Oxford (1863–76); dean of Chichester (1875).

[50]Thomas Henry Huxley (1825–95), the expounder of Darwinism and self-named "agnostic." He was a friend of the laureate's, despite the wide disparity in their most fundamental beliefs. After the poet's death Huxley addressed to him a poem entitled "To Tennyson: The Tribute of His Friends."

[51]Probably John MacLaren (1815–93), the publisher, who was later established at Prince's Street, Edinburgh.

[52]I cannot identify the particular paper Tennyson was reading at this time. Maurice, of course, wrote quite a large number of theological essays dealing with the Incarnation, the Atonement, the Resurrection and Ascension, divine inspiration, and various other "supernatural" subjects.

20th. He reads to me the beginning of "Sir Gareth."[53] Full of youth & vigour & beauty, I think it.

21st. I drive with him to the Station for his Metaphysical dinner.

22nd. Good, kind Mr. Locker writes to me that he has enjoyed it much. His letter finished about midnight. A. lunches with him to-day.

23rd. I have just managed to finish arranging & cataloguing his books before driving to meet him.

26th. A. walks every day & is very cheerful. We pack for our departure to Farringford.

December

5th. Bright but extremely cold. We drive to Farnham & in a comfortable carriage warmed by hot water we reach Lymington well. Delightful to see Mrs. Cameron at the Station rushing toward one with open arms. Then came Henry, then Capt. Speedy who wraps me up in the cabin.

6th. Nanny & Agnes & than several of our friends come.

8th. Mrs. Cameron & Hardinge dine with us. A sad parting that of Hardinge & his parents.

11th. More anxious telegrams about our Prince.[54] Very touching accounts of the Princess. . . . how when [she] was allowed to go into his room she stood for 6 or 7 hours looking at him thro' a hole in a screen.

A.'s new rooms not yet finished. An innocent sight to see him drying places where the wet showed with a hot poker.

15th. Our Lionel comes & on the 19th our Hallam.

21st. The last day poor Agnes comes here I think before her dreadful illness. For weeks I can write nothing & for a fortnight my voice quite leaves me. My Hallam is a perfect nurse. One day he writes fifteen letters for me & my Lionel tucks me under his arm in his own dear fashion & writes for me too some-

[53] Like "The Last Tournament," "Gareth and Lynette" was first published in *Gareth and Lynette* in December 1872.

[54] On November 21, 1871, the Prince of Wales was stricken with a near fatal attack of typhoid fever.

times. A. says "I leave you to your sons" but he does not. [He] works on as affectionately & carefully as ever.

26th. I am able to see Mrs. Bradley nearly every day & Louy Simeon & Miss B.

1872

January

I see Lady Florence Herbert & one day she lunches here. Pinkie & the Cornishes & Bradleys have all gone—15th.

19th. Sister Clara comes to help poor Nanny in nursing Agnes & Charlie & Louy arrive while A. & Hallam are away at Brighton with the Herberts to see his fossils.

20th. Our Lionel goes as Mr. Herbert comes here to see Hallam & see him [Tennyson]. They both dine here.

29th. They go to-day. We hear of Margaret Rawnsley's marriage to Mr. Arden about this time. Hallam who is the great patron of all children goes from the Terrace to the little Bradleys to play with them. Lionel too played with them.

February

1st. The little Bradleys go.

4th. Agnes prayed for in Church.

5th. Mrs. Cameron takes up snowdrops & violets gathered by A. for Isabel Cock's marriage to-day.

6th. He decides on having the Chapel built at Aldworth.

17th. We have the offer of tickets for St. Paul's on the Thanksgiving day.[1] Very sorry not to be able to accept it.

19th. A. & Hallam drive to Osborne to leave our names on the Queen's book & the Prince's. Hallam leaves his accustomed crown of Daffodils for the Dowager at Norton Lodge.

24th. To-day he leaves us. The house very forlorn without him.

27th. The Thanksgiving day. Another kind letter from Sophy Cracroft about Gore Lodge. Our Aunt gives us till the end of March to know whether we can leave Agnes. I read the 3rd

[1] On February 27, 1872, a service of thanksgiving for the recovery of the Prince of Wales was held in St. Paul's Cathedral.

vol. of Pressensé & delight to find my own thoughts clothed in magnificent language. . . .

March

22nd. Mrs. Cameron shows us the Norman crosses from Frome.[2] Sellwood & Charley & Louy see them before they leave us. They all go. Lou Prinsep's bridesmaids & we take our [*illegible*] gift to Margaret Rawnsley. Mrs. Cameron comes to say good-bye to Charley & Louy. Scarcely can there be more heavenly beings.

28th. Our Lionel comes home.

April

1st. Lionel goes with Mrs. Cameron's party to Lymington for the acting. Mr. St. Barbe kindly gives him a bed. . . .

2nd. They return. Annie Thackeray and Pinkie Ritchie with them.

3rd. Our Hallam gives up his chance of the cup at Marlboro' that he may [honour?] our wish that he should return. He has won all races to this last day, his farewell to Marlboro'. Thankful are we for what it has done for him. Mrs. Smith & her daughter Meta, Col. White, May Prinsep, Frederick Pollock, Mrs. Cameron, & Charlie dine with us.[3]

4th. The bride looks very charming & her twelve bridesmaids with their bunches of primrose on their hair & on their white serge dresses. Altogether it is like a scene in a fairy story. . . . A. & I at the breakfast. The boys also at the ball. We give an almost general invitation to the guests as Mrs. Cameron says that she does not know what she will do with them.

5th. The boys polish the floor & Pinkie helps to decorate the room. Everybody admires it. To-night Johnnie Barrington Si-

[2] At least one branch of the Sellwood family originally came from the East Woodlands, near Frome, Somerset.

[3] Colonel White may be George Stuart White (later Sir; 1835–1912), the field-marshal. White served gallantly in the Indian Mutiny and in the Afghan War and was made major-general in 1889.

Lou Prinsep's sister, May, was a bridesmaid at her wedding on April 4.

meon's fate is decided in the boys' study. He betrothed himself to Miss Dutton & so our ball-room is opened. The dance is pronounced most successful.

18th. We have another also got up in a hurry.

23rd. Margaret Rawnsley's wedding day. Louy Simeon is staying with us.

25th. Our Lionel goes back to Eton. We hear from Archibald Peel of his sister Adelie Biddulph's death. She said to her children that she was happier than they had ever been on their happiest holiday.

June

13th. Our 22nd wedding day. Perfectly lovely. A. & Hallam walk to Newton & back.

18th. Barrington Simeon's wedding. His Ella makes a magnificent looking bride we hear. Farewell to our dear friends here & to poor Nanny & Agnes. In some ways we feel leaving home more than ever this time. Merwood sends us a photograph of himself & his cats.

20th. To-day we go. A beautiful day. Aldworth looks rather sad outside for want of flowers. Tilly meets us in the drive. A. reads some Shakespeare to us.

21st. Our Lionel has had chicken-pox & comes to-day.

22nd. I superintend filling the flower-baskets on the lawn. Every night except Sunday A. has read Shakespeare to us. Also before we left Farringford he read some and some Pascal & Montesquieu besides. Now he is reading *Hamlet* magnificently.

July

1st. Our Lionel returns to-day & Mr. Jowett comes. A pleasant little visit but he goes on the 3rd.

11th. Hallam meets A. & Annie Thackeray & an American lady at the Paddington Station for Annie's party at Taplow. . . . Hallam rows thro' thunder & lightning & rain & gets thoroughly wet. They find Lionel, Cornishes & Mr. Prothero waiting for them under umbrellas at the dock. The ladies drive to Taplow. The gentlemen walk. A. returns to Clapham. Hallam sleeps at the Cornishes'. He clears a room of Hat boxes & she makes his bed for him. Most kind they are. The Cornishes go to Lords and Lionel also. He has invitation from his cousins d'Eyncourt & is most hospitably entertained by them the two days. Hallam lunches with his Father at the Gardens. They go afterwards to Lambeth Palace.[4] Mr. & Mrs. Knowles also go. The Archbishop & Mrs. Tait extremely kind. He shows them all about until obliged to leave for the House & then [*illegible*] his people to let them see everything in the Palace. The Lollards' Tower[5] & the Illuminated books of Hours have an especial interest for A. & Hallam. Hallam, resisting invitations to Garden parties here at the Gladstones, returns to me.

15th. A. comes with Mrs. Brookfield. Very delighted we are to have her both for her own sake & for the sake of the Hallam connection. A. reads Shakespeare to us every night. Many thunderstorms. . . .

25th. Thunderstorm again. A. reads me some of Proctor. Willingham Rawnsley,[6] Mr. Knowles & Mr. Spedding.

29th. Willingham & Mr. Knowles go.

30th. Tremendous thunderstorm.

August

1st. Mr. Spedding, very glad we are to have had our dear old friend here.

2nd. Our Lionel returns home.

5th. Mrs. Grosvenor Hood & her friend Miss Lindesay come. It rains. Very sorry are we that one for whom we care so much should have so little enjoyment of a visit she has come so far to pay.

[*7th.* We went to Paris. A.T. said that the hollow eyes of the ruined Tuileries looked out very ironically, with "Liberté, Egalité, Fraternité" written above them. The bonne told us how she

[4]Lambeth Palace, the London residence of the archbishops of Canterbury, was begun by Archbishop Langton (1207–29).

[5]The Lollards' Tower (1434–45) derives its name from the belief that the Lollards, followers of John Wyclif, were imprisoned in it.

[6]The younger son of Kate and Drummond Rawnsley; author of "Personal Recollections of Tennyson," *Nineteenth Century*, 97 (1925), 1–9.

had lived during the siege for four months in the cellars.[7] A. and the boys went to the Louvre. A.T. told the boys that in 1848 he saw two Englishmen come to look at the Venus of Milo. They were discussing Peel and the corn laws. "This is the finest statue in the whole world." "Yes, but about Peel now," and so back they went to the corn laws, and the statue was left unheeded. He immensely admired the portraits by Velasquez with a far away look in the eyes: and Titian's Entombment.][8]

We all go later to the Convent d'Oiseaux to see Della. She can scarcely believe that we are there. Afterwards we go to the Sainte Chapelle to see its wonderful jewelled windows.[9] Nothing hurt there inside or out tho' all around is in ruins. We drove past the Hôtel de Ville. The French seem to me sad & kind & subdued. A. buys many vols. of Victor Hugo & Alfred de Musset.

9th. We go to Fountainbleau. Hallam spares us all trouble in the journey.

10th. They all go to see the Palace & afterwards I drive with them in the Forest. We notice how tall & straight & Palm-like the oaks grow with beautiful bark all regularly marked not at all like our gnarled oaks. . . . A. reads some Victor Hugo in the evening. We all go to the Palace gardens & are amused to see the Swans & the [*illegible*] fight for the bread thrown to them. We hear the military band.

14th. Our Hallam goes to Pasteur Brand's for the sake of French conversation. Sad to part from him.

We go to Dijon.

15th. A. takes me to the Chartreuse which we saw & admired 21 years ago when scarcely anyone thought of it, also to the Cathedral & another Church.[10] There were divine strains in the

[7]The siege of Paris began about September 17, 1870. Paris was compelled to capitulate on January 28, 1871, and the Treaty of Frankfurt, officially ending the Franco-Prussian War, was ratified on May 23, 1871.

[8]*Materials*, III, 187. Titian's *Entombment* dates from about 1570.

[9]Sainte Chapelle was the ancient palace-chapel erected in 1245–48 during the reign of St. Louis by Pierre de Montereau for the reception of the sacred relics now preserved at Notre Dame. In 1871 it narrowly escaped destruction by fire.

[10]The Chartreuse de Champnol was founded by Philippe le Hardi in the fourteenth century.

The Gothic Cathedral of St. Bénigne dates substantially from the thirteenth

Cathedral being the feast day of the Assumption. Lionel & I long to stay. He finds out everything which will interest us to see & does everything that has to be done admirably. We do not stay at Lyons because of the Exposition but go on to Macon & thence to Vienne. Deeply interesting with its Corinthian Temple built in honour of Augustus & his wife. Its Cathedral a fine building partly of the Merovingian time & above all its St. Maurice & St. Pierre where are the ancient Christian tombs.[11] The old damp church reminded me a little of that of St. Ambrose at Milan. On one of the stone sarcophagi we see the old Emblem of the Good Shepherd with a lamb on his shoulders. There were also tablets with branches of laurel on them & one with what seemed to me our Lord rising from the tomb. A being with large wings & somewhat in the floating attitude of our picture of the Resurrection. One Sarcophagus had two places in it & two skulls side by side. No wonder I thought this is how I should like A. & myself to lie in our grave.

19th. A. said that "this is our best day" as to the journey & we quite agree. The drive along the valley of the Isère to Grenoble is so beautiful. A magic dreamy light on the crags which stretched far away into the distance. Here & there patches of gold colour give them an additional splendour. Beneath are Vines & fruit-trees & crops. At Grenoble the hostess & the waiter look distracted & say "La Salette, La Salette" reminding of "The Sparrow Hawk."[12] It seems that there is an unusual number of pilgrims to-day. Their voices are as the sound of many waters. Our Lionel gets something into his eye which we cannot remove. A kind Pharmacien cuts a bit of writing paper into a point & takes it out cleverly.

We drive about the Town & are charmed with the view of the mountains, rosy from sunset. The cemetery is a beautiful one, the public gardens pleasant. We drive to Sassenaye. A. &

---

century. A few yards to the right of the cathedral is the twelfth-century church St. Philibert.

[11]The Cathedral (St. Maurice) is a fine Gothic church dating from the twelfth to sixteenth centuries. The little Church of St. Pierre, a Romanesque building of the ninth century, now contains the Musée Lapidaire.

[12]"La Salette" undoubtedly refers to the Grenoble cathedral, Notre-Dame-de-la-Salette, begun in 1861. The site was chosen because of the supposed visitation of the Virgin there in 1846 to two shepherds to whom she announced the impending punishment of several countries. The Virgin's prophecy must have been linked in the public mind with the Franco-Prussian War and the invasion of the "épervier," the sparrow hawk—that is, the Hun. The sparrow hawk is a predator, and the symbolism clearly points to Prussia.

Lionel charmed with the view from the mountain which they climb while I sit part of the time under a tree in a little field.

21st. A. & Lionel go to La Chartreuse. A. tells me to read Victor Hugo's "Burgraves."[13] He wants to know what I thought of the "strange confusion of times." There seems to me something fine in the ideas tho' to be sure Uther Pendragon is somewhat out of place. Fortunately for me Mary[14] loves travelling & can get on without English maids. One night here she dines in the room with thirty or forty priests. That night A. & Lionel saw a puppet show of L'Enfer, the Greek Patriarch & John Bull in spite of strong remonstrance taken down and as each fell a smoke arose.

22nd. Glad am I to see A. & Lionel. They have both been interested. Lionel said that the dim view of the two lines of white cowled monks at the midnight mass was very striking. There was a carefully shaded lamp to each three monks so much could not be seen of them.

Next day the Procureur showed them over the convent & every now & then open doors disclosing officiating brethren or Fathers in embroidered garments.

23rd. We go to Chambéry. A showery evening, the mountains grand in purple gloom & here & there stern with their bare cliffs & crags. A French lady & gentleman got into our carriage, the only lady & gentleman I think we have met during this visit to France. He showed us the Château.[15]

A. & Lionel go to Aix les Bains to look for rooms & find some in the Garden of Maison Dameur looking towards the mountains. While we have been in Chambéry A. has most kindly been to the Café Chant and with Lionel two evenings not liking to let him go alone. This tho' dirty is a charming town as to situation & A. has taken me to the Cathedral[16] & the ruins of the Dukes of Savoy & the Fountain of Elephants. At Aix he takes me to see the Jousts on the lake.[17] A pretty sight

[13] *Les Burgraves* (1843).

[14] Mary is apparently Mary Ker, who accompanied the Tennysons on their August 1872 French excursion.

[15] Of the original thirteenth-century Château at Chambéry, only three towers and the late-Gothic and Renaissance chapel remain.

[16] The Chambéry Cathedral, the interior of which is noted for its painted imitations of flamboyant sculptures, dates from the twelfth and fifteenth centuries.

[17] Aix-les-Bains lies on the shore of Lake Bourget.

the Jouteurs fine men clothed in white with shields & long spears. Our pleasure spoilt by one of the poor men being hurt when tumbled out of the boat at the first encounter.

29th. After other walks A. & Lionel go up the Dent du Chat with Jean d'Anthelme as guide & do not return till about eleven which makes me anxious, seven or half past was talked of. I send for the waiter but he thinks there is nothing wrong & they come back very pleased with their day. They have had a beautiful sight of Mont Blanc, A. saying it "looked like a great cathedral with three naves."

30th. Neither the worse for their climb tho' the mountain is more than six thousand feet high & steeper than any part of Mont Blanc. Anthelme says he praised both A. & Lionel as good Montagnards & says that Lionel is like a bird. A. takes me for a row on the lake & then they go to the tombs of the Dukes of Savoy at Hautecombe.[18] A. tells me that from the Dent du Chat [Mont Blanc] looks like a Cathedral with three naves as we watch the sunset colouring on the mountains this evening. He goes to see the things found in the lake of the bronze & stone age but some pots or vases of the stone age are the only things he has not seen elsewhere.

September

2nd. We go to Geneva. A fine view of Mont Blanc at Latigny. Our companion, a French lady, excited about the "originalité" of the Rhone. A. takes me to the meeting of the Aisne & the Rhone. The clear stream with the muddy one. The waters of the lake most lovely. As the night deepens so the rushing of the Rhone grows louder & louder.

A. takes Lionel & me out in a boat. A. rows a little, Lionel rows hard. We hear the echoes of Sir Robert Peel's cannon rolling from mountain to mountain.

5th. We go by boat to Lausanne. The landlord & Mr. Fleece find out who A. is. Both very kind. The landlord gives him some most choice tobacco.

6th. In spite of its beauty we leave Lausanne &, sleeping at Fontaine, reach Dijon again.[19] We just look into the church of Fon-

[18] Hautecombe Abbey was the burial place for the princes of Savoy until 1788, when the Superga, near Turin, was chosen for that purpose.

[19] A mile and a half northwest of Dijon, Fontaine-Française is the birthplace of St. Bernard (1091–1153).

taine but do not like to disturb the congregation & we see the ruins of the Castle of St. Bernard's Father simple & interesting standing on their hill. . . . The old lady showed us the Chapel built by Louis XIV partly over the room where St. Bernard was born & told us how bienveillant the Prussians had been, much more than many French, but that the Church had suffered from shells. We returned by the beautiful Park or wood as one should call it after having seen the tombs of the Dukes which I saw more than 21 years ago with A. A delightful drive & a happy morning reading the service & "Le Lendemain de la Mort." Not that one cared much for this except for the fact that people dream or may dream under chloroform & ether.

We telegraph to our Hallam to meet us at Melun, no train that suits stopping at Fountainbleau. He not there. Our Lionel gets up soon after five to go & look for him. To my joy I see both boys in the court of Hôtel Windsor. Hallam had interpreted Melun to mean the Station for Melun at Fountainbleau & had walked about five hours waiting for us until the Station master set a gendarme to watch him thinking that he meant to throw himself under a train. My letter to him from Dijon had been taken out of the envelope & the envelope sent empty so all his packing had to be done in a great hurry. The young ladies helping vigourously.

Sleeping at Amiens & Boulogne we reach home comfortably on the 12th.

14th. Our friends call. Mr. Burdon & Mr. Mangles again most kind in giving Lionel shooting. A. has to go to Town about American publishing business but returns on the 16th. A. reads some *Coriolanus* to us.

19th. We all go down to the Farm cottage to look what shall be done with it. Lionel makes a mistake about his train to Eton & has to be driven to Guildford. He goes thro' the [*illegible*] & A. & Hallam hold only the pony carriage behind to keep him from being overthrown. A beautiful moonlight night & the journey is well performed.

22nd. Mr. Mangles kindly calls bringing Fungi poisonous & not poisonous, A. having talked to him about the name of one. He dines with us & A. reads "Gareth" to him.

24th. He sends it off to the Press, sorry to be so hurried & we sorry that he should be but he has promised & keeps his promise. He finishes *Coriolanus* to us, which he reads dramatically & magnificently.

25th. Louy & Mary Simeon come & as we find that it is the birthday of Louy's betrothed, Mr. Ward, we telegraph for him & he comes. We are glad to like the future husband of our well beloved friend so well.

October

1st. Julia Lennard[20] & her daughter Julia come to-day & Mr. Locker also. We find that his father & Mr. Hallam were friends which makes the meeting pleasant. For ourselves it is of course something apart from all other feelings to have Arthur Hallam's sister our guest.

Nanny & Agnes come. The recovery of Agnes little short of a miracle.

4th. The two Julias go.

7th. Nanny & Agnes go & Mary & Alan & Walter Ker.[21] Emilia Tennyson[22] comes. Hallam drives with his cousins & makes the dullness of a country house tolerable to Emilia as long as he stays but we have to part from our boy for Trinity, Cambridge, on the 8th. No son could well be more missed by his parents or more deserve it. Mary & Alan have also to part from their son for Trinity.

21st. All leave us except Tilly.

22nd. Archibald Peel & Lady Georgiana arrive.

24th. They are so good & kind we enjoy having them but they have to cross to Cowes on this stormy day.

25th. A. reads me some of Ford's *Broken Heart* again this evening. Our one day alone for a month.

27th. Our Lionel comes & later Mr. Knowles. Lionel looks pale but is very charming, almost more simple than ever. He tells me so innocently of his little triumphs at school. To my exceeding joy Hallam walks in about ten o'clock at night. His leave for the wedding begins to-day so he posted off here. I think that his talks with the bright young spirits round him

[20] The only surviving sibling of Arthur Henry Hallam and later the wife of Sir John Farnaby.

[21] The only child of Mary and Alan Ker, Walter was later a barrister and scholar and an occasional poet.

[22] A daughter of the Frederick Tennysons.

make up for the want of reading. I began to be alarmed at the number of suppers & dinners given him. He too seems to me more than commonly charming.

November

14th. Lady Strangford comes. Poor thing, these years of grief & suffering have sadly changed her but she is full of faith.[23]

15th. A. returns, the printers having at last released him. He reads me his glorious War Song, "The Song of the Knights."[24] A happy evening. Thankful for these evenings alone with him. . . .

22nd. Mr. Locker & Eleanor and Franklin Lushington.

23rd. Frank goes but a great pleasure to have had him even for this little visit. Lady Simeon comes. Poor thing, her loss seems to press on her [*illegible*] as much as at first.

26th. Mr. Locker & Eleanor leave us. Dear little Eleanor very loveable.

27th. Lady Simeon goes.

December

4th. Clearing A.'s study that the floor may be once more taken up. We have such difficulty in keeping the room quiet.

[23]The day after Lady Strangford's visit Emily wrote to Hallam about her, praising her generosity and remarking particularly on her devoted care of Emanuel Deutsch, the Semitic scholar. Though "very ill & sad" since her husband's death in 1869, Lady Strangford appeared to Emily to be "full of faith in things divine & of the love which comes of it." "She helps to support some once wealthy relations of her own now ruined but the most romantic story is this that a year & a week ago there was a consultaton of 6 doctors on the care of Deutz. . . . They all said he could not live three weeks. Her husband had said to her 'Milly remember one of your missions is to take care of Deutz,' to whom he had always been a great friend during his life. So accordingly she . . . said—well—he shall not feel friendless in his last hours he shall be made as comfortable as I can make him so as she had let her own house she hired two floors in another & put him in one & herself in another & there they are still" (November 15, 1872, T.R.C.).

[24]The song of Arthur's knights is in "The Coming of Arthur," ll. 481–501. Tennyson wrote the song, which, he said, gave "the drift and grip" of the *Idylls* as a whole, in November 1872.

5th. Fine till after we have crossed to Ryde. Nanny, Agnes & Miss Forde come.

6th. Hard work getting A.'s books arranged in his new study.

8th. A fearful storm & shipwreck. The tar-barrel & lights are seen to burn a few minutes or a quarter of an hour as some say and wild cries are heard or fancied & then all is silent & dark. A board floats in with "The Hope" on it. Every soul on board has perished within sight of many on shore.

9th. A. goes to see the wreck & calls on Mr. Cameron & Lady Florence Herbert, who comes riding alone soon after to return the call.

10th. I finish A.'s books.

11th. Do the other books to-day.

13th. Our Lionel arrives to luncheon earlier than we expected so the flags are not out for him nor the flowers in his room. He goes to meet Hallam in the afternoon. . . .

19th. They meet dear Lady Hamond on her last drive—asleep in the carriage. She was coming with Miss Wayrey to call on me. Mrs. Grosvenor Hood comes instead in wretched spirits. Inquiries at Norton Lodge.

24th. Lady Hamond passes away quietly at half past seven just as the birds . . . begin to sing. Her last words were "beautiful, beautiful, Cherubim & Seraphim." All thro' her illness she kept [saying], "I am sorry to give you so much trouble, my children," & she repeated her hymns & sentences tho' she could not hear the XIVth chapter of St. John which she asked to have read.

25th. I copied out the "Epilogue" to the *Idylls of the King*. Having been interrupted yesterday I made a mistake.

28th. A. & Mr. Bradley drive to the funeral. Less mournful looking than funerals in general having her Husband's flag for the Pall.

30th. Pleasant evening with Lady Florence & Mr. Herbert.

31st. Mr. Clark comes.

1873

January

1st. Mr. Locker & Eleanor come. The Bradleys & Lady Florence & Mr. Herbert dine with us. . . .

5th. We have most kind letters from Lady Augusta who seems extremely pleased with the Epilogue which we sent on the 3rd.[1]

7th. The boys go with Eleanor to the boat & bring back Mr. Paul. The Herberts & Bradleys dine with us. A. so unwell from cold he goes to bed. Lionel to rehearse at the Camerons. . . . All so kindly exert themselves to be pleasant that the evening passes better than I had expected.

9th. Lady Augusta copies a delightful bit from the Queen's letter about the "Epilogue" which we receive to-day.

Yesterday Lady Florence, who is going to her Aunt at Broadlands, came to say goodbye. We have a great liking for her.

13th. Mr. Bradley says goodbye. I believe no better man breathes & few with so clear an intellect. The play goes off very well, I hear. Lionel's acting much praised & Hallam's singing. . . . Battledore these days in which A. joins.

15th. After a game he reads "The Passing of Arthur." We call on the Wards.[2]

20th. The Butlers go to-day. The last of our pleasant Christmas gathering.

Our boys make their farewell visits. Lionel leaves us on the 27th, Hallam next day. On the 27th we send off the printed

[1]For an advance copy of the *Idylls'* dedicatory Epilogue "To the Queen" Tennyson received a message of thanks through Lady Augusta Stanley, now the wife of Arthur Stanley, dean of Westminster. Although no longer a member of the queen's household, Lady Augusta remained her intimate friend and confidante. On January 31 Emily informed Hallam that his father had received another message from Lady Augusta expressing her delight with the "'beautiful wholesome words'" of the epilogue. "So after all," Emily concluded, "it seems that our fears of the anger [the Epilogue] would excite are groundless" (T.R.C.).

[2]Richard and Louy Simeon Ward.

"Epilogue" to Lady Augusta for the Queen. One feels dumb in heart & brain losing the boys. That it should be so seems almost sad to me having my A. & I reproach myself but at night he says what implies the same thing for himself & when I think of it this is not sad. We have surely grown & developed a new love, for the old is not less but larger in trust in some ways than it was even at first.

We see the death of Professor Sedgwick in the *Pall Mall.*[3]Our Hallam will be very sorry that the dear old man's words have come true that he should never see him again.

Lady Florence stays about two hours with me. I always like to talk with her. He stays also a great part of the time.

30th. Lady Florence & Mr. Herbert come to tea. A. reads "Maud" to them.

31st. The "Epilogue" very much praised at Sir Henry Taylor's where Hallam was kindly pressed to go on his way to Cambridge. He greatly excited by the fact of his Cambridge party having resulted in the Bethrothal of Wilke Ritchie to Magdalene Brookfield.

February

1st. The day of Professor Sedgwick's funeral. To-day Florence and Mr. Herbert walk with A.

3rd. A beautiful letter from Hallam describing the funeral. It touched us all that a parrot should have said "Good Night" as the procession entered the Chapel.

A. walks with the Herberts part of the way to the boat. We shall miss them much. He practices what he preaches & they both deny themselves much for the sake of others.

Very pleasant letters from the Duchess of Argyll & Lady Augusta Stanley about the "Epilogue." The Leader in yesterday's *Times* also was courteous. . . .

A. walks these days with Agnes.

15th. Glad & sad at A.'s going to Town to-day. Glad that he should be with the dear Lockers for he needs a change & they will take all possible care of him & there is much to be settled in more ways than one. Mr. Locker most kindly writes of his arrival. My daily letters from himself. Agnes & Mrs. Cameron are so good as to come to me continually.

[3]Adam Sedgwick died on January 27.

20th. My letter from A. & also one from Louy Ward telling of dear little Charlie Simeon's death & of the way in which his mother bears it. Read a little of the Holy Roman Empire (by Bryce)[4] but my eyes still too weak to read much. A fine book, I think. The true idea of Empire if only one put God in the place of the Pope.

25th. A letter from Annie Thackeray telling what a delightful [time] she has had with A. & Hallam who took her to see the Old Masters. . . . A very happy letter from [Hallam] in Town and one from A. Poor Hallam's from Cambridge next day very different. He had just heard of the death of his friend Congreve. He had been his constant companion during the two happiest years of his life at Marlboro'. He has hurried off at once to the funeral being entreated to do so. . . .

[A.] dines at the Pollocks yesterday & the day before the Lockers had a dinner party for him. The Stanleys, Mr. Lecky, & the Bishop of Manchester.[5]

March

Mr. Locker has most kindly copied the Queen's autograph letter to A. for me. A precious treasure for our boys. Mr. Locker tells me that he is to offer to go to Windsor next week, the Queen having so graciously expressed a wish to show him the Mausoleum at Frogmore.

3rd. Every day letters from A.[6]

4th. He tells me that next Thursday is the day fixed for his visit to Windsor. . . .

[4]James Bryce, Viscount Bryce, *The Holy Roman Empire* (London and Cambridge, 1864).

[5]James Fraser (1818–85) was bishop of Manchester from 1870 until his death.

[6]In her fascinating March 3, 1873, letter to Hallam, Emily expressed some particularly interesting thoughts on human love, reflecting in part on her own experience. Apparently responding to some question put to her on the subject by her son, she wrote: "Yes I do think that if a man *can love* a woman who has refused the love of many for him he ought to marry her. I suppose it very much depends on character whether love begets love. The love which sought to make all its own from those who in mind & character did not suit me was repellent to me but I believe it is far from being always so & I quite think if the person be to be respected & admired heart & mind tho' not naturally the very person most attractive to one it is quite possible to be won entirely by love from that person" (T.R.C.).

6th. A beautiful morning. A. goes with Lady Augusta & the Queen to Windsor. After talking with the Queen at the Castle, where he saw the Duchess of Sutherland & the Duchess of Roxburghe,[7] he walked with the Queen & Lady Augusta & waited until the Queen & Princess Beatrice arrived, walking also. . . . H.M. took him into the building & explained everything to him & pointed out his own lines.[8] He dined at the Deanery & met the Duke of Argyll.

9th. He is to meet Mr. Markham, the secretary of the Hakluyt Society, who is to tell him about Sir Richard Grenville, A. wishing to make a ballad about him.[9]

10th. I am putting up some pictures & photographs in A.'s room & run down to see what o'clock it is when, while I am drying my hands in my room, he opens my door. What a delight [to] have him only I should like to have met him at the House door. He looks well & cheerful tho' rather thin. I find all things beautifully packed by Mrs. Locker's own hand. He reads me the account of Sir Richard Grenville in Froude.[10]

While I am dressing for dinner a telegram comes from Mr. Locker asking if some honour were offered whether it would be pleasing. A. writes that as far as he knows his own feeling he does not himself care for any honour except as a symbol of the Queen's kindness but that if it were hereditary it would be prized by him for his boys independently of this. We neither of us desire anything for ourselves. The old life has been too good for me to wish any change even in outward things & the thought of it depresses me.[11]

[7]Susanna Stephanie Innes Ker, 6th duchess of Roxburghe (1814–95), a lady of the bedchamber, 1868, and acting mistress of the robes to Queen Victoria, 1892.

[8]Tennyson's lines ("Long as the heart beats life within her breast") on the statue of the duchess of Kent.

[9]In 1873 Clements Markham was secretary of the Hakluyt Society, which was founded in 1846 for the purpose of publishing accounts of early voyages and travels. Tennyson first published "The Revenge: A Ballad of the Fleet" in the *Nineteenth Century* in March 1878 under the title "Sir Richard Grenville: A Ballad of the Fleet."

[10]Tennyson first read about the heroic 1591 fight of Sir Richard Grenville and the *Revenge* against the entire Spanish fleet in J. A. Froude's "England's Forgotten Worthies" in the July 1852 *Westminster Review*.

[11]As a result of his meeting with the queen on March 6, Tennyson was again sounded as to whether he would accept a baronetcy. He declined the honor after unsuccessfully attempting to have the title conferred on Hallam.

It is indeed a blessing to think that [the "Epilogue"] may have done good & helped somewhat to a more perfect union of England & her colonies which we all four here so much desire.[12] A card from Mr. Locker telling of the letter sent by the Dean to Mr. Gladstone. How very good Mr. Locker & the Dean have been!

21st. Lord Dufferin's first letter comes to-day. Extremely interesting. He uses the strongest language about the loyalty of Canada & says that A.'s noble words have struck responsive fire in every heart, have been in all the newspapers & have quite healed the wounds inflicted by the foolish words of the *Times*. A blessing to know this!

25th. This day brought the kindest of letters from Mr. Gladstone offering a baronetcy. A. asks leave to consider the matter a day or two.

29th. Asks if might be so that the baronetcy should be for his descendants, not for himself, but adding that if the Queen preferred that he should take it he hoped that he had enough of old world loyalty in him to wear his Lady's favours against all corners. The boys both object because both cannot be baronets & both wish to be the same. Mr. Gladstone kindly says innovation might be attempted in favour of Hallam's having it during his Father's lifetime but says he does not wish for an innovation on his account.

April

4th. Our Lionel comes.

5th. Our Hallam, Emily Jesse arrived before with her [*illegible*] & her dog.

8th. The Herberts come to the Terrace. A great pleasure to have them there. The Wards, Mr. Leslie Stephen & Minnie, Mrs. Brookfield, & Charlie. The Deffells[13] & Frederick Pollock all here. Pinkie & Richmond Ritchie all in the place. I rather in a

[12] See "To the Queen" ("O loyal to the royal in thyself"), ll. 14–33, where Tennyson suggests his strong disagreement with a recent article in the *Times* which had indicated that a severance of Canada from the empire would be to England's financial advantage.

[13] Probably George Herbert Deffell (1819–95), the barrister, and his wife. Deffell was chief commissioner of insolvent estates from 1865 until 1888, when he became puisne judge of the supreme court.

fidget about our dance on the 18th so many balls & so much gaiety going on. Emilia Tennyson & Mr. Prothero come to us. The dance after all said to be very successful. Some officers kindly come from Parkhurst in spite of theatricals there & we have good music. Mr. Myers is also here & Mr. Coleridge who sings "Total Eclipse" & other things, Pinkie accompanying.[14] A great delight to have such grand music so finely sung. Mr. Herbert & Lady Florence persuade Hallam & his friends to sail round the cliffs in the early morning & the sea birds awake & feed their young. They are enchanted tho' they are too late for the awaking.

20th. The Herberts go. We shall miss them much. Mr. Coleridge sings sacred music to us again. The Cornishes succeed the Herberts at the Terrace. There are dinners & walks in which A. & the boys join. Mr. FitzJames Stephen & his brother, Annie Thackeray dine with us.[15] The rest come in the evening. Mr. FitzJames Stephen very agreeable. He interests me much by what he says of India.

May

2nd. A. & I call on Lady Lilford.

3rd. She & Annie & Mrs. Cornish dine with us. Others in the evening.

4th. Our friends have most of them gone. It is well that the dinners are now at end for A. has grown tired of them. Very delightful people but one's strength very much overtaxed by the numbers to be entertained & all the work besides. . . .[16]

[14] Arthur Duke Coleridge (1830–1913), the barrister and author, was a friend of George Grove and Arthur Sullivan. A devoted admirer of Bach, Coleridge was the chief promoter of the scheme which resulted in the first performance in England of the *B Minor Mass.* Among other works, he wrote *Eton in the Forties* (1896) and translated *The Life of Franz Schubert* from the German of Kreissle von Hellborn (1869).

[15] James FitzJames Stephen (later Sir; 1829–94), a judge and friend of Froude and Carlyle, was judge of the high court from 1879 until 1891, when, upon retirement, he was created a baronet.

[16] Within a fortnight Emily further tired herself working with Tennyson's always disheveled wardrobe, the care and cleaning of which she found it impossible to leave either to servants or to the poet himself. "I have been cleaning Papa's clothes," she informed Hallam on the sixteenth. "Yesterday having noticed them in a very disgraceful state, I had another suit put out for him &

8th. Mr. Browning's "Cotton Night Cap"[17] comes to A. from himself. In the mornings Lionel is busy for his examinations. He helps me so kindly & affectionately inventing stories for the children & acting charades with them. A. reads us Milton's war in Heaven[18] magnificently.

9th. The two Annies (Thackeray, Prinsep) dine with us & A. reads Milton again.

10th. A. & Lionel take me to see the Rhododendrons & then the Apple blossoms in the garden & the orchard. I never saw the blossoms fuller or richer. Afterwards they lead me to the newly planted trees.

11th. To-day they take me over the bridge & into the wilderness. We hear the great Fog horn which makes us think of Ariosto. Annie Thackeray dines with us. A. reads "Scipio's Dream" to us & then some chapters in Isaiah, the "Song of Deborah" & our Lord's woe to the Pharisees.[19] We watch the moon in the mist. This partly clears & makes a smile on her face. We admire the young green at the end of the evening thro' its misty veil. A weird evening because of the mist. A. & Lionel walk with the two Annies & Emily[20] to see the moon & hear the nightingales. The moon on the sea, they see but do not hear the nightingales.

14th. A. walks again at night.

16th. Lionel goes to meet his Uncle Edmund. Annie dines with us. A very refreshing evening. Interesting conversation, chiefly metaphysical.

19th. Edmund obliged to go. We are all extremely sorry. A croquet party & a small dance afterwards in honour of the Miss Peacocks of Efford.

---

sent them down again to Frank. They were returned as far as I could see in the same state & in the evening Frank expressed his sorrow that he could not suit me about the clothes & said that he did his best & if he could not suit me about the clothes he wished to go etc. To which I replied 'very well Frank' & resolved on trying what my own weak hand could do. The clothes are presentable now inspite of long neglect" (T.R.C.).

[17] Robert Browning, *Red Cotton Night-Cap Country* (1873).

[18] See *Paradise Lost*, Book VI.

[19] "Scipio's Dream" is Cicero's "Somnium Scipionis," in Book VI of his *Republic*, written around 54 B.C. For the "Song of Deborah," see Judges 5.2–31. For "our Lord's woe to the Pharisees," see Matthew 23.

[20] Emily Ritchie.

28th. Arthur & Harriet[21] come. Mr. Barrington & his son here with a horse. All the ladies at the trying & buying of it. A pretty sight. William galloping it up & down in the Park, the three colts scampering after it.

31st. Very cold. The thermometer about fifty in the study with a fire.

June

2nd. A. brings me beautiful branches of red & white lilacs. Other days lilies of the valley. The Judas tree beautiful & the green chestnut & the monthly roses near Lionel's window a sight to make an old man young.

10th. The Bishop of Winchester, Bishop of Albany.[22] A. reads me a Romanzero of Heine ("Don Pedro").

11th. Our Lionel leaves for Cambridge by the early boat, but the new horse frightened by an omnibus runs up a bank & throws him out of the dogcart. William (thank God) not hurt & Lionel with only a few slight wounds on hands & legs. He feels shaken but leaves again by the 12 o'clock boat.[23]

12th. We hope for a telegram but none comes & A. drives to Yarmouth for letters.

13th. Hallam writes that Lionel has got over his first day's examination well & that he feels sure he will pass. Good news for our wedding day. Most thankful am I & for the pleasant evening greeting of the day. A. & I set off driving for Yarmouth in hope of letters. Thunder drives us back.

14th. To-day he walks thro' the rain for letters.

15th. To-day a letter comes from Mr. Mier enclosing a list of successful candidates, Lionel's name amongst them. A letter also from Hallam saying how warmly Lionel has been received at Eton by numerous school fellows & telling of their own kind welcome by the Cornishes.[24]

[21] Arthur and Harriet Tennyson.

[22] Probably the Rt. Rev. John J. Conroy, who was appointed bishop of Albany, New York, in 1865 and served in that capacity until 1877.

[23] Lionel Tennyson took initial entrance examinations at Trinity College, Cambridge, in June 1873, when he was nineteen. Hallam Tennyson had entered Trinity College the previous October at the age of twenty.

[24] The day before Emily had written a joint letter to her boys at Trinity College,

16th. A. laughs at me for watching for our Hallam but I do not think that he cares less than I do to have him.

18th. A. & I go to meet our Lionel. Hallam has to accompany his Uncle Arthur Tennyson & so misses going with us.

21st. A. has invitations from Aunt Franklin, Baroness Rothschild & the Goschens who have heard that he would like to see the Shah.[25] He cared most to see the popular demonstration on his entrance into London. A. & Hallam tell me how beautiful the view is from the Afton Causeway bridge with the sunset glow on the yard & the tide with the reflection of trees. Their description makes me think of the (23rd) servants and all go except Tilly & myself to see the Naval review in honour of the Shah & all enjoy themselves much. The servants not having returned, Mrs. Cameron & A. & I help to bring in the dinner cooked by the Charwoman.

24th. The day not fine but at Windsor it is better & we must suppose that the Shah is pleased with the review since he presents the Duke of Cambridge[26] with his beautiful jewelled sword. The Henry Taylors & the Snows[27] at dinner. I enjoy my talk with Sir Henry & the party altogether very pleasant.

July

1st. A grand expedition to Carisbrooke in honour of the boys' three cousins Elise, Emilia, & Mathilde Tennyson.

---

sending her greetings to the Cornishes and indicating her appreciation of Euripides' *Alcestis*, a copy of which the Cornishes had apparently sent to Farringford for the poet: "Papa and I both like the Alcestis very much. Tell Mrs. Cornish with my love that I do not call it quite unhappy. To sacrifice all for one we love can never be altogether unhappy" (T.R.C.).

[25] Baroness Juliana Rothschild (1831–77) is the wife of Baron Mayer Amschel de Rothschild (1818–74).

The Goschens are George Joachim Goschen and his wife, the former Lucy Dalley.

In late June 1873 the shah of Persia came to England, making the first visit ever of a Persian sovereign to the courts of Europe. On June 23 the shah visited Portsmouth and received the British fleet assembled at Spithead for his inspection.

[26] William Frederick Charles George, 2d duke of Cambridge (1819–1904), who succeeded to the dukedom in 1850.

[27] Herbert Snow (later Kynaston; 1835–1910) and his second wife, the former Charlotte Cordeaux. Snow, who assumed the surname of Kynaston in 1875, was assistant master at Eton from 1858 until 1874. He served as principal of Cheltenham College from 1874 until 1888.

5th. They go. Willie Peel[28] comes.

17th. Farewell visits.

18th. We go to Aldworth.

20th. A. & the boys go up for a garden party at Aunt Franklin's.

23rd. Mrs. Greville & Mr. Lionel dine with us & A. reads part of "Maud" to them.

26th. Mr. Butcher[29] comes. We all like him very much & are interested by his conversation. Mr. Herbert & Lady Florence come on their way to a farm they think of buying. They are driving all the way in a pony cart. Mr. Herbert talks to me most kindly about the boys, asks whether he may mention that Hallam would like a private secretaryship. I am only too grateful that he should.

29th. He & Lady Florence go. We have very much enjoyed having them.

31st. Aubrey DeVere comes. Kind & affectionate as ever & as delightful as ever in conversation. Lord & Lady Middleton[30] & their daughter call. Mr. Roderick with them. Mr. DeVere knows them already.

August

2nd. Fain would we ask Mr. DeVere to stay but we have not room. Sir Frederick & Lady Pollock are coming to-day. They sit out of doors most of this lovely day. A. reads the new Poem[31] to the Pollocks who think it as good as anything he has done.

6th. We may not say many happy returns to A. but we think he rather likes to see that his birthday is not forgotten. Hallam puts a pretty little salver on his table & I have ordered a little inkstand for travelling. Mr. & Mrs. Knowles come to-day & go to-morrow. A. & the boys take me in my little carriage in-

[28] The Alexander Peels' son.

[29] Probably Samuel Butcher (1811–76), who was incumbent of Ballymoney, Cork, from 1854 until 1866, when he became bishop of Meath.

[30] Henry Willoughby, 8th Baron Middleton (1817–77), and his wife, Julia Louisa, the daughter of Alexander William Robert Bosville.

[31] Perhaps "To the Queen" ("O loyal to the royal in thyself").

tending to drive me to the end of the Down but I get so wearied that the boys make me a seat with their hands, the most luxurious carriage I ever had, & we reach home before the storm, of which an old man on the down warned us, comes. I have enjoyed my outing exceedingly. . . .

11th. Our Hallam's 21st birthday. We take a table into his room before the curtains are drawn with our gifts on it. Glad indeed are we all that he likes them & among them the beautiful little book slide[?] . . . from dear Andrews who has known him nearly all (by far the greater part of) his life. We drink his health in the "Waterloo Sherry" which I have kept for the occasion but the day is saddened by his departure with his Father for Switzerland.[32] My Lionel very careful & attentive.

13th. A letter from our Hallam at Folkestone & letters from Nanny & Agnes giving an account of the little festivity at Farringford in honour of our Hallam's 21st birthday. Lionel's friend Cator comes. They drive to Petworth & the Punch Bowl & ride to Whitley to inquire after Sir Charles Trevelyan & the Hollands. They were to have come to us on the 4th only two or three days before Lady Trevelyan's death but had to put off the visit on account of her illness.

16th. Mr. Cator goes.

17th. My Lionel reads *In Memoriam* beautifully to me.

18th. He goes to Stinage Park.[33] Hallam writes every possible day.

23rd. To my great delight Lionel arrives as I am dressing for dinner. After his three days of Cricket & every night dancing & up till past two . . . he looks ill & is glad to be home again tho' everyone has been very kind. He has walked up from the Station notwithstanding his weariness. He having taken up the dream of Gerontius on his way to Stinage was so struck by it that he asks me about it & as it struck me too when I read it last year he reads it to me this evening and beautifully.[34]

25th. This morning brings a letter from Mr. Locker saying that A. & Hallam have walked with Mr. Feshfield[?] from Pontre-

[32]Tennyson and Hallam also toured the Engadine and the Italian lakes; they arrived back at Farringford on September 11.

[33]Stinnage's Wood, Cambridgeshire.

[34]John Henry Newman's *Dream of Gerontius* first appeared in the May-June 1865 issue of *The Month*.

sina to see them but that Eleanor having a cold could only greet them out of her bed-room window. Hallam too has a cold, he says, but looks well. Not one of my many letters has been received. Very disappointing! Lionel meets Sophy Cracroft who to our regret can only stay one night. My cousins Cracroft being the only cousins with whom my sisters & myself had early intimate associations.

28th. Extremely stormy morning on our height but Dr. & Mrs. Butler[35] & their Agnes who come to luncheon & do not seem to have felt the storm much. They are delighted with the place & the view & we very pleased to have them. Lionel reads me "The Torrent" & "Autumn" & the end of "Winter" in Thomson & some of Shelley's minor poems.

29th. He goes to meet Mr. Jowett.

30th. Interesting talk with Mr. Jowett who rejoices me by saying that Lionel is very good company & has very good ability. Mr. Jowett goes to-day. I finish my list of A.'s books. He & Hallam happy at Pontresina.

September

1st. I read two of Stopford Brook's sermons.[36] I like them. A letter from Hallam dated Chiavenna. A. thinks from the suite of rooms we had 22 years ago. He sends me flowers.

2nd. Magdalene Brookfield's wedding day. Lionel and I arrayed in our best, but I wrapt in a large brown shawl to hide my splendours, set off on this bright fresh morning to be present. Sophy Cracroft in her magnificent Indian Shawl, red embroidered in gold, the gift of some Indian magnate, meets us in the carriage & helps Lionel to choose a fan for the Bride & accompanies me to the church. We stop at the corner of [*illegible*] Square & send Laurence, once Uncle Franklin's invaluable steward & now Aunt Franklin's equally invaluable butler, ([*illegible*] Factotum, half English, half Portuguese) to inquire whether Lionel is expected at the house or is to go to the church. Laurence is enjoined secrecy for tho' I wish to be pres-

[35] The Henry Montague Butlers.

[36] Stopford Augustus Brooke (1832–1916), minister of the proprietary chapel of St. James, London, 1866–76, published several volumes of sermons. He later wrote *Tennyson, His Art and Relation to Modern Life* (1894).

ent at the wedding I cannot go to the breakfast. However, while we are waiting, a carriage with two little white hats trimmed with sky blue & another larger the same & one mauve & violet passed by, immediately there was a clapping of hands & then exclamations & the carriage returned & I was betrayed & Lionel was summoned to the house & went off with his fan. Sophy & I hid behind the pulpit, Lionel standing by us but the Bride & the Bridesmaids & Mrs. Brookfield & all came & greeted me lovingly, so I was glad that I was there. . . . Sophy takes Lionel & myself to the Station & we have a pleasant journey home. By far the finest day we have had for some time.

3rd. Lionel goes to Farringford for a little shooting.

8th. Louy & Mr. Ward come to-day.

9th. A telegram asking if Lionel may stay for Highland games. He does not wait for an answer, but to my joy returns.

10th. He drives Louy & Mr. Ward to the Punch Bowl & to-day they go with him to Guildford to look at Williamson's beautiful things. They row on the river & like their day. Two letters from Hallam. He is indeed most good in writing. Just a hope that they may return to-morrow but they do not come. Lionel takes our guests thro' Lord Egmont's Park by Fernhurst & they like their drive very much. Our guests are just going when A. & Hallam, our beloved ones, come home. Sorry that it should be rainy & misty but fires make the house look comfortable & they are glad to come home & we are more than glad to have them. Lionel has taken the place left for him by their absence wonderfully well. . . .

16th. Mrs. Mangles brings me flowers & asks the boys to go with her to an Amateur Concert at Midhurst. Hallam is not well. Lionel goes. He drives there, walks back with a lantern. I misdoubt his being able to open the Hall door with the big key he has taken so I only lie down dressed. I am on my bed & go down to look at the state of the candle just as he comes to the door in his Ulster, lantern in hand. In vain he tries to open the door so I let him in by the window. Hallam reads me two choruses from the *Agamemnon* that about Iphigenia & that on Helen.[37] I take exceeding pleasure in these prose viva voce translations by my A. & my boys. I can I am sure shape the original Poems out of them as I never can from the best poetic translations, even my A.'s.

[37] See ll. 102–276 and 760–866.

Admiral Tatham[38] calls. He was with Colonel Grosvenor Hood when he died & wrote to prepare the family when he was wounded. He speaks in the most enthusiastic terms of Lady Hood & Mr. Grosvenor. Hallam reads me Palgrave's Essay on Mohammedanism[39] & A. some *Macbeth*. He & the boys walk or drive paying visits to our friends in the neighbourhood or they take me out.

21st. Hallam reads me one of Stopford Brook's sermons before we went out & reads me another now. He reads me the Archbishop of York's sermons before the British Association. . . . Hallam also reads Ferrier's [*illegible*] experiments on the brain & their results.[40]

23rd. Early in the morning a voice in the Hall which proves to be Mr. Digby, always welcome. Lionel goes with him to Hind Head where he has to meet his cousins for a Pic Nic & enjoys his day. A. reads some *Hamlet* to us from Clark's *Hamlet*.

25th. He reads Stirling Maxwell's Atomic Theory to us received as something very important by the British Association.[41] I read Stopford Brook's first Sermon on Immortality which very much expresses both A.'s feeling & my own, I think, on the subject. Julia Lennard & La Julia & Pennie come to-day.[42]

26th. All except myself have luncheon in the Cowdray Park. A. & Hallam call on Mr. Mitford[43] & Hallam has an interesting talk with him. All say that they have enjoyed their day very much.

27th. The Lennards go to-day. Delightfully simple girls.

29th. To-day Dr. & Mrs. Bradley & Edith & Daisy come.

30th. Rains. No one gets out much.

[38] Admiral Edward Tatham (1811–80).

[39] William Gifford Palgrave, *Essays on Eastern Questions* (London, 1872).

[40] David Ferrier (later Sir; 1843–1928), the scientist and author, published his *Experimental Researches in Cerebral Physiology and Pathology* in 1873. Ferrier delivered his Croonian lectures on the same subject at the Royal Society in 1874–75 and published *The Functions of the Brain* in 1876.

[41] Emily apparently meant James Clerk Maxwell (1831–79), the scientist, rather than Sir William Stirling-Maxwell (1818–78), the historian. Clerk Maxwell published his *Matter and Motion* in 1873.

[42] These were Lady Lennard's daughters.

[43] Perhaps Algernon Bertram Mitford, who was created Baron Redesdale in 1902.

October

2nd. To-day Dr. Bradley has to our great regret to go.

3rd. The rest drive to Petworth & have luncheon in the Tower of the Park. A. & Hallam call on Mr. Mitford. Our guests thoroughly liked the day, I think.

4th. The boys drive with them to Guildford.

5th. A. & the boys take me out & we have a most happy talk with A. in the evening.

6th. He is interested in having part of the Garden grubbed up & planted with shrubs. In the evening he reads some of Shakespeare's sonnets to us.

7th. This evening *Pericles.*

Lionel goes for a day's shooting most kindly offered by Mr. Mitford. How [good] our friends have been to him, both Mr. Hodgson & Mr. Mangles. A. reads us some *Henry VIII.* Hallam persuades him to these readings so delightful to us all.

9th. Mr. Roden Noel comes to-day.[44] A. & Hallam drive to meet him. We have a pleasant day with him. I wish the weather had been finer—he might have seen the views. Lionel drives him to the train.

10th. A. reads some *Henry IV* to-night.

11th. Lionel shoots at Vale Wood & Hallam, A., & I watch the men at work with the shrubs & trees. A. reads some *Henry IV* & *Henry VIII* in the evening.

12th. A rainy Sunday. We have the Litany at home & one of Stopford Brook's sermons & A. reads a little of the *Mystery of Matter*[45] & we talk.

13th. To-day our boys leave us for Trinity. A. wanders forlorn & one feels forlorn enough the four being separated for even so short a time. But we have indeed cause to be thankful for all that makes it thus. A. takes me out & comes down early & talks to me.

[44]Roden Berkeley Wriothesley Noel (1834–94), the poet and critic, was the son of the 1st earl of Gainsborough. Noel published, among other works, *Behind the Veil, and Other Poems* (1863), *A Philosophy of Immortality* (1882), and *Essays on Poetry and Poets* (1886); the last contains a perceptive and enthusiastically appreciative chapter on Tennyson.

[45]James Allanson Picton, *Mystery of Matter, and Other Essays* (London, 1873).

14th. We watch the men at work this sunny day.

15th. To-day he is very busy with them.

16th. Archibald Peel comes to dinner but has to go to-morrow. Very good in him to come so far to see us.

18th. A. and I are on the Terrace watching the making of what is to be my rose garden when Mrs. Greville comes, a welcome guest. She brings him a Meerschaum & each of us a pretty pen-holder from Hamburg. A. comes down early & talks. It is so delightful to have him to oneself or with the boys as I had a few days.

20th. German Backgammon or talk.

22nd. He reads Alfred de Musset to me.

23rd. *Un Caprice.*

24th. *La Mouche.* Surely Boccaccio could scarcely have told the tale more perfectly. He takes me out these days to see the work.

25th. *La Carmosine* as far as he can.

26th. We look after the work & he reads to me *Un Souvenir.*[46]

27th. Mr. & Mrs. Craik[47] come to call on Tilly. Very attractive people.

28th. To-day we go to Seamore Place.[48] A lovely day. Sunshine all the way to the verge of London & then thick fog.

29th. Cissy & Lucy with us. Emily Jesse, Tilly, & Annie Thackeray dine.

30th. I see Tilly off by the early train & A. & I call on Aunt Franklin at Notting Hill Vicarage. . . . She comes from her room to see us & is exceedingly affectionate & talks delightfully as usual. We also call on Mr. Forster & find him very suffering, poor man. Mr. & Mrs. Knowles call. He wants A. to have his bust done for Baron Grant's[49] house which he is building, desir-

[46] Musset's comedies *Un Caprice* and *La Carmosine* appeared in 1837 and 1850, respectively. His short poem "Un Souvenir" was published in 1841, and the novella *La Mouche* in 1853.

[47] George Lillie Craik and his wife, the former Dinah Maria Mulock (1826–87), the celebrated author of *John Halifax, Gentleman* (1857).

[48] During this London visit the Tennysons took a house in Seamore Place.

[49] Albert Grant (1830–99), known as Baron Grant, M.P. for Kidderminster, 1865–68 and 1874–80.

ing to adorn the hall with busts of the chief men of the day. We know nothing but this of the Baron. We call on the George Howards, Kate Rawnsley & Margaret Arden are with us. Bad news of Drummond.

November

8th. Major Moncrieff, Mr. Venables, Mr. Twisleton, Mr. & Mrs. Brookfield dine with us.[50] To my delight Hallam comes just as we are dressing for dinner. Lionel comes to-morrow. A. & the boys go with Annie Thackeray to *Richelieu*[51] & the actors come to their box having recognized A. A. goes daily to Mr. Woolner's because of the bust & drives about returning the many kind visits we have had.[52] Among them we have been delighted to see the Dean & Lady Augusta who were most kind. Mr. & Mrs. Woolner, Mr. Holyoake[53] & Mr. Knowles dine with us. Mrs. Cameron & Henry come unawares one evening. . . .

15th. [*One line cut*] to Cambridge & after luncheon. One thinks that it may help Mrs. Cameron to bear the parting from Henry.[54] Hallam gives a grand dinner.

16th. A. does not dine in hall not being very well but dines at the Inn with Mrs. Cameron & Henry.

17th. He returns with Mr. Knowles who dines with us.

18th. Our Lionel comes at Mrs. Cameron's earnest entreaty to accompany her & Henry to Southampton.

20th. He dines with us on his way back to Cambridge having

[50] Major Moncrieff was Alexander Moncrieff (later Sir; 1829–1906); he joined the army in 1855, served in the Crimea, and was raised to the rank of colonel in 1878.

Twisleton was Edward Turner Boyd Twistleton (1809–74), the barrister and politician. In 1873 Twistleton published *The Tongue Not Essential to Speech.*

[51] Henry Irving's production of Edward Bulwer-Lytton's *Richelieu, or the Conspiracy* (1838).

[52] Woolner completed his draped bust in plaster of Tennyson in 1874.

[53] George Jacob Holyoake (1817–1906), who edited successively the *Reasoner*, 1846, the *Leader*, 1850, and the *Secular Review*, 1876. Holyoake's most important books include *A History of Cooperation* (1875–77) and *Self-Help by the People* (1855).

[54] Henry Herschel Hay Cameron first went to London in February 1873 to pursue an acting career, but finding little success, he left England that November for his father's estates in Ceylon.

seen Henry into the small steamer but not having had time to go on board the [*illegible*] with him.

22nd. Our Hallam comes with his friend Macaulay for our five o'clock tea.

23rd. Franklin Lushington, Mr. Barrett, the Duke of Argyll call & also the [*illegible*], Annie Thackeray & Mrs. Saunderson. The boys go to tea with the Taylors. Everybody very kind.

25th. Hallam & his friend go by the early train. I very much like Mr. Macaulay. Mr. Locker comes to us most evenings & is brotherly in his kindness. . . .

December

8th. Hallam comes for his holidays.

12th. Our Lionel.

13th. Mr. Leigh Smith lunches with us & shows us the Spitsbergen photographs.[55]

17th. We have Mr. Browning, Annie Thackeray, Pinkie, the George Howards. Our boys are, of course, with us, & their friends Mr. Jebb[56] & Mr. B[*illegible*]. One cannot well desire better & more agreeable. A very pleasant dinner, I am thankful to say. An evening party afterwards. Brookfields, Ritchies, Speddings, Sir James & Lady Colville, Lord & Lady Arthur Russell, Mr. Leicester Warren[57] & his sister, Sir Frederick & Lady Pollock, the Leckys with a Dutch friend, the Leaders, Mr.

[55] Benjamin Leigh Smith (1848–1913), the explorer, made five voyages to the Arctic regions, during the most important of which (1871) he determined the extreme western point of Spitzbergen and discovered several islands in nearly the same latitude.

[56] Richard Claverhouse Jebb.

[57] The Colviles were Sir James William Colvile (1810–80), the judge, and his wife, the former Frances Elinor Grant, daughter of Sir John Peter Grant. Colvile served as chief justice of Bengal, 1855–59, and was a member of the judicial committee of the privy council from 1859 until his death.

Lord Arthur Russell was Arthur John Edward Russell (1825–92), the second son of Lord George William Russell and M.P. for Tavistock, 1857–85; he was raised to the rank of a duke's son in 1872.

Warren was John Byrne Leicester Warren, 3d baron de Tabley (1835–95), the poet and barrister. Warren published several small volumes of poetry under the pseudonyms "George F. Preston," 1859–62, and "William Lancaster," 1863–68. He succeeded to the peerage in 1887.

Fletcher, Mr. & Mrs. Hatton, Mr. Allingham & a few others. Mrs. Greville almost [*illegible*]. Mr. Browning asks if he may come again on Sunday. He has kindly come several Sundays, so have Sir Frederick Pollock & Mr. Allingham.

Mr. Furnivall has been about the Shakespeare Society which he wishes to found & to make A. President.[58] This he declined but agrees to join the society. The boys walk with A. to call on Mr. Carlyle. The next day he kindly called on me. Fortunately A. & Hallam come in from seeing Miss Helen Faucit[59] act in *As You Like It* before he has left & Lionel from the Oval where he has had to play instead. He goes with Mr. Carlyle to an omnibus. Mr. Carlyle has been very interesting & touching. Mr. Browning lunches with us & Pinkie & Nelly Ritchie[60] & afterwards I drive with Lionel to the Oval & call on Aunt Franklin. Mr. Jebb has had to go earlier.

19th. Mr. Browning very affectionate & delightful. He consents to stay [for] dinner on the moment. Mrs. Clough & Arthur also stay. Emily Jesse & two friends of hers come to five o'clock tea. Mrs. Proctor also & her daughter. It was a great pleasure to hear Mr. Browning say that he has not had so happy a time for a long while.

Since we have been in Town, everybody has been very kind to us & so many have called that I have not had time to put down daily doings. Sir Andrew Clark[61] comes to smoke a pipe with A. in the evening. He has been devoted in his attendance on him. All as a friend. He will take no fee. He believes in diet & well he may having recovered himself by this from ten or eleven attacks of hemorrhage of the lungs.

22nd. Mr. Milnes calls. The Bradley Hall opened to-day.[62]

23rd. We return home. A lovely day.

[58] Furnvivall was, of course, Frederick J. Furnivall (1825–1910), the scholar, editor, and founder, in 1873, of the New Shakespeare Society. Furnivall regularly sought and accepted Tennyson's opinion on the authenticity of Shakespeare texts.

[59] Helen Faucit was Helena Saville Faucit, the actress.

[60] Nelly was Eleanor Ritchie.

[61] Sir Andrew Clark (1826–93), the renowned Scottish physician.

[62] Charles Popham Milnes (1833–91), author of *Lectures on the Book of Daniel* and *The Marine Geology of the Clyde*, among other works, was vicar of St. Peter's, Monk Wearmouth, Durham, from 1867 until 1883. The Bradley Memorial Building at Marlborough College, dedicated to George Granville Bradley, was opened on December 22, 1873.

24th. The boys and myself give away the meal as usual. A. reads some of *The Tempest* to us.

26th. He reads the rest of *The Tempest.*

28th. A. reads some of Isaiah to us to-day. The boys see the Master of Trinity & Mrs. Thompson at Church & Hallam calls at the Hotel with a note from me asking them to come & stay with us. No doubt it is good for one to be a little in London but how glad & thankful I am to be in our peaceful home.

29th, 30th, 31st. The Thompsons lunch with us these days. Mrs. Thompson drives with me & the Master walks with A. We have been troubled again by publishing affairs. It is a great pity that these splittings of partners must drive him from one publisher to another. However let us hope that he has found a steadfast publisher now in Mr. King with whom he may stay to the end. That he is most liberal there can be no doubt.

1874

January 1st

The Thompsons & Nanny & Agnes lunch with us as Nanny & Agnes do from time to time and are very good in calling to see us. We say goodbye to the Thompsons, for pleasant they have been. They go, most kind. A. reads some of *A Midsummer's Night's Dream*. Lionel refuses a great many invitations. Hallam still more to the Houghtons, the Lennards, to London Balls, & the Estcourts. Our time passes most peacefully & delightfully. In the evenings A. reads to us *Lear*, *Antony & Cleopatra*, *Macbeth* & one of Mr. Fitzjames Stephens' Articles in *The Contemporary*. To ourselves we are reading Motley again.[1] Hallam generally walks with his Father & Lionel drives with me to return our calls.

5th. The boys go to a dance at the Wards.

8th. They lunch with Mrs. Freeman to meet Miss Claughton & Hallam dines at the Camerons to meet them. In the mornings Lionel reads for his [*illegible*]. I, of course, am very busy with bills & letters but I am more happy than I can say & more thankful to be at home alone with my three.

13th. A. brings me the first snowdrops.

15th. Mr. King becomes A.'s Publisher.

23rd. The Duke of Edinburgh's Wedding day.[2] A splendid morning. Hallam reads me an account of the blessing of the Nova. A. finishes *Julius Caesar* to us.

24th. A Paper from Mr. Holyoake, so he does not forget his kind promise of giving me news of the co-operative proceedings from time to time.

[1]Motley's *Rise of the Dutch Republic* was the first of his works on Dutch history.

[2]Prince Alfred, duke of Edinburgh, married Marie Alexandrovna, granddaughter of Czar Nicholas I of Russia, on January 23, 1874. Tennyson celebrated the marriage in his "A Welcome for Her Royal Highness Marie Alexandrovna, Duchess of Edinburgh," which was first published in the *Times* on March 7, 1874.

25th. A. reads the beginning of *Othello*.

26th. Hallam drives with me & then walks with his Father. I finish making manuscript books for his library. This vacation seems to me more like the days before school with my boys in many ways than it has been since they first went to school. Their relations to each other are now so very much the same as they were when little boys. I am so thankful that they are together once more, not parted as they were almost entirely from difference of holidays.

27th. Another splendid morning after the early frost & that delicious bird I always hear in spring. Is it a storm thrush? Those few sad notes most like the saddest notes of that nightingale I heard so long ago at Hale but never elsewhere.[3] We agree that *Othello* is too tragic to be read aloud. A. reads us *Henry IV*.

February

2nd. The boys not well enough to go from colds. I telegraph to Mr. [*illegible*].

3rd. They go to-day tho' Hallam's throat is not right & the typhoid still in Cambridge which adds to one's anxiety. Both sleep in Town.

5th. A line from Lionel to say that Hallam is better. We send our carriage to meet the Prinseps who take possession of their new house the Briary to-day. A. reads on with 2nd part of *Henry IV*.

12th. He reads to me every night & Agnes accompanies him daily in his walk. Drummond & Kate Rawnsley come & Edward Rawnsley lunches with us one day. Drummond & Kate are very affectionate & agreeable. Mrs. Cameron is much charmed with him. They leave on the 19th.

September

I had to answer many letters from unknown correspondents, asking advice from A. as to religious questions, and desiring criti-

[3] When she married, Emily was living with her father at Hale, near Farnham, in West Surrey.

cism of poems, etc. and I became very ill and could do but little, so my Journal ends here.[4]

[4]This entry completes Lady Tennyson's Journal, though there is an addendum of Hallam Tennyson's penned in at the end of her Journal book. This addendum, which offers sketchy coverage of major events between 1874 and 1892, is entirely in Hallam's hand and was for the most part written after the laureate's death. Hallam's initial entry in this addendum offers a wistful comment on the ending of his mother's Journal and the consequent need for him to set down something additional from notes and memory, since he "no longer" had the Journal "on which to depend." "I did not return to Cambridge after the long vacation of this year," he continued, "but remained at home as my Father's secretary. Otherwise our life did not undergo much change."

Emily was periodically unwell from the beginning of 1874, but it was apparently the trip to France in August and overwork upon the return home in early September that precipitated her physical collapse. Despite Hallam's indication that life changed little after the incursion of his mother's illness, he did in fact give up all plans for taking his degree at Cambridge, and surely family spirits must have been subdued when it at first appeared that Emily might not recover. But "Lady Farringford," as Pinkie Ritchie often called her, did recover to a considerable degree, and though the Journal was never resumed, she lived on for more than twenty years.

Genealogical Tables

The Tennyson Family

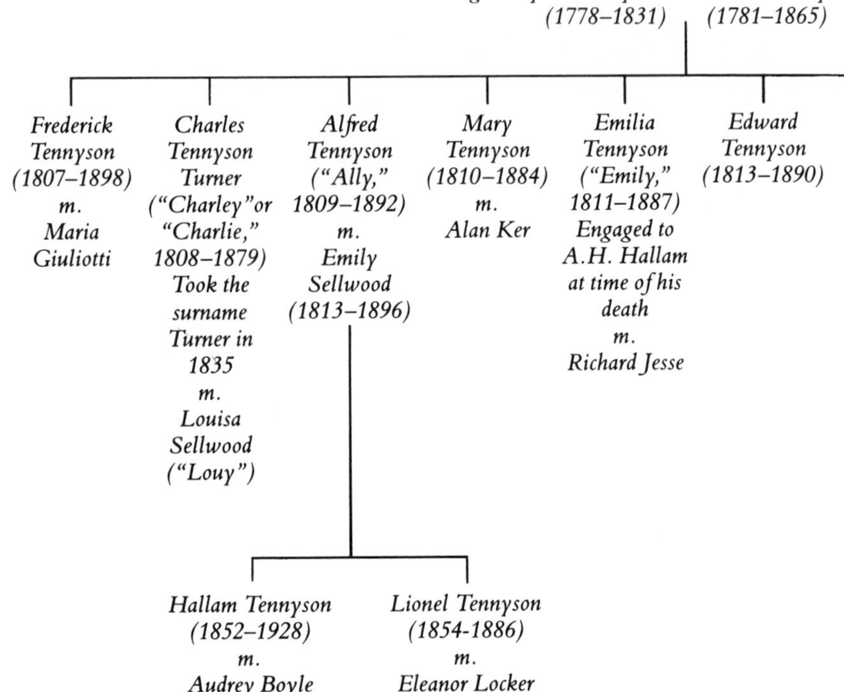

The Rev. Dr. George Clayton Tennyson m. Elizabeth Fytche
(1778–1831) (1781–1865)
Frederick Tennyson (1807–1898) m. Maria Giuliotti
Charles Tennyson Turner ("Charley"or "Charlie," 1808–1879) Took the surname Turner in 1835 m. Louisa Sellwood ("Louy")
Alfred Tennyson ("Ally," 1809–1892) m. Emily Sellwood (1813–1896)
Mary Tennyson (1810–1884) m. Alan Ker
Emilia Tennyson ("Emily," 1811–1887) Engaged to A.H. Hallam at time of his death m. Richard Jesse
Edward Tennyson (1813–1890)
Hallam Tennyson (1852–1928) m. Audrey Boyle
Lionel Tennyson (1854-1886) m. Eleanor Locker

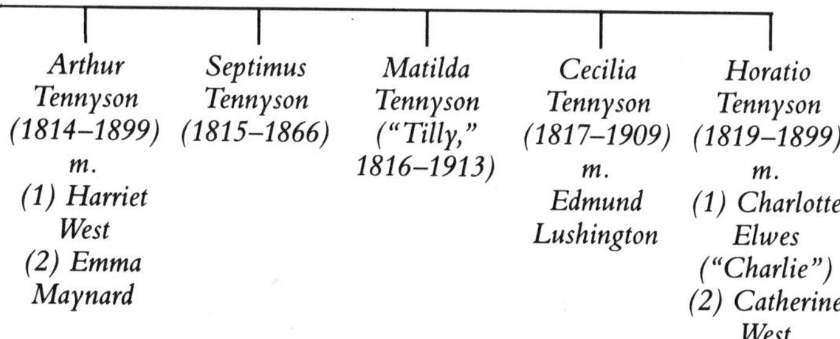
Arthur Tennyson (1814–1899) m. (1) Harriet West (2) Emma Maynard
Septimus Tennyson (1815–1866)
Matilda Tennyson ("Tilly," 1816–1913)
Cecilia Tennyson (1817–1909) m. Edmund Lushington
Horatio Tennyson (1819–1899) m. (1) Charlotte Elwes ("Charlie") (2) Catherine West

The Sellwood Family

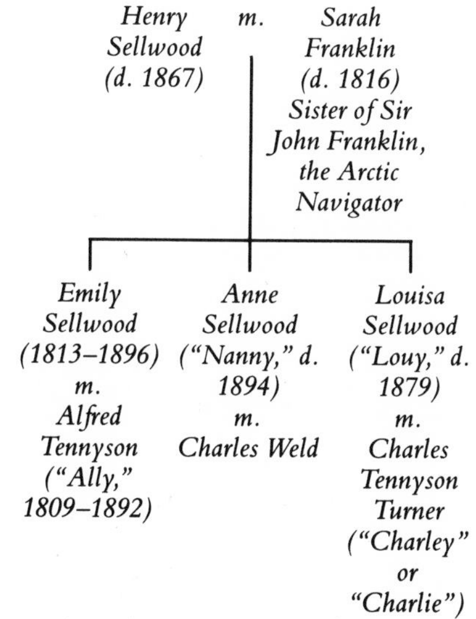
Henry Sellwood (d. 1867)
m.
Sarah Franklin (d. 1816) Sister of Sir John Franklin, the Arctic Navigator
Emily Sellwood (1813–1896) m. Alfred Tennyson ("Ally," 1809–1892)
Anne Sellwood ("Nanny," d. 1894) m. Charles Weld
Louisa Sellwood ("Louy," d. 1879) m. Charles Tennyson Turner ("Charley" or "Charlie")

Index